Lecture Notes of the Institute for Computer Sciences, Social-Informatics and Telecommunications Engineering 18

Editorial Board

Ozgur Akan
Middle East Technical University, Ankara, Turkey
Paolo Bellavista
University of Bologna, Italy
Jiannong Cao
Hong Kong Polytechnic University, Hong Kong
Falko Dressler
University of Erlangen, Germany
Domenico Ferrari
Università Cattolica Piacenza, Italy
Mario Gerla
UCLA, USA
Hisashi Kobayashi
Princeton University, USA
Sergio Palazzo
University of Catania, Italy
Sartaj Sahni
University of Florida, USA
Xuemin (Sherman) Shen
University of Waterloo, Canada
Mircea Stan
University of Virginia, USA
Jia Xiaohua
City University of Hong Kong, Hong Kong
Albert Zomaya
University of Sydney, Australia
Geoffrey Coulson
Lancaster University, UK

Peter Mueller   Jian-Nong Cao
Cho-Li Wang (Eds.)

Scalable Information Systems

4th International ICST Conference
INFOSCALE 2009
Hong Kong, June 10-11, 2009
Revised Selected Papers

 Springer

Volume Editors

Peter Mueller
IBM Zurich Research Laboratory
8803 Rueschlikon, Switzerland
E-mail: pmu@zurich.ibm.com

Jian-Nong Cao
Hong Kong Polytechnic University
Department of Computing
Hung Hom, Kowloon, Hong Kong
E-mail: csjcao@comp.polyu.edu.hk

Cho-Li Wang
The University of Hong Kong
Department of Computer Science
Pokfulam Road, Hong Kong
E-mail: clwang@cs.hku.hk

Library of Congress Control Number: 2009939932

CR Subject Classification (1998): B.8, C.4, D.2.8, H.3.4, D.2, C.2, C.1.2, C.1.4

ISSN   1867-8211
ISBN-10   3-642-10484-3 Springer Berlin Heidelberg New York
ISBN-13   978-3-642-10484-8 Springer Berlin Heidelberg New York

This work is subject to copyright. All rights are reserved, whether the whole or part of the material is concerned, specifically the rights of translation, reprinting, re-use of illustrations, recitation, broadcasting, reproduction on microfilms or in any other way, and storage in data banks. Duplication of this publication or parts thereof is permitted only under the provisions of the German Copyright Law of September 9, 1965, in its current version, and permission for use must always be obtained from Springer. Violations are liable to prosecution under the German Copyright Law.

springer.com

© ICST Institute for Computer Science, Social Informatics and Telecommunications Engineering 2009
Printed in Germany

Typesetting: Camera-ready by author, data conversion by Scientific Publishing Services, Chennai, India
Printed on acid-free paper   SPIN: 12799060   06/3180   5 4 3 2 1 0

Preface

In view of the incessant growth of data and knowledge and the continued diversification of information dissemination on a global scale, scalability has become a mainstream research area in computer science and information systems. The ICST INFOSCALE conference is one of the premier forums for presenting new and exciting research related to all aspects of scalability, including system architecture, resource management, data management, networking, and performance. As the fourth conference in the series, INFOSCALE 2009 was held in Hong Kong on June 10 and 11, 2009.

The articles presented in this volume focus on a wide range of scalability issues and new approaches to tackle problems arising from the ever-growing size and complexity of information of all kind. More than 60 manuscripts were submitted, and the Program Committee selected 22 papers for presentation at the conference. Each submission was reviewed by three members of the Technical Program Committee.

The resulting excellent proceedings required a lot of effort from a great team. First, we thank all the authors for their hard work in preparing the submissions to the conference. We deeply appreciate the effort and contributions of the Technical Program Committee members, who worked very hard to review the papers in the short period of time allotted for the review. The efforts of our external reviewers is also deeply appreciated. We are also very grateful to Xianhe Sun, Cheng-zhong Xu, and Minglu Li for accepting our invitation to present a keynote speech. Their enlightening talks on trailblazing issues will continue to inspire our work.

The Organizing Committee thanks Imrich Chlamtac and Ophir Frieder, who served as the Steering Committee for this conference. Our thanks also go to ICST for their effort and continuous help with the organization of the conference and the support provided during the preparation of the conference. In particular, we thank Maria Morozova, the conference coordinator, and Eszter Hajdu, the proceedings coordinator, for their professional support and guidance at all stages.

We hope that the INFOSCALE 2009 proceedings will serve as a valuable reference resource for researchers and developers in both academia and industry.

June 2009

Jiannong Cao
Beihong Jin
Li Li
Peter Mueller

Organization

Steering Committee Chair

Imrich Chlamtac   Create-Net, Italy

Steering Committee

Ophir Frieder   Illinois Institute of Technology, Chicago, USA

General Chair

Jiannong Cao   The Hong Kong Polytechnic University, Hong Kong, China

Program Committee Chairs

Cho-li Wang   The University of Hong Kong, Hong Kong, China
Robert Steele   University of Sydney, Sydney, Australia

Workshops Chair

Alvin Chan   The Hong Kong Polytechnic University, Hong Kong, China

Tutorial Chair

Xiaolin (Andy) Li   Oklahoma State University, USA

Publications Chair

Peter Mueller   IBM Zurich Research Lab, Switzerland
Beihong Jin   Institute of Software, Chinese Academy of Science, China
Li Li   Communications Research Center Canada, Canada

Local Arrangements Chair

Alan Wong   The Hong Kong Polytechnic University, Hong Kong,
                                    China

Web Chair

Daqiang Zhang   The Hong Kong Polytechnic University, Hong Kong,
                                    China

Conference Coordinator

Maria Morozova   ICST

Technical Program Committee

Anne Cregan   Intersect, Australia
Ashfaq Khokhar   University of Illinois at Chicago, USA
Bin Xiao   Hong Kong Polytechnic University, China
Bo Hong   Georgia Institute of Technology, USA
Changai Sun   Beijing Jiaotong University, China
Chao-Tung Yang   Tunghai University, Taiwan
Ching-Hsien, Hsu   Chung Hua University, Taiwan
Christopher Lueg   University of Tasmania, Australia
Chuan Wu   University of Hong Kong, China
Dion Goh Hoe Lian   Nanyang Technological University, Singapore
Dongman Lee   Information and Communications University, Korea
Ernesto Damiani   University of Milan, Italy
Feilong Tang   Shanghai Jiao Tong University, China
Feng Ling   Tsinghua University, China
Frank Kargl   Ulm University, Germany
Gang Pan   Zhejiang University, China
Hamid Laga   Tokyo Institute of Technology, Japan
Jianliang Xu   Hong Kong Baptist University, China
Jong Hyuk Park   Kyungnam University, Korea
Joshua Huang   University of Hong Kong, China
Ju-Wook Jang   Sogang University, Korea
Lei Chen   Hong Kong University of Science and Technology,
                                    China
Li Zha   Chinese Academy of Sciences, China
Michael Sheng   University of Adelaide, Australia
Ming Xu   University of National Defense, China
Minghua Chen   Chinese University of Hong Kong, China
Pangfeng Liu   National Taiwan University, Taiwan

Paul Coulton	Lancaster University, UK
Qun Li	College of William and Mary, USA
Rajkumar Buyya	University of Melbourne, Australia
Shengzh Feng	Shenzhen Institute of Advanced Tech., China
Tanveer Zia	Charles Sturt University, Australia
Tzung-Shi Chen	National University of Tainan, Taiwan
Vijay Varadharajan	Macquarie University, Australia
Wang-Chien Lee	Pennsylvania State University, USA
Weijia Jia	City University of Hong Kong, China
Weisong Shi	Wayne State University, USA
Wenbin Jiang	Huazhong University of Science and Technology, China
Wenguang Chen	Tsinghua University, China
Yu Chen	Tsinghua University, China
Yuchee Tseng	National Chiao-Tung University, Taiwan
Yuzhong Sun	Chinese Academy of Sciences, China
Zhi-Hua Zhou	Nanjing University, China
Zoe Wong	Griffith University, Australia

Table of Contents

A Fully Data-Driven Reconfigurable Architecture with Very Coarse-Grained Execution Units

Yuzhong Jiao[1,2], Xin'an Wang[1,2], and Xuewen Ni[2]

[1] Reconfiguring DSP Research Center, Shenzhen Graduate School of Peking University
Shenzhen 518055, P.R. China
[2] Element of Microelectronics, Peking University
Beijing 100871, P.R. China
jiaoyz04829@szcie.pku.edu.cn, wangxa@szpku.edu.cn,
nxw@pku.edu.cn

Abstract. There is a clear turning point in the development history of reconfigurable architectures. Larger execution units (EU) used to be adopted in special domain applications to improve the cost performance of programmable architectures. However, after the granularity of EUs came up to the level of arithmetic logic unit (ALU) and multiplication accumulation unit (MAC), the trend almost stopped. At present, a great number of reconfigurable architectures make use of simple Von-Neumann-architecture processing elements (PE) with such EUs as ALU and MAC. Actually, today's application algorithms are far different from the previous counterparts with the development over the last decades. Larger operation units can be extracted from common application algorithms. Without the coherent enhancement of EUs, it is difficult for reconfigurable architectures to replace the application specific integrated circuits (ASIC) used for most of current high-throughput applications. In order to further improve the performance/cost ratio, this paper presents a novel architecture with very-coarse-grained EUs and fully-data-driven mechanism.

Keywords: Reconfigurable architecture, Processing element (PE), Execution unit (EU), Very-coarse-grained, Fully-data-driven.

1 Introduction

An important force driving the electronics industry is the growing demand for increasingly complex multimedia computing and baseband processing devices [1]. Based on the natural parallelism of the algorithms in the devices [2], [3], [4] and [5], a great number of reconfigurable architectures have been proposed by the industry and academia to fulfill such a demand over the last decade [6], [7], [8] and [9]. These architectures combine the advantages of the efficiency (in terms of area, power and performance) of ASICs and the flexibility of the programmability of conventional programmable processors with Von Neumann architecture. The granularities of the reconfigurable architectures have evolved from gate-level circuits to more coarse-grained functional blocks [10] and [11] or even program-controlled PEs [12], [13] and

P. Mueller, J.-N. Cao, and C.-L. Wang (Eds.): Infoscale 2009, LNICST 18, pp. 1–13, 2009.
© Institute for Computer Science, Social-Informatics and Telecommunications Engineering 2009

[14]. With the advancement of the granularities of basic PEs, the computation capacities of reconfigurable architectures have increased significantly.

In this paper, we propose a novel reconfigurable architecture with very-coarse-grained EUs. Both the control circuits of PEs and the interconnection network are very simple. Weakly programmability is provided to realize enough functions in some special domain applications. In order to obtain a high-cost-performance reconfigurable architecture, data-driven concept is used not only in interconnection networks but also in each PE.

The paper is organized as follows: in section 2 the adaptability of reconfigurable architectures to current high-throughput applications is analyzed; in section 3 the novel architecture with fully-data-driven mechanism and very-coarse-grained EUs is presented; section 4 gives the configurations of the proposed reconfigurable architecture; section 5 presents the design flow of special domain applications by using the new architecture; the performance analyses are shown in section 6 and finally the conclusion is given.

2   Design Consideration

Although lots of reconfigurable architectures have been designed and have revealed the potential high computing performance, they have achieved rather limited success. The main reason is that their performance/cost ratios are not good enough for most high-throughput custom devices. Thus, reconfigurable architectures are limited in the narrow fields such as the signal processing of radar and base station, and the prototyping development of high-throughput systems [11], [15] and [16].

In fact, ASICs or traditional system-on-a-chips (SOC) are used more widespread in the computation-intensive signal processing systems. However, ASIC approaches often have high nonrecurring engineering (NRE) costs, and take considerable time, even months, to fabricate. And with the development of microelectronics technologies, the NRE cost is increasing. On the other hand, the lifetime of electronic products has shortened. Therefore, programmability must be emphasized in high-performance architectures to reduce risks and to increase profits.

A trend is easily seen that new reconfigurable architectures will be more flexible to program than their previous counterparts. That is, the programmability of reconfigurable architectures continues increase. Since the advancement of technologies enables more complex logic blocks to be integrated on one chip, the basic PEs in reconfigurable architectures vary from simple controllable logic blocks to configurable ALUs and MACs, and further to smaller RISC-type programmable DSP cores. Now, a great number of reconfigurable architectures use one array structure and contain hundreds of simple DSP cores [9]. However, the basic EUs (like addition and multiplier, or ALU and MAC) in PEs seem to have been holding a relatively steady size and do not change as quickly as PEs. Maybe this can account for the limited successes of reconfigurable architectures.

The primary aim of reconfigurable architectures is to exploit the concurrency of algorithms and to reduce control overhead for conventional microprocessors, and configuration overhead for FPGAs. Originally, the larger execution units were designed

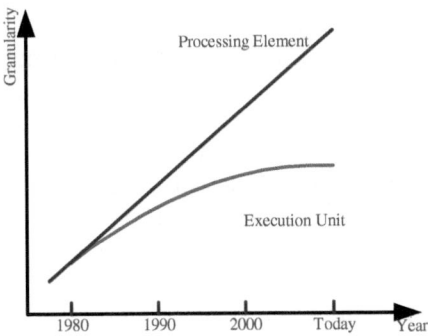

Fig. 1. The trends of PEs and EUs

on the basis of the data flow graphs (DFG) of applications, or optimized for some special blocks [17], [18] and [19]. However, such attempts almost came to a standstill after the emergence of ALUs and MACs [20] and [21]. The evolutionary trends of PEs and EUs are shown in Fig. 1. PEs varying from configurable coarse-grained EUs to DSP cores implies the return of control overhead. Although the advancements in technology make it possible to integrate more PEs, the reconfigurable architectures do not offer satisfactory performance/cost ratios to replace ASICs in high-throughput applications.

The problem partly stems from the knowledge mismatch between computing architectures and application algorithms. More attentions are given to the exploration of reconfigurable architectures in order to get the best solution in multiple-dimension design space. At the same time, the aboriginal viewpoint of disassembling applications algorithms is still held that all application systems can be ultimately divided into some basic operation units like adder, multiplier, multiplexer and logic shift. Therefore, almost all reconfigurable architectures use these basic units to process algorithms. However, the features of application systems have changed. The following are the main differences between current and former applications.

- Current innovating points mainly locate at the combinations of various algorithms.
- One single mainstream algorithm may be adopted in multiple different standards and specifications. For instance, orthogonal frequency division multiplexing technique (OFDM) is used in more than 10 communication standards and specifications.
- Mainstream algorithms are presenting more advantages, which results in just few algorithms existing in similar application systems.
- With the fast development of global economy, hundreds of million persons can benefit from one mainstream technique.

Thus it can be seen that the basic functional blocks of current application systems are much larger than those of former algorithms. Larger operation units can be extracted from common application algorithms.

We suppose that ASICs are composed of tightly coupled basic operation units like the assemblage of one multiplier, adder and register in FIR filters. Thus, the area overhead of an ASIC can be estimated according to the implementation structures of application algorithms. Based on the sampling rate of one algorithm, the minimum working frequency of one ASIC unit can then be obtained. Furthermore, the demand of an algorithm for millions instructions per second (MIPS) can be solved by the product of the sampling rate and the number of operation units. Due to the large area overhead for programming, control and communication, the area overhead of all EUs account for only a small part of the area overhead of whole reconfigurable architectures. We define the area overhead ratios of reconfigurable architectures to all EUs in the chips as k, if we use programmable architectures to realize the same algorithms. Thus, we can infer that for an application, programmable architectures will occupy k times area as that of ASIC to obtain the same MIPS, provided that the frequency is identical; similarly, programmable architectures will run at the frequency of k times as that of ASIC to keep the same area and performance.

The aforementioned relationship is easy to understand. Unfortunately, less attention is paid to the ratio value of k, which is often much larger than 10. It may be acceptable to use conventional reconfigurable architectures to implement the special applications such as prototyping development mentioned above. However, replacing ASICs in high-performance customer devices by current reconfigurable architectures on a large scale is still impossible. Therefore, it becomes the key to extend the successes of reconfigurable architectures how to reduce the ratio value of k. Thus, we attempt to adopt larger EUs in the PEs of a reconfigurable architecture.

3   Architecture

3.1 Array Structure

Most of real-life multimedia and baseband computations in custom devices belong to stream applications [4] and [5]. Besides computation intensity, they exhibit two other characteristics: concurrency and regularization. Fig. 2 shows the concurrency of stream applications. It includes two concepts:

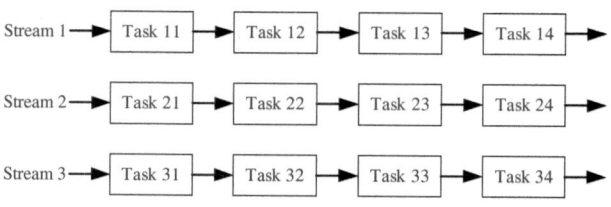

Fig. 2. The concurrency of a stream application

- Pipelined data path, in which every task can be processed simultaneously to form an efficient pipeline, similar to systolic structures [3];
- And data parallelism, where multiple data streams can be computed simultaneously.

Similarly, the regularization also has two concepts as follows:

- Producer-consumer locality, which embodies the relationship between task kernels. Each kernel receives the result data produced by its front kernel, consumes (processes) them, produces new data, and sends to its back kernels.
- Regular connection, which means there are no feedback and long-distance interconnection at unit or subsystem levels.

Based on the characteristics of current high-throughput applications, we propose an array structure shown in Fig. 3. It consists of a heterogeneous array of tens (or even hundreds) of PEs. The architecture is a template that can be instantiated for a given application. As a result, the function of every processing element depends on the mapping results of application algorithms at synthesis-time. Due to the locality of computation and communication, every PE just connect directly with its four nearest neighborhoods at the locations of the east, west, south and north. Besides direct interconnections, indirect connections can be formed by bypassing the ports of some PEs. Data-driven mechanism is employed in both interconnection network and PEs. One PE does not work until the needed data arrive. The networks of most reconfigurable architectures are synchronized by this way [8] and [9]. In our architecture, the EUs in PEs are also synchronized by data. Therefore, we call the architecture we propose as fully-data-driven reconfigurable architecture.

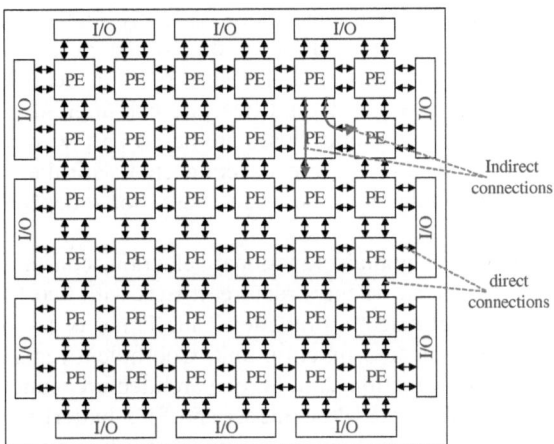

Fig. 3. The proposed heterogeneous array structure

3.2 Processing Elements

The functions of each PE are to configure a special interconnect network on the basis of a certain application, and to execute very-coarse-grained computations like multi-tap

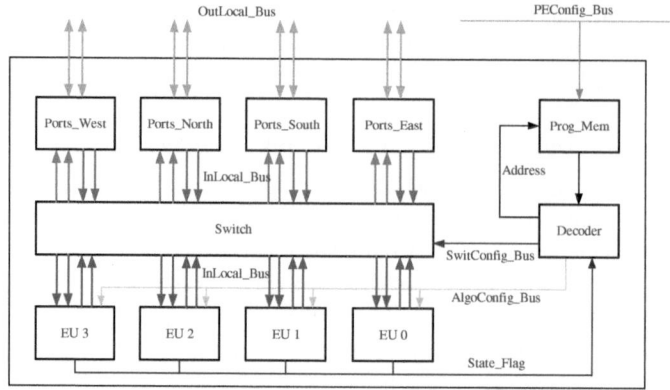

Fig. 4. The structure of the processing elements

FIR segments and FFT butterfly units. Fig. 4 presents the general structure of the PEs in proposed reconfigurable architecture, mainly including program memory (Prog_Mem), instruction decoder (Decoder), multiple ports (Ports_West, Ports_North, Ports_South and Ports_East), EU, and switch (Switch).

Instructions can be written through PE configuring bus (PEConfig_Bus) from embedded microprocessor or outside. Decoder is made use of to decode instructions, then to get the configuration information. Decoder does not work cycle by cycle, but actively fetch next instruction in term of the last instruction and the EU state flags (State_Flag).

There are four kinds of directional ports, namely Ports_West, Ports_North, Ports_South and Ports_East. Each cluster of directional ports includes two dual-direction ports connecting with other PE. The directions of dual-direction ports and the connections between the two ports and two internal single-direction input buses and two internal single-direction output buses are based on the configuration instructions. The input ports of one PE are directly connected with the output ports of its neighborhoods. The communications between these ports depend on their FIFOs states.

The configurations of EUs contain functional selection, constant coefficients, operation times, and etc. Fig. 5 shows the structure of EUs with two functions. Function select register is in charge of selecting function unit. Timer is responsible for setting the operation times of the selected function unit. Coefficient registers provide some constant coefficients to the function unit. In our architecture, function units include large-scale circuits like multi-tap FIR segments and FFT butterfly units. Small function units like adder and multiplier are also supported. The scale of function unit is based on actual applications. There is at least one FIFO in every EU. These FIFOs are used to save the input data from other PEs or input ports. The FIFOs in EUs as well as ports are very small. They can be composed of register files. The EU number of each PE may be different, which is relative to the input and output signals and the area overhead of EU.

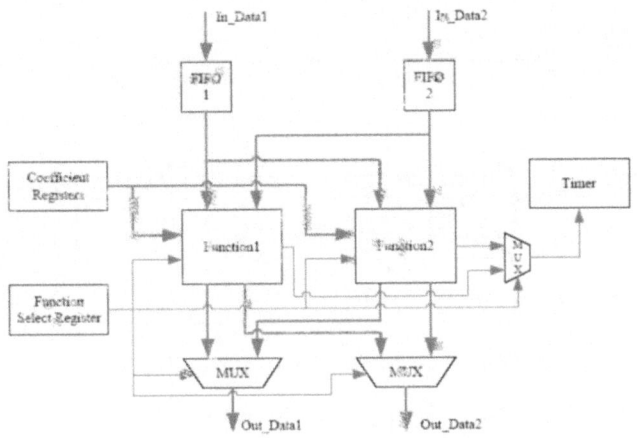

Fig. 5. The structure of execution units

Switch is the most important part that specifies the connections among all EUs and Ports, which will be introduced in the following section.

All PEs own the same Decoders, program memories, Ports, and Switches, though their roles are very different in the whole reconfigurable architecture. The only different is the execution units.

After finishing all configurations of Ports, EUs and Switch, Decoder will stay in a waiting state and continuously detect State_Flag. At this time, all the interconnection relations between Ports, EUs and Switch are static similar to an ASIC circuit driven by data. When the given number of operations has been done, EUs will give some certain signals to inform the decoder to reconfigure.

3.3 Switch

Three kinds of signals need to be routed. They are Data, Data-valid, and FIFO Near-full respectively. Data and Data-valid are always produced together. PEs or output ports receive data from other PEs or input ports on the basis of the indication of Data-valid. They can be treated with the same circuit structures. Fig. 6 shows the routing scheme of port output data. The scheme of EU input data is similar to this. The difference lies in the positions of No Connections.

When the FIFOs in EUs and output ports are close to be full, the input data signal's producers must stop to wait until the corresponding near-full signal is invalid. Otherwise, useful data will be lost. The routing of the near-full input signals is somewhat different from Fig. 6, mainly because the needed configuration signals are not the same. A translator is needed to translate the configuration information of data signals and data-valid signals to those of near-full input signals.

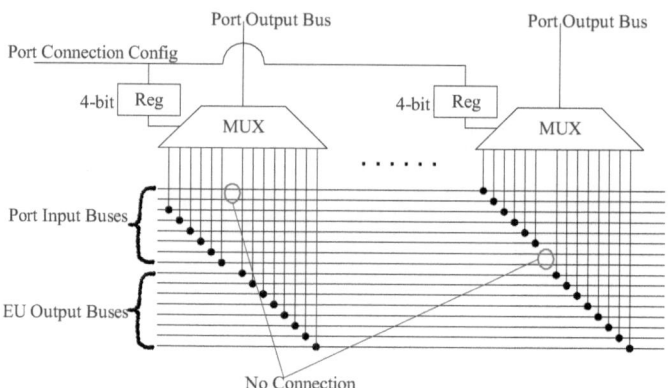

Fig. 6. The part of the Switch structure

4 Reconfiguration

Four types of instructions are distinguished as follows:

- Switch configuration instructions: Configure the connections between different EUs, between different ports, and between EUs and ports.
- Ports configuration instructions: Define the connections between ports and local interconnection buses, and the directions of the local dual-direction interconnection buses.
- EU configuration instructions: Specify the functions of EUs and the number of processing samples, and send the needed coefficients.
- Register clear instructions: Clear the data in ports FIFOs, EU registers, and EU FIFOs.
- Branch instructions: Jump to the initial address of a new application on the basis of the state flags of EUs.

Because of the simplification of PEs, the instruction operations are actually a series of sequential configurations. After configurations, the whole circuits of PE will be static. For next task, new configurations begin. According to the orderliness, we use the format of instruction packet to simplify the instruction decoders and minimize the instruction memories. The format is shown in Fig. 7. Due to the invariable sequence and format, the opcodes become implicit. Decoders can understand the meanings of codes in the packets, and send the corresponding configurations to the different parts of PEs. When a new state flag comes, Decoder begins to read next instruction packet.

By configuring the ports and switches, almost all PEs can communicate with each other. In fact, this may not be necessary due to the features of current high-throughput applications. As to the connections in each PE, the communications are multiform. For instance Ports_West can communicate with Ports_North, Ports_South or Ports_East in the one-to-one form. On the other hand, broadcasting communications can be provided. For instance, Ports_West can send data to Ports_North, Ports_South and Ports_East at the same time.

Commonly, there are multiple EUs in each PE. By different configurations, these EUs can work in parallel like Fig. 8 (a), and in pipeline like Fig. 8 (b). This multiformity benefits from the reconfigurable switches which are able to form various connections among PEs and ports. When a task is over, PE can be reconfigured to implement a new task.

Task 1: Code Length
Ports Configuration
Switch Configuration
EU Function Selection
EU Operation Times
EU 1 Coefficient
EU 2 Coefficient
... ...
Task 2
... ...

Fig. 7. The format of instruction packet

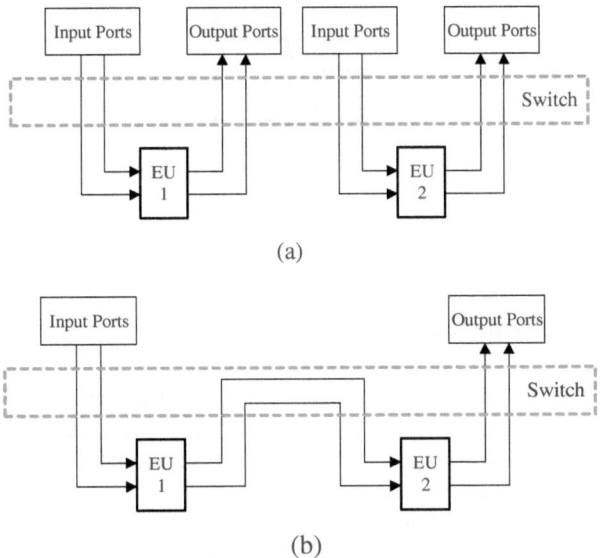

(a)

(b)

Fig. 8. The connections between EUs, (a) in parallel, and (b) in pipeline

5   Design Flow

The aim of the proposed reconfigurable architecture is not to provide a general processor, but to simply the design flow of ASICs and SOCs, for a narrow special application domain, and to lower the TTM and NRE cost. The design flow of the proposed architecture is shown in Fig. 9. The application codes in the form of MATLAB or C language are translated into the data flow graph with basic operations like multiplication and addition. Based on the area overhead demands, performance/cost ratio and programmability, some basic operations are combined together to form a function unit like FFT butterfly unit and Viterbi add-compare-select unit. Then, larger function units will be mapped as EUs onto the array architecture we proposed. The function units in different data paths can also be combined to form an execution unit with multiple functions if the application model is time-multiplexing. An optimizing process is needed in order to obtain the minimum processing elements. The results of optimization are a certain architecture and configuration instructions.

Because the interconnection network and PE configuration structure are fixed, and a set of execution units have been placed in a library, the design time of a chip will be shortened by reusing these predefined resources.

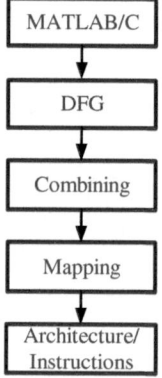

Fig. 9. The design flow of the proposed architecture

6   Performance Analysis

For illustrative purposes, let us consider the implementation of FIR digital filter on the proposed architecture. Fig. 10 gives the FIR filter structure and the possible execution units used to process the corresponding convolution tasks. We name the computation of one delay, multiplication and addition in Block A as one-tap operation, and similarly name the computation in Block B as two-tap operation. Clearly, the execution unit with the function of two-tap operation has the advantages over the execution unit with the function of one-tap operation in processing capability.

As is stated above that the reconfigurable architectures with less k can achieve higher performance/cost ratio. In order to estimate k, we design a configurable architecture with few PEs in the FPGA chip of Altera Cyclone II. Fig. 11 shows the k values under the condition of different grained EUs used in the proposed architecture. When the EU has the capability of one-tap operation, k is close to 10, while the value is about 2 when the EU has eight-tap operation function. With the increment of the granularity of EUs, the k value decrease gradually.

Several EUs can be cascaded to run a more-tap operation by configurating the Switch. Furthermore, several PEs can be cascaded to realize an ASIC-like digital FIR filter. Based on actual applications, the filter with different tap numbers and tap coefficients can be reconfigurated easily and quickly.

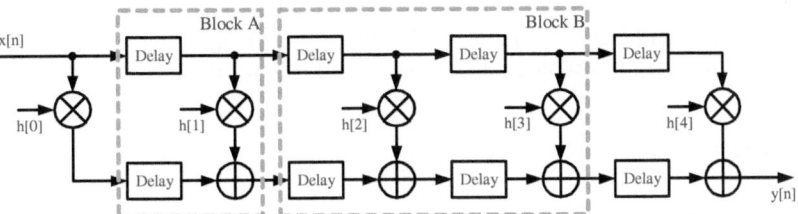

Fig. 10. A five-tap FIR filter

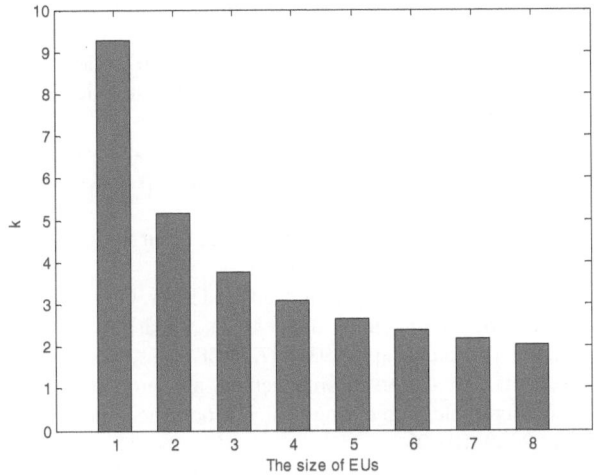

Fig. 11. The relation between k and the size of EUs

7   Conclusion

We have presented a reconfigurable architecture of high-throughput digital signal processing, with the characteristics of fully-data-driven mechanism and very-coarse-grained EUs. In the light of the trend of current application algorithms, a data-driven array structure or interconnection network is employed, which permits the direct connections between one PE and its four neighbors and also support the indirection connections between any two neighboring PEs by configurations. Unlike most coarse-grained reconfigurable architectures, each PE may contain very-coarse-grained EUs. By the configurations of PEs, the ASIC-like connections can be formed among EUs and ports with the data-driven mechanism to realize the mapping of special domain applications. The corresponding design flow of the reconfigurable architecture has also presented. In order to illustrate the role of very-coarse- grained EUs, we analyzed the relationship between the area overhead ratio of the whole architecture to all EUs and the granularity of the EUs. The analysis results showed that the area overhead ratio can be raised with the enhancement of EU granularity.

Future work is focused on further evaluation of the high-throughput processing capabilities of real-life applications such as WiMAX baseband processing and H.264 video system. In addition, a suitable methodology for mapping special domain applications onto the reconfigurable architecture should be explored.

References

1. Abnous, A., Rabaey, J.: Ultra-low-power domain-specific multimedia processors. In: 1996 Workshop on VLSI Signal Processing, pp. 461–470. IEEE Press, New York (1996)
2. Dennis, J.B.: Data flow supercomputers. Computer 13(11), 48–56 (1980)
3. Kung, H.T.: Why systolic architectures? Computer 15(1), 37–46 (1982)
4. Kapasi, U.J., Rixner, S., Dally, W.J., Abn, J.H., Mattson, P., Owens, J.D.: Programmable stream processors. Computer 36(8), 54–62 (2003)
5. Srikanteswara, S., Palat, R.C., Reed, J.H., Athanas, P.: An overview of configurable computing machines for software radio handsets. IEEE Communications Magazine 41(7), 134–141 (2003)
6. Hartenstein, R.: A decade of reconfigurable computing: a visionary retrospective. In: 2001 Conference on Design, automation and test in Europe, pp. 642–649. ACM Press, New York (2001)
7. Compton, K., Hauck, S.: Reconfigurable computing: a survey of systems and software. ACM Computing Surveys 34(2), 171–210 (2002)
8. Todman, T.J., Constantinides, G.A., Wilton, S.J.E., Mencer, O., Luk, W., Cheung, P.Y.K.: Reconfigurable computing: architectures and design methods. In: 2005 IEE proceedings of Computers and Digital Techniques, pp. 193–207. IEEE Press, New York (2005)
9. Abdin, Z., Svensson, B.: Evolution in architectures and programming methodologies of coarse-grained reconfigurable computing. Microprocessors and Microsystems (2008), doi:10.1016/j.micro.2008. 10.003
10. Koren, I., Mendelson, B., Peled, I., Silberman, G.M.: A data-driven VLSI Array for Arbitrary Algorithms. Computer 21(10), 30–43 (1988)
11. Chen, D.C., Rabaey, J.M.: A reconfigurable multiprocessor IC for rapid prototyping of algorithmic-specific high-speed DSP data paths. IEEE Journal of Solid-State Circuits 27(12), 1895–1904 (1992)
12. Taylor, M.B., Lee, W., Miller, J., et al.: Evaluation of the RAW microprocessor: an exposed-wire-delay architecture for ILP and streams. In: 31st Annual International Symposium on Computer Architecture, pp. 2–13. IEEE Press, New York (2004)
13. Duller, A., Towner, D., Panesar, G., Gray, A., Robbins, W.: PicoArray technology: the tool's story. In: 2005 Conference on Design, Automation and Test in Europe (DATE 2005), pp. 106–111. IEEE Press, New York (2005)
14. Yu, Z.: High performance and energy efficient multi-core systems for DSP applications. Ph.D. Thesis, University of California, Davis (2007)

15. Vejanovski, R., Stojcevski, A., Singh, J., Faulkner, M., Zayegh, A.: A highly efficient reconfigurable architecture for an UTRA-TDD mobile station receiver. In: 2003 International Symposium on Circuits and Systems (ISCAS 2003), pp. II45–II48. IEEE Press, New York (2003)
16. El-Rayis, A.O., Arslan, T., Erdogan, A.T.: Addressing future space challenges using reconfigurable instruction cell based architectures. In: 2008 NASA/ESA Conference on Adaptive Hardware and Systems (AHS 2008), pp. 22–25. IEEE Press, New York (2008)
17. Cherepacha, D., Lewis, D.: DP-FPGA: an FPGA architecture optimized for datapaths. VLSI Design 4(4), 329–343 (1996)
18. Yeung, A.K.W., Rabaey, J.M.: A reconfigurable data-driven multiprocessor architecture for rapid prototyping of high throughput DSP algorithms. In: The Twenty-sixth Hawaii International Conference on System Sciences, pp. 169–178. IEEE Press, New York (1993)
19. Marshall, A., Stansfield, T., Kostarnov, I., Vuillemin, J., Hutchings, B.: A reconfigurable arithmetic array for multimedia applications. In: 1999 ACM/SIGDA Seventh International Symposium on Field Programmable Gate Arrays, pp. 135–143. ACM Press, New York (1999)
20. Mirsky, E., Dehon, A.: MATRIX: a reconfigurable computing architecture with configurable instruction distribution and deployable resources. In: 1996 IEEE symposium on FPGAs for custom computing machines, pp. 157–166. IEEE Press, New York (1996)
21. Singh, H., Lee, M., Lu, G., Kurdahi, F.J., Bagherzadeh, N., Chaves, F.E.M.: MorphoSys: an integrated reconfigurable system for data-parallel and computation-intensive applications. IEEE Transactions on Computers 49(5), 465–481 (2000)

Identify Intimate Social Relationship in Blogsphere

Li Han[1,2], SongXiang Cen[2], Jian Ma[2], and Yan Ma[1]

[1] Beijing University of Posts and Telecommunications, China
hanli_bupt@126.com, mayan@bupt.edu.cn
[2] Nokia Research Center Beijing, China
csx008@gmail.com, jian.j.ma@nokia.com

Abstract. Weblog has become a kind of important information resource on the Internet for it can make people publish individual experiences and opinion easily. Blogsphere has evolved vast and complex social network through blogrolls, citation, reading, comments and other social activities. More attentions are paid on related research for the prevalence of blog. The paper proposes the definition of intimate relationship based on comments links to analyze social network in the blogsphere. Blog social network is modeled as weighted directed graph and every weight depends on the frequency of social relationship between bloggers. And then blog intimate friends circle can be extracted with identification algorithm proposed by the paper. Blog data from one of famous blog sites (Hibaidu) in China is collected and taken as our study object. Through analyzing the blog dataset, we found that the intimate relationships are kept more stably and different bloggers maintain intimate relationship with the same blogger but they have no social interactions, which is named as the phenomena of familiar strange friends. These findings will contribute to the understanding of blogsphere and providing better blog services for users.

1 Introduction

Weblog has become a prominent social medium on the Internet. But so far, blog has no recognized definition. According to "Glossary of Internet Terms" [1], basically a blog is a journal that is available on the web. The activity of updating a blog is "blogging" and someone who keeps a blog is a "blogger". Blogs are typically updated daily through software that allows people with little or no technical background to update and maintain the blog. Postings on a blog are almost always arranged in chronological order. Weblog has many particular features compared with regular web pages so specific attentions should be paid on weblog. At the same time, as a kind of popular social medium, Blogsphere gestates gigantic social network through social activities, such as blogrolls, citation, comments, reading and so on. Increasing interests from research and industrial communities about blog harness much research work along with the prevalence of weblog. Ongoing research in the area includes mining blog content [2] [3] [4] [5] and analysis of blog social network. Our work is more related to the latter. Traditional analysis of social network always carried out based on static graph [2]. But there is variability in the social network so subsequent works pay more attention on social network evolution. Now most of the blog research has focused on

P. Mueller, J.-N. Cao, and C.-L. Wang (Eds.): Infoscale 2009, LNICST 18, pp. 14–25, 2009.
© Institute for Computer Science, Social-Informatics and Telecommunications Engineering 2009

blogrolls and citation links [6] [7] [8]. But comments links is also an important social relationship, the focus of this paper will paid on comments links.

The study of intimate relationships is a relatively new area within the field of social psychology. Intimate relationship is a particular close interpersonal relationship, which plays a central role in our overall human experience. According to Miller *et al* [9], the intimate relationship consists of people that we are attracted to, whom we like and love, and those who we marry and provide emotional and personal support. This paper extends intimate relationship to characterize social relationship in the blogsphere, more specifically, the definition of intimate relationship will be proposed based on comments link to weight social relationship among bloggers. We think only when there are the same interest things among bloggers, they will keep intimate relationship. So the research of intimate relationship in the blogsphere will help understanding of blog social network and propose new added services based on findings, such as, personalized blog search engine or recommendation of blog.

The paper is organized as follows. Section 2 reviews related work on blog community and information diffusion. Section 3 gives the definition of intimate relationship and intimate friends circle and proposes corresponding identification algorithm. Section 4 conducts experiment based on dataset from China Hibaidu website. The summarization and the direction of future work are given in the final section.

2 Related Work

Analysis of blog social network can be applied to research of blog community and information diffusion of blogsphere. Kumar *et al.* [8] aimed to experimentally observe and model the highly dynamic and temporal community structure. So they defined time graphs to extend the traditional notion of evolving directed graph, capturing link creation as a point phenomenon in time. Their algorithm for community extraction based on time graph consisted of pruning and expansion. The blog graph would be first scanned for all vertices of degree at most two. Vertices of degree zero and one were removed and vertices of degree two were checked to determine whether their two neighbors were connected. If so they were passed through as a seed in the expansion step and the resulting community was output. The aim of the expansion step was to grow the seed into a set of nodes that constituted a potential community. They analyzed the evolution of structural properties of blog time graph and the results showed that the macroscopic structure and the microscopic structure of the graph began to change dramatically. They also presented analysis of bursty behavior within the blog communities and showed that this burstiness was a fundamental property of link creation in blogspace. Tseng *et al* [10] aimed to capture the community landscape on a specific topic and allow users to explore these important blog communities. When users identified a query of interest and fetched relevant entries, and then the impact scores of relevant entries were calculated. The ranking scores for the blogs were derived from the entry scores. The community structure could be extracted through rank-based connectivity analysis. Given different thresholds of ranking score, different slices of the community structure were given as a set of clusters. Tomographic clustering algorithm generated an ordered sequence of blogs, which could be drawn into a curve called mountain view with blog scores on the vertical axis. Mountain view could be seen as the contour of the community structure since the curve showed upper bounds of paths within social network. Peaks and valleys of the view depicted representive blogs as community authorities and community connectors respectively. Kazunari [11] proposed the concept of a latent weblog community, which was a meeting space for bloggers who wrote about similar or closely related topics but did not know each other. To extract latent weblog communities, a new method to partition a bipartite graph into subgraph was proposed, which removed the highest frequency edges to go through the shortest paths between the weakest pairs. Because the method tried to divide node pairs which had the weakest relation among all nodes paris, the authors named it as Weakest pair algorithm. Experimental results explained that the weakest pairs algorithm was more effective than shortes path betweenness in extracting latent weblog community from Blogspace in terms of information loss and structure completeness. Backstorm et al [12] aimed to resolve the basic questions about evolution of social community based on source data from LiveJournal and DBLP and found that the propensity of individuals to join communities and the development of communities depended in subtle ways on the underlying network structure.

Another problem of information diffusion in the blogsphere is also related to our work. Gruhl et al [13] studied the dynamics of information propagation in the blogsphere and presented a characterization of topic propagation from individual to individual respectively at macroscopic and microscopic level. Adar et al [14] defined a set of features appropriate for infection inference in the blogsphere and constructed infection tree to visualize the information flow.

Our works analyze blog social network and identify intimate friendship from Blogsphere. We extend intimate friendship in the social psychology and firstly give the definition of intimate relationship for the blogsphere. Based on the definition, intimate relationships are extracted by the weight of social interaction among blogger. Previous research paid more attention on the number of neighbours in the blogsphere when finding blog communities. But we take not only the number of social relationship but also the intensity and frequency of social interaction between blogers into consideration. Additionally, as a kind of social medium from Internet, Blog has specific regional for different culture. The paper utilizes real blog dataset from China website HiBaidu as research object. The findings are more suitable for the status of China Blog than research works based on other blog datasets.

3   Model Blog Social Network

Blogsphere can be described by blog graph, a directed graph $B(V, E)$, where V is the set of all the blogger and a directed edge $(v_x, v_y) \in E$ suggests there is social relationship between blog v_x and blog v_y. The social relationship can be citation, comments, blogroll and trackback but the paper will pay more attention on comments relationship. So there will be a directed edge from v_x to v_y when blog v_x give

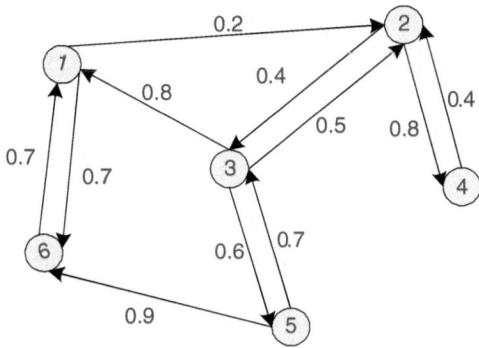

Fig. 1. Weighted Directed Blog Graph

comments to any post of blog v_y during studied time, where v_y is called the head

and v_x is called the tail. But in the blog graph, v_y can be named as blogger and v_x is named as reviewer. In order to identify intimate friendship in the blogsphere, directed blog graph is extended to weighted directed blog graph. The label or weight of directed edge from v_x to v_y denotes the percentage of comments gived by v_x to

blog v_y in the total number of posts of blog v_y.

Next, we will discuss what can be named as intimate relationship in the blogsphere based on weighted directed blog graph. The degree of intimate relationship between bloggers depends on the weight. There will be threshold value set, and if the weight of a directed edge is above the threshold value, it can be thought that there is intimate relationship between the blogger and reviewer. If the threshold value is set to 0.6, there are two bidirectional intimate relationships between blog 1 and 6, blog 3 and 5 as Figure 2. But the relationships from blog 3 to 1, from blog 5 to 6, and from blog 2 to 4 can not be thought as intimate relationship for its undirectivity.

3.1 Definition of Circle of Intimate Relationship

Let $V = \{v_1, v_2, \ldots v_x, \ldots v_n\}$ be the set of blog node, N be the set of neighbour blog

nodes, such as $N(v_x) = \{v_a, v_b, \ldots v_i, \ldots v_z \mid (v_x, v_i) \in E, or, (v_i, v_x) \in E\}$ be the

neighbour set of blog node v_x .   The blog dataset

$D = R \cup W = \{r_1, w_1, r_2, w_2, \ldots r_m, w_m\}$ is a blog relationship dataset of blogger

reviewing relationship itemset R and weight itemset W. Every item pair (r_i, w_i) be

$(r_i, w_i) = \{v_x, v_y, w_{xy}(v_x, v_y)\}$, $w_{xy}(v_x, v_y)$ means the first blogger v_x give

comments to the second blogger v_y and the number of comments is w_{xy} percent of the number of posts published by the second blogger . Every $r_i = (v_x, v_y)$ is ordered pair and has the unique corresponding value of w_i .

Definition 1 (Intimate Relationship)

There is intimate relationship in the $p = (v_x, v_y) \in R$ if $w_{xy}(v_x, v_y) > \sigma$ and $w_{yx}(v_y, v_x) > \sigma$, where σ is the threshold value. And $p = (v_x, v_y)$ can be named as intimate relationship pair, which is not ordered pair. So the intimate relationship is bidirectional.

According to social psychology, intimate relationship comes into being gradually so there is a kind of social relationship, which can not be divided into intimate relationship but will be likely to become intimate relationship in the future. We name this relationship as promising intimate relationship and give its definition in the definition 2. Decay factor α is utilized to reduce criteria for classifying.

Definition 2 (Promising Intimate Relationship). There is promising intimate relationship in the $p = (v_x, v_y) \in R$ if $w_{xy}(v_x, v_y) > \alpha\sigma$ or $w_{yx}(v_x, v_y) > \alpha\sigma$. So promising intimate relationship is directive.

Definition 3 (Intimate Friends Circle). Intimate friends circle is made up of center and edge. $q = \{v_{mx}, v_{my}, ... v_{mz}\}$ is the center of intimate friends circle, when $\forall v_{ma}, v_{mb}$, v_{ma} and v_{mb} must be intimate relationship pair. The edge of circle $NE(q) = \{v'_{ux}, v'_{uy}, ... v'_{uz}\}$, $\forall v'_{ux}$, $\exists v_{my} \in q$, there must be promising intimate relationship between v'_{ux} and v_{my} . So $q \cup NE(q)$ constitutes intimate friends circle, and $|q|$ is the size of intimate friend circle.

Definition 4 (Intimate Friends Circle Set)

$Q_{ifc} = \{Q_1, Q_2, ... Q_m\}$ is the intimate friends circle set for the blogsphere, every item Q_i is $q_i \cup NE(q_i)$, q_i is the center of intimate friends circle and $NE(q_i)$ is the edge of circle.

3.2 Identify Intimate Friends Circle Set

The definition of intimate friends circle set has been given above. How to identify intimate friends circle set from the vast and complex blog social network, the corresponding algorithm is proposed in Table 1. According to the above definition, every intimate friends circle is made up of center and edge. There may be no edge under certain value of threshold and decay factor but circle must have a center. For blogsphere, the quantity of intimate friends circle depends on the number of center.

Table 1. Algorithm to identify intimate friends circle set

Algorithm Identify Intimate Friends Circle Set

Input : Blog relationship dataset D
    Threshold σ Decay factor α
Output: Intimate friends Circle Set Q$_{ifc}$
1: Initialize 0 intimate friendship pair set P
2: For each $(r_i, w_i) = (v_x, v_y, w_{xy}(v_x, v_y)) \in D$
3:    if $w_{xy}(v_x, v_y) > \sigma$
4:       Find $(r_i', w_i') = (v_y, v_x, w_{yx}(v_y, v_x))$
5:          if $w_{yx}(v_y, v_x) > \sigma$
6:             add (v_x, v_y) to P
7: end
8: Initialize $j = 1$
9: for $p_i = (v_x, v_y) \in P$
10:    add v_x, v_y to q_j
11:    if $\exists v_z$ satisfy$(v_x, v_z) \in P \& (v_z, v_y) \in P$
12:       add v_z to q_j
13:    for each $v_{x'} \in q_j$
14:       if $\exists (r_i, w_i) = (v_{x'}, v_a, w(v_{x'}, v_a)) \& w(v_{x'}, v_a) > \alpha\sigma$
15:          add v_a to $NE(q_j)$
16:       if $\exists (r_i', w_i') = (v_a, v_{x'}, w'(v_a, v_{x'})) \& w'(v_a, v_{x'}) > \alpha\sigma$
17:          add v_a to $NE(q_j)$
18:    $j = j + 1$
19:    add $q_j \cup NE(q_j)$ to Q$_{ifc}$
20: end

4 Experiment

To analyze intimate relationship in the blogsphere, we crawled blog data from one of the famous blog website Hibaidu (http://hi.baidu.com) as our research object and collected a set of 3484 blogs containing 536351 posts until sep 11th 2008. Baidu space is a Chinese blog publication platform whose web pages are well organized with unified templates. This enables us to extract the posts, comments and other information such as published date simply by regular expressions. Because we pay more attention on the comments relationship in the blogsphere, we extract corresponding reviewing relationship from every post and construct blog social relationship dataset D as the description in the section 3. Every item includes two blog nodes (A, B), which means that blog A give comments to blogger B during studied time, and there will be a directed line from A to B.

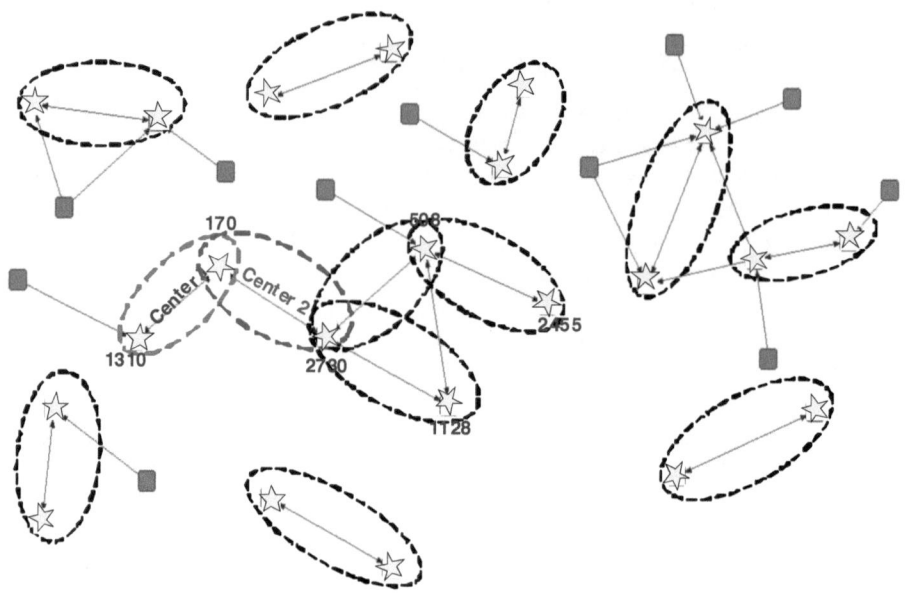

Fig. 2. Intimate Friends Circle Set

Based on the blog social network, we extract intimate friends circle from Hibaidu blog dataset with our algorithm under $\sigma = 0.6$ and $\alpha = 0.5$. The final results are given by Figure 2. In order to describe our findings, every blog is given to a unique serial number in the following parts. It is easily concluded that there is few indeed intimate relationship in the blogsphere. A blog can belong to two or three intimate friends circle concurrently but no so many social activities exist among his initiate friends within different communities, for example blog 170 and 1310 form the center of circle 1, blog node 170 and 2730 form center 2 but there is no intimate relationship between node 1310 and 2730. Similar situation also exists between 170 and 1128, 170 and 508, 2730 and 2455. We name the phenomenon as familiar strange friends. But there is a pair of blog node 1128 and 508, which form different intimate friend circle with node 2730, but have more social interaction. In order to study the phenomena of familiar strange friends further, we pay more attention on the social relationship between node pair 1128 and 508. Here we adopt two indicators $SR(B,R)$ and $DP(B,R)$ to weight the social relationship between blog nodes as formula (1) and (2).

$$SR(B,R) = \frac{number\_comment\_(R\_to\_B)}{number\_post(B)} \qquad (1)$$

$$DP(B,R) = \frac{number\_comment\_(R\_to\_B)}{number\_comment(R)} \qquad (2)$$

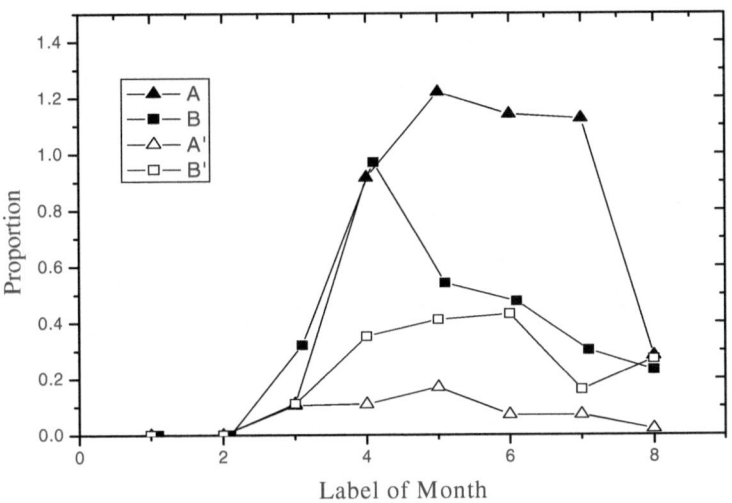

Fig. 3. Social Relationship between Blog Node 1128 and 508

number_post(B) denotes the number of post of blog *B* during studied time, *number_comment(R)* denotes the number of comments of reviewer *R* and *number_comment_(R_to_B)* is the number of comments from reviewer *R* to blog *B*. Line *A* and *A'* denote *SR*(1128,508) and *DP*(1128,508) respectively, and line B and B' is *SR*(508,1128) and *DP*(508,1128) in Figure 3.

It can be found that the social relationship between 508 and 1128 will be kept once the relationship has been established. But it is found that there is changing tendency in the relationship during May to July 2008. In order to uncover the reason, we study the activity of blog node 1128 and 508 in the blogsphere. For every blog node, the degree of activity is measured according to the number of post and comments from blogger as formula (3).

$$DA(B) = number\_post(B) \times number\_comment(B) \qquad (3)$$

Figure 4 gives the degree of activity for blog node 1128 and 508 from January to August. We analyze the social interaction between node 1128 and 508 by combining Figure 3 with 4. Node 508 keeps his attention about node 1128 since he gives comments to node 1128. The attention has decreasing tendency on August but the degree

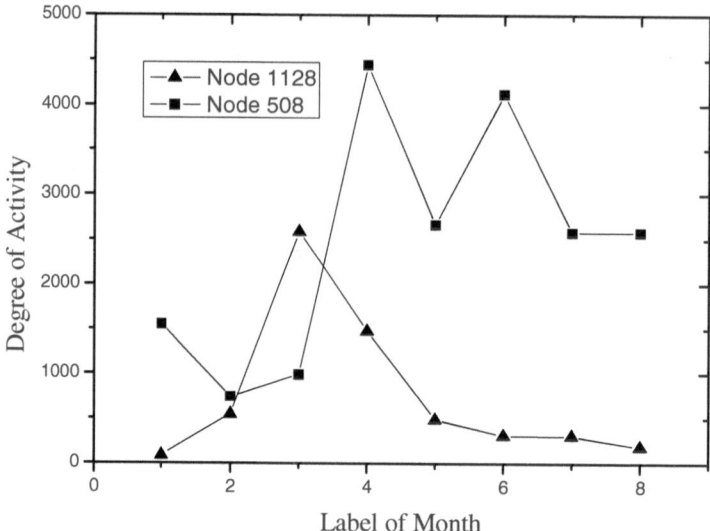

Fig. 4. Degree of Activity of blog node 1128 and 508

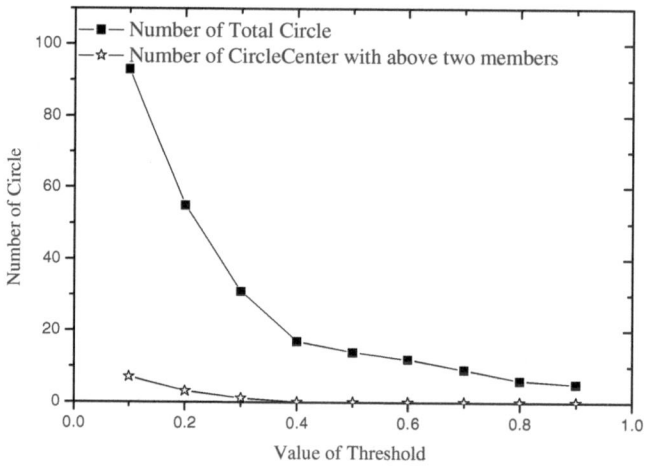

Fig. 5. Number of Circle in the Blogsphere

of activity of node 508 also drops. Node 1128 pays less attention on node 508 from May to August at the same time the active degree of node 1128 has the similar tendency during the same time. Based on the observed result, it is believed that there should be more social relationship between these familiar strange friends. We will provide recommendation among these familiar strange friends found and follow the status of relationship to verify the conjecture in the future research work.

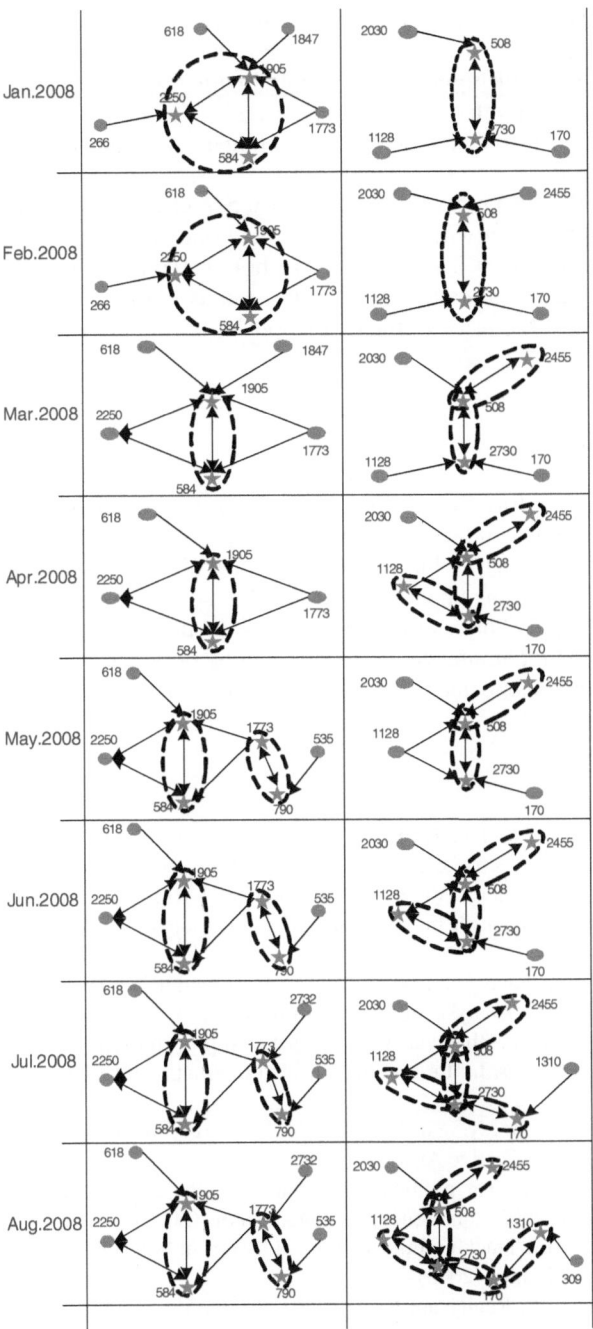

Fig. 6. Evolution of Intimate Friends Circle in Blogsphere

According to the above definition, every circle has unique center, which depends on the value of threshold, so we study the number of circle when changing threshold value. From the results of Figure 5, the simple interaction social relationship is common so the number of circle will drop significantly when value of threshold change from 0.1 to 0.4. It is also concluded that the number of circle center with above two members is very few.

In order to study the process of intimate friends circle, we extract two intimate friend circle groups, which will include more than one circle, to visualize the formation of circle set as Figure 6. The value of threshold is 0.6 and decay factor is 0.5. The intimate relationship in the center of intimate friends circle can be kept stably than that of circle edge, so the basic intimate relationship in the intimate friends circle has the slow evolution.

5   Conclusions

The paper pays more effort on analyzing the social relationship among bloggers in the blogsphere. The intimate relationship depends on frequency of interaction between blogger. Through studying the blog dataset from Hibaidu, we found the constancy of intimate relationship and the phenomena of familiar strange friendship. The finding of phenomena will help to characterize social network in the blogsphere. At the same time, individual blog recommendation service can be provided for users through identifying intimate relationship and the results of mining content of blog.

References

1. Matisse's Glossary of Inernet Terms,
   http://www.matisse.net/files/glossary.html
2. Bar-llan, J.: An Outsider's View on Topic-oriented Bloggiing. In: Proceeding of the Alt.Papers Track of the 13th International Conference on World Wide Web, paper 28-34 (May 2004)
3. Mishhe, G.: Experiments with Mood Classification in Blog Posts. In: Style 2005-1st Workshop on Stylistic Analysis of Text for Information Access, at SIGIR 2005 (2005)
4. Mei, Q., Liu, C., Su, H., Zhai, C.: A Probabilistic Approach to Spatiotemporal Theme Pattern Mining on Weblogs. In: Proceedings of 15th International Conference on World Wide Web (2006)
5. Ni, X., Xue, G.-R., Ling, X., Yu, Y., Yang, Q.: Exploring in the Weblog Space by Detecting Informative and Affective Articles
6. Adamis, L., Glance, N.: The political blogosphere and the 2004 U.S. election: divided they blog. In: LinkKDD 2005 Conference, Chicago, Illinois (2005)
7. Adar, E., Adamic, L.: Tracking infromation epidemics in blogsphere. In: Web Intelligence 2005, Compiegne, France (2005)
8. Kumar, R., Novak, J., Raghavan, P., Tomkins, A.: On the bursty evolution of blogspace. In: Proceedings of 12th International Conference on World Wide Web (WWW), pp. 568–576 (2003)
9. Miller, R.S., Perlman, D., Brehm, S.S.: Intimate Relationship. McGraw-Hill, Toronto

10. Tseng, B.L., Tatemura, J., Wu, Y.: Tomographic clustering to visualize blog communities as mountain views. In: Proceedings of 2nd Annual Workshop on the Weblogging Ecosystem (2005)
11. Ishida, K.: Extracting latent weblog communities: A partitioning algorithm for bipartite graphs. In: Proceedings of 2nd Annual Workshop on the Weblogging Ecosystem (2005)
12. Backstrom, L., et al.: Group formation in large social networks: membership, growth and evolution. In: Proceedings of 12th ACM SIGKDD, pp. 44–54. ACM Press, New York
13. Gruhl, D., Guha, R.V., Liben-Nowell, D., Tomkins, A.: Information diffusion through blogsphere. SIGKDD Explorations 6(2), 43–52 (2004)
14. Adar, E., Adamic, L.A.: Tracking information epidemics in blogspace. In: Web Intelligence (2005)

Local vs. Global Scalability in Ad Hoc and Sensor Networks

András Faragó

The University of Texas at Dallas,
Richardson, Texas 75080, USA
farago@utdallas.edu

Abstract. We address large, random network topologies that are typical in ad hoc and sensor networks. In these systems we need at least two different types of scalability. First, we want that with growing network size the topology remains connected, so that communication is possible between nodes. Second, it is also necessary that the individual nodes can operate with limited energy and complexity, which requires that the number of neighbors of any node remains bounded. Unfortunately, these global vs. local scalability requirements conflict with each other, as it is known, under very general conditions, that full connectivity can only be achieved with infinitely growing node degrees. Therefore, it is important to quantify how large part of the random topology can be still expected to belong to a connected component if the nodes are confined to some bounded degree. We investigate this issue in a model that is more general than previously investigated random wireless network topology models. In our general model we derive an asymptotically optimal trade-off between node degrees and the fraction of nodes that form a connected component.

Keywords: Scalability, network topology, connectivity, node degrees.

1 Introduction

Large wireless networks with random topology and no supporting infrastructure, such as ad hoc and sensor networks, are expected to be an important part of the future communications landscape. The network topology of these systems is often modeled by various random graph models, most typically by geometric random graphs. (For general background on such models see, e.g., the books [5], [10].)

Due to the randomness of the network topology, it is not at all guaranteed that any two nodes can send messages to each other, since the random graph that represents the network topology may not be connected. If we want to ensure that all nodes can reach each other, then, as a minimum requirement, we have to make sure at least that the network topology (which is usually represented by an undirected graph) is connected.

The connectivity requirement, however, is not as innocent as it may look, due to random node positions and limited wireless transmission ranges. It turns out (see,

P. Mueller, J.-N. Cao, and C.-L. Wang (Eds.): Infoscale 2009, LNICST 18, pp. 26–45, 2009.
© Institute for Computer Science, Social-Informatics and Telecommunications Engineering 2009

e.g., Gupta and Kumar [6,7]) that in typical cases, such as placing the nodes in a planar disk independently and uniformly at random, the price of connectivity is very high: the transmission range needs to be set such that it asymptotically results in an infinitely growing number of neighbors.

This phenomenon is a serious threat to scalability in these networks. One might hope at this point that for different geometric random graph models the situation may perhaps improve. For example, one may try different deployment domains, different probability distributions, different distance metrics, etc. Unfortunately, however, it has been proven in a very general model that none of these can relieve the scalability bottleneck, see Faragó [3]. It appears that unbounded node degrees are unavoidable whenever full connectivity is required in the limit in a random, geometrically induced topology. This is, of course, bad news for scalable implementation, since a node with finite processing power cannot be expected to handle an unbounded neighborhood with bounded delay.

It is therefore of keen importance whether better scalability can be achieved if we are willing to give up full connectivity and substitute it with the milder requirement of *partial connectivity*. This means, as a price for keeping the node degrees bounded, we accept that only most, but not all, nodes are in a connected component. The motivation is that in many potential applications, such as a network of randomly placed sensors, it is acceptable to have only a majority (say, 99%) of nodes in a connected component and the rest are possibly disconnected.

We investigate the fundamental limits related to such partial connectivity, under very general modeling assumptions. Building on the work we have started in [3,4] on connectivity issues, now we explore the asymptotically optimal trade-off between the fraction of nodes that can be kept in a connected component as a function of the bound on the expected node degrees.

We look for the possibly most general conditions under which we can still prove such a trade-off. It turns out that aiming at generality does pay off: we are able to prove that certain very mild conditions on the otherwise unrestricted model already suffice for the proof. The level of generality also makes the proofs much more transparent than the usual stochastic geometry based analysis of random geometric graphs or percolation models, and allows to easily answering questions that would otherwise be quite hard. To illustrate it, a motivating example is presented in the next section.

2   A Motivating Sample Problem

In this example we model a mobile wireless ad hoc network. The initial position of each node is chosen in the following way. Let P be a probability measure over a planar domain D. First we choose k pivot points independently at random, using P. Then the actual node positions are generated such that each potential node is chosen independently at random from P, but it is kept only if it is within a given distance d_0 to at least one of the random pivot points, otherwise it is discarded. Note that this way of generating the nodes makes them dependent, as the non-discarded ones cluster around the random pivot points, thus modeling a clustered, non-independent node distribution.

The mobility of the nodes in this example is modeled in the following way. Over some time horizon T_n, that may depend on n, the number of nodes, each node moves along a random curve from its initial position with a constant speed v_0. The curve is chosen from a set C of available potential trajectories in D. For simplicity, it is assumed that each curve can be identified by a real parameter. This parameter is chosen using a probability distribution $Q_{x,y}$ that depends on the initial position (x, y) of the node. Then the randomly obtained curve is shifted so that its start point coincides with the random initial position of the node and then the node will move along this random trajectory. It is assumed that C and D are such that the shifted curves still remain in the domain.

Let $d(x, y)$ be a nonnegative real valued function over $D \times D$, with the only restriction that $d(x, x) = 0$ holds for any x. This function is intended to measure "radio distance" in D. The assumption is that whenever $d(x, y)$ is small enough, then two nodes positioned at x and y can receive each others' transmissions. The function $d(x, y)$, however, does not have to satisfy the usual distance axioms, it may reflect complex radio propagation characteristics, such as expected attenuation and fading, it may account for the heterogeneity of the terrain, for propagation obstacles etc. We may also include random effects, making $d(x, y)$ a random variable, reflecting special conditions of interest, such as the random presence of eavesdroppers that can trigger the inhibition of certain links. We assume, however, that if there is randomness in $d(x, y)$, then it is independent of the other random variables in the model.

We now define the links of the network, as follows. Consider two nodes with initial position vectors $X_1(0), X_2(0)$, respectively. As they move along their random trajectories, their positions at time t is denoted by $X_1(t), X_2(t)$, respectively. The two nodes are considered connected by a link, if there is a closed subinterval of length at least t_n within the time horizon $[0, T_n]$, such that $d(X_1(t), X_2(t)) \leq r_n$ holds for every time t within the subinterval, with the possibly complicated radio distance. Here t_n and r_n are parameters that may also depend on the number n of nodes. The motivation for this link definition is that the nodes should be within range at least for the time of sending a packet.

Now the question is this: for given P, D, C, $Q_{x,y}$ and $d(x, y)$, and for the described way of dependent node generation, can we somehow choose the model parameters, such that the expected node degrees remain bounded by, say, 4 and still at least 99% of nodes belong to a connected component?

We believe that it would be rather hard to answer this question with a direct analysis for arbitrary complex choices of P, D, C $Q_{x,y}$ and $d(x, y)$. On the other hand, in view of our general results that we build up in the subsequent sections, it becomes quite straightforward.

3   On a Bottleneck of Scalability

Before presenting our results, let us briefly analyze how the considered issue imposes a *general* scalability bottleneck for large wireless networks.

It is well known that network connectivity is of primary concern in large, random ad hoc networks, since a connected network topology is a fundamental condition for successful operation. Another, less obvious, important reason for taking a closer look at connectivity is its role in the limiting behavior of the *transport capacity* of ad hoc networks.

Reseach interest in the fundamental limits on the transport capacity of ad hoc networks had an upsurge after the the the seminal paper of Gupta and Kumar [6] on the capacity of wireless networks. Many results followed on how much traffic can an ad hoc network support in different modes of operation, which values of local parameters can guarantee global connectivity, what can topology control principally achieve etc.

One of the key results of Gupta and Kumar [6] considers the achievable throughput per source-destination (S-D) pair in a large network, where n nodes are placed independently and uniformly at random in a planar disk of unit area. The nodes have the same (positive) transmission radius r which, in principle, can be chosen arbitrarily. The nodes can transmit with a fixed maximum rate (bit/sec), but they are allowed to divide the channel into subchannels without any constraint, in any domain (e.g., frequency, time, code). The nodes communicate using arbitrary protocols for channel access and routing, with the only restriction that there is a minimal requirement of interference avoidance in the same (sub)channel to ensure successful receptions. The considered traffic pattern is that each node has a randomly chosen destination in the network. The authors prove that in this general model the achieveable throughput per S-D pair is $\Theta\left(\frac{1}{\sqrt{n \log n}}\right)$.

Regarding scalability, the key message of this result is that the achievable throughput per S-D pair tends to zero as the network size grows to infinity. We call this the *vanishing throughput effect*. It means, the network is fundamentally not scalable, since it becomes unable to usefully operate when it grows very large.

To better understand a fundamental reason for the vanishing throughput and its key relationship to asymptotic connectivity, let us briefly discuss what causes it and how in the Gupta-Kumar model [6].

The transmission radius r of nodes has two opposite effects. If r is small, then more hops are needed to deliver a packet to its destination, since in each hop the packet can advance at most a distance of r towards its destination. Therefore, small r causes a growing burden of nodes to serve as relays, which decreases the end-to-end throughput. This would justify choosing r as large as possible. On the other hand, large transmission radius increases interference which causes the throughput to decrease again, so interfence reduction would require to choose r as small as possible.

The detailed analysis of the above conflicting tendencies in [6] shows that the forwarding burden is proportional to $1/r$, since the average route hop-length is proportional to $1/r$. On the other hand, the interference increases quadratically with the radius, due to the area involved, which is proportional to r^2. Balancing the two effects yields the conclusion that r has to be chosen as small as possible, as the interference reduction, due to its quadratic nature, brings more benefit than what is lost by longer routes. Specifically, the joint effect results in the formula

$$\lambda(n) = O\left(\frac{1}{nr(n)}\right) \tag{1}$$

where n is the number of nodes, $\lambda(n)$ is the throughput in bit/sec for each S-D pair and $r(n)$ is the transmission radius (as a function of n). It is clear from (1) that if we want to avoid $\lambda(n) \to 0$, then $r(n)$ has to tend to 0 at least as fast as $O(1/n)$, so that $nr(n)$ does not grow to infinity.

There is, however, an effect that does not allow choosing the transmission radius arbitrarily small. This is the requirement that the network topology must be *connected*, since otherwise communication between certain endpoints becomes impossible. The discussed model uses an earlier result of the same authors [7] about the needed transmission radius for asymptotic connectivity. They show that if the nodes are placed uniformly at random in a unit disk, then the network is connected with probability approaching 1 if and only if the transmission radius satisfies

$$\pi r^2 = \frac{\ln n + c(n)}{n} \tag{2}$$

with $c(n) \to \infty$. According to (2), it is necessary for connectivity that

$$r > \sqrt{\frac{\ln n}{\pi n}}$$

holds for all large enough values of n. Combining it with (1), we obtain

$$\lambda(n) = O\left(\frac{1}{n\sqrt{\frac{\ln n}{n}}}\right) = O\left(\frac{1}{\sqrt{n \ln n}}\right)$$

clearly showing the vanishing throughput effect.

According to the above discussion, the lower bound on the transmission radius, enforced by the network connectivity requirement, can be viewed as an important factor in the vanishing throughput effect, since without it the transmission radius could be chosen small enough to gain arbitrarily more from reduced interference than what is lost by longer hop-distances.

To obtain a graph theoretical view of the network topology, we can translate (2) into the expected node degrees. If the nodes are placed uniformly at random in a unit disk, then πr^2 is the expected number of nodes that fall in the range of a node that is not at the border of the disk, so that its range is fully in the domain. This is also the probability that a random node falls in this range, so the expected number of neighbors is $n\pi r^2$ and by (2) we have $n\pi r^2 > \ln n$. Since only a vanishing fraction of nodes are close to the border, we can asymptotically ignore the border effect and reformulate (2) in the following way: for the Gupta-Kumar model, *connectivity requires that the node degrees grow to infinity at least logarithmically with the network size.*

It is worth mentioning that infinitely growing node degrees alone, even without the capacity analysis, can kill scalability, since the processing requiments of a node are likely to grow at least proportionally with the size of the neighborhood.

Thus, we can conclude that an important factor in the vanishing throughput phenomenon is that the connectivity requirement does not allow the transmission radius to shrink too fast, which, if translated to a graph view, means that the node degrees must tend to infinity, whenever *full* connectivity is required. This naturally leads to the idea of relaxing the full connectivity requirement and it makes important to investigate the trade-off between the fraction of nodes that can be kept in a connected component versus the expected node degrees.

4   Random Graph Models

Let us first explain what we mean by random graphs and a random graph model in the most general sense.

In full generality, by a *random graph* on a fixed number of nodes (n) we mean a random variable that takes its values in the set of all undirected graphs on n nodes. We use the notation G_n for a random graph on n nodes. At this point, it is still completely general, it can be generated by any mechanism, with arbitrary dependencies among its parts, it is just *any* graph-valued random variable, taking its values among undirected graphs on n nodes.

A *random graph model* is given by a sequence of graph valued random variables, one for each possible value of n:

$$\mathcal{M} = (G_n;\ n \in \mathbf{N}).$$

Let us now consider some important general parameters and properties. Let G_n be any random graph on n nodes and denote by $e(G_n)$ the number of edges in the graph. We characterize the degrees of G_n by the expected degree of a randomly chosen vertex, which we call he *expected average degree* of G_n. It is denoted by $\overline{d}(n)$ and defined by

$$\overline{d}(n) = \frac{2\mathrm{E}(e(G_n))}{n}$$

based on the fact that the actual average degree in any graph G on n nodes is $2e(G)/n$. Often the expected degree of each individual node is also equal to $\overline{d}(n)$, but in a general model it may not hold. (Note that even if the expected degree of each node is equal to the expected average degree, it does not mean that the *actual* random degrees are also equal.)

Ideally, we would like a random graph model in which $\overline{d}(n)$ remains constant and the model is *asymptotically almost surely (a.a.s.)* connected, meaning

$$\lim_{n \to \infty} \Pr(G_n \text{ is connected}) = 1.$$

Note: Whenever we write down a limit, such as the one above, we also assume that the limit exists.

Since, as mentioned in the Introduction, asymptotic connectivity is not possible in most models without unbounded degrees, therefore, one may hope that if less than full connectivity is required, then there is a better chance to keep the node degrees bounded. To this end, let us define a weaker version of connectivity.

Definition 1. (β-connectivity) *For a real number $0 \le \beta \le 1$, a graph G on n nodes is called β-connected if G contains a connected component on at least βn nodes.*

When we consider a sequence of graphs with different values of n, then the parameter β may depend on n. When this is the case, we write β_n-connectivity. Note that even if $\beta_n \to 1$, this is still weaker than full connectivity in the limit. For example, if $\beta_n = 1 - 1/\sqrt{n}$, then we have $\beta_n \to 1$, but each graph on n nodes can still have $n - \beta_n n = \sqrt{n}$ nodes that are not part of the largest connected component.

Let us now introduce a model class that reflects a typical feature of geometric random graph models. This feature is that in geometric random graphs the primary random choice is picking random nodes from some domain and then the edges are already determined by some geometric property (typically some kind of distance) of the random nodes. We elevate this approach to an abstract level that includes many special cases of interest. Based on this high level of abstraction, we call it *abstract geometric random graph model*.

The most general version of our abstract geometric model is built using the following components:

- **Node variables.** The nodes are represented by an infinite sequence $X_1, X_2, \ldots$ of random variables, called *node variables*. They take their values in an arbitrary (nonempty) set S, which is called the *domain* of the model. In most practical cases the domain is a simple subset of the Euclidean plane or of the 3-dimensional space. In general, however, S can be any abstract set from which we can choose random elements[1]. When we want to generate a random graph on n nodes, then we use the first n entries of the sequence, that is, $X_1, \ldots, X_n$ represent the nodes in G_n. It is important to note that we do not require the node variables to be independent.

- **Edge functions.** We denote by $Y_{ij}^{(n)} \in \{0, 1\}$ the indicator of the edge between nodes X_i, X_j in the random graph G_n. Since loops are not allowed, we always assume $i \neq j$, without repeating this condition each time. The (abstract) geometric nature of the model is expressed by the requirement that the random variables $Y_{ij}^{(n)}$ are determined by the nodes $X_1, \ldots, X_n$, possibly with additional independent randomization. Specifically, we assume that there exist functions $f_{ij}^{(n)}$, such that

$$Y_{ij}^{(n)} = f_{ij}^{(n)}(X_1, \ldots, X_n, \xi_{ij})$$

where ξ_{ij} is a random variable that is uniformly distributed on $[0, 1]$ and is independent of all the other defining random variables of the model (i.e., the node variables and all the other ξ_{kl} variables). Henceforth the role of ξ_{ij} is referred to as *independent randomization*[2]. The undirected nature of the graph is expressed by the requirement $Y_{ij}^{(n)} = Y_{ji}^{(n)}$, which can simply be enforced by

---

[1] To avoid mathematical complications that would only obscure the main message, we assume that all considered sets, functions etc. are measurable with respect to the used probability measures and all considered expected values exist. This is satisfied in in every practically relevant model.

[2] Note that the specified distribution of ξ_{ij} does not impose a restriction, since the functions $f_{ij}^{(n)}$ are arbitrary.

computing all values for $i < j$ only and defining the $i > j$ case by exchanging i and j.

Regarding the abstract geometric random graph model in the presented very general form, it is clear that allowing *totally arbitrary* node variables and edge functions offers little hope for meaningful analysis. Therefore, next we introduce some restricting conditions. Later we are going to see that one has to make only surprisingly mild restrictions to meaningfully analyze the trade-off between node degrees and β-connectivity.

Up to now we allowed that an edge in G_n can depend on all the nodes, and the dependence expressed by the $f_{ij}^{(n)}$ functions can be arbitrary and different for each edge. To get a little closer to the usual geometric random graph model, let us introduce the following property, called locality. Informally, it restricts the dependence of an edge to its endpoints, in a homogeneous way, but still via an *arbitrary* function.

Definition 2. (Locality) *An abstract geometric random graph model is called local, if for every n and $i, j \leq n$ the existence of an edge between X_i, X_j depends only on these nodes. Moreover, the dependence is the same for every i, j, possibly with independent randomization. That is, there are functions $f^{(n)}$ such that the edge indicators are expressible as*

$$Y_{ij}^{(n)} = f^{(n)}(X_i, X_j, \xi_{ij})$$

where ξ_{ij} represents the independent randomization.

Our second condition called *name invariance* refers to the joint distribution of nodes. If we allow totally arbitrary joint distribution, then it offers little chance for meaningful analysis. On the other hand, restricting ourselves only to independent, identically distributed (i.i.d.) node variables would exclude important cases, such as clustering. Therefore, we introduce a condition that allows more general than i.i.d. node variables, but still makes meaningful analysis possible. To introduce it, let us first recall a useful concept from probability theory, called exchangeability.

Definition 3. (Exchangeable random variables) *A finite sequence $\xi_1, \ldots, \xi_n$ of random variables is called* exchangeable *if for any permutation σ of $\{1, \ldots, n\}$, the joint distribution of $\xi_1, \ldots, \xi_n$ is the same as the joint distribution of $\xi_{\sigma(1)}, \ldots, \xi_{\sigma(n)}$. An infinite sequence of random variables is called exchangeable if every finite initial segment of the sequence is exchangeable.*

Exchangeability can be equivalently defined such that for any $k \geq 1$ among the random variables, say, $\xi_{j_1}, \ldots, \xi_{j_k}$, their joint distribution is always the same (for a given k), it does not depend on which particular set of k indices is selected. Note that i.i.d. random variables are always exchangeable, but the converse generally does not hold, so this is a larger family.

Now let us introduce the condition that we use to restrict the arbitrary dependence of node variables.

Definition 4. (Name invariance) *An abstract geometric random graph model is called* name invariance, *if its node variables are exchangeable.*

We call it the *name invariance* of the model because it means the names (the indices) of the nodes are irrelevant in the sense that the joint probabilistic behavior of any fixed number of nodes is invariant to renaming (reindexing) the nodes. In particular, it also implies that the node variable are identically distributed, but they do not have to be independent.

Name invariance is naturally satisfied with the most frequently used random node choices, such as uniform independent random points in a planar domain, or a Poisson point process in the plane, or in higher dimension. We allow, however, much more complex node generation (over an arbitrary set!) since dependencies are not excluded by name invariance.

A simple example for a dependent, yet still name invariant, node generation process is a "clustered uniform" node generation. As an example, let S be a sphere in 3-dimensional space, i.e., the surface of a 3-dimensional ball. Let R be the radius of the ball. Let us first generate a pivot point Y uniformly at random from S. Then generate the nodes $X_1, X_2, \ldots$ uniformly at random and independently of each other from the neighborhood of radius $r \ll R$ of the random pivot point Y (within the sphere). It is directly implied by the construction that exchangeability holds. Moreover, any particular X_i will be uniformly distributed over the *entire* sphere, since Y is uniform over the sphere. On the other hand, the X_i are far from independent of each other, since they cluster around Y, forcing any two of them to be within distance $2r$. The setting can be generalized to applying several pivot points and non-uniform distributions, creating a more sophisticated clustering.

5   Example Models

Before turning to the results, let us present some example models to show the usefulness and comprehensiveness of the generalization provided by our abstract geometric random graphs. Since the results will apply to local and name invariant models, we restrict ourselves to such models in the examples.

Geometric random graphs. All the usual geometric random graph models fit naturally in our general framework. For example, the base set S can be chosen as a unit disk or square in the plane or a unit ball or cube (or any other domain) in higher dimension. Let us choose i.i.d. points $X_1, X_2, \ldots$ from S, according to some probability distribution. Let $\rho(x, y)$ denote the distance of the points $x, y \in S$, it can be any distance function. Finally, let $r > 0$ be a radius (possibly depending on n). Then the edge function

$$f^{(n)}(X_i, X_j, \xi_{ij}) = \begin{cases} 1 & \text{if } \rho(X_i, X_j) \leq r \\ 0 & \text{if } \rho(X_i, X_j) > r \end{cases} \tag{3}$$

defines a geometric random graph in the usual sense. (The independent randomization is not used here, so the edge function does not depend on ξ_{ij}.) It is clear that this includes all the usual geometric random graph models, allowing any metric space as the basis. Moreover, we can also use non-independent points, such as the "clustered uniform" example in the previous section, as long as the distribution is exchangeable.

Erdős-Rényi random graphs. The by now classical random graph model of Erdős and Rényi (see, e.g., [1,8]), where each possible edge is included independently with some probability p is also included as a direct special case. We can set $S = \{1, \ldots, n\}$ and for $X_i, X_j \in S$

$$f^{(n)}(X_i, X_j, \xi_{ij}) = \begin{cases} 1 & \text{if } \xi_{ij} \leq p \\ 0 & \text{if } \xi_{ij} > p \end{cases}$$

Note that now the edge function depends only on the independent randomization, so indeed each edge is included independently with probability p.

A geometric but non-metric example: battery levels. In the geometric random graph models ρ satisfies the triangle inequality. This, however, cannot capture all situations that occur in ad hoc or sensor networks. As an example, assume the nodes are located in the plane. Let x_i, y_i be the coordinates of the ith node. Furthermore, we also characterize a node with its battery level $E_i > 0$. E_i represents the remaining energy, assuming the node is not fully out of energy. Thus, a node is represented by a triple $X_i = (x_i, y_i, E_i)$. Let $d(E_i)$ be the distance over which a node can communicate, given its energy level E_i. (The function $d(E_i)$ can be derived from the physical characteristics of the node and from radio propagation conditions.) Now, a possible example of a "distance" function is

$$\rho(X_i, X_j) = \frac{\sqrt{(x_i - x_j)^2 + (y_i - y_j)^2}}{\min\{d(E_i), d(E_j)\}}$$

If we take $r = 1$ and use the above ρ function in (3), then it expresses the condition that a link exists if and only if its end nodes are at most at a distance that can be bridged by the energy levels of both nodes. Note that the above function ρ does not satisfy the triangle inequality, so it does not lead to a geometric random graph model in the usual sense. On the other hand, it still fits in our framework, as in (3) we did not require the triangle inequality to hold for ρ.

Another non-metric example: link blocking. We can capture some features of traffic dependent network characteristics, as well. Let each node i be characterized by a triple $X_i = (x_i, y_i, \lambda_i)$, where x_i, y_i are planar coordinates and λ_i is the traffic demand of the node. Let B_{ij} be the blocking probability of the link (i, j), given that the link exists. We may compute B_{ij} as a function of λ_i, λ_j from some traffic model. For example, if we use Erlang's well known formula, assuming a capacity of C units on the link and its load is taken as the sum of its end nodes' traffic load $\lambda_i + \lambda_j$, then we obtain

$$B_{ij} = \frac{(\lambda_i + \lambda_j)^C / C!}{\sum_{i=0}^{C} (\lambda_i + \lambda_j)^i / i!}.$$

(Of course, we may use other traffic models, as well, this is just an example.) Now we can take the "distance" function

$$\rho(X_i, X_j) = \frac{1}{1 - B_{ij}} \sqrt{(x_i - x_j)^2 + (y_i - y_j)^2}$$

and use it in (3) with some radius r. We can observe that for small blocking probability ($B_{ij} \ll 1$) $\rho(X_i, X_j)$ will be approximately the same as the Euclidean distance. On the other hand, as B_{ij} approaches 1, the factor $\frac{1}{1-B_{ij}}$ tends to infinity and, therefore, high blocking probability makes the existence of the link in the model less likely, even if the physical distance is small. This example also violates the triangle inequality, so it is not a geometric random graph.

Log-normal shadowing. A typical phenomenon in the radio environment is *fading*. An example of fading is a relatively slow random fluctuation in the signal strength, which occurs even if the locations are fixed. Measurements show that this random variation can be accurately modeled by a log-normal distribution (see, e.g., [9]). Hence the name *log-normal shadowing*, which is widely used for this phenomenon. A way to capture it in our model is this. Let us characterize a node i by a triple $X_i = (x_i, y_i, \eta_i)$, where x_i, y_i represent a random position in the plane and each η_i is an infinite sequence of independent, log-normally distributed random variables:

$$\eta_i = (\eta_j^{(i)}; \ j = i, i+1, i+2, \ldots).$$

The "distance" is defined as

$$\rho(X_i, X_j) = \eta_b^{(a)} \sqrt{(x_i - x_j)^2 + (y_i - y_j)^2}$$

where $a = \min\{i, j\}$ and $b = \max\{i, j\}$. (The reason for we need an infinite sequence of log-normal random variables is that this way we can have independent log-normal shadowing for every link.) This distance can express the fact that from the radio communication point of view we really perceive an "effective distance", which is a log-normally modulated random variant of the physical distance. Using this ρ in (3) leads again to a random graph that is not geometric, as ρ does not satisfy the distance axioms.

6   Threshold Function for Partial Connectivity

Let us now define a concept that will characterize the trade-off between node degrees and the type of partial connectivity that we introduced as β-connectivity in Definition 1. The set of nonnegative real numbers, extended with ∞, will be denoted by $\mathbf{R}_0^\infty$. Real functions are also extended to ∞ by $f(\infty) = \lim_{x \to \infty} f(x)$, whenever the limit exists (it will always exist in our cases). The value of β is always assumed to be in $[0, 1]$.

Before the formal definition let us explain the concept informally. We define a threshold function for β-connectivity, such that whenever β is above the threshold, then it is impossible to achieve a.a.s. β-connectivity for any model in the considered family of random graph models. On the other hand, if β is below the threshold, then this is not the case anymore, that is, there is at least one model in the family that achieves a.a.s β-connectivity with this β. Now let us present the formal definition. Recall that the expected average degree in a random graph G_n is defined as $\overline{d}(n) = 2\mathrm{E}(e(G_n))/n$.

Definition 5. (Threshold for β-connectivity) *Let $\mathcal{F}$ be a family of random graph models. For any model $\mathcal{M} \in \mathcal{F}$ let G_n denote the random graph on n nodes generated by $\mathcal{M}$ and set*

$$D_{\mathcal{M}} = \limsup_{n \to \infty} \overline{d}(n).$$

A function $f : \mathbf{R}_0^{\infty} \mapsto [0,1]$ is called a β-connectivity threshold function for $\mathcal{F}$ if the following two conditions are satisfied:

(i) For any model $\mathcal{M} \in \mathcal{F}$ and for every $\beta > f(D_{\mathcal{M}})$

$$\lim_{n \to \infty} \Pr(G_n \, is \, \beta\text{-connected}) < 1$$

holds, where G_n is generated by $\mathcal{M}$.

(ii) If β is below the threshold, then (i) does not hold anymore, in the following sense. For every $\epsilon > 0$ there exists a model $\mathcal{M}_0 \in \mathcal{F}$ and a

$$\beta \leq f(D_{\mathcal{M}_0}) - \epsilon$$

such that

$$\lim_{n \to \infty} \Pr(G_n \, is \, \beta\text{-connected}) = 1$$

where G_n is generated from $\mathcal{M}_0$.

The importance of this concept is the following. If for a considered class $\mathcal{F}$ of random graph models we can find out what the corresponding β-connectivity threshold function is, then we can tell precisely what range of expected average degrees allow a.a.s. β-connectivity for a given β. Or, conversely, if we know the (asymptotic) expected average degree for a particular model $\mathcal{M}$ in the considered class, then we can decide what level of connectivity can be asymptotically achieved for this model.

7   Results

Now we show that for the quite general class of abstract geometric random graph models we can find the precise β-connectivity threshold function, if we assume that the models satisfy the conditions of locality and name invariance. The previously presented examples all satisfy these conditions, so they show that even with these restrictions we can still include many complex and practically important models.

Theorem 1. (Threshold function for local and name invariant abstract geometric graphs) *Let $\mathcal{F}$ be the family of local and name invariant abstract geometric random graph models For any model $\mathcal{M} \in \mathcal{F}$ set*

$$D_{\mathcal{M}} = \limsup_{n \to \infty} \overline{d}(n).$$

Then the β-connectivity threshold function for $\mathcal{F}$ is

$$f(D_{\mathcal{M}}) = 1 - e^{-D_{\mathcal{M}}}.$$

The proof is based on another theorem, which is interesting on its own right. As a further notation, the (random) number of isolated nodes in G_n is denoted by I_n.

Theorem 2. (Lower bound on the expected number of isolated nodes) *The expected number of isolated nodes in a local and name invariant abstract geometric random graph G_n always satisfies*

$$\mathrm{E}(I_n) \geq n \left(1 - \frac{\overline{d}(n)}{n-1}\right)^{n-1}. \tag{4}$$

Proof of Theorem 2. First we note that since our model is abstract and does not involve any real geometry, one has to be careful to avoid using such intuition that may appeal geometrically, but does not follow from the abstract model.

As a first step, observe the following: name invariance implies that for any function g of the node variables and for any permutation σ of $\{1, \ldots, n\}$ we have

$$\mathrm{E}(g(X_1, \ldots, X_n)) = \mathrm{E}(g(X_{\sigma(1)}, \ldots, X_{\sigma(n)})).$$

Since the probability that a particular node has any given degree k is also expressible by such a function, therefore, the probability distribution of the node degree must be the same for all nodes (but the degrees, as random variables, may not be independent). As a consequence, the expected degree of each node is the same, which then must be equal to the expected average degree $\overline{d}(n)$.

Let us pick a node X_i. We derive a lower bound on the probability that X_i is isolated, i.e., its degree is 0. Due to the above symmetry considerations, it does not matter which node is chosen, so we can take $i = 1$. Let $\mathcal{I}_n$ be the (random) set of isolated nodes in G_n. What we want to compute is a lower bound on $\Pr(X_1 \in \mathcal{I}_n)$. Then we are going to use the fact that

$$\mathrm{E}(I_n) = \mathrm{E}(|\mathcal{I}_n|) = \sum_{i=1}^{n} \Pr(X_i \in \mathcal{I}_n)$$

Note that, due to the linearity of expectation, this remains true even if the events $\{X_i \in \mathcal{I}_n\}$ are not independent, which is typically the case. Then, by the symmetry considerations, we can utilize that $\Pr(X_i \in \mathcal{I}_n)$ is independent of i, yielding $\mathrm{E}(I_n) = n \Pr(X_1 \in \mathcal{I}_n)$.

In order to derive a lower bound on $\Pr(X_1 \in \mathcal{I}_n)$, we need a fundamental result from probability theory, called *de Finetti's Theorem*[3]. This theorem says (in its

---

[3] It was first published in [2]. Being a classical result, it can be found in many advanced textbooks on probability. Interestingly, it seems that, despite its usefulness, it is rarely applied by the networking community.

simplest form that is already sufficient for our purposes) that if an infinite sequence $\xi_1, \xi_2, \ldots$ of 0-1 valued random variables is exchangeable, then the following hold:

(i) The limit

$$\eta = \lim_{N \to \infty} \frac{\xi_1 + \ldots + \xi_N}{N} \tag{5}$$

exists with probability 1. Note that exchangeability implies that all ξ_i have the same expected value, so in case they were independent, then the strong law of large numbers would apply and the limit would be the common expected value, with probability 1. Since, however, the ξ_i are not assumed independent (only exchangeable), therefore, the average may not tend to a constant, it can be a non-constant random variable in $[0, 1]$.

(ii) For any N and for any system $a_1, \ldots, a_N \in \{0, 1\}$ of outcomes with $s = \sum_{i=1}^{N} a_i$

$$\Pr(\xi_1 = a_1, \ldots, \xi_N = a_N) = \int_0^1 x^s (1 - x)^{N-s} dF_\eta(x)$$

holds, where F_η is the probability distribution function of η.

(iii) The ξ_i are conditionally independent and identically distributed (conditionally i.i.d.), given η, that is,

$$\Pr(\xi_1 = a_1, \ldots, \xi_N = a_n \,|\, \eta) = \prod_{i=1}^{N} \Pr(\xi_i = a_i \,|\, \eta).$$

Informally, de Finetti's theorem says that exchangeable 0-1 valued random variables, even if they are not independent, can always be represented as a mixture of Bernoulli systems of random variables. It is important to note, however, that even though the statements (ii) and (iii) refer to finite initial segments of the sequence $\xi_1, \xi_2, \ldots$, it is necessary that the entire *infinite* sequence is exchangeable. For finite sequences the theorem may not hold, counterexamples are known for the finite case [11].

Let us now define the infinite sequence of 0-1 valued random variables

$$e_j = f^{(n)}(X_1, X_j, \xi_{1j}), \quad j = 2, 3 \ldots$$

Of these, $e_2, \ldots, e_n$ are the indicators of the edges with one endpoint at X_1. But the function $f^{(n)}$ is defined for any $(x, y, z) \in S \times S \times [0, 1]$, so nothing prevents us to define the *infinite* sequence e_j; $j = 2, 3, \ldots$, by taking more independent and uniform $\xi_{1j} \in [0, 1]$ random variables.

Observe now that the sequence e_j; $j = 2, 3, \ldots$ is an infinite exchangeable sequence of 0-1 valued random variables. Only the exchangeability needs proof. If we take any k indices $j_1, \ldots, j_k$, then the joint distribution of $e_{j_1}, \ldots, e_{j_k}$ depends only the joint distribution of $X_{j_1}, \ldots, X_{j_k}$, plus the independent randomization. If we replace $j_1, \ldots, j_k$ by other k indices, then it will not change the joint distribution of the k node variables, due to their assumed exchangeability. The independent randomization also does not change the joint distribution, since the ξ_{1j}

are i.i.d., so it does not matter which k are taken. Furthermore, the locality of the model implies that each e_j depends on one X_j (besides X_1) so taking another k cannot change how many node variables will any subset of the e_j share. Thus, for any k, the joint distribution of $e_{j_1}, \ldots, e_{j_k}$ does not depend on which k indices are chosen, proving that e_j; $j = 2, 3, \ldots$ is an infinite exchangeable sequence of 0-1 valued random variables.

Now, by de Finetti's Theorem, there is a random variable $\eta \in [0, 1]$, such that the e_j are conditionally i.i.d., given η. Then we can write

$$
\begin{aligned}
\Pr(X_1 \in \mathcal{I}_n) &= \Pr(e_2 = \ldots = e_n = 0) \\
&= \mathrm{E}(\Pr(e_2 = \ldots = e_n = 0 \,|\, \eta)) \\
&= \mathrm{E}\left(\prod_{j=2}^{n} (\Pr(e_j = 0 \,|\, \eta)) \right) \\
&= \mathrm{E}\left(\prod_{j=2}^{n} (1 - \Pr(e_j = 1 \,|\, \eta)) \right).
\end{aligned}
\tag{6}
$$

Notice that $\Pr(e_j = 1 \,|\, \eta)$ is the probability that an edge exists between X_1 and X_j, conditioned on η. Consequently, $\xi = \Pr(e_j = 1 \,|\, \eta)$ is a random variable, depending on η. At the same time, it does not depend on j, as by de Finetti's theorem, the e_j are conditionally i.i.d., given η, so it does not matter which j is taken in $\xi = \Pr(e_j = 1 \,|\, \eta)$. Thus, we can continue (6) as

$$
\Pr(X_1 \in \mathcal{I}_n) = \mathrm{E}\left(\prod_{j=2}^{n} (1 - \xi) \right) = \mathrm{E}\left((1 - \xi)^{n-1} \right).
\tag{7}
$$

We can now observe that $\xi \in [0, 1]$ and the function $g(x) = (1 - x)^n$ is convex in $[0, 1]$, so we may apply Jensen's inequality. Jensen's well known inequality says that for any random variable ζ and for any convex function g the inequality $\mathrm{E}(g(\zeta)) \geq g(\mathrm{E}(\zeta))$ holds, which is a consequence of the definition of convexity. Thus, we can further continue (7), obtaining

$$
\Pr(X_1 \in \mathcal{I}_n) = \mathrm{E}\left((1 - \xi)^{n-1} \right) \geq (1 - \mathrm{E}(\xi))^{n-1}.
$$

Note that $\mathrm{E}(\xi) = \mathrm{E}(\Pr(e_j = 1 \,|\, \eta)) = \Pr(e_j = 1)$ is the probability that an edge exists between X_1 and X_j. By name invariance, this is the same probability for any two nodes, let p_n denote this common value. Thus,

$$
\Pr(X_1 \in \mathcal{I}_n) \geq (1 - p_n)^{n-1}
$$

follows. We know that there are $n - 1$ potential edges adjacent to each node, each with probability p_n. Therefore, despite the possible dependence of edges, the linearity of expectation implies the expected degree of each node under our conditions is $(n - 1)p_n$, which is also equal to $\overline{d}(n)$. We can then substitute $p_n = \overline{d}(n)/(n - 1)$, which yields

$$\Pr(X_1 \in \mathcal{I}_n) \geq \left(1 - \frac{\overline{d}(n)}{n-1}\right)^{n-1},$$

implying

$$\mathrm{E}(I_n) = n \Pr(X_1 \in \mathcal{I}_n) \geq n \left(1 - \frac{\overline{d}(n)}{n-1}\right)^{n-1},$$

completing the proof.

♠

Now, using Theorem 2, we can prove the threshold claimed in Theorem 1.

Proof of Theorem 1. Fix any model $\mathcal{M} \in \mathcal{F}$. Since $D_{\mathcal{M}} = \limsup_{n\to\infty} \overline{d}(n)$ and

$$\left(1 - \frac{D_{\mathcal{M}}}{n-1}\right)^{n-1} \to e^{-D_{\mathcal{M}}},$$

therefore, there must exist a sequence $a_n \to 1$, such that

$$\left(1 - \frac{\overline{d}(n)}{n-1}\right)^{n-1} \geq a_n e^{-D_{\mathcal{M}}}.$$

Hence, by Theorem 2,

$$\mathrm{E}(I_n) \geq a_n e^{-D_{\mathcal{M}}} n \tag{8}$$

holds for every n.

Now fix a β with $1 \geq \beta > 1 - e^{-D_{\mathcal{M}}}$. (We can assume $D_{\mathcal{M}} < \infty$, since otherwise there is no such β.) We are going to show that $\Pr(G_n$ is β-connected) cannot tend to 1.

Set $s_n = \Pr(I_n \leq (1-\beta)n)$, i.e. s_n is the probability that at most $(1-\beta)n$ nodes are isolated. Then $\Pr(G_n$ is β-connected) $\leq s_n$ must hold, since β-connectivity implies that there may be at most $(1-\beta)n$ isolated nodes. Consider now the random variable $\gamma_n = n - I_n$, which is the number of non-isolated nodes. Then $\gamma_n \geq 0$ and $\mathrm{E}(\gamma_n) = n - \mathrm{E}(I_n)$. Therefore, (8) implies that

$$\mathrm{E}(\gamma_n) \leq (1 - a_n e^{-D_{\mathcal{M}}})n$$

holds for every n. Furthermore, by the definition of γ_n, the events $\{I_n \leq (1-\beta)n\}$ and $\{\gamma_n \geq \beta n\}$ are identical. Thus, we can write, using the well known Markov inequality for nonnegative random variables:

$$s_n = \Pr(I_n \leq (1-\beta)n) = \Pr(\gamma_n \geq \beta n)$$

$$\leq \frac{\mathrm{E}(\gamma_n)}{\beta n} \leq \frac{(1 - a_n e^{-D_{\mathcal{M}}})n}{\beta n} = \frac{1 - a_n e^{-D_{\mathcal{M}}}}{\beta}.$$

Since $a_n \to 1$, β is constant and $\beta > 1 - e^{-D_{\mathcal{M}}}$, we can conclude that $\limsup_{n\to\infty} s_n < 1$ must hold. This, together with $\Pr(G_n$ is β-connected) $\leq s_n$ yields that the probability of β-connectivity cannot tend to 1.

Next we prove the other side, i.e., that with β below the threshold by an arbitrarily small fixed $\epsilon > 0$, a.a.s. β-connectivity does occur at least for some model $\mathcal{M}_0 \in \mathcal{F}$. Let us chose the model $\mathcal{M}_0$ as follows. Generate G_n such that each edge is added with some fixed probability p, independently of the others. This is a classical Erdős-Rényi random graph model (see Section 5), which is part of the model family $\mathcal{F}$, since it clearly satisfies name invariance and locality. We use the following result from [8] about the Erdős-Rényi model: If $np = c$ for a constant $c > 1$, then there is a sequence $h_n \to 0$, such that G_n a.a.s. contains a connected component of size $(1 + h_n)\beta_0 n$, where β_0 is the unique root of the equation

$$\beta_0 + e^{-\beta_0 c} = 1. \tag{9}$$

For this model we have

$$\overline{d}(n) = (n-1)p = \frac{n-1}{n}c$$

implying $D_{\mathcal{M}} = c$.

Now let us fix an arbitrary $\epsilon > 0$. Since the root $\beta_0 = \beta_0(c)$ of equation (9) is less than 1 for any fixed c, but approaches 1 as $c \to \infty$, therefore, due to continuity, we can choose c such that

$$\beta_0 = 1 - e^{-\beta_0 c} = 1 - e^{-c} - \epsilon/2$$

holds. Then, by the above cited result, G_n a.a.s. has a connected component of size $(1 + h_n)\beta_0 n$ with $h_n \to 0$. To compensate the effect of $h_n \to 0$, we can slightly decrease β_0 to some $\beta < \beta_0$. Let us choose $\beta = 1 - e^{-c} - \epsilon < \beta_0$. Then we have proved that G_n, with the appropriately chosen c, a.a.s. contains at least βn connected nodes. Moreover, due to $D_{\mathcal{M}} = c$,

$$\beta = 1 - e^{-D_{\mathcal{M}}} - \epsilon$$

holds, which completes the proof.   ♠

It is worth mentioning that the definition of the treshold function and Theorem 1 directly imply that bounded expected average degrees in $\mathcal{F}$ exclude a.a.s. β_n-connectivity when $\beta_n \to 1$. Then, of course, a.a.s. full connectivity, which corresponds to $\beta = 1$, is also excluded.

Corollary 1. *Let β_n be a sequence in $[0, 1]$ with $\beta_n \to 1$. Then for any local and name invariant abstract geometric random graph model $\mathcal{M}$ it holds that if $D_{\mathcal{M}} < \infty$, then the random graphs generated by $\mathcal{M}$ cannot be a.a.s. β_n-connected.*

8   Solving the Sample Problem

Our results are derived through a more general approach than what is usual in this context. In particular, it is purely probabilistic, geometry is replaced by a higher level abstraction. To illustrate that despite the relative simplicity, the results can have a surprising strength, let us apply them to the motivating sample problem of Section 2.

As noted in the exposition of the sample problem, it would be hard to solve it for arbitrary choices of $P, D, C, Q_{x,y}$ and $d(x, y)$ with directly analyzing the stochastic geometry of the model (the notations are re-used from Section 2). On the other hand, we can easily check that it satisfies our general conditions, as shown below.

Let us choose the model domain S as a 3-dimensional phase space, in which each node is represented by a point such that the first two coordinates describe the initial position of the node and the last coordinate encodes which random trajectory was chosen from C for the node. Let $X_1, X_2, \ldots$ be the representations of the nodes in this phase space.

We can now check that, for any n, the joint distribution of $X_1, \ldots, X_n$ is invariant to re-indexing them. The reason is that both the initial positions and the trajectory choices are generated by processes in which the indices do not play any role. Therefore, the model is *name invariant*. Interestingly, this remains true despite having a lot of dependencies among the nodes: the initial positions of different nodes are not independent (due to clustering), and the trajectory of a given node is also not independent of its initial position, as it is drawn from a probability distribution that may depend on the location. Through this, the trajectories and initial positions of different nodes also become dependent, making their whole movement dependent. Yet, the model is still name invariant.

Let us now consider the links. As defined in Section 2, two nodes are considered connected if during their movement over the time horizon $[0, T_n]$ there is a subinterval of time, of length at least t_n, such that they remain within "radio distance" $\leq r_n$ during the entire subinterval. The radio distance, however, may be very different from the Euclidean distance, it may be described by an arbitrary function that may account for complex propagation characteristics, attenuation, obstacles, and it may also contain independent randomness.

Given some possibly complicated radio distance $d(x, y)$ and the node generation and movement process with possibly complex trajectories, it may not be easy to compute whether a link actually exists between two nodes according to the above definition. On the other hand, for us it is enough to note that once the phase space representations X_i, X_j of any two nodes are given, plus the realization of the independent randomness of the distance, they together determine whether a link exists between the two nodes or not. The reason is that the initial positions and the trajectories, given in the phase space representation, fully determine the movement of the nodes. Once this is known, it determines, along with the realization of the independent randomness of the distance function, whether the link definition is satisfied, i.e., if there is a subinterval of length $\geq t_n$ in $[0, T_n]$, such that the nodes stay within radio distance $\leq r_n$ during the entire subinterval. To actually compute it may not be easy for a sophisticated case, but for our purposes it enough to know that it is *determined* by the listed factors, without knowing anything about the other nodes. This implies that the model is *local*.

Thus, we have established that the problem can be described by a local and name invariant abstract geometric graph model, for any choice of the parameters.

Then, by Theorem 1, the threshold function for β-connectivity is

$$f(D_{\mathcal{M}}) = 1 - e^{-D_{\mathcal{M}}}.$$

If we require that node degrees are bounded by, say, 4, then we have $D_{\mathcal{M}} \leq 4$, implying

$$f(D_{\mathcal{M}}) = 1 - e^{-D_{\mathcal{M}}} \leq 1 - e^{-4} < 0.9817.$$

Thus, the threshold in this case falls below 0.99, so by Theorem 1, it is impossible to achieve that asymptotically 99% of the nodes belong to a connected component, no matter how the other parameters are chosen.

Note that the direct application of our general results was able to cut through a lot of complexity that would otherwise arise if we wanted to reach the same conclusions by directly analyzing the stochastic geometry of such a model.

9   Conclusion

We have quantified the precise trade-off between expected node degrees and the fraction of nodes that belong to a connected component in a large wireless network topology, under very general conditions. Our conditions can be easily checked in most specific cases. Therefore, the approach can serve as a powerful method to explore the degree vs. partial connectivity trade-off in possibly complicated random network topology models, which would be otherwise hard to analyze directly.

Acknowledgment

The author is grateful for the support of NSF Grant CCF-0634848.

References

1. Bollobás, B.: Random Graphs. Cambridge University Press, Cambridge (2001)
2. de Finetti, B.: Funzione Caratteristica di un Fenomeno Aleatorio. Atti della R. Academia Nazionale dei Lincei, Serie 6, Classe di Scienze Fisiche, Mathematice e Naturale 4, 251–299 (1931)
3. Faragó, A.: On the Fundamental Limits of Topology Control in Ad Hoc Networks. Algorithmica 49, 337–356 (2007)
4. Faragó, A.: Scalability of Node Degrees in Random Wireless Network Topologies. In: IEEE JSAC (in press, 2009)
5. Franceschetti, M., Meester, R.: Random Networks for Communication. Cambridge University Press, Cambridge (2007)
6. Gupta, P., Kumar, P.R.: The Capacity of Wireless Networks. IEEE Trans. Information Theory 46, 388–404 (2000)
7. Gupta, P., Kumar, P.R.: Critical Power for Asymptotic Connectivity in Wireless Networks. In: McEneany, W.M., Yin, G., Zhang, Q. (eds.) Stochastic Analysis, Control, Optimization and Applications: A Volume in Honor of W.H. Fleming, pp. 547–566. Birkhauser, Boston (1998)

8. Janson, S., Luczak, T., Rucinski, A.: Random Graphs. Wiley, Chichester (2000)
9. Pahlavan, K., Krishnamurty, P.: Principles of Wireless Networks. Prentice-Hall, Englewood Cliffs (2002)
10. Penrose, M.: Random Geometric Graphs. Oxford University Press, Oxford (2003)
11. Stoyanov, J.M.: Counterexamples in Probability. Wiley, Chichester (1987)

Measuring IP Address Fragmentation from BGP Routing Dynamics

Xia Yin[2], Xin Wu[1,2], and Zhiliang Wang[3]

[1] Tsinghua National Laboratory for Information Science and Technology
[2] Department of Computer Science & Technology, Tsinghua University, Beijing, China
[3] Network Research Center of Tsinghua University, Beijing, China
yxia@mail.tsinghua.edu.cn, tun-x03@mails.tsinghua.edu.cn,
wzl@cernet.edu.cn

Abstract. Address Fragmentation plays a key role in the exponential growth of DFZ routing table, known as the scalability problem of current Internet. In this paper, we measure the severity of address fragmentation, and try to figure out the relationship between Prefix-Distance and Network-Distance of current Internet by taking Geographic-Distance as an approximation of Network-Distance. We focus our measurement on the prefixes with relatively small Geographic-Distance, and get Prefix Groups from BGP routing dynamics. This method reduces the number of active probes required in active measurement, and results a more detailed prefixes' distribution analysis. We find out that there are two extreme allocations of IP address blocks in current Internet. Some of the blocks with small Geographic-Distances have small Prefix-Distances, while others with small Geographic-Distances have rather big Prefix-Distances. This is the direct reason of the BGP routing table's inflation. We further conclude that by reallocating IP address blocks according to geography, we could significantly reduce the size of the global routing tables.

Keywords: Prefix Distance, Geographic Distance, BGP.

1 Introduction

The global Internet consists of tens of thousands of autonomous systems (ASes). The Border Gateway Protocol (BGP) [1] is the defacto inter-domain routing protocol, which transfers reachability information, i.e. update messages, between ASes.

It is commonly recognized that current Internet routing and addressing system is facing serious scaling problems. The growth of Default Free Zone (DFZ, the collection of all Internet ASes that do not require a default route to route a packet to any destination) routing table size is at an alarming rate [2]. Internet Architecture Board (IAB) claims that there are four main driving forces behind the rapid growth of the DFZ RIB (Routing Information Base, an electronic database storing the routes and sometimes metrics to particular network destinations) [2]: suboptimal RIR address allocations, multihoming, traffic engineering and business events such as mergers and acquisitions, among which address allocation policies contribute significantly to routing table size.

P. Mueller, J.-N. Cao, and C.-L. Wang (Eds.): Infoscale 2009, LNICST 18, pp. 46–57, 2009.
© Institute for Computer Science, Social-Informatics and Telecommunications Engineering 2009

Address Fragmentation refers to the phenomena that the set of prefixes originated by the same AS cannot be summarized by one prefix. More than 75% of BGP routing table items are because of address fragmentation [3]. Analyzing the composition and distribution of address fragmentation can enhance our understanding of address allocation and aggregation.

In this paper, we propose a method to analyze address fragmentation. More specifically, we try to figure out the relationship between Prefix-Distance and Network-Distance of current Internet by taking Geographic-Distance as an approximation of Network-Distance. Instead of active probing, we use only passive monitoring of BGP message. By clustering prefixes based on similarities between their routing event start times, we cluster prefixes into groups. Prefixes in one group always have close logical relationships, e.g. they may be connected to the same ISP Point of Presence (PoP) or located in the same place. If prefixes in one group also have small Prefix-Distance, i.e. their IP address blocks are adjacent, they may get the chance to be well aggregated. However, according to our measurement result, there are two extreme allocations of IP address blocks in current Internet. Some of the blocks with small Geographic-Distances have small Prefix-Distances, while others with small Geographic-Distances have rather big Prefix-Distances.

The rest of the paper is organized as follows. We summarize some related work in Section 2, state the problem formally in Section 3. We propose a method to measure address fragmentation in Section 4, and analyze measurement results in Section 5. Finally, in Section 6, we summarize this paper.

2   Related Works

David G. Andersen [4] utilizes BGP dynamics to infer network topology. By clustering prefixes based upon similarities between their update times, He infers logical relationship between network prefixes within an Autonomous System (AS). Comparing with active method, this passive measurement method reduces the number of active probes required in traditional traceroute-based Internet mapping mechanisms. We also measure IP address distribution from BGP dynamics, however, we cluster prefixes into groups according to the similarities between their routing event start times. This significantly reduces the complexity.

Tian Bu [5] explore various factors contribute to the routing table size and characterize the growth of each contribution, including multihoming, load balancing, address fragmentation, and failure to aggregate. They find out that the contribution of address fragmentation is the greatest and is three times that of multihoming or load balancing. The contribution of failure to aggregate is the least. In our work, we further find out that there are two extreme allocations of IP address blocks in current Internet. Some of the blocks with small Geographic-Distances have small Prefix-Distances, while others with small Geographic-Distances have rather big Prefix-Distances. This is the direct reason of the BGP routing table's inflation.

M. Freedman [6] measures the geographic locality of IP prefixes using traceroute. He concludes that (1) address allocation policies and granularity of routing contribute significantly to routing table size, and (2) the BGP routing table can get aggregated significantly by reallocating IP addresses according to geographic locality. Our work not only validates Freedman's conclusions, but also enhances his measurement methodology and results. Instead of active probing, we only utilize passive measurement method, which reduces active probe monitors significantly. Besides Freedman's findings, we also identify two extreme allocations of address blocks in current Internet. Blocks with relatively small Geo-Distances have either very small or large Prefix-Distances.

Xiaoqiao Meng [7] quantitatively characterize the IPv4 address allocations made between 1997 to 2004 and the global BGP routing table size changes during the same period of time. 45% of the address allocations during that period were split into fragments smaller than the original allocated blocks. He claimed that without these fragmentations, the current BGP table would have been about half of its current size.

3 Prefix-Distance, Network-Distance and Geographic-Distance

In this section, we propose the basic assumptions of our measurement, state our purpose formally and define some related parameters which will be referenced frequently in the following of this paper.

Assumption 1: hosts within an IP prefix are topologically close.

This assumption is adopted by many researches [6, 8]. Even though shorter prefixes (large address blocks) tend to comprise more geographic locations [6], for most prefixes (/24 and longer) this assumption is reasonable [8].

Assumption 2: Prefixes that always have routing events simultaneously have close logical relationship, i.e. they are always connected to the same ISP Point of Presence (PoP) or located in the same place.

A similar assumption first appeared in [4]. It clustered prefixes based upon similarities between their update times, but not routing event start times. According to [4]'s evaluation, in more than 95% of the case, prefixes belonging to the same group share the same ISP PoP. Our assumption is a little different from [4]. Comparing with update arriving time, we believe taking routing event start time as clustering standard is also reasonable. We evaluate this assumption in Section 5.

Definition 1: D_p, D_n, and D_g

D_p: The *Prefix-Distance* of two address blocks. Firstly, we list the IP address from 0.0.0.0 to 255.255.255.255 alphanumerically. Then suppose there are two address blocks A and B, which cover two parts of the array. $D_p(A, B)$ refers to the number of addresses between A and B. Fig. 1 illustrates the definition of $D_p(A, B)$. If two blocks are overlapped, $D_p = 0$.

Fig. 1. Definition of D_p

D_n: The Network-Distance of two address blocks. A and B are two address blocks. i_A is one address in A, and j_B is one address in B. $t_{i_A j_B}$ stands for the round trip time (RTT) between i_A and j_B. n_A is the number of addresses in block A. n_B is the number of addresses in block B. The definition of D_n is shown in (1). Intuitively, it is the arithmetic mean value of all RTTs between A and B at the same time.

$$D_n(A,B) = \frac{1}{n_A n_B} \sum_{i_A \in A, j_B \in B} t_{i_A j_B} \tag{1}$$

D_g: The Geographic-Distance of two address blocks. A and B are two address blocks. i_A is one address in A, and j_B is one address in B. $d_{i_A j_B}$ stands for the shortest spherical distance between i_A and j_B. n_A and n_B are also the numbers of addresses in block A and B. The definition of D_g is shown in (2), which is the arithmetic mean value of all shortest spherical distances between A and B.

$$D_g(A,B) = \frac{1}{n_A n_B} \sum_{i_A \in A, j_B \in B} d_{i_A j_B} \tag{2}$$

We are trying to figure out the relationship between D_p and D_n. Ideally, the smaller D_p is, the smaller the D_n should be. That is to say, if two blocks have small Prefix-Distance, their Network-Distance should be small as well. This is good for aggregation. If two blocks have small Prefix-Distance, but their Network-Distance is large, these two blocks will not get aggregated in the routing table. As shown in Fig. 2, there are three districts in the D_p-D_n coordinates: Abnormal D_1, Normal D_2 and Abnormal D_3. If block A and B's D_p-D_n point lies in Abnormal D_1, they have small Prefix-Distance but relatively big Network-Distance, and cannot get aggregated. On the other hand, if block A and B's D_p-D_n point lies in Abnormal D_3, they have big Prefix-Distance but relatively small Network-Distance, and cannot get aggregated either. Only when A and B's D_p-D_n point lies in Normal D_2, they may get the chance to get aggregated. The slopes of the two boundaries l_1 and l_2 are variable parameters in our method. We leave it for out future research.

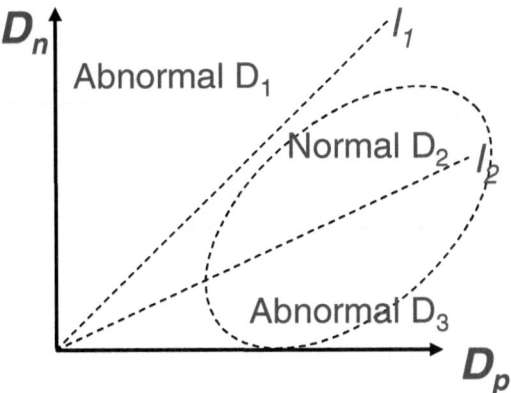

Fig. 2. D_p-D_n Coordinates

In this work, we focus on Normal D_2 and Abnormal D_3.(we leave Abnormal D_1 as our future work) The Network-Distance between any two address blocks is not trivial to obtain, thus we utilize Geographic-Distance D_g as an approximation of D_n. According to Oliveira [8]'s research, geographic distance is in direct proportion to end-to-end delay in most of the case, as a result this approximation is reasonable to some extend. There are also several other mechanisms estimating arbitrary end-to-end delays, such as IDMaps, GNP, Vivaldi and iPlane [11-14]. We plan to fit one of them into our system in the future.

4   Measuring D_p and D_g

4.1   Collect Prefix Groups

To collect prefix groups belonging to Normal D_2 and Abnormal D_3, we utilize the passive measurement method described in [4], but with a different prefix clustering algorithm. The basic assumption of this method is that prefixes that always have routing events simultaneously may have close relationship with each other (*Assumption 2*) . By grouping the prefixes that always have routing events together, we get the prefix groups that have relatively small D_n, which belong to Normal D_2 and Abnormal D_3.

There are two steps, as shown in Fig. 3, to get the prefix groups belonging to Normal D_2 and Abnormal D_3. The input is a time series of routing updates. An update is a BGP routing message that is specific to a prefix, such as an announcement or withdrawal. Each update contains a timestamp indicating the receive time and the prefix that is affected. The updates are ordered by timestamp. The first step is to use threshold T_1 to cluster BGP updates into *Routing Events*. Updates in one routing event are generated by the same reason, for example a link is down / up, or a router finds a better path to a destination. The second step is to group the prefixes that frequently have routing events in the same time window, whose width is T_2. The result of the clustering is groups of prefixes, each of which contains tightly correlated prefixes. Prefixes within one group always share administrative or topology features.

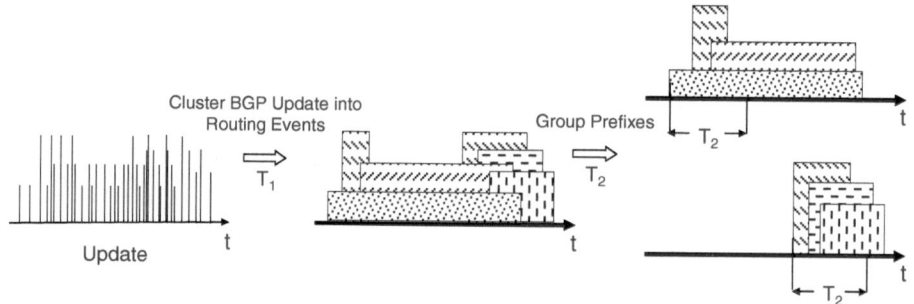

Fig. 3. Two Steps to Get Prefix Groups

Step 1: Cluster BGP Update into Routing Events

The basic idea of this process is to cluster consecutive BGP updates of the same prefix into one routing events if the updates are separated by a time interval less than a threshold. Fig. 4 illustrates this process.

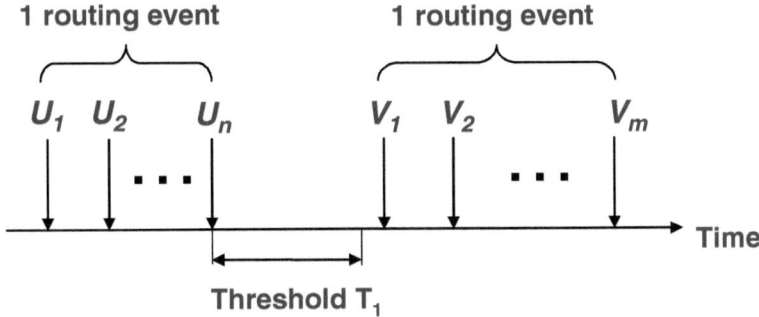

Fig. 4. The process of clustering BGP updates into routing events using threshold T_1. The horizontal axis stands for time. The vertical arrows stand for updates of the same prefix and the same observation point, which are represented by U_i (i = 1 ... n) and V_j (j = 1 ... m). The threshold value in this example is T_1. The time intervals between consecutive U_is and V_js are smaller than T_1, while the time interval between U_n and V_1 is bigger than T_1, thus, all U_is constitute a routing events and all V_js constitute another.

The threshold T is crucial in this process. We utilize a dynamic threshold method proposed in [10] to cluster BGP updates into routing events. Comparing with static threshold method, this dynamic approach can get more accurate clustering results.

Step 2: Cluster Prefixes that Always Have Routing Events Simultaneously into One Group

As shown in Fig. 3, after the first step, updates are clustered into different routing events. Some of the events happen almost simultaneously, while others do not. We introduce anther threshold T_2 to indicate the width of the time window. If start times of different routing events locate within one time window, we cluster the prefixes that cause these routing events into the same group.

If prefix P_A and prefix P_B are clustered into one time window for only once, but for most of the time, P_A and P_B have their own routing events independently, we will not say P_A and P_B have relatively small Network-Distance. As a result, we introduce another parameter F in (3) to indicate the frequency of clustering different blocks into one time window. p_i stands for address block. $W(p_i)$ stands for the number of time windows that contain p_i. $W(p_i \cap p_j)$ stands for the number of time windows that contain both p_i and p_j. If F is bigger than a certain threshold f, we say p_i, p_{i+1}...and p_{i+k} belong to the same *Prefix Group*. In our experiment $f = 100\%$. That is to say, only those prefixes which have routing events within one time window all the time can be grouped into one prefix group.

$$F = \frac{W(p_i \cap p_{i+1} \cap ... \cap p_{i+k})}{W(p_i) \cup W(p_{i+1}) \cup ... \cup W(p_{i+k})} \tag{3}$$

4.2 Calculate D_p^g and D_g^g

Suppose k prefixes belong to the same Prefix Group, there will be C_k^2 points generated by prefix pairs in Fig. 2. However, information contained in these points is redundant. We are focusing on the features of a Prefix Group but not any pair in the Group. Only one point, instead of C_k^2 points, is required to characterize a Prefix Group. As a result, we further define D_p^g, D_n^g and D_g^g, where the superscript g stands for the name of the Prefix Group.

***Definition 2**: D_p^g, D_n^g and D_g^g of Prefix Group g*

Prefixes $p_{i+1}...p_{i+k}$ belong to the same Prefix Group g. D_p^g, D_n^g and D_g^g are defined as the arithmetic means of D_P, D_n and D_g, as shown in (4), (5) and (6).

$$D_p^g = \frac{1}{C_k^2} \sum_{p_l \in g, p_m \in g, l \neq m} D_p(p_l, p_m) \tag{4}$$

$$D_n^g = \frac{1}{C_k^2} \sum_{p_l \in g, p_m \in g, l \neq m} D_n(p_l, p_m) \tag{5}$$

$$D_g^g = \frac{1}{C_k^2} \sum_{p_l \in g, p_m \in g, l \neq m} D_g(p_l, p_m) \tag{6}$$

We collect BGP updates from RouteViews [15]. Our dataset contains all updates from route-views.linx in January and February, 2009. The time span should not be too long in case of any significant topology change. We firstly cluster these BGP updates into routing events (we get around 60790000 routing events in total). Then we group prefixes with time window of 5 seconds. After calculating different groups' F values, we choose the groups whose F values are 100% as the Prefix Groups. In this work, we utilize D_g^g as an approximation of D_n^g, and compute Geographic-Distance of prefixes using GeoLite City database from Maxmind [16], which maps each IP address to a geographic location. . Finally, we put all the (D_p^g, D_g^g) points in Fig. 2 to find out the relationship between Prefix-Distance and Geographic-Distance.

5 Measurement Results

5.1 Clustering Result

Fig. 5 shows the result when time window is 5 seconds. There are around 50,000 points and two areas: ZONE 1 near the origin and ZONE 2 far from D_g. This measurement result indicates that there are basically two kinds of Prefix Groups. One is that with small Prefix-Distance and small Geographic-Distance, represented by ZONE 1. The other is that with small Geographic-Distance but significant Prefix-Distance, represented by ZONE 2. Situations in between are very rare.

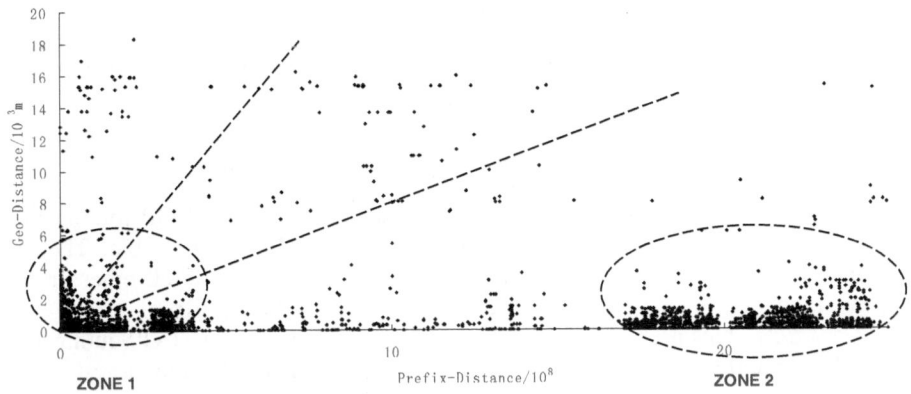

Fig. 5. Prefix-Distance and Geo-Distance when Time Window is 5 Seconds

Prefixes Groups in both ZONE 1 and 2 have relatively small Geographic-Distance. That is to say blocks in one Prefix Group are very likely to get connected to the Internet through the same Point of Presence (PoP). For ZONE 1, blocks in one Prefix Group have small Prefix-Distance, thus they are very likely to get aggregated. On the other hand, for ZONE 2, blocks in one Prefix Group are hardly to get aggregated because of big Prefix-Distance. This measurement result shows an interesting phenomenon: there are two extreme block allocations in current Internet. Some of the blocks with small Geographic-Distances have small Prefix-Distances, while others with small Geographic-Distances have rather big Prefix-Distances.

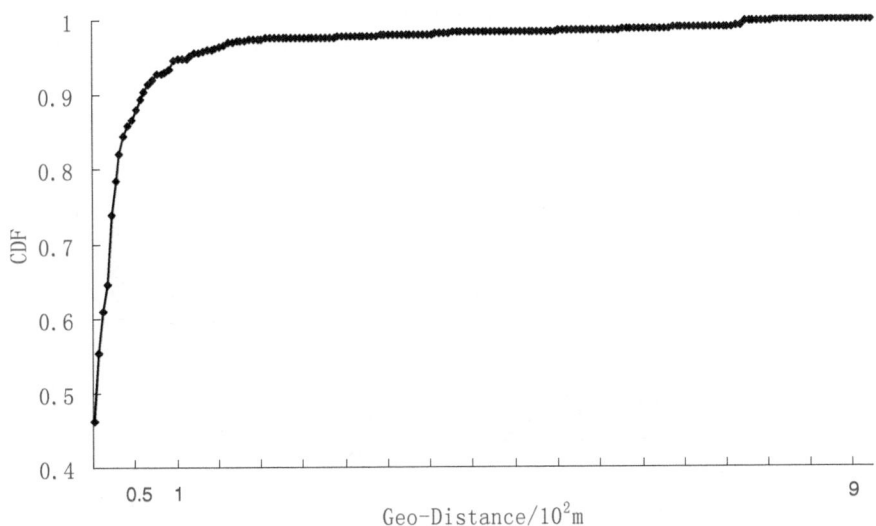

Fig. 6. Geo-Distance Distribution of Prefixes within One Group

We further calculate the Geo-Distance of each prefix group. Fig. 6 shows the Geo-Distance's distribution. More than 90% of the prefix groups' Geo-Distances are less than 100 meters. This indicates that prefix groups generated by our clustering method do have relatively small Geo-Distances. Thus, *Assumption 2* is reliable.

5.2 Prefix-Distance and Geo-Distance in BGP Routing Tables

We also calculate Prefix-Distance and Geo-Distance of current BGP routing table. Firstly, we choose one prefix from route-views.linx BGP routing table. Then, we calculate the Prefix-Distance and Geo-Distance of this prefix with all other prefixes appears in the routing table. In our experiment, we choose two prefixes.

24.143.8/24: This prefix is announced by AS6389, belonging to BellSouth.net Inc. According to CIDR-REPORT [18]'s statistic, AS6389 announces the largest number of prefixes, i.e. around 4322. 24.143.8/24 is one of the prefixes. It first appears in BGP routing table on Oct. 16th, 1999. Fig. 7 shows the Prefix-Distance and Geo-Distance of this prefix and other prefixes in March-4th-2009's BGP routing table download from RouteViews [15] (There are around 291003 prefixes). Even though AS6389 announced the largest number of prefixes, we find out that most of the points locate in Normal D_2. We also draw the Prefix-Distance and Geo-Distance graph of 24.143.8/24 and the other prefixes announced only by AS6389. However, as shown in Fig. 8, almost all the points are located in Abnormal D_3. This indicates the reason why AS6389 announces the largest number of prefixes: because its prefixes are near from each other geographically, but are separated address blocks.

59.252.0.0/16: This prefix is announced by AS37937, belonging to China eGovNet Information Center. According to CIDR-REPORT's statistic, AS37937 only announces this one prefix. It first appears on May 8th, 2007. Fig. 9 shows the Prefix-Distance and Geo-Distance of this prefix and other prefixes in March-4th-2009's BGP routing table download from RouteViews. Most of the points are located in Abnormal D_1, where Prefix-Distance is small but Geo-Distance is relatively large. This indicates

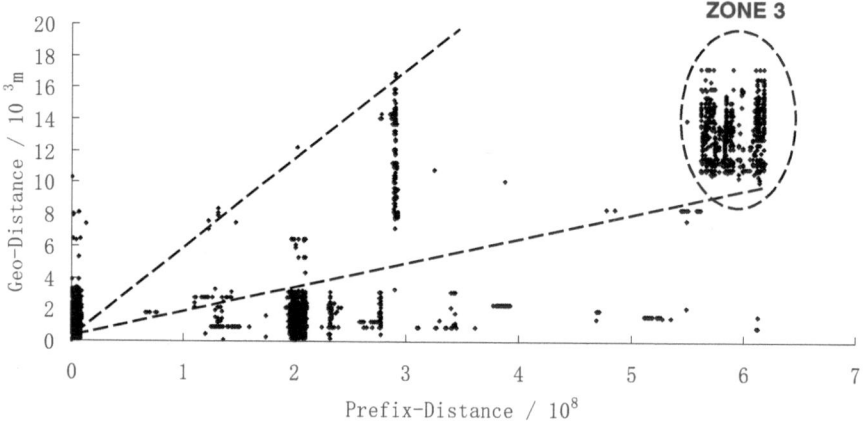

Fig. 7. Prefix-Distance and Geo-Distance of 24.143.8/24 and other Prefixes

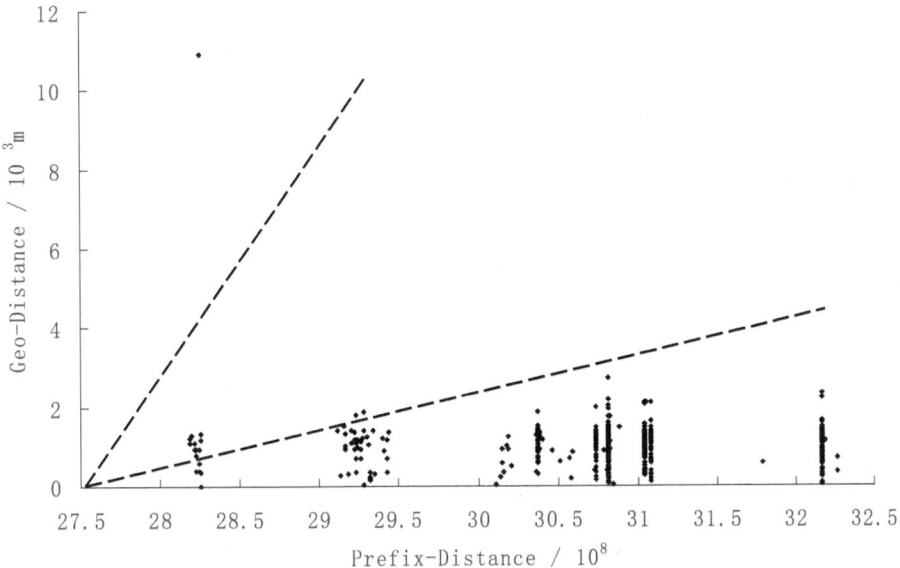

Fig. 8. Prefix-Distance and Geo-Distance of 24.143.8/24 and other Prefixes in AS6389

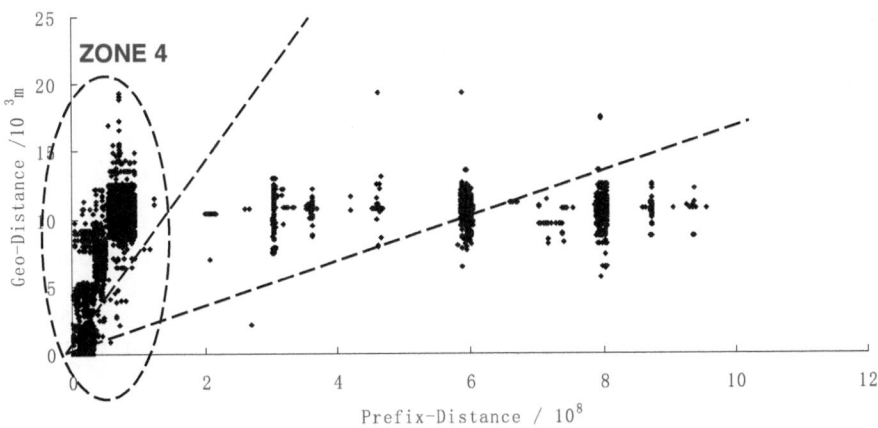

Fig. 9. Prefix-Distance and Geo-Distance of 59.252.0.0/16 and other Prefixes

that aggregatable prefixes are far away from each other, and thus cannot get aggregated. Comparing with prefix 24.143.8/24 (whose measurement result shows in Fig. 7), 59.252.0.0/16 first appears in BGP routing table eight years later. During these eight years BGP table size grows from 6000 entries to 290000 entries. According to Xiaoqiao Meng [7]'s conclusion that 45% of the address allocations from 1997 to 2004 were split into fragments smaller than the original allocated blocks, we speculate that failing to allocating IP address blocks according to geographic information is the most possible reason. This speculation is identical with M. Freedman [6]'s conclusion.

6   Conclusion and Future Work

In this paper, we try to figure out the relationship between Prefix-Distance and Network-Distance of current Internet by taking Geographic-Distance as an approximation of Network-Distance. We focus our measurement on the prefixes with relatively small Geographic-Distance, and get Prefix Groups from BGP routing dynamics. Comparing with previous active probing methods, our method 1) reduces the number of active probes required in active measurement. And 2) results a more detailed prefixes' distribution analysis. Our measurement result shows that 1) there are two extreme allocations of IP address blocks in current Internet. Some of the blocks with small Geographic-Distances have small Prefix-Distances, while others with small Geographic-Distances have rather big Prefix-Distances. 2) Failing to allocating IP address blocks according to geographic information in the past eight years is one of the driving forces of BGP tables' inflation.

There are two directions for our future work. Currently, the reliability of our measurement lies on the correctness of MaxMind [16]. Firstly, we will try to fit some tools that can estimate Network-Distance into our system. Secondly, we are trying to do some quantitative analysis about our measurement results.

Acknowledgments. We would like to thank Professor David Lee from the Ohio State University for his great suggestions on our problem statement, measurement and analysis. This work is supported by the National Basic Research Program of China (973 Program) (Grant No. 2009CB320502).

References

1. Rekhter, Y., Li, T.: A Border Gateway Protocol 4 (BGP-4). IETF, Request for Comments 4271 (January 2006)
2. Meyer, D., Zhang, L., Fall, K.: Report from the IAB Workshop on Routing and Addressing. In: Routing and Addressing Workshop, Amsterdam, Netherlands, December 15 (2006)
3. Bu, T., Gao, L., Towsley, D.: On Routing Table Growth. In: ICNP (2003)
4. Andersen, D., Feamster, N., Bauer, S., Balakrishnan, H.: Topology Inference from BGP Routing Dynamics. In: SIGCOMM IMW 2002 (2002)
5. Bu, T., Gao, L., Towsley, D.: On Characterizing BGP Routing Table Growth. Computer Networks: The International Journal of Computer and Telecommunications Networking 45, 45–54 (2004)
6. Freedman, M., Vutukuru, M., Feamster, N., Balakrishnan, H.: Geographic Locality of IP Prefixes. In: IMC 2005 (2005)
7. Meng, X., Xu, Z., Zhang, B., Huston, G., Lu, S., Zhang, L.: IPv4 address allocation and the BGP routing table evolution. Computer Communication Review 35(1), 71–80 (2005)
8. Oliveira, R., Lad, M., Zhang, B., Zhang, L.: Geographically Informed Inter-Domain Routing. In: ICNP 2007, Beijing, China (2007)
9. Chang, H., Jamin, S., Willinger, W.: Inferring AS-level Internet topology from router-level path traces. In: Proc. of SPIE ITCom, August 2001, pp. 19–24 (2001)

10. Wu, X., Yin, X., Wang, Z., Tang, M.: A Three-step Dynamic Threshold Method to Cluster BGP Updates into Routing Events. In: ISADS 2009 (2009)
11. Francis, P., Jamin, S., Jin, C., Jin, Y., Raz, D., Shavitt, Y., Zhang, L.: IDMaps: An architecture for a global internet host distance estimation service. In: Proc. IEEE INFOCOM, March 1999, vol. 1, pp. 210–217 (1999)
12. Ng, E., Zhang, H.: Predicting Internet network distance with coordinates-based approaches. In: INFOCOM (2002)
13. Shavitt, Y., Tankel, T.: On the curvature of the Internet and its usage for overlay construction and distance estimation. In: INFOCOM (2004)
14. Madhyastha, H.V., Anderson, T., Krishnamurthy, A., Spring, N., Venkataramani, A.: A Structural Approach to Latency Prediction. In: IMC 2006 (October 2006)
15. The RouteViews project, http://www.routeviews.org/
16. MaxMind GeoLite City, http://www.maxmind.com/app/geolitecity

On Improving Network Locality in BitTorrent-Like Systems

Yun-Chiu Ching[1], Ching-Hsien Hsu[1], and Kuan-Ching Li[2]

[1] Department of Computer Science and Information Engineering
Chung Hua University, Hsinchu, Taiwan 300, R.O.C.
{mali,robert}@grid.chu.edu.tw
[2] Department of Computer Science and Information Engineering
Providence University, Shalu, Taichung 43301, Taiwan
kuancli@pu.edu.tw

Abstract. The emerging Peer-to-Peer (P2P) model has become a very popular paradigm for developing Internet-scale systems. The BitTorrent is an example of P2P system for sharing resources, including files and documents. Owing to the peer does not have the capability of locality aware, it cannot differentiate its neighbors belong to which Internet Service Provider (ISP), file sharing results in a large number of cross-ISP traffic (about 70%). ISPs often control BitTorrent traffic by bandwidth limiting for reducing cross-ISP traffic. In this paper, we propose an adaptive peer collaboration strategy to reduce cross-ISP traffic without additional equipment and backup mechanism, which means decreasing the cost of additional equipment. Internal peers can collaborate indirectly. In peer collaboration strategy, a peer chooses most of its neighbors from internal ISP as itself, and only a few from external ISPs for reducing transfer of cross-ISP by biased neighbor selection. Second, in order to decrease redundancy, we employ Advanced Tracker (AT) to record the information of pieces that owned by each ISP. Finally, we adopt dynamic priority allocation for improving the file download time. Experimental results show that our peer collaboration strategy outperforms previous approaches, decreases redundancy and decreases the file download time remarkably.

Keywords: Peer-to-Peer, cross-ISP traffic, peer collaboration strategy, biased neighbor selection.

1 Introduction

BitTorrent [1, 11] file sharing system has become the most popular application in recent years. The early P2P file sharing systems are like Napster [2], Gnutella [3] and eMule [4]. Unlike the client-server model, BitTorrent divides a file into a number of equal-sized pieces, where each peer simultaneously downloads and uploads via its neighbors. BitTorrent has the special character, which the more users join BitTorrent, the faster download rate. Hence, file sharing creates a lot of BitTorrent traffic. The research [20] shows that BitTorrent generates cross-ISP traffic occupy most of Bit-Torrent traffic (about 70%). Each peer's neighbors are selected randomly from the

P. Mueller, J.-N. Cao, and C.-L. Wang (Eds.): Infoscale 2009, LNICST 18, pp. 58–75, 2009.
© Institute for Computer Science, Social-Informatics and Telecommunications Engineering 2009

tracker, which indicates that each peer cannot decide its neighbors from the same ISP as itself. Additionally, each peer gets a lot of pieces from external peer [20]. Therefore, BitTorrent traffic has become a large number of cross-ISP traffic. ISPs often control BitTorrent traffic by bandwidth limiting for reducing cross-ISP traffic. However, bandwidth limiting will increase the file download time and worsen the user download experience, the fundamental concern of the ISP which is to improve the locality of BitTorrent traffic.

In this paper, we propose peer collaboration strategy, which includes three parts. First, we let a peer choose a lot of its neighbors from internal ISP as itself, and only a few from external ISPs by modifying trackers and clients [9]. This conception is doing a similar grouping BitTorrent peers into clusters [10] and let most of pieces of exchange rely on internal ISP, and only a few of pieces rely on external ISP, improving traffic locality in BitTorrent and reducing the times of cross-ISP. Besides, the approach of modifying trackers and clients can come to biased neighbor selection [9] without additional equipment, it conform our spirit that as economic as possible and avoid the equipment had a breakdown, and decreasing cost of equipment. Moreover, the biased neighbor selection is key to the success of reduces cross-ISP traffic and rely on BitTorrent adopts the local rarest first (LRF) algorithm [11, 19] as the piece selection strategy, where each peer downloads piece which is least replicated pieces among its neighbors.

The purpose of BitTorrent peers into clusters is to solve redundancy problem [9] and it is valid for reducing cross-ISP traffic. Owing to each peer's neighbors are selected randomly from the tracker, the redundancy is very high as start to share the file. The optimal redundancy is 1 [9], which means each piece will only be transferred once from initial seed to other ISPs. Even if there is no backup mechanism, our goal in this paper is to let redundancy down as low as possible (close to 1). We present peer collaboration strategy, the lower redundancy, inspired by FPFR [18] and MOB [10]. They are both multicast approach and their redundancy are 1. The distribution of MOB in grid is similar to BitTorrent. Unlike the BitTorrent, MOB adds teamwork among the nodes of a cluster to improve collaboration. BitTorrent employs incentive mechanisms such Tit-For-Tat (TFT) [11, 19] to improve ratio of upload. However, BitTorrent is based on the personal benefit. Many users always leave as finishing their download and some of users are free-riding [13]. In order to decrease redundancy, each peer needs to collaborate. For example, each peer downloads different piece from external ISPs and does not download the piece if it is in internal ISP already. BitTorrent has no teamwork among peers according to the above-mentioned statement. We propose a strategy and it let each peer know whether the piece in internal ISP to avoid downloading the redundant piece, which is exist in internal ISP. Thus, second part of peer collaboration strategy is that decreasing redundancy is close to 1. We employ Advanced Tracker (AT) to maintain a list, which records the information of pieces that owned by each ISP presently. Each peer can know whether the piece in internal ISP in terms of a list, and needs to get the piece by external peer if there is no that piece in internal ISP.

Peer collaboration strategy may cause some peers are waiting for the internal piece rather than external piece, and increase the file download time. On the other hand, all the download process of BitTorrent, especially in the first piece scenario and last piece scenario, because of the choke algorithm the paradox of supply and demand exists in

BitTorrent [16], which is increasing the file download time. Finally, we adopt dynamic priority allocation to decrease the file download time.

The rest of this paper is organized as follows. We present an overview of BitTorrent and the relate work of cross-ISP traffic in section 2. We present the preliminaries in section 3. We present peer collaboration strategy in section 4 and give the experimental evaluation in section 5. We conclude this paper and future work in section 6.

2 Related Work

2.1 BitTorrent Overview

The BitTorrent P2P system has become the most popular sharing resources, and its kernel source code had been written by Bram Cohen in 2002[11]. Unlike the HTTP/FTP model, a large number of files were shared by BitTorrent via Internet without increasing the loading of publisher's server and bandwidth. The performance of BitTorrent outperforms the traditional approaches remarkably. The main idea of BitTorrent is that each peer simultaneously downloads and uploads. Therefore, the download rate does not restrain by publisher's upload bandwidth, and much more users join the torrent can supply more upload bandwidth. BitTorrent is that a shared file is divided into a number of equal-sized pieces (typically 256 KB in size), and each piece is split in sub-pieces (typically 16 KB in size) to avoid a delay among pieces being sent, and always keeping some number (typically 5) requests pipelined at once. Sub-pieces are the transmission unit on the network, but the protocol only accounts for transferred pieces. Each peer simultaneously downloads and uploads after get first piece from its neighbors, and each peer is a serve as well as a client. Therefore, BitTorrent can distribute the pieces quickly and it has a higher transfer rate than the traditional approaches, and it also does not increase the loading of publisher's server.

Figure 1 shows that the file download process of BitTorrent is as follows. (1) A user downloads a metadata file (called the torrent file) was generated by publisher from a web server, which contains IP address of tracker and the SHA-1 hash values of each piece, and the piece size and so on. (2) A user starts the BitTorrent client software to join and contacts the tracker as a new peer. Tracker is s central server, which keeps track of all peers downloading the file. The new peer requests a part of peers from the tracker, which responds to the new peer with a list of randomly chosen peers (typically 50), then the new peer attempts to establish connection with these peers as its neighbors. (3) The new peer starts to exchange pieces with its neighbors. BitTorrent let tracker keep an up-to-date state, and every 30 min each peer reports to the tracker its state. Figure 1 shows that the Seed is initial seed, which means the file publisher, and there are two types of Peer, namely leechers and seeders. Leechers also called downloaders, are peers who only have a part (or none) of the pieces of the file, which seeders are peers who have all pieces of the file. Leechers simultaneously download and upload pieces, and seeders only upload piece. A leecher turns into a seeder when it obtains all the pieces. At this moment, a seeder can leave BitTorrent or stay online to upload pieces continually. When the number of its neighbors dips below the threshold (typically 20), the peer again contacts the tracker to obtain a list of additional neighbors.

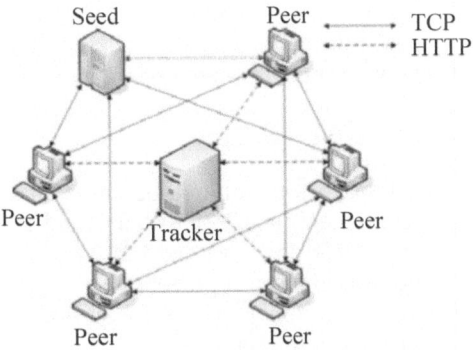

Fig. 1. The framework of BitTorrent

BitTorrent does not the central sharing resources, so it needs a great algorithm to improve fairness and optimizing the whole download rate. BitTorrent adopts choke algorithm includes TFT and Optimistic Unchoke (OU) as the peer selection strategy, where each peer can upload pieces to five peers, so each peer has five upload quotas, among which each peer allocates four quotas for the TFT and the fifth for the OU. Process of Choke algorithm as follows, every 10 seconds, a peer employs the TFT to evaluates which of its interested neighbors have been giving pieces to it with the high rates and the four highest peers are preferred to unchoke. Every 30 seconds, a peer employs OU to randomly unchoke from the remaining set of peers. OU allows boot-strap new peers and explores other peers which potentially upload to it with the higher rates. Existing BitTorrent employs the static quota allocation to fixedly allocate upload quotas for the TFT and OU. The peer starts to send <request> message to request pieces when the other side sends <unchoke> message to it. How to choose the piece is also very important. A poor piece selection may cause the last pieces problem [11,19] and let peers obtain the incomplete file, and furthermore it may cause the low download rate or increase the loading of upload peer. BitTorrent employs four strategies as piece selection as follows.

(1) **Strict Priority:** In BitTorrent, a complete piece is the exchange unit for file sharing, but sub-pieces are the transmission unit on the network. Hence, once a single sub-piece has been requested, the remaining sub-pieces from that particular piece are requested before sub-pieces from any other piece.

(2) **Rarest First:** Under this strategy, a peer downloads the piece, which is least replicated among its neighbors is chosen first. Even if there are no seeds in BitTorrent, the peer may get piece from its neighbors to avoid the last pieces problem.

(3) **Random First Piece:** If a new peer has nothing to upload and exchange, it is important to get one piece as quickly as possible, and the new peer starts to employ the rarest first policy until it gets first piece.

(4) **Endgame Mode:** When a user has most of pieces already, which means only a few of pieces does not obtain, the peer sends requests for all sub-pieces to its neighbors. Cancels are sent for sub-pieces as one of its neighbors starts to upload the sub-pieces, to avoid redundant sends and the end of the file can download quickly.

As shown in Figure 1, there are two types of protocol in BitTorrent, one is the connection between peers and tracker, its protocol is based on HTTP, and the other is the connection among peers, its protocol is based on TCP.

2.2 Existing Studies on Cross-ISP Traffic

There are many previous approaches to solve issue about cross-ISP traffic, some of them need higher cost of equipment, and P2P systems and ISPs need collaboration closely [5,6,7,22], others only spend low cost and P2P systems collaborate with ISPs indirectly [9,12,20]. The purposes of these approaches are improving the file download time and decreasing redundancy. In this paper, a peer inside the same ISP we called internal peer, conversely, we called external peer.

In [5], positional at the gateway of ISP to the Internet, a cache stores pieces sent by external peers to internal peers, and as internal peer wants to get the piece from external peer, the cache interrupts and sends the copy to internal peer. In [6,7], ISP supplies an oracle service to users. ISP employs the equipment to manage each peer to avoid a lot of BitTorrent traffic. Likewise, users can obtain a great download rate. However, they need the user supplies the oracle with a list of possible neighbors, and then oracle ranks them according to certain criteria such as distance and bandwidth. Another approach is to employ the gateway peer [20], and it is the only peer inside internal ISP that can connect to external peers. But gateway peer needs high upload bandwidth to avoid increasing download time [9], and gateway peer needs to keep stable performance. P2P traffic shaping devices [9] can intercept and modify the responses from the tracker to the peer, and let peers drive to biased neighbor selection. P4P [22] supplies the inter-active interface to P2P system and ISP, and it allows ISP to manage the underlying physical network and supplies the real- time network to P2P system. Furthermore, it can integrate network command into P2P system, improving the network utility ratio and performance of P2P system. The content distribution networks (CDN) [12] to drive biased neighbor selection without collaboration between users and ISPs. A peer only needs to have the ability to perform local DNS queries for CDN names, and then it can find its neighbors. Modifying trackers and clients is another approach [9], and this approach allows each peer to get most of peers from internal ISP, only a few from external ISP, and it is a direct and efficient approach. Using bandwidth limiting to control BitTorrent traffic is the simple and direct approach, but it is not efficiency.

These approaches are the same principle, which let BitTorrent peers into clusters and improving the traffic in internal ISP. Consequently, several users can decrease the file download time and ISP does not employ bandwidth limiting to reduce cross-ISP traffic. However, various approaches need to raise the cost of hardware except modifying trackers and clients and CDN [12]. For example, Cache, P2P traffic shaping devices, Oracle service and P4P portal, and it needs the particular peer to have highest band-width and stable performance, such as gateway peer. In this paper, our peer collabora-tion strategy can reduce cross-ISP traffic without sacrificing system performance and is based on the premise that as economic as possible. Besides, our peer collaboration strategy only needs to modify original framework of BitTorrent, and it does not need additional equipment. Experimental results show that our peer collaboration strategy can decrease redundancy and decrease the file download time efficiently.

3   Preliminaries

Generally, BitTorrent goes through three stages in its life: flash crowd, steady state and winding down [8, 15, 17, 21]. Among the three stages, flash crowd stage creates a lot of traffic and is the most challenging for ISPs to control, so we focus on the flash crowd stage in this paper. We assumed that each peer leaves as finishing its download, only initial seed always stays online until terminating the simulation, and initial seed does not employ the biased neighbor selection. In this paper, the main evaluation criteria are redundancy and download time. Improving traffic locality can reduce cross-ISP traffic, but the lower redundancy, the lower cross-ISP traffic.

In section 2, we can find three problems about original BitTorrent. (1) Each peer's neighbors are selected randomly from the tracker, and file sharing creates a lot of BitTorrent traffic. (2) BitTorrent adopts the LRF algorithm as the piece selection, and it cannot avoid redundancy is increasing even if we solve problem (1). (3) The whole download process of BitTorrent in the first piece scenario and last piece scenario, because of the choke algorithm the paradox of supply and demand exists in BitTorrent [16], which is increasing the file download time. We present the peer collaboration strategy as follows, and it has three parts, which solve the above problems.

(1) **Biased neighbor selection:** According to the above-mentioned statement, each peer's neighbors are selected randomly from the tracker. Hence, file sharing may create a lot of cross-ISP traffic. ISPs employ bandwidth limiting in order to reduce cross-ISP traffic to decrease cost. Therefore, we may not have a great performance even if we use the high bandwidth. Some factors affect the performance such as network congestion, ACK delay, and smaller bandwidth, etc. Likewise, ISPs also need to control BitTorrent traffic. In order to create a win-win situation, using biased neighbor selection is a direct and efficient approach, and ISPs do not worry about the cross-ISP traffic all the time but users have a better download experience. We adopt the approach of modifying trackers and clients to finish biased neighbor selection [9]. Modifying tracker we called Advanced Tracker (AT). When a new peer join the torrent. According to the new peer's ISP, AT let the new peer chooses M-N neighbors from internal ISP as itself, and only N neighbors from external ISPs, where M is the maximum connection of peer, and N is the number of external peers.

(2) **Unique piece selection:** BitTorrent adopts the LRF algorithm as the piece selection. Even if BitTorrent had been employed the biased neighbor selection, each peer may get the redundant piece, which means the piece had downloaded by some internal peer. Because BitTorrent only employs the LRF algorithm as the piece selection and is affected by choke algorithm. Our method as follows, we let AT maintain a table, we called Global Unique Piece Table (GUPT). It records the information of pieces that owned by each ISP and peers can observe the GUPT to avoid downloading the redundant piece. Therefore, each peer get the piece from external peer is unique inside internal ISP every time. Internal peers can collaborate indirectly, and decrease redundancy significantly. Also, we present the two approaches to solve the problem that the paradox of supply and demand in terms of GUPT. We detailed introduce it in section 4.2.

(3) **Dynamic priority allocation:** In unique piece selection, GUPT will probably make some peers are waiting for the inside piece rather than outside piece, so increasing download time. On the other hand, the whole download process of BitTorrent in the first piece scenario and last piece scenario, because of the choke algorithm the paradox of supply and demand exists in BitTorrent [16], which is increasing the file download time. The advantages of Dynamic Quota Allocation (DQA) [16] are preserved in our dynamic priority allocation, and we let OU allocate quota to external peer, improving the download rate via optimizing the upload quota utility ratio. It is noted that we do not make the backup mechanism, dynamic priority allocation needs each peer to upload more 2-4 pieces in terms of it follows the DQA, and it can complementary to the problem that ISP lost pieces. Dynamic priority allocation can let pieces spread to different ISP as quickly as possible because of external peer has a higher priority.

4   Peer Collaboration Strategy

In this section, we present our Peer Collaboration Strategy (PCS). We explain how internal peers to collaborate indirectly in terms of the whole framework and flowchart in section 4.1 and section 4.2. We propose an approach to improve the download time in section 4.3.

4.1   Biased Neighbor Selection

The basic approach to solve the problem of cross-ISP traffic is grouping BitTorrent peers into clusters so as to reduce the connection of external ISP. In BitTorrent, each peer's neighbors are selected randomly from the tracker, and most of neighbors spread to different ISPs. Hence, file sharing creates a lot of cross-ISP traffic. Internal peers can let a lot of exchange inside internal ISP, and only unique piece rely on external peer after BitTorrent peers into clusters.

In order to let BitTorrent peers into clusters, we choose the approach of modifying trackers and clients to drive biased neighbor selection [9], and this is a direct and efficient approach. Modified tracker we called Advanced Tracker (AT). When a new peer join the torrent, According to the new peer's ISP, AT let the new peer choose M-N neighbors from internal ISP as itself, and only N neighbors from external ISPs, where M is the maximum connection of peer, and N is the number of external peers, and we set N = 1.

Figure 2 shows that the biased neighbor selection is different from random neighbor selection. As shown in Figure 2, biased neighbor selection reduces a lot of external connection significantly. Thus, it does not need additional equipment to drive biased neighbor selection and conform to the principle of economic. Also, the redundancy will decrease.

However, BitTorrent adopts the LRF algorithm as the piece selection. The rarest piece cannot present the unique piece inside internal ISP. Therefore, each peer has many chances to get redundant piece in external ISP even if BitTorrent peers into clusters already. The choke algorithm also acts the important roles, and they are keys to reduce the redundancy. In section 4.2, we propose a strategy to restrain the redundancy

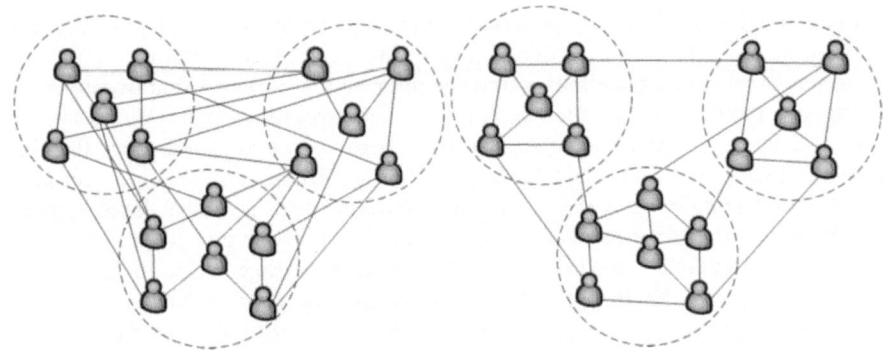

Fig. 2. Random neighbor selection vs. biased neighbor selection

efficiently. Let each peer get the piece from external peer is unique inside internal ISP every time, besides an exception. For example, several peers may simultaneously leave, so there is no seed in internal ISP, and ISP lost pieces. At that time, the peer needs to send request to external peer if initial seed does not in internal ISP.

4.2 Unique Piece Selection

4.2.1 Global Unique Piece Table

In section 4.1, we use AT to drive biased neighbor selection. However, we find some scenario, which would increase redundancy after biased neighbor selection.

(1) **LRF algorithm:** The definition of rarest piece is least replicated among its neighbors [19], which indicates rarest piece is not unique in internal ISP except the rarest piece first travels into internal ISP. Once the rarest piece travels into internal ISP which it had downloaded by internal peer, the redundancy will increase gradually. The LRF algorithm does not use to solve the problem of choosing unique piece. Thus, we need a strategy to get unique piece from outside.

(2) **Choke algorithm:** If some peer is interested in internal peer and external peer simultaneously, the redundancy may increase via choke algorithm. For example, internal peer sends <choke> message and external peer sends <unchoke> message in terms of TFT. The redundancy will increase as the particular piece had been downloaded before.

(3) **ISP lost pieces:** Internal peer needs external peer to get some rarest piece again when ISP lost pieces happened, which was due to several peers may simultaneously leave and peers include seed or initial seed is not here. ISP lost piece cannot prevent, besides the system uses the backup mechanism [5] or network coding [14]. The redundancy will increase deservedly when ISP lost pieces.

(4) **Synchronal request:** When there are no records on GUPT (in internal ISP, a piece had not been downloaded yet), internal peers may download pieces via external peers simultaneously because no records on GUPT for references.

We present the second part of peer collaboration strategy is that we let redundancy close to 1. Internal peers cannot collaborate to decrease redundancy according to (1)(2)(3)(4). Our unique piece selection can solve (1)(2). We organize (3)(4) into exception because it cannot avoid the redundancy is increased in our strategy. We do not discuss the matter and allow the redundancy is increased in (3)(4). In unique piece selection, our method is that we let AT maintain GUPT to record the information of pieces that owned by each ISP. Initially, the file was allocated by initial seed and spread it around. When a peer has received <bitfield> or <have> message from internal peer, it does not check the GUPT and it only uses the incentive mechanisms of original BitTorrent. When a peer has received the <bitfield> or <have> message from external peer, it checks the record of the particular piece whether it had been recorded on GUPT. If there is no record about the particular piece on GUPT, the peer sends <interested> message and waiting to have the <unchoke> message with the opposite side. Conversely, sends <not interested> message directly to inform the opposite side. If the peer is unchoked by the opposite side, it informs AT to record the particular piece on GUPT as it has done to request the piece. Figure 3 depicts the flowchart of unique piece selection, and this scheme can prevent the redundant pieces from external ISPs except ISP lost piece and synchronal request.

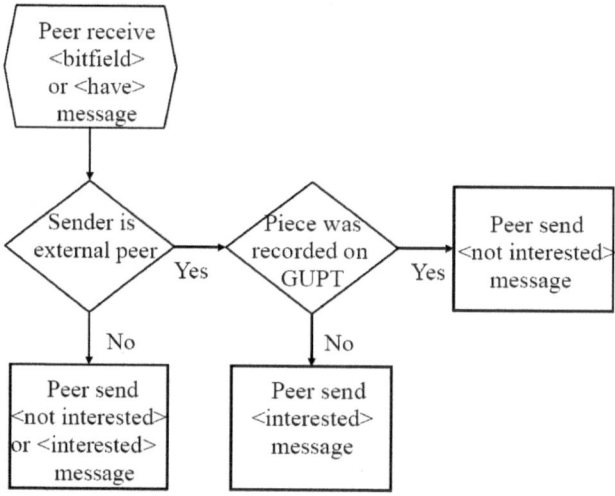

Fig. 3. Flowchart of unique piece selection

4.2.2 Solution of ISP Lost Pieces Problem

Some internal peers only rely on external peer to get the piece from external peer when ISP lost pieces happened. Some peers cannot get piece from external peer because of the record on the GUPT. Peers cannot complete their download except initial seed inside the same ISP. Therefore, ISP lost pieces happened, our solution as follows.

(1) **Peer contacts AT again:** Generally, ISP lost pieces is due to several peers may simultaneously leave, and let ISP lost some rarest piece. In BitTorrent, when the number of its neighbors dips below the threshold (typically 20), the peer again contacts the tracker to obtain a list of additional neighbors. If the peer get piece at once after reconnection, which indicates that locality lost piece rather than whole ISP. And if no action in the long time, which indicates that the peer only rely on external peer to get the piece (maybe external peer is a seed or lecher who has lost

piece, even initial seed). Our method as follows, the peer does not consult GUPT anymore as the peer does not send any <interested> message after get a list from AT again in 30 seconds.

(2) **GUPT records the number of piece:** GUPT also record the number of each piece. Our method as follows, each peer informs AT to count the number of piece as get the piece from internal ISP, and subtract the one unit with all pieces as leaves, if the number of some piece is zero, which indicates a peer can request the loss piece from external peer again.

4.3 Dynamic Priority Allocation

It is not difficult to find issue in unique piece selection scenario, which GUPT will probably make some peers are waiting for the inside piece rather than outside piece, so increase download time or ISP lost pieces happened. On the other hand, the previous studies show that the whole download process of BitTorrent in the first piece scenario and last piece scenario, because of the choke algorithm the paradox of supply and demand exists in BitTorrent [16], which is increasing the file download time. Each new peer can only rely on the upload peer uses the OU algorithm to randomly upload to one of these new peers, which causes many new peers to be starving. Unfortunately, Bit-Torrent adopts the static quota allocation, TFT cannot allocate pending upload quota to OU. In DQA, OU can use more upload quotas that upload quotas are located at pendency, to optimize the upload quota utility ratio and solve the problem that the paradox of supply and demand.

Although there are two approaches to solve ISP lost pieces in unique piece selection. We prefer to adopt the zealous approach to prevent ISP lost pieces. First, Dynamic Priority Allocation (DPA) adopts the strategy of DQA let the system allocate the piece to neighbors more quickly. DQA let each peer has a smooth, average and steady download rate. The new peer follows procession to download, it can avoid most of peers download very slowly, and only a few of peers download very quickly. It is easy to cause ISP lost pieces via several peers simultaneously leave. Each peer has a smooth download rate, which indicates it has smaller standard deviation that the interval of the download time among peers. Thus, a large amount of seeds can be produce in a short time. Moreover, we preserve advantages of DQA that adopt a weight allocation scheme to adaptively allocate upload quotas for TFT and OU in our dynamic priority allocation and let external peer has a higher priority to allocate the quota of OU in terms of the different piece is allocated to different ISP as quickly as possible and is suited to the our condition (cross-ISP). Formulas (1) to (8) are the deduction of DQA. Q denotes the total upload quotas, Q_{tft} and Q_{ou} denotes the upload quota for the TFT and OU separately. Furthermore, we set Q_{ou} divided into Q_{urg} and Q_{norm}. They are allocated by the following formula:

$$F = \left| P_{fast} \right| \cdot \alpha \tag{1}$$

$$L = \left| P_{low} \right| \cdot (1 - \alpha) \tag{2}$$

$$Q_{tft} = \frac{F}{F + L} \cdot Q \tag{3}$$

$$Q_{ou} = \frac{L}{F+L} \cdot Q \tag{4}$$

$$U = |P_{urg}| \cdot \beta \tag{5}$$

$$N = |P_{norm}| \cdot (1-\beta) \tag{6}$$

$$Q_{urg} = \frac{U}{U+N} \cdot Q_{ou} \tag{7}$$

$$Q_{norm} = \frac{N}{U+N} \cdot Q_{ou} \tag{8}$$

Where $|P_{fast}|$ denotes the number of the set P_{fast} and $|P_{low}|$ denotes the number of the set P_{low}. Likewise, $|P_{urg}|$ denotes the number of the set P_{urg} and $|P_{norm}|$ denotes the number of the set P_{norm}. α denotes the weight of P_{fast} and β denotes the weight of P_{urg}, and we set $\alpha = 0.7$ and set $\beta = 0.8$ in terms of dynamic quotas allocation, which means P_{fast} has a higher priority than P_{low} and means P_{urg} has a higher priority than P_{norm} separately.

We use formula (7) to allocate the urgent upload quotas Q_{urg} divided into Q_{ex} and Q_{in}. In formula (9)~(12), $|P_{ex}|$ denotes the number of the set P_{ex} and $|P_{in}|$ denotes the number of the set P_{in}. γ denotes the weight of P_{ex}, and we set $\gamma = 0.7$, which means P_{ex} has a higher priority than P_{in}. Dynamic priority allocation mainly solved the download time and ISP lost pieces problem.

$$E = |P_{ex}| \cdot \gamma \tag{9}$$

$$I = |P_{in}| \cdot (1-\gamma) \tag{10}$$

$$Q_{ex} = \frac{E}{E+I} \cdot Q_{urg} \tag{11}$$

$$Q_{in} = \frac{I}{E+I} \cdot Q_{urg} \tag{12}$$

5   Experimental Evaluation

This section presents our experimental evaluation. First, we introduce our simulation environments and methodology, and then analyze our experimental results to prove PCS is effectiveness.

5.1   Methodology

ISP traffic redundancy and download time are the main evaluation criteria in our simulation experiments. The term ISP traffic redundancy means the average number of times each piece crosses the ISP, until all peers inside the ISP finish their download. The lowest redundancy is 1. The highest redundancy is R, where R is the number of peers inside the ISP. Measurement of the file download time uses the cumulative distribution function (CDF). We design a discrete event driven simulator for BitTorrent, which primarily simulates the peer behavior such as (1) peer joining/leaving, (2) peer obtains a list and connects its neighbors, (3) piece transfer, (4) peer reports the tracker periodically, and the main incentive mechanisms such (5)choke algorithm, (6)LRF algorithm in the flash crowd stage. The framework of network consists of 14 ISPs, they are assumed to be completely connected and we combine bandwidth limiting with our simulation environments. It is noted that we ignore the simulation of the underlying physical network characteristics such as propagation delay, congestion control and flow control, etc. This approach also assumes idealized performance of TCP, and does not model the dynamics and traits of TCP implementations. Each ISP have 50 peers, and we simulate 700 peers including 1 initial seed and use one tracker, and the initial seed bandwidth is 400Kbps and does not use biased neighbor selection.

Our simulation environments examine two network settings, the upload/download bandwidth for peers (100Kbps/1Mbps) in the homogeneous network and the heterogeneous contain a high-bandwidth peers (we called extra peers) with the homogeneous, the upload/download bandwidth for extra peers (1Mbps/1Mbps) in the heterogeneous. We assume all extra peers have point-to-point links with each ISP and also with each other. Each peer leaves as finishing its download, only initial seed always stays online until terminating the simulation. The shared file with size of 64 MB is divided into 2000 equal-size pieces with each piece size 32KB. Each peer has five upload quotas, four quotas for the TFT algorithm and the fifth quota for the OU algorithm. In DPA, we set $\alpha = 0.7$, $\beta = 0.8$ and $\gamma = 0.7$. Biased neighbor selection (BNS), GUPT and DPA are to combine to the PCS. Our simulation environments and previous approach [9] are the same because we primarily compare with it.

5.2 Performance Analysis

PCS compare with previous approaches in terms of redundancy and the file download time. In [9], we know only bandwidth limiting cannot restrain the redundancy and decrease the file download time. Table 1 shows that we set ISP bandwidth from 2.5Mbps to 500Kbps, the redundancy still higher (about 21), and the redundancy is decreased only slightly between 1.5Mbps and 500Kbps. It appears that ISP bandwidth limiting cannot reduce cross-ISP redundancy anymore, and the download time increase 2.6 factor. The performance can does better as long as we use the BNS.

Table 1. Normalized download time and ISP traffic redundancy under ISP bandwidth limiting in the homogeneous networks

ISP bandwidth limiting	Time	ISP traffic redundancy
No limiting	7932s	47.13
2.5Mbps	8675s	31.47
1.5Mbps	10891s	25.23
500Kbps	18738s	21.95

Figure 4 depicts the ISP traffic redundancy of each approach without using ISP bandwidth limiting in the homogeneous networks. As shown in Figure 4, the redundancy of BitTorrent is about 47 (total internal peer is 50, so the highest redundancy is

50). It is noted that each peer almost downloads piece from external peer, it is a poor traffic locality inside the ISP. The redundancy immediately down to 4 after the original BitTorrent uses the BNS. Our PCS is based on GUPT and it combines with GUPT, which indicates that peers can collaborate indirectly, so the redundancy of PCS can keep to about 3. Factors of increasing redundancy are only ISP lost pieces and synchronal request. Our PCS has unique piece selection strategy, so the redundancy is lower than BitTorrent only uses the BNS in the homogeneous. Moreover, we combine BNS and GUPT with DQA and DPA separately to examine. These strategy are used to decrease download time, there is no effect upon the redundancy in this state except do not use BNS. Also, Figure 4 shows that the redundancy is almost the same as the strategy adds DQA and DPA. The average redundancy of DPA is lightly better than DQA, the key is DPA can let pieces spread to different ISP as quickly as possible because of external peer has a higher priority, which indicates that each peer has a smooth, average and steady download rate to avoid a few of peers leave as finishing their download and ISP lost pieces happened.

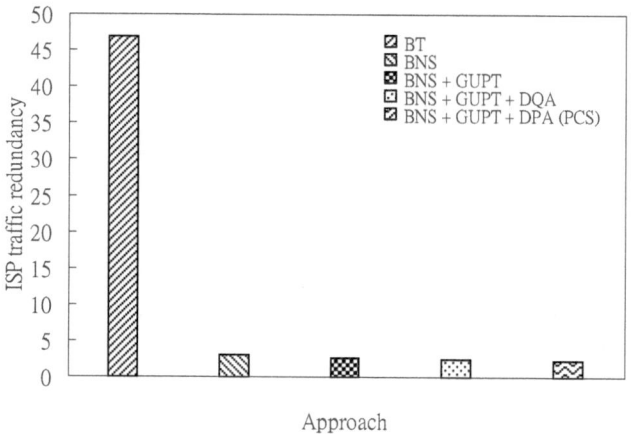

Fig. 4. ISP traffic redundancy of each approach in the homogeneous networks

Figure 5 depicts the file download time of each approach in the homogeneous. We can find our PCS outperforms BNS. For example, in 4000s, the PCS has about 95% peers completing all pieces while the BNS has only 5% peers. DPA is based on DQA, so each peer can maintain smooth download time among all pieces includes in the first piece scenario and last piece scenario. As shown in Figure 5, also we find the DPA and DQA allocate pieces quickly in the early phase, and each peer keeps smooth download rate. Several peers finish their download simultaneously in a short time. They have a great performance about the file download time, and they are faster than BNS and original BitTorrent. Besides, DPA can let pieces spread to different ISP as quickly as possible because of external peer has a higher priority, DPA is faster than DQA by about 1.1 factor and faster than BNS by about 1.6 factor, and faster than original BitTorrent by about 1.77 factor.

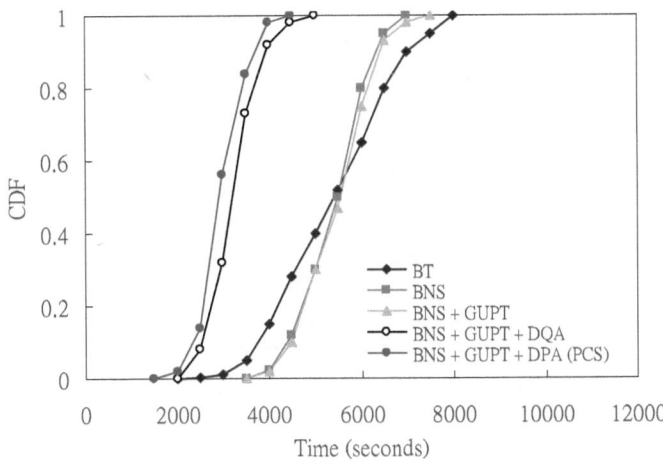

Fig. 5. Download time of file in the homogeneous networks

Figure 6 depicts the effect upon the redundancy of additional extra peers in the heterogeneous, we add extra peers from 10 to 50 and extra peers do not use BNS, and leave as finishing their download. As shown in Figure 6, we find the redundancy will increase gradually with BNS because of additional extra peers. PCS combines with GUPT, so it can restrain the redundancy. The redundancy of PCS keeps 5 as adds extra peers until 50, but the redundancy of BNS is >10 already.

Figure 7 shows that we contrast the download time of all approaches in heterogeneous networks, and the performance of all approaches in the heterogeneous networks outperform in the homogeneous networks due to extra peers have the high upload

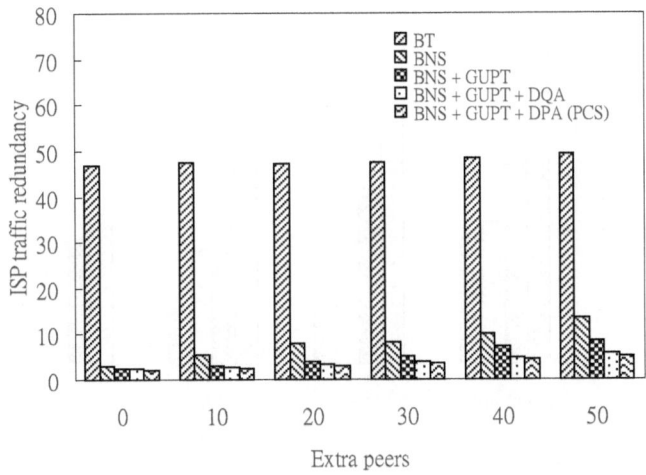

Fig. 6. ISP traffic redundancy of approach in heterogeneous networks

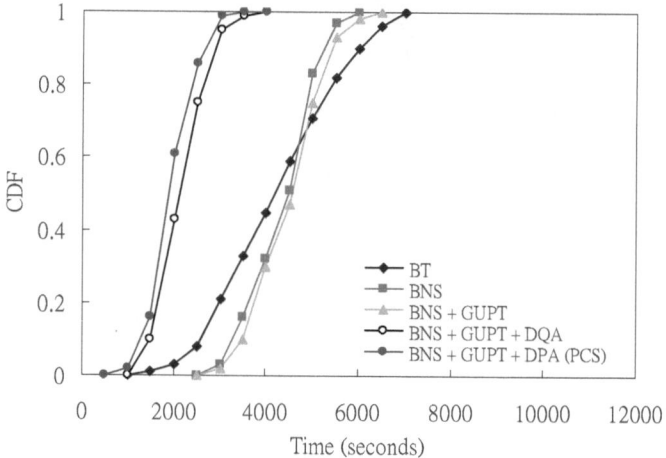

Fig. 7. Download time of file with 50 extra peers in heterogeneous networks

bandwidth, and PCS has the fastest download time. We can find our PCS not only restrain the redundancy as shown in Figure 6, but the download time of PCS still outperforms others in Figure 7.

Figure 8(a) shows that we let all approaches add bandwidth limiting to reduce redundancy except original BitTorrent. We look into the performance of BitTorrent in the heterogeneous networks through bandwidth limiting. Because of the reality of truth, ISP needs to restrain the P2P traffic by bandwidth limiting. We set bandwidth limiting from 2.5Mbps to 500Kbps.

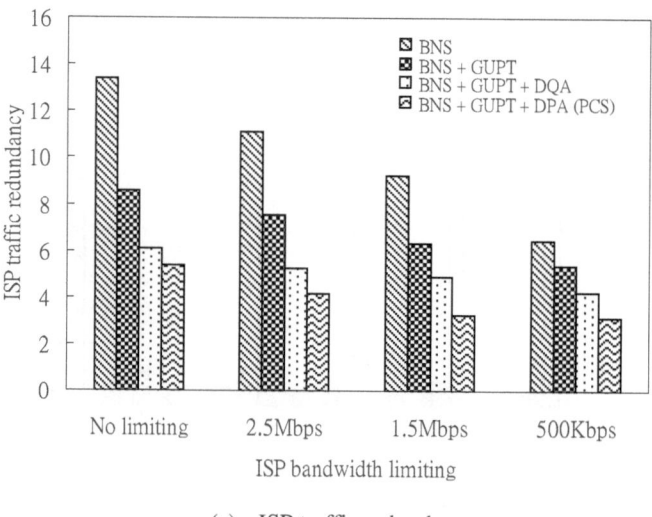

(a)   ISP traffic redundancy

Fig. 8. Combination of bandwidth limiting with 50 extra peers in the heterogeneous networks

As shown in Figure 8(a), all approaches can reduce redundancy through bandwidth limiting, and PCS has the lowest redundancy. Figure 8(b) shows that PCS maintains the fast download rate after PCS adds bandwidth limiting. The file download time of PCS is increased only slightly (about 5%), and it has a fewer effect upon the users. But BNS increase by about 13%.

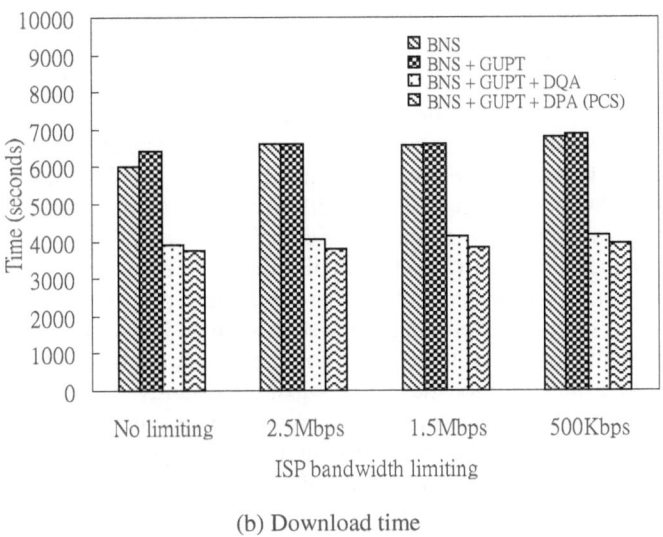

(b) Download time

Fig. 8. (*Continued*)

6 Conclusions and Future Work

We have presented Peer Collaboration Strategy (PCS), which integrates the advantage of biased neighbor selection (decrease redundancy) and DQA (decrease the file download time) into our strategy, and combines with GUPT to let redundancy down. PCS can ensure redundancy is controlled, besides the status of ISP lost pieces. Experimental results show that our peer collaboration strategy can reduce cross-ISP traffic without sacrificing system performance, and we have to modify original framework of BitTorrent, and it does not need additional equipment and backup mechanism. In terms of the user perspective, they only care about the file download time and if the seed does not exist. Therefore, a lot of previous approaches only focus on the file download time and most of the ideas are based on personal demand, and they do not consider cross-ISP traffic. However, the reality of truth, a large number of cross-ISP traffic will let ISPs adopt bandwidth limiting, and it brings the low download rate and redundancy out of control. In this paper, we consider the whole performance of BitTorrent in terms of the ISPs perspective, and we focus on the reduce cross-ISP traffic and the next is the whole performance of BitTorrent. Improving the BitTorrent peers into clusters and we conform to the principle of economic. Experimental results show that we adopt PCS is based on biased neighbor selection and DQA to solve cross-ISP traffic, not only restrain the redundancy but users can obtain a great performance, and decrease the file download time significantly. We have concluded that reforming the performance of BitTorrent should be considering the whole ISP first. Instead of only improving the download rate, we also need to consider the cross-ISP traffic. Thus, ISPs can reduce cross-ISP traffic without sacrificing system performance, and let ISPs and users create a win-win situation. We expected to accommodate the more complex network to our simulator in the future, and make the more complete analysis and consider the factors of influence, which causes the cross-ISP traffic.

Actually, we cannot only rely on decrease redundancy to reduce the cost of equipment in the reality. Because of the lowest redundancy indicates reduce redundancy of only one file. However, a large number of files were shared by P2P systems. We cannot avoid the P2P traffic has been increasing gradually. Thus, ISPs still need to economize on cost of extended equipment by bandwidth limiting. But, the cross-ISP traffic may get out of control if there is no strategy, which reforms the P2P system. We thought an approach combines PCS with bandwidth limiting can reduce cross-ISP traffic and conform to the principle of economic. There are many proposals intend to integrate CDN into P2P system or developing the system such as P4P now, even more let P2P system merge with monitor system. They promote Qos through this equipment manage the files and users, and monitor the traffic. Most importantly, they also the advantages of P2P are preserved, such as scalability, expansibility and arbitrariness. It depends on the consideration of ISPs between the cost and the service. On the other hand, desire of collaboration between ISPs and users, and the incentive that let users adopt the new P2P system also should be considering.

References

1. BitTorrent, http://www.bittorrent.com/
2. Napster, http://www.napster.com/
3. Gnutella, http://www.gnutelliums.com/
4. eMule, http://www.emule.org/
5. CacheLogic, http://www.cachelogic.com/
6. Aggarwal, V., Feldmann, A., Scheideler, C.: Can ISPs and P2P Users Cooperate for Improved Performance. In: Proceedings of ACM SIGCOMM Computer Communication Review, July 2007, vol. 37(3), pp. 29–40 (2007)
7. Aggarwal, V., Akonjang, O., Feldmann, A.: Improving User and ISP Experience through ISP-aided P2P Locality. In: Proceedings of IEEE Conference on Computer Communications Workshops, INFOCOM 2008, April 13-18, pp. 1–6 (2008)
8. Bharambe, A.R., Herley, C., Padmanabhan, V.N.: Analyzing and improving a BitTorrent network's performance mechanisms. In: Proceedings of the 25th IEEE International Conference on Computer Communication, INFOCOM 2006, April 2006, pp. 1–12 (2006)
9. Bindal, R., Cao, P., Chan, W., Medved, J., Suwala, G., Bates, T., Zhang, A.: Improving traffic locality in BitTorrent via biased neighbor selection. In: Proceedings of the 26th IEEE International Conference on Distributed Computing Systems (ICDCS), July 2006, p. 66 (2006)
10. Burger, M.D., Kielmann, T.: MOB: zero-configuration high-throughputmulticasting for grid applications. In: Proceedings of the 16th international symposium on High performance distributed computing, Monterey, California, USA, June 25-29, pp. 159–168 (2007)

11. Cohen, B.: Incentives Build Robustness in BitTorrent. In: Proceedings of First Workshop on Economics of Peer-to-Peer Systems (2003)
12. Choffnes, D.R., Bustamante, F.E.: Taming the torrent: a practical approach to reducing cross-isp traffic in peer-to-peer systems. In: Proceedings of the ACM SIGCOMM 2008 conference on Data communication, Seattle, WA, USA, pp. 363–374 (2008)
13. Feldman, M., Papadimitriou, C., Chuang, J., Stoica, I.: Free-riding and whitewashing in Peer-to-Peer systems. In: Proceedings of the ACM SIGCOMM workshop on Practice and theory of incentives in networked systems, Portland, Oregon, USA, pp. 228–236 (2004)
14. Gkantsidis, C., Rodriguez, P.R.: Network coding for large scale content distribution. In: Proceedings of the 24th Annual Joint Conference of the IEEE Computer and Communications Societies, INFOCOM 2005, March 13-17, vol. 4, pp. 2235–2245 (2005)
15. Guo, L., Chen, S., Xiao, Z., Tan, E., Ding, X., Zhang, X.: Measurements, Analysis, and Modeling of BitTorrent-like Systems. In: Proceedings of the 5th ACM SIGCOMM conference on Internet Measurement, Berkeley, CA, p. 4 (2005)
16. Huang, K., Wang, L., Zhang, D., Liu, Y.: Optimizing the BitTorrent performance using an adaptive peer selection strategy. In: Proceedings of Future Generation Computer Systems, July 2008, vol. 24(7), pp. 621–630 (2008)
17. Izal, M., Urvoy-Keller, G., Biersack, E.W., Felber, P., Hamra, A., Garces-Erice, L.: Dissecting bittorrent: Five months in a Torrent's lifetime. In: Proceedings of the 5th Passive and Active Measurements Workshop, France, pp. 1–11 (2004)
18. Izmailov, R., Ganguly, S., Tu, N.: Fast Parallel File Replication in Data Grid. In: Proceedings of Future of Grid Data Environments workshop (GGF-10), Berlin, Germany (March 2004)
19. Legout, A., Urvoy-Keller, G., Michiardi, P.: Rarest first and choke algorithms are enough. In: Proceedings of the 6th ACM SIGCOMM conference on Internet Measurement, Rio de Janeriro, Brazil, pp. 203–216 (2006)
20. Karagiannis, T., Rodriguez, P., Papagiannaki, K.: Should internet service providers fear peer-assisted content distribution. In: Proceedings of the 5th ACM SIGCOMM conference on Internet Measurement, Berkeley, CA, p. 6 (2005)
21. Tian, Y., Wu, D., Ng, K.W.: Modeling, analysis and improvement for BitTorrent-like file sharing networks. In: Proceedings of the 25th IEEE International Conference on Computer Communications, INFOCOM 2006, Barcelona, Spain, April 2006, pp. 1–11 (2006)
22. Xie, H., Yang, Y.R., Krishnamurthy, A., Liu, Y., Silberschatz, A.: P4P: Provider Portal for Applications. In: Proceedings of the ACM SIGCOMM 2008 conference on Data communication, Seattle, WA, USA, pp. 351–362 (2008)

Parallel File Transfer for Grid Economic

Chia-Wei Chu[1], Ching-Hsien Hsu[1], His-Ya Chang[2], Shuen-Tai Wang[2],
and Kuan-Ching Li[3]

[1] Department of Computer Science and Information Engineering,
Chung Hua University, Hsinchu, Taiwan
{cwc,robert}@grid.chu.edu.tw
[2] National Center for High-Performance Computing,
Hsinchu, Taiwan
{jerry,stwang}@nchc.org.tw
[3] Department of Computer Science and Information Engineering,
Providence University, Taichung, Taiwan
kuancli@pu.edu.tw

Abstract. In data grid environments, datasets are usually replicated to many servers when taking into consideration its efficiency. Since these files are usually huge in size, how to efficiently transmit and access between servers and grid users is an important issue. In this paper, we present an economy-based parallel file transfer technique using P2P co-allocation scheme, aiming to service grid applications efficiently and economically in data grids. Taking into consideration the cost factor, we present a novel mechanism for selection of appropriate server, by combining with an adaptive file decomposition scheme and the dynamic adjustment method. In order to evaluate the performance of the proposed method, we have implemented the proposed algorithm and compared with several other previous published techniques. Simulation results demonstrate that the proposed technique is economically effective.

Keywords: Data Grid, Parallel File Transfer, Dynamic Adjustment, Co-allocation, P2P.

1 Introduction

Grid technology has the great ability to interconnect computational and storage resources scattered at various locations, mutually communicating via networks to share computations and data stores of parallel applications. A number of scientific experimentations with large amount of data analysis such as high-energy physics, gene and protein in biology, simulation of earth science, and other macro issues like origin of cosmos are able to be solved efficiently.

Due to its high efficiency, research for this technology has been broadly performed recently. With this perception, grid computing is viewed as one of important applications for the next-generation network that resource exchanges and knowledge sharing are materialized through the grid technology employed by people. By effectively integrating various specialized tools like computation equipment, databases, software via broadband networks, the grid technology is also a safe, stable, yet simple platform.

P. Mueller, J.-N. Cao, and C.-L. Wang (Eds.): Infoscale 2009, LNICST 18, pp. 76–89, 2009.
© Institute for Computer Science, Social-Informatics and Telecommunications Engineering 2009

Based on the fact that a single computer's performance cannot deal with requirements in scientific applications with enormous amount of data derived from scientific experiments, the grid technology is possibly favorable to these applications by distributing available computations and resources around the world, based on its geometric locations. Presently, the grid technology has been extensively applied in computation and data storage.

In this paper, an efficient scheme for parallel file transfer is proposed, where datasets are replicated to several server stations in data grid environments as copies containing large-size files usually whose efficient distribution and transmission have become a critical issue. Facing this topic [2, 12, 14], one scholar argued the co-allocation architecture [15] and multiple co-allocation manners to fulfill data or files parallel-downloaded in multiple server stations.

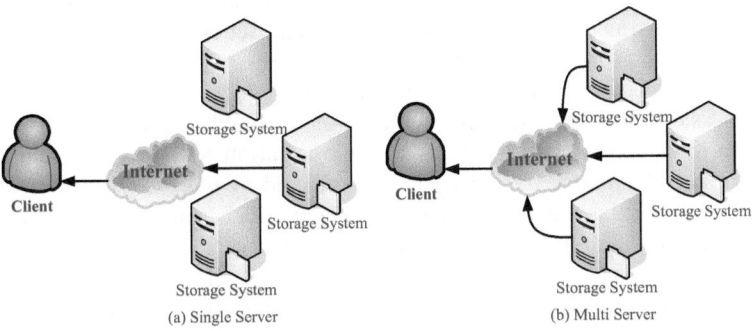

(a) Single Server

(b) Multi Server

Fig. 1. Single Server vs. Multi-Server

Owing to the possibility of worse efficiency in transmission of data downloaded from one server by a client within popular Internet with jam occurring, one method of adopting multiple servers for improvement in efficiency of downloading data (see Figure 1) is available to the data grid environment for solving this issue. In this way, the transmission manners extensively employed for multiple servers have been recommended. As a result of data stored in different locations [2, 15], the concept of agent servers argued by some scholars is able to stabilize the efficiency of parallel transfer [1, 6, 7].

There exist several related works ongoing. Identical-size file blocks distributed in each transmission server make a faster server to spend more time than a slower one while transferring the last file block [15], another approach is to use different servers for transmission of identical file blocks but consuming more network resources [9], ways to minimize differences in time consumed by all servers completing transmission and manage unnecessary waste of network resources for transmission of identical file blocks has become one important issue.

In this paper, the proposed research is to take into account a server's efficiency in transmission and to propose a novel mechanism that effectively and dynamically distribute transmission in which is accessed by cost effects to avoid excessive waste. Knowing that the Grid technology is being employed to various enterprises and even daily lives in the future, enterprisers shall comprehend the importance of effectively improving service quality and increasing customers' satisfaction.

The rest of this paper is organized as follows. The co-allocation architecture and related work is introduced in Section 2, while in Section 3 the mechanism of improving co-allocation scheme is presented. Section 4 describes our approach (*EEPT*), and experimental result performance analysis is done in Section 5. Finally, Section 6 provides the conclusions and future work of this research.

2 Related Work

2.1 Co-Allocation Architecture

As one of most common technology used in the development of data grids, the Co-Allocation Architecture [15] is also taken as the main scheme in this investigation and partially improved at its architecture. As shown in Figure 2 for operations of the Co-Allocation architecture, a client applying for one request will hand over necessary data and messages to one broker that acquires the available target files' resource contents via an information server such as Grid Information Service (*GIS*) and Monitoring & Discovery System (*MDS*). Servers are selected by the broker, the co-allocation is able to download data and files requested by the client from system-storage servers via GridFTPs. Files are then forwarded to the client from the broker for completion of downloading.

Other transmission mechanisms such as Brute-Force, History-Based and Dynamic Load Balancing are also provided [15]:

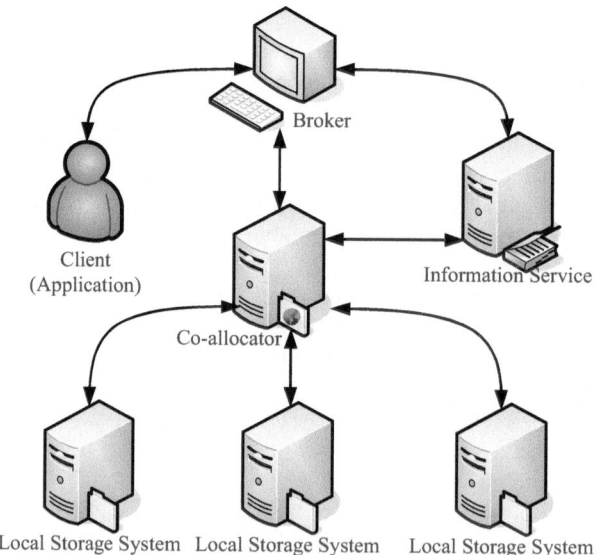

Fig. 2. Co-Allocation Architecture

(1)   Brute-Force: According to the number of servers, data files are divided into n blocks with an identical size apiece.

(2)   History-Based: As a method derived and improved from Brute-Force, History-Based with "more" identical-size blocks are separated from data files and able to distribute those blocks according to the status of server networks.

(3)   Dynamic Load Balancing: With more and smaller segmented blocks from data files, the transmission of one block is completed by one server only it is assigned to conduct the next transmission after the previous one is finished.

However, these transmission methods as presented are available to networks with complete quality but possibly change effect of transferring files in case of some problems observed in network system. Furthermore, the contingent efficiency for transmission on realistic networks prompts some scholars to offer other improved transmission mechanisms matching realistic situations.

2.2   The Recursive-Adjustment

The Recursive-Adjustment Co-Allocation [3, 4, 5] is an option to reduce the waiting time consumed in transmission of the last block by the slowest in speed server. At the initial stage, this operation is to divide data files into several blocks as a server's references for measurement of bandwidths and then decide the quantity of blocks needed to be delivered by each server, according to computed bandwidths. With the fast-speed server completing its transmission, the blocks for each server's next transmission can be recomputed until the remained block is less than a threshold set to end this recursive-adjustment mechanism for blocks to be transmitted. The Recursive-Adjustment Co-Allocation is presented in Figure 3, where $E(T_i)$ is the expected time for completion of transmission and T_i the realistic time for completion.

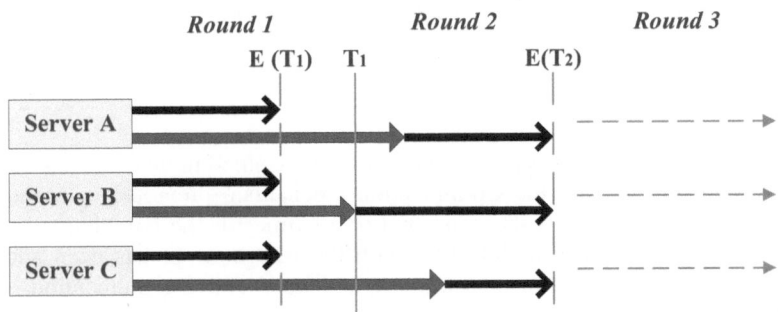

Fig. 3. Recursive-Adjustment Co-Allocation

2.3   Dynamic Co-Allocation Scheme with Duplicate Assignments

Without the presence of a forecast mechanism or adjustment in a server's variable bandwidths, the Dynamic Co-allocation Scheme with Duplicate Assignments (*DCDA*) [9, 10] has excellent performance. Using a ring-sorting algorithm, *DCDA* divides D datasets into k identical-size blocks which can be delivered by each server without data intersection. Once one assigned block is completely transmitted, another unde-livered block will be assigned to this server in accordance to the algorithm which is employed recursively until all k blocks of D dataset are completely transmitted. With this method, possible idle time such as time consumed in communication between a server and a broker will be neglected without exception.

According to the author's algorithm for transmission, there is one problem in *DCDA*. Multiple servers repeatedly transferring identical blocks and therefore occupy large amount of network resources. As result, network jam between other clients and servers is generated. In contrast to above, when not taking into consideration a server's status or selecting servers within above mentioned studies, other studies in-corporating selection of servers are described next.

2.4 Co-Allocation with Server Selection

The main objective of the Abort and Retransfer mechanism [8] is to improve the worst-efficient server's transmission for the last block. Despite distributed data files, this mechanism allows terminating the worst-efficient server's unfinished operations halfway and transfers undelivered blocks with inspections completed to higher-efficient server makes consumption in time improved for a successful transmission.

Having a P2P environment as the background architecture, the Adaptive Dynamic Parallel Download (*adPD*) [16] distributes each identical-size block segmented from data files, which need to be transferred to individual servers whose transmission tasks can be assisted by the fast transmission-completed server by replacing the slower one. This mechanism's advantage is that no excessive time is consumed in the adjustment of data when transferred in a P2P environment.

Based on algorithms for Co-Allocation mechanism, the Efficient and Adaptive (*EA*) [11] simultaneously access a server's performance as a reference of selecting a server for data transmission and able to reduce consumption in time for selecting servers and fulfills requirements for efficient parallel downloading.

3 Research Architecture

Despite quick and temporary communication time consumed in links and communica-tions among all units under the Co-allocation mechanism previously presented, the time accumulated also affects the consumption of time for the completion of trans-mission. Due to this, a new architecture with the P2P concept has been added for reduction of time consumed in data transfer and links and communications among different units, as shown in Figure 4.

To receive a request for a file with data formats and features to be downloaded from a client, a broker is able to acquire a detailed list of servers owning the requested file by linking to an information server. Once the request for this detailed list is ac-cepted, the client can actively link the file server based to P2P concept. In this fash-ion, the time consumed in links and communications is drastically reduced, since no data downloaded from a broker but a file allocation conducted by a client.

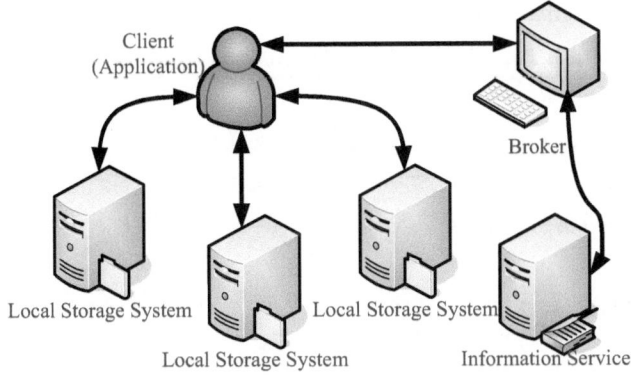

Fig. 4. P2P Co-Allocation Architecture

Under considerations in economic costs consumed in server selection of a client for the purpose of downloading files from a server, a mechanism matching given requirements in costs is developed in this proposed research, for the selection of servers which may permit efficient download of requested data files. Maintained at normal running status, all servers mentioned in the paper are guaranteed to be compliant with information servers.

4   Efficient and Economic Parallel File Transfer (EEPT)

One of main factors that affect a client's costs with transmission costs included, a client's bandwidths beyond considerations of a transmission mechanism previously is taken into account in this investigation. A server selected in accordance with a client's bandwidths will reduce costs without transmission efficiency being influenced.

4.1   Server Selection and File Decomposition

For the case of a server's costs under consideration, the way to select a server becomes the first priority as a result of consumption in costs correlated with a mechanism for the selection of servers. Restricted conditions for this selection of the most beneficial information server are shown as follows: β^{avg} (a server's average network bandwidth), β^{max} (a server's maximum network bandwidth), β^{min} (a server's minimum network bandwidth), C (a server's consumed cost), and β_{client} (a client's bandwidth).

As for the first condition for selection, we employ the most common algorithm, Greedy Knapsack Problem, for the determination of a *CP (Capacity Price)*, which will be selected first while having the maximum value. Because of an identical value acquired for *CPs*, the second condition with available information about servers such as β^{max} and β^{min} for a stable value guaranteed is indispensible. In this way, a stable value is expected to 0 as closed as possible. In order to simplify the presentation in the following section, we have some definitions:

Definition 1

β_i^{avg} is the average bandwidth of server i.

Definition 2

β_i^{max} is the maximum bandwidth of server i.

Definition 3

β_i^{min} is the minimum bandwidth of server i.

Definition 4

C_i is the price to use server i to download file per time unit.

Definition 5

β_{client} is the limitation of client bandwidth.

By deducing a server's *CP* which is acquired from Equation (1), a β_{client} equal to or close to zero signifies that the Greedy Knapsack Problem fulfills and serve as an efficient server for transmission. However, considering possible identical *CPs*, we may obtain a server's stable value by means of Equation (2), since one server with a stable value is instrumental to provide a better transmission and efficient use costs. Higher performance server with lower price means higher *CP* value. To simplify

$$CP_i^{avg} = \beta_i^{avg} / C_i \tag{1}$$

In addition, an influence factor α is used for evaluating reliability of a data server. A smaller α is equivalent to less undulation at network's bandwidth which is ideal for one server, especially selected to stabilize transmission efficiency due to slight undulation at bandwidths, and corresponds to economic benefits in costs. The influence factor is defined as follows.

$$\alpha_i = \left(\beta_i^{max} - \beta_i^{min}\right) / \beta_i^{avg} \tag{2}$$

The usage of α in Equation (2) also reflects the definition of average deviation (μ), in probability and statistics, as show in Equation (3). A smaller μ is equivalent to a more stable network's bandwidth.

$$\mu = \frac{\Sigma\left|\beta_i^{nt} - \beta_i^{avg}\right|}{n} \tag{3}$$

Where β_i^{nt} denotes the network bandwidth at the ith time interval; and n is the total amount of time intervals.

Depending on our mechanism on selecting of servers, we are able to distribute blocks from data files directly proportional by using servers' average bandwidth. The example is shown as follows.

For data (1000MB) downloaded by one client, β_{client} is 100MB/s and information of servers is listed in Table 1.

Table 1. Information of storage serve

	β_i^{avg}	$\beta_i^{min} \sim \beta_i^{max}$	C	CP	α
Server 1	20 MB/s	15~25	2	10	0.5
Server 2	30 MB/s	20~40	2	15	0.67
Server 3	50 MB/s	45~55	4	12.5	0.2
Server 4	50 MB/s	30~70	4	12.5	0.8

As a result of CP=15, Server 2 is taken as one of transmission servers ($\beta_{client} - \beta_2^{avg} = 70$). According to this architecture, $\beta_1^{avg} = 20$Mbps and $\beta_3^{avg} = 50$Mbps can be chosen as servers for transmission. With these servers considered for transmission, the bandwidths (average) designated to all servers are respectively 20MB/s (server 1), 30MB/s (server 2) and 50MB/s (server 3), and the sizes divided for each block are 200MB, 300MB and 500MB

4.2 Dynamic File Transfer

Despite the size of each server's block to be transmitted and target for transmission simultaneously completed by all servers are known, dynamic adjustments are still required due to a network's dynamic bandwidths. To avoid excessive economic costs wasted in idle time, an easily-understood dynamic adjusted mechanism can reduce idle time and make all servers complete transmission almost at the same time, as shown in Fig. 5.

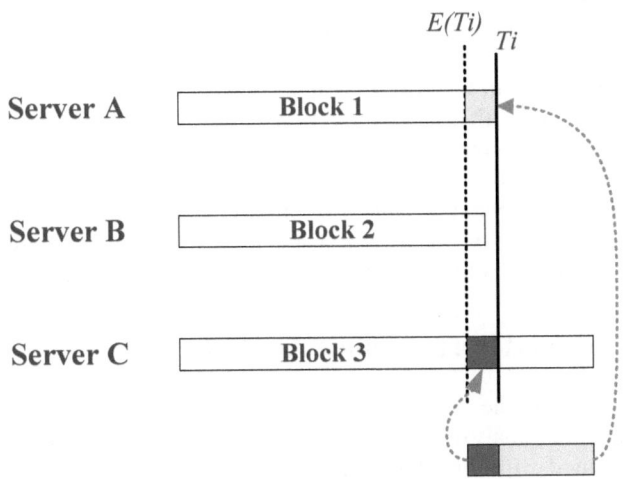

Fig. 5. *EEPT* Dynamic Adjustment

With the transmission of one block first completed by one better-efficient server which will be informed for the ongoing progress in block transmission conducted by other servers, this server is able to assist the server completing the least block transmission by sharing the remained block to be transmitted. According to the bandwidth traffic last observed, the remained block to be transmitted shall be redistributed directly proportional. When transmission is simultaneously completed by all servers with minimized consumption in economic costs caused by idle time for the situation of an identical expected target, the whole transmission will be the most efficient. However, it is necessary to set threshold conditions for the sake of avoiding endless development in the adjustment mechanism. To this end, two threshold conditions under this dynamic adjustment mechanism are set. The former one is Remained block to be transmitted, and the latter one is the transmission progress.

While assisting another server's transmission, a server has to check whether the remained traffic is less than or equal to the remained block to be transmitted. For that matter, since the minimum designated to the lowest one of all servers β^{max}, an assistant transmission will not be conducted for a remained block less than β^{min} and all transmission tasks will be ongoing until completion. As threshold, the minimum β^{min} is used for selecting one server matching economic costs also being efficient. On the other hand, to complete transmission before an expected schedule, the minimum, β^{min} as one threshold condition, is used for excluding endless dynamic adjustments.

In order to avoid termination of networks out of the first threshold condition with a transmission task failed before an expected schedule, a client has to monitor the transmission progress to exclude terminated networks affecting the whole efficiency. Against this requirement, the progress for transmission of other blocks shall be monitored with one transmission completed by the fastest server and an ongoing dynamic adjustment is conducted. In case of no expected transmission progress within a preset period, the remained blocks will be designated to other servers for transmission forthwith and distributed directly proportional according to servers' bandwidth traffic observed last.

Continue the example in Section 4.1. Segmentation of blocks' sizes is based on the selected average bandwidth for servers: Block1 (200 MB), Block2 (300 MB) and Block3 (500 MB) are designated to Server1, Server2 and Server3 for transmission, respectively. For the case of Server3 completing transmission of block3 before the expected schedule, the client is able to comprehend the transmission progress of Server1 and Server2 simultaneously. Next, for the sake of materializing transmission simultaneously, a block shall be adjusted according to threshold conditions.

5 Experiments and Performance Analysis

Experimental results on the efficiency for completion time, idle time, cost, and overhead are obtained and analyzed in this section. The study is based on discussions of our proposed method with other mechanisms argued by relevant studies, as: (1) Single, (2) Brute Force, (3) History, (4) Recursive and (5) Dynamic Co-allocation Scheme with Duplicate Assignments (*DCDA*).

The given conditions in this simulation include β_{client} =100 Mbps, the information of servers (shown in Table 2) and the network status of servers (shown in Figure 6).

Table 2. Experiment setup

	β_i^{avg}	$\beta_i^{min} \sim \beta_i^{max}$	C	CP	α
Server 1	30 MB/s	10~ 50	2	15	1.34
Server 2	60 MB/s	40 ~ 80	4	15	0.67
Server 3	20 MB/s	10 ~ 30	1	20	1
Server 4	20 MB/s	15 ~ 25	1	20	0.5
Server 5	50 MB/s	40 ~ 60	4	12.5	0.4

According to the server selection policy of *EEPT*, server 4 is firstly chosen as one server for transmission, owing to server 4 has the highest *CP* value and its α value is lower than server 3 when both server 3 and server 4 have *CPs* equal to 20. As the transmission flow of selected servers (β_4^{avg} =20 Mbps) does not exceed the bandwidth of client (β_{client} 100 Mbps), more servers should be selected for parallel file transfer. As a result, server 3 will be chosen in next, resulting a 40 Mbps transmission flow ($\beta_4^{avg} + \beta_3^{avg}$ =40 Mbps); and finally, server 2 is chosen, making a 100 Mbps transmission flow ($\beta_4^{avg} + \beta_3^{avg} + \beta_2^{avg}$ = 100 Mbps).

Experimental simulation results for detailed comparison between our proposed mechanism and other mechanisms listed early this section are presented next. Experimental simulation results are obtained utilizing the proposed mechanism for the

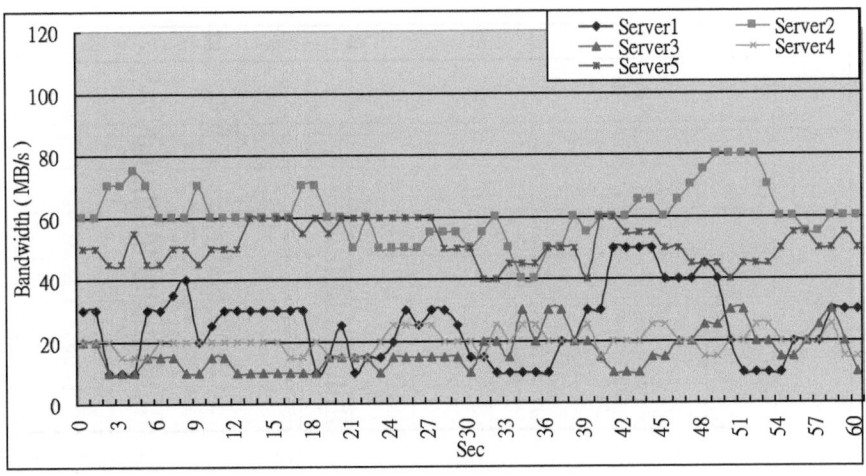

Fig. 6. Varying network bandwidth variations

selection of servers, employed for the purpose of corresponding to requirements in efficient servers and avoiding payments at the expense of extra economic costs. In experimental simulations, the sizes of files to be transmitted are 512MB, 1GB, 1.5GB and 2GB.

As shown in Figure 7 for experimental simulations, our mechanism has been verified that the consumption in time for completion of transmission approaches to our expected target and is significantly reduced when compared with other methods. As shown in Figure 8 for comparisons of idle time, the consumption in time with the Dynamic Adjustment technology employed is decreased significantly. In this regard, depending on the degree of simultaneous completion for files transmitted by servers, the performance in idle time will be excellent with minimum time difference.

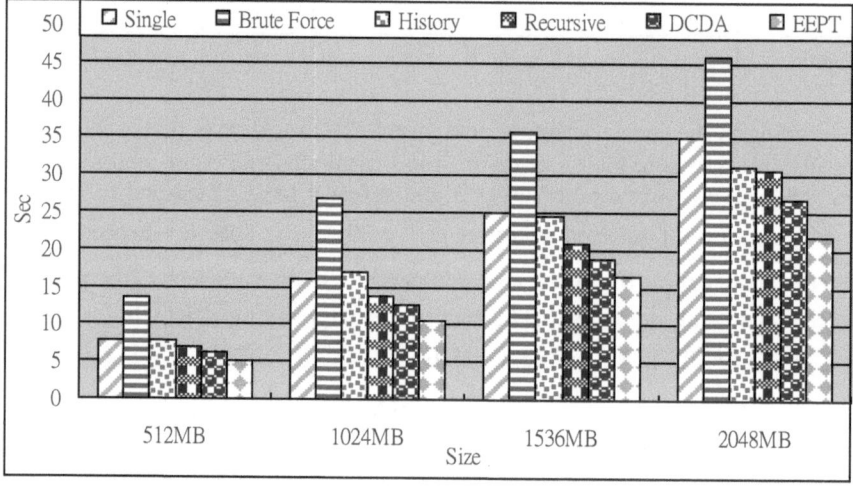

Fig. 7. Performance comparisons - Completion time

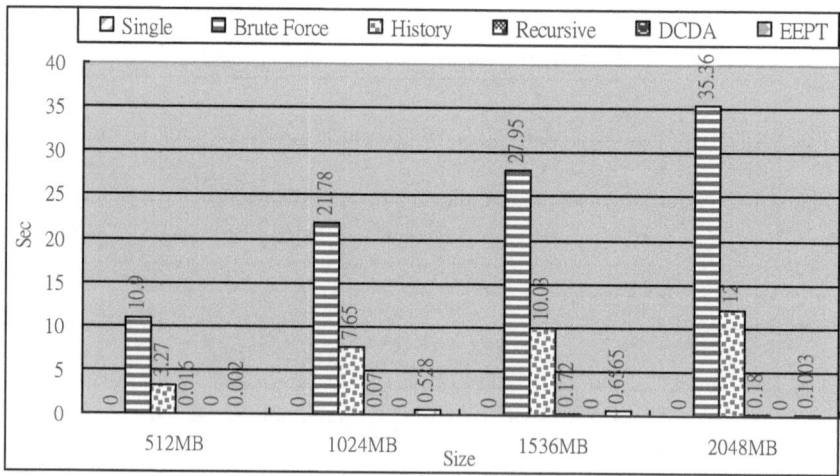

Fig. 8. Performance comparisons - Idle time

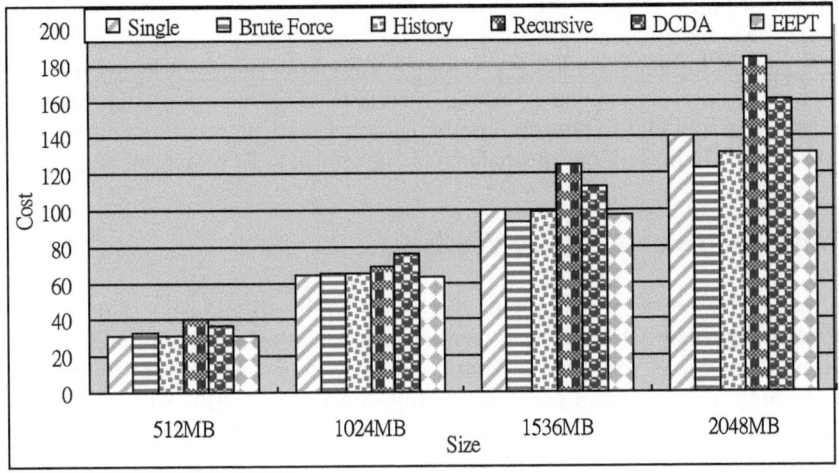

Fig. 9. Performance comparisons - Transmission cost

Figure 9 indicates costs consumed by all methods, according to conditions listed in Table 1 wherein the cost from the Dynamic Adjustment technology is higher than others due to larger number of high-efficient servers used in transmission. As set data (costs per second) closing the realistic situations, costs of one high-efficient transmission server indicated in Table 1 are higher than others. Due to possible unfair evaluation to the Dynamic Adjustment technology based on data shown in Figure 9 only, the overhead is designed for fair comparisons:

$$Overhead = Completion\ time \times Cost \qquad (4)$$

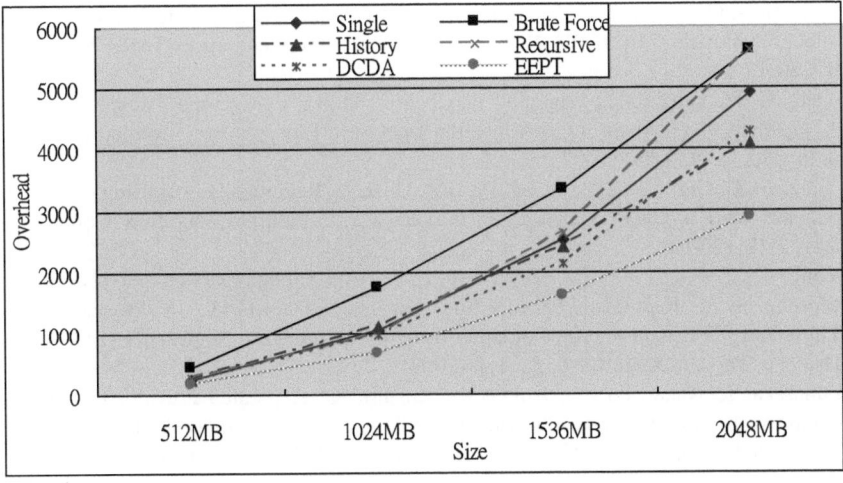

Fig. 10. Performance comparisons - Transmission overhead

As shown in Figure 10, a smaller value for overhead is equivalent to a transmission efficiency matching completion time and costs. Based on simulation data with costs incorporated taking into consideration, we can find more servers selected for transmission which do not correspond to better transmission efficiency though higher costs. Therefore, it is required to choose servers matching realistic requirements in transmission. From data indicated, our mechanism is one choice to fit requirement in costs.

6 Conclusions and Future Work

With the consideration of economic issues for parallel file transfer in data grids, the proposed mechanism which is the dynamic adjustment scheme combined with server selection method was verified that is able to significantly curtail costs without affecting transmission quality and can maintaining transmission efficiency. As one easily-understood concept and matching realistic requirements in transmission, the dynamic adjustment technology mentioned here along with our P2P Co-Allocation architecture is able to reduce time spent in communication during distribution of blocks conducted by servers.

As future work, a forecasting mechanism executed with exact algorithms will be favorable to the dynamic adjustment technology when precisely segmenting blocks and distributed to other servers. Thus, to reach the final target, researchers shall focus on detailed designs in addition to successful transmission completed synchronously by servers.

References

1. Kawano, A., Funasaka, J., Ishida, K.: Parallel Downloading Using Variable Length Blocks for Proxy Servers. In: 27th International Conference on Distributed Computing Systems Workshops (ICDCSW 2007), pp. 59–66 (2007)
2. Gkantsidis, C., Ammar, M., Zegura, E.: On the Effect of Large -Scale Deployment of Parallel Downloading. In: IEEE Workshop on Internet Applications (WIAPP 2003), pp. 79–89 (2003)
3. Yang, C.-T., Yang, I.-H., Wang, S.-Y., Chen, C.-H., Li, K.-C.: Improvements on Dynamic Adjustment Mechanism in Co-Allocation Data Grid Environments. Journal of Supercomputing 40(3), 269–280 (2007)
4. Yang, C.-T., Chi, Y.-C., Yang, M.-F., Hsu, C.-H.: A Recursively-Adjusting Co-Allocation Scheme with a Cyber-Transformer in Data Grid. Future Generation Computer Systems 25(7) (2009)
5. Yang, C.-T., Chi, Y.-C., Fu, C.-P., Hsu, C.-H.: An Anticipative Recursively-Adjustment Mechanism for Redundant Parallel File Transfer in Data Grids. In: Proceedings of the Thirteenth IEEE Asia-Pacific Computer Systems Architecture Conference (ACSAC 2008), Hsinchu, Taiwan, August 4-6, pp. 1–8 (2008)
6. Funasaka, J., Nakawaki, N., Ishida, K., Amano, K.: A parallel downloading method of coping with variable bandwidth. In: Proceedings of the 23rd International Conference on Distributed Computing Systems Workshops (ICDCSW 2003), pp. 14–19 (2003)

7. Funasaka, J., Kawano, A., Ishida, K.: Implementation issues of parallel downloading methods for a proxy system. In: Proceedings of the 25th IEEE International Conference on Distributed Computing Systems Workshops, ICDCSW 2005 (2005)
8. Chang, R.-S., Wang, C.-M., Chen, P.-H.: Replica Selection on Co-allocation Data Grids. In: Cao, J., Yang, L.T., Guo, M., Lau, F. (eds.) ISPA 2004. LNCS, vol. 3358, pp. 584–593. Springer, Heidelberg (2004)
9. Bhuvaneswaran, R.S., Katayama, Y., Takahashi, N.: Dynamic Co-allocation Scheme for Parallel Data Transfer in Grid Environment. In: Proceedings of the First International Conference on Semantics, Knowledge, and Grid (SKG 2005), pp. 19–24 (2005)
10. Bhuvaneswaran, R.S., Katayama, Y., Takahashi, N.: Coordinated Co-allocator Model for Data Grid in Multi-sender Environment. In: Dan, A., Lamersdorf, W. (eds.) ICSOC 2006. LNCS, vol. 4294, pp. 66–77. Springer, Heidelberg (2006)
11. Chang, R.-S., Lin, C.-F., Ruey, J.-H., His, S.-C.: An efficient and bandwidth sensitive parallel download scheme in data grids. In: 3rd International Conference on Communication Systems Software and Middleware and Workshops, 2008 (COMSWARE 2008), pp. 296–301 (2008)
12. Vazhkudai, S., Schopf, J.: Predicting Sporadic Grid Data Transfers. In: Proceedings of 11th IEEE International Symposium on High Performance Distributed Computing (HPDC 2002), July 2002, pp. 188–196 (2002)
13. Vazhkudai, S., Schopf, J.: Using Regression Techniques to Predict Large Data Transfers. International Journal of High Performance Computing Applications (IJHPCA 2003), 249–268 (August 2003)
14. Vazhkudai, S.: Enabling the Co-Allocation of Grid Data Transfers. In: Proceedings of the Fourth International Workshop on Grid Computing (GRID 2003), November 17, pp. 44–51 (2003)
15. Xu, Z., Xianliang, L., Mengshu, H., Chuan, Z.: A Speed-based Adaptive Dynamic Parallel Downloading Technique. In: Proceedings of ACM Special Interest Group Operating, pp. 63–69 (2005)

Performance Evaluation of Identity and Access Management Systems in Federated Environments

Frank Schell, Jochen Dinger, and Hannes Hartenstein

Steinbuch Centre for Computing & Institute of Telematics,
Karlsruhe Institute of Technology, Universität Karlsruhe (TH), Karlsruhe, Germany
{frank.schell,jochen.dinger,hannes.hartenstein}@kit.edu

Abstract. Identity and access management (IAM) systems are used to assure authorized access to services in distributed environments. The architecture of IAM systems, in particular the arrangement of the involved components, has significant impact on performance and scalability of the overall system. Furthermore, factors like robustness and even privacy that are not related to performance have to be considered. Hence, systematic engineering of IAM systems demands for criteria and metrics to differentiate architectural approaches. The rise of service-oriented architectures and cross-organizational integration efforts in federations will additionally increase the importance of appropriate IAM systems in the future. While previous work focused on qualitative evaluation criteria, we extend these criteria by metrics to gain quantitative measures. The contribution of this paper is twofold: i) We propose a system model and corresponding metrics to evaluate different IAM system architectures on a quantitative basis. ii) We present a simulation-based performance evaluation study that shows the suitability of this system model.

Keywords: identity and access management, federated identity management, access control, scalability.

1 Introduction

The task of assuring authorized access to services in distributed environments is performed by an identity and access management (IAM) system. The distinctive feature of IAM systems to other distributed systems is the handling of sensitive user data that raises privacy concerns. The setup of such a system leads to challenges in making fundamental design decisions that have significant impact on the properties of the overall system. This is getting even more complex in federated environments where identities can be exchanged between different security realms based on trust relationships established in advance. The challenges here are the correlation of the spatial distributed identity information of single users to a federated identity and the exchange of security-related information in this heterogeneous environment.

P. Mueller, J.-N. Cao, and C.-L. Wang (Eds.): Infoscale 2009, LNICST 18, pp. 90–107, 2009.
© Institute for Computer Science, Social-Informatics and Telecommunications Engineering 2009

For example, in a scenario that uses a sophisticated access control policy, e.g., attribute-based access control [25], there will certainly be a so called policy decision point (PDP) stating authorization decisions about access requests of users. This component can be implemented in different ways and positioned at different hierarchical levels in a federated environment: A PDP could be realized as a component in a service itself, in an application server hosting the protected service, in an outsourced organization-wide service, in a service of another federation partner or even as a federation-wide service. The implications of such fundamental design decisions comprise in particular on the one hand impact on performance and scalability issues and on the other hand actuality, correctness, and confidential usage of identity information.

Looking at the extremes, a PDP could be positioned directly at each service provider. This decision ensures a fast runtime behavior with a high chance that this component is available. But each service provider would need all identity information for all users that want to use this service. This raises privacy concerns and demands for synchronizing this data, which can lead to failures and can also be a complex task. Another possible arrangement is to outsource a PDP from the single service providers to a trusted partner that handles all the access decision requests for them. With respect to the identity information stored at this central provider this leads to less inconsistencies due to the more up-to-date user attributes needed for determining the access control decisions and to easier operation and maintenance of the PDP. But this causes more network traffic, an increased latency, and leads to less autonomy of the service providers.

To guide the systematic engineering of identity and access management systems regarding their underlying architectures we thoroughly analyze the characteristics of these architectures in service-oriented environments. Therefore, we extend known qualitative evaluations with quantitative metrics. We address the implications of the architectural decisions in federated environments like the number of necessary IAM components for a specific user load and a given number of services. This also helps determining on which level the different IAM components concerning authentication and authorization processes are located. To our best knowledge there is not yet a methodology defined for determining the fitting identity and access management architecture for a specific use case. Therefore, we propose such a methodology in this contribution by showing how system architects of IAM systems can choose the right architecture for their specific scenario.

The paper is organized as follows. Section 2 describes the related work. The third Section introduces the methodology used to evaluate the different IAM approaches. In Section 4 we present evaluation criteria and metrics for IAM systems. Section 5 introduces the system model by specifying components, operations, messages, and dependencies of IAM. In Section 6 we evaluate different scenarios starting from a local approach to an outsourced AAI provider and we show how the design decision affects the system behavior. A conclusion and an outlook on future work in this area conclude the paper.

2   Related Work

There are different approaches for realizing access control like discretionary access control (DAC), mandatory access control (MAC) or more sophisticated ones like role-based access control (RBAC) [14] or attribute-based access control (ABAC) [25] that are more likely to be used in a distributed environment [2]. The basic principle behind ABAC is to use attributes for making authorization decisions to achieve more scalability than identity-based access control [19]. All necessary information is represented by a set of attributes and their values, which can be gathered dynamically if required, like user attributes, (e.g. roles, date of birth), environmental attributes (e.g. actual date and time), or attributes of resources (e.g. actual usage). Access control policies are typically specified as rules, which are evaluated with these attributes to allow or deny access to protected resources. An ABAC model for web services is introduced in [25].

The eXtensible Access Control Markup Language (XACML) is an XML-based standard for specifying access control policies, which can be processed to determine authorization decisions [23]. Furthermore it defines an architecture consisting of different components called XACML entities and a sequence of operation for these components. The XML entities comprise amongst others a policy enforcement point (PEP) for intercepting access requests and a policy decision point (PDP) for making authorization decisions. These components are well-known from policy-based networking [24]. In [19] an ABAC model is combined with language and architecture standards provided by the XACML specification, which uses automated trust negotiation mechanism to address the nondisclosure of sensitive attributes.

Federated identity management (FIM) enables the dynamic exchange of identity information across security domains based on trust relationships established in advance and therefore increases the portability of digital identities. [3], [12] and [9] show the fundamental concepts of federations and give an overview of federation protocols. In [15] the authors present the benefits using the federation paradigm for establishing an identity management system at large organizations.

Authentication and authorization infrastructures (AAI) support service providers to outsource security services to 3rd party providers [18]. This raises the overall level of security, provides a flexible access control model like ABAC, and eases the usability through, e.g., single sign-on (SSO) mechanisms [17]. Furthermore specific user data, e.g., user profiles, buying patterns, and earned privileges, can be gathered and transferred federation-wide for authorizing access to service providers based on actual data of federation members. Differences between the AAIs result from the chosen architecture depending on the level of outsourcing of security-related services [4]. Surveys of existing AAIs can be found on a technical level in [8], more detailed for b2c Commerce in [18], and with effects of architectural decisions in [16]. Here, the architectures of Shibboleth [20], Liberty Alliance [7], Passport [11], etc. are evaluated. In addition, the authors of [17] propose a reference architecture for an AAI respecting privacy and flexibility and [5] conducts user centric identity management architectures supporting, e.g., SSO, on a conceptual basis.

The authors of [10] propose a comprehensive approach for simulating IAM systems. They are setting the context for *Identity Analytics* in enterprises by adopting the scientific method [22] to approach this domain. The authors use discrete-event stochastic models for simulating various human activities and behavior, policies, social aspects, legislation, etc. This approach is used to give CIOs of an enterprise support in deciding on new or existing IAM investments by predicting their impact on relevant key factors to these decision makers, e.g., operational costs, reputation, compliance and so on. Though aiming at various aspects of IAM systems in complex enterprise contexts the authors do not focus on the consequences of using different IAM architectures and they do not support system architects with their approach.

3   Methodology

In [4] we presented some evaluation dimensions for access control architectures. We examined different architectural approaches for access control on a more conceptual basis using these criteria. Now we have done another step in evaluating such architectures by extending the qualitative results with quantitative results for differentiating these architectures. To achieve this, we use the following methodology to evaluate IAM architectures.

First, we define criteria as depicted in Fig. 1 that describe an area of interest of IAM systems. We have identified several major criteria, like scalability, robustness, and proliferation of security-relevant data. These criteria are a starting point for the further investigation of IAM systems. The next step is to define metrics for each criterion, which can be used to evaluate instances of different IAM approaches. The single metrics should reflect relevant characteristics of an IAM system that enable the differentiation of the single IAM approaches. The metrics can then be used for measuring systems in operation to provide input

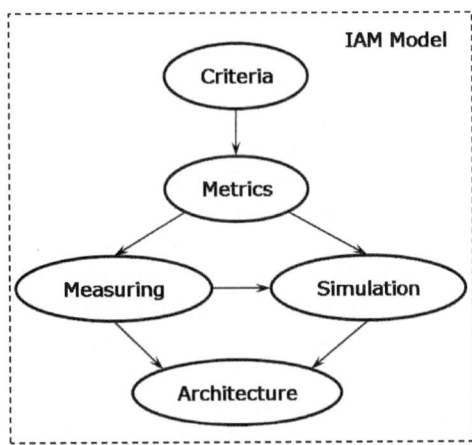

Fig. 1. Methodology for the Evaluation of IAM System Architectures

parameters for the model, e.g., duration and resource demand for determining authorization decisions. Another application of measurement is the calibration and validation of similar simulated scenarios that need to have an analogous behavior like the measured systems. The values for the metrics are gathered with measurement tools like web request tests, performance counters and network traffic analyzing tools. The metrics are also used in simulations to evaluate specific scenarios with the former specified metrics. The measuring and simulation help system architects to find the right architecture for their specific situation by matching their requirements with the results of the measurements and the simulation runs to determine their fitting scenario. Furthermore, simulation enables system designers, system architects, and other responsible persons for an IAM system to test new architectures of IAM systems before they are being deployed at all.

These activities demand for an IAM system model that describes all necessary parts of an IAM system, like the system components or the behavior of these components as it is described in section 4. The measuring and simulation can both lead to new insights about IAM systems, to new criteria that have to be followed, and to new metrics that have to be evaluated in subsequent measurements or simulation runs. This can lead to an improved overall evaluation process by a step-by-step refinement of the IAM system model.

We will further elaborate in this contribution on the aspect of simulation by specifying a basic model for IAM systems and by presenting results of simulation runs regarding aspects of scalability.

4   System Model for Identity and Access Management

The simulation model for IAM architectures comprises components, messages, processes and also dependencies between these elements.

4.1   Components

First, the components of the model are introduced.

- *Authentication Provider.* An authentication provider (AuthN-P) handles requests for user authentication. An AuthN-P provides an operation *authenticate*, which validates given user credentials like login and password, certificates, tokens or a combination of them.
- *Authorization Provider.* The component to decide on requests for access to a specific service is an authorization provider (AuthZ-P) or policy decision point (PDP). Therefore it gets all necessary information from attribute providers to determine these access control decisions. An authorization provider needs to implement an operation *authorize*, which determines to grant or deny access to a specific resource.
- *Attribute Provider.* An attribute provider (Attr-P), also called policy information point (PIP), provides data about specific users for authentication providers or authorization providers.

- *Enforcement Provider.* A component called policy enforcement point (PEP) or enforcement provider (Enf-P) restricts the access to a service provider. Therefore it intercepts access requests and asks for authentication and authorization statements at corresponding components.
- *Synchronization Provider.* A synchronization provider (Sync-P) detects changes of identity information in repositories and synchronizes these changes to connected repositories. Therefore, the synchronizer needs a rate for detecting changes. A Sync-P can be used to synchronize all or just parts of the data stored in the connected stores. The synchronization provider can be implemented using different technologies [13].
- *Data Repository.* There are a few kinds of data repositories, e.g., directory or database, defined. A credential store (Cred-S) is the repository for user credentials. Next, there is an attribute store (Attr-S) that serves as a repository for attributes about a user. The third type of data repository is the policy store (Policy-S), which stores the access control policies that are necessary for the AuthZ-P to state authorization decisions. Last, there could be some service repository (Serv-S) for storing information about all services of the federation. The availability of certain user data is modeled here.
- *Service Provider.* Any kind of resource that needs to be protected can be provided by a service provider (SP). This comprises infrastructure services as well as application layer services.
- *Client.* A user needs a client to consume certain services. A client can be a browser or any other application able to interact with the service provider.

Each provider has a rate for availability and the provided operations have resource costs (cpu, memory, network). On a more abstract view each operation should have modeled at least a duration for its execution. The providers communicate with messages that should have a certain latency of exchange, some size, and a rate for message losses.

4.2 Process Model

We present a basic process that may vary depending on the arrangement of the involved components in a specific scenario. All components can be arranged together to form the authentication and authorization processes.

A client starts the process by requesting a resource provided by a service provider. This request is intercepted by the Enf-P of the service provider, which checks the request for specific access control assertions, i.e., an authentication assertion and an authorization assertion. If not a valid authentication assertion is delivered, the client is requested to authenticate at a trusted AuthN-P. After a successful authentication process an authentication assertion is delivered to the Enf-P, which checks the authentication assertions for validity. After a successful validation the AuthZ-P is requested for stating an authorization decision. Therefore, the AuthZ-P gets the appropriate access control policies and the necessary attributes to decide on the request. An authorization assertion is delivered to the Enf-P that can now grant or deny the request of the client, which initiated this access control process.

An option that has to be cleared is the sequence of enforcement, authentication, and authorization processes. There are two possible sequences:

$$Enforcement \rightarrow Authentication \rightarrow Authorization(E1)$$

$$Authentication \rightarrow Enforcement \rightarrow Authorization(E2)$$

In sequence (E1) the enforcement provider is intercepting access requests and asking for authentication and authorization of the corresponding users. Sequence (E2) allows the user to first authenticate at the authentication provider before asking for access to a certain service provider. Some IAM systems allow both approaches so both scenarios can be mixed if required. There are two options for attribute retrieval in case (E1). There is the possibility to already get user attributes while authenticating users and send these to the enforcement provider (UAR1). Another way is to let only the authorization provider get all necessary attributes (UAR2).

5   Evaluation Criteria and Metrics for IAM Systems

The evaluation dimensions specified in [4] served as a fundament for the following defined categories and metrics.

5.1   Performance and Scalability

A substantial requirement for an IAM architecture is a high performance in most conditions. Therefore, the IAM system should be able to handle a certain constant or increasing number of users and a specific amount of service providers with low delays. To rate performance and scalability issues we deal with the following performance metrics for the evaluation of different IAM approaches.

- *Response time.* Keeping track of the response time of the IAM system components as a whole is an early indication of the capabilities of an architecture. An increasing response time of single components can also give a hint for overloaded components in tense situations. This also comprises the elapsed time for authenticating single users, determining access control decisions, searching user attributes, and so on.
- *Resource usage.* The measurement of the utilization of each component like usage of CPU/memory or incoming/outgoing network-load enables the detailed analysis of single IAM components and identification of bottlenecks.

5.2   Robustness, Reliability and Autonomy

The service providers should be available even if IAM components break down due to malfunction or any other reason. Robustness comprises correct authentication and authorization decisions under these circumstances. This demands for evaluating the degree of autonomy of foreign security domains with the following metrics.

- *Wrong access control decisions.* The single components have an imperfect view on necessary access control information like out-dated user attributes, credentials, etc. due to limited synchronization capabilities or unavailable information providers. Evaluating the number of wrong authentication or authorization decisions in tense situations gives information about the robustness of the underlying IAM architecture.
- *Attribute authorities.* An authorization process depends on up-to-date user attributes that can be spread over a number of attribute providers storing this information. The aggregation of this information from too many entities can be time-consuming and lead to erroneous results due to out-dated data.
- *Trusted components.* Access control is a sensible task that requires a minimum amount of trust between cooperating entities. Therefore a metric that lists all trusted components for an access control decision is helpful to determine possible data leakage.

5.3 Proliferation and Quality of Security-Relevant Data

Regarding privacy issues the dissemination of user data in the overall system has to be analyzed for the different IAM approaches. Also the timeliness and accuracy of the distributed user data and access control policies has a direct impact on making correct authentication and authorization decisions. Therefore we define the following metrics for evaluating the proliferation and certain quality aspects of security-relevant data.

- *Access to user attributes.* The number of components with access to user attributes in plaintext gives a hint for the risk of revealing this information. The more components the attributes can access or the more clients can access a service the more it is likely that a security breach may occur.
- *Timeliness of user data.* Access control decisions should be based on up-to-date identity information, so we need a metric for evaluating the actuality of this information. This comprises the timeliness of synchronized access control policies, too.
- *Accuracy of user data.* The data stored in a repository is likely to be not exactly, e.g., due to typos at data acquisition. This leads to erroneous or wrong access control decisions. This also includes faulty specified access control policies.

5.4 Integration Costs

A protected service is to be integrated in the overall IAM system. The different IAM approaches demand for a varying effort in the development phase of a service, e.g., programming of security-related code, and in the operation phase due to configuration effort like the configuration of SSL in the application server or the configuration of more sophisticated technologies like parameters of the Windows Communication Foundation [21].

5.5   Costs of Operation

The establishment of an IAM demands for specific knowledge and time in an organization. This also comprises the installation of the overall system or the definition of administrative processes like the specification of security policies or access control policies. Furthermore, the operation of an IAM system demands, e.g., specification of roles, definition of access control policies or configurations of IAM components, and documentation of the system.

The integration and operational costs are hard to evaluate as it is known from the software development discipline. The focus of this paper are scalability issues of IAM systems. Thus, we will evaluate different performance parameters of IAM systems. Evaluation results of the remaining metrics will be presented in further publications.

6   Evaluating Identity and Access Management Systems

Each of the specified components of the system model for IAM can be arranged locally at a service provider or at one or more external provider(s). Based on the AAI security sub-services decision tree of [16], there are three possibilities for realizing external providers of a component.

For simplicity reasons, we locate in a first step the associated stores with their respective components. For example the credential store is located at a AuthN-P, i.e., if the AuthN-P is local then the credential store is positioned locally, too. The authorization provider has a policy store and if positioned externally also a service store, which holds information for resolving access control policies concerning specific service providers. Furthermore, each attribute provider has a co-located attribute store.

A brief discussion of the pros and cons of the positioning of authentication providers, authorization providers, attribute providers and enforcement providers either local, single central, few central, and distributed can be found in [16]. The possible arrangements for each specific type of the formerly defined providers of an IAM system are as follows.

- Authentication Provider: local, single central, multiple central, distributed
- Authorization Provider: local, single central, multiple central, distributed
- Attribute Provider: local, single central, multiple central, distributed
- Enforcement Provider: local, single central, multiple central as a proxy
- Synchronization Provider: between service providers or multiple central providers

Figure 2 depicts the fundamental positioning possibilities for providers of the system model for IAM. The AuthN-P, AuthZ-P and Attr-P can be arranged in all shown arrangements. The Enf-P has no store that needs to be synchronized, so the possibilities for this component can be reduced to (1A), (2), (3A) and (4A).

(1A) shows a local provider at the service provider don't having dependencies to other service providers at all. (1B) depicts the same local providers, but the

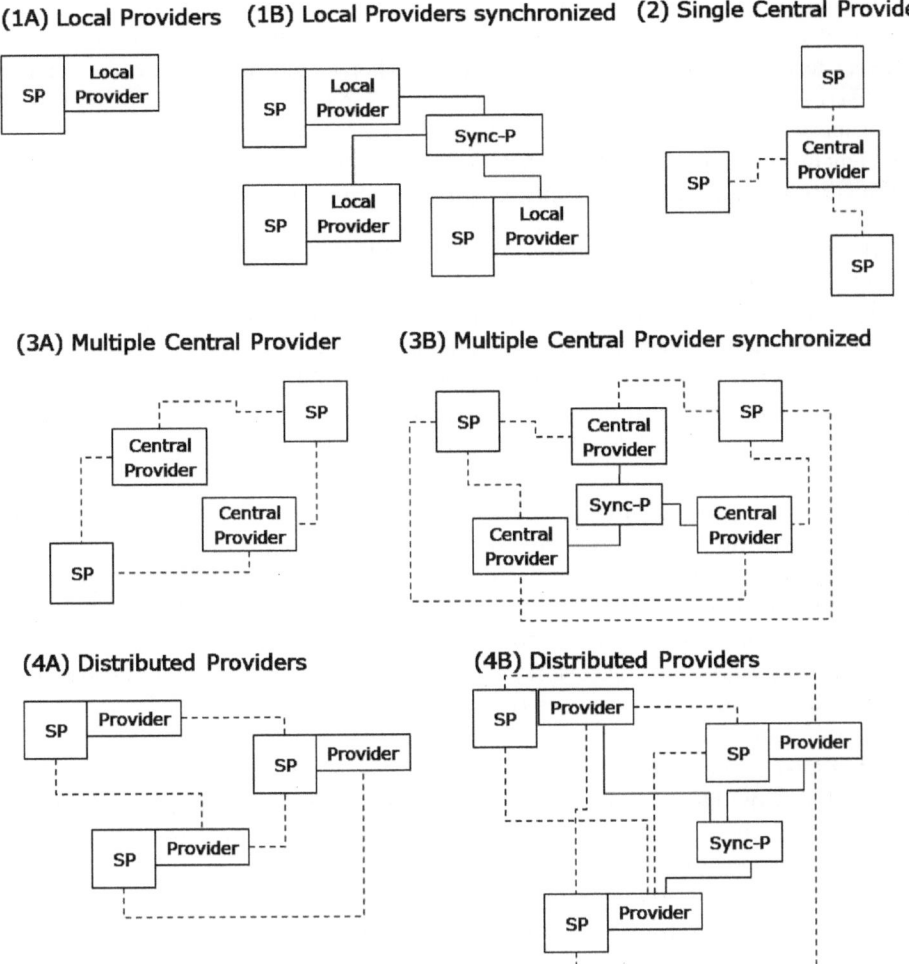

(1A) Local Providers   (1B) Local Providers synchronized   (2) Single Central Provider

(3A) Multiple Central Provider   (3B) Multiple Central Provider synchronized

(4A) Distributed Providers   (4B) Distributed Providers

Fig. 2. Possiblities for the Arrangement of Providers

stores of the local providers are synchronized. Arrangement (2) describes a single central provider that is used by all participating service providers. So there is just one single central entity that provides this functionality. This could be an authentication provider like it is known from Passport [6].

Next, a few, still centralized, providers might provide this kind of component like a few Identity Providers given in a typical Shibboleth Federation [20]. (3A) shows these multiple central providers, which can be used by different service providers. The service providers may use more than one of these providers. In Arrangement (3B) there is a Sync-P added that can synchronize all or parts of the data stored at the multiple central providers to achieve consistent data.

Another possibility is the total distribution of this type of component to all participating services providers, so that each of the service providers are able to act, e.g., as an authentication provider for another service provider. (4A) depicts this distributed case, where all service providers have recourse to the providers of the other service providers. The arrangement (4B) shows an additional Sync-P that synchronizes data for this provider between the service providers.

We state the following assumptions for the simulated scenarios.

– *Workload.* We observe all scenarios with different user workloads trying to get access to a specific service provider. For each scenario we are evaluating different conditions, e.g., from 1 up to 1000 users working in parallel on a single provider. The time for the single users between two runs is set to zero.
– *CPU processing rate.* The processing rate of the CPUs is set to 1 GHz. Each service provider and outsourced provider has a single CPU available.
– *CPU resource demands.* We state the following resource demands for the single operations.
  • *AuthN-P.* We assume a distribution of 90% usage of passwords for authentication with a resource demand of 1000 cycles and a 10% usage of certificates, e.g., authentication of administrators or access request to more restricted resources, with a resource demand of 2000 cycles, due to the higher computational costs of asymmetric encryption.
  • *AuthZ-P.* An authorization provider aggregates the necessary access control policies and computes them with a resource demand of 2000 cycles, due to the inherent complexity of the rules.
  • *Attr-P.* The task of transforming attributes requested by an authorization provider is relatively expensive due to the given complexity of evaluating these policies by specific rules. We assume a resource demand for each policy of 2000 cycles.
  • *Enf-P.* An enforcement provider intercepts access requests and validates assertions given by the user for validity. This operation costs 500 cycles.
  • *Stores.* We assume the same costs for all of the operations provided by the stores with 500 cycles.
– *Dependencies.* All simulated scenarios use the sequence of enforcement (E1) and the user attribute request strategy (UAR2), so that the enforcement provider intercepts the access requests and asks for the authentication of the requesting principal and demands for an authorization decision at the AuthZ-P, which aggregates the necessary attributes for determining the access control decision.

For conducting the simulations we use the Palladio Component Model (PCM) [1]. PCM is designed to enable early performance predictions by specifying a domain specific modeling language for component-based software architectures. Therefore, PCM uses UML-like models that allow different roles involved in the overall development process of software systems, like developers, software architects, system deployers, and domain experts, to specify their respective part of a system.

The components of a system are specified in a repository that uses service effect specifications (SEFF) to model the internal behavior of the single components. A system model declares the components used for a specific simulation and the connections between the components to realize the desired system. The resource environment model describes the provided hardware like cpu, memory, and network resources. The system model and the resource environment model are used by the allocation model to define the resources that will be used by specific components. Furthermore, the usage model specifies the behavior of the users that use the system.

PCM is implemented as an Eclipse plugin, which allows the creation of PCM model instances in a graphical editor that is based on the Eclipse Modeling Framework. With that, it enables developers to derive performance metrics from the models using analytical techniques and simulation.

6.1 Scenarios

We define the following scenarios as fundamental IAM architectures based on the aforementioned model. All the scenarios are depicted in Fig. 3.

Scenario (A) - Local Providers. The service providers act in this scenario as Enf-P, AuthN-P, AuthZ-P and Attr-P for themselves. They do not share any provider with other service providers, so each service provider has to implement its own providers and there is no interaction necessary to a central provider or between the single service providers.

Scenario (B) - Single Identity Provider. Like scenario (A) all service providers are acting as enforcement and authorization provider for themselves here, but the authentication and attribute provider are outsourced to a single entity called identity provider (IdP) as it is known, e.g., from Passport. There is no need to update the credentials, due to the single, centralized identity provider. Furthermore the service providers don't need a service repository for storing information about the other service providers, because they don't use capabilities of any other service provider.

Scenario (C) - Single AAI Provider. The next scenario is a single authentication and authorization infrastructure (AAI) provider, which provides authentication and authorization processes for the federated service providers. It stores the needed information, credentials, attributes, and access control policies, in central repositories. It also uses a service repository to find the right service provider for retrieving attributes, which are demanded for access control decisions. Therefore, the single service providers just need to implement an enforcement provider to use the AuthN-P, AuthZ-P, and Attr-P of the AAI provider.

Scenario (D) - Identity Provider and Policy Decision Point. Scenario (D) is an outsourced identity provider, i.e., AuthN-P and Attr-P, and an outsourced policy decision point, i.e., AuthZ-P, each as a single service, but all

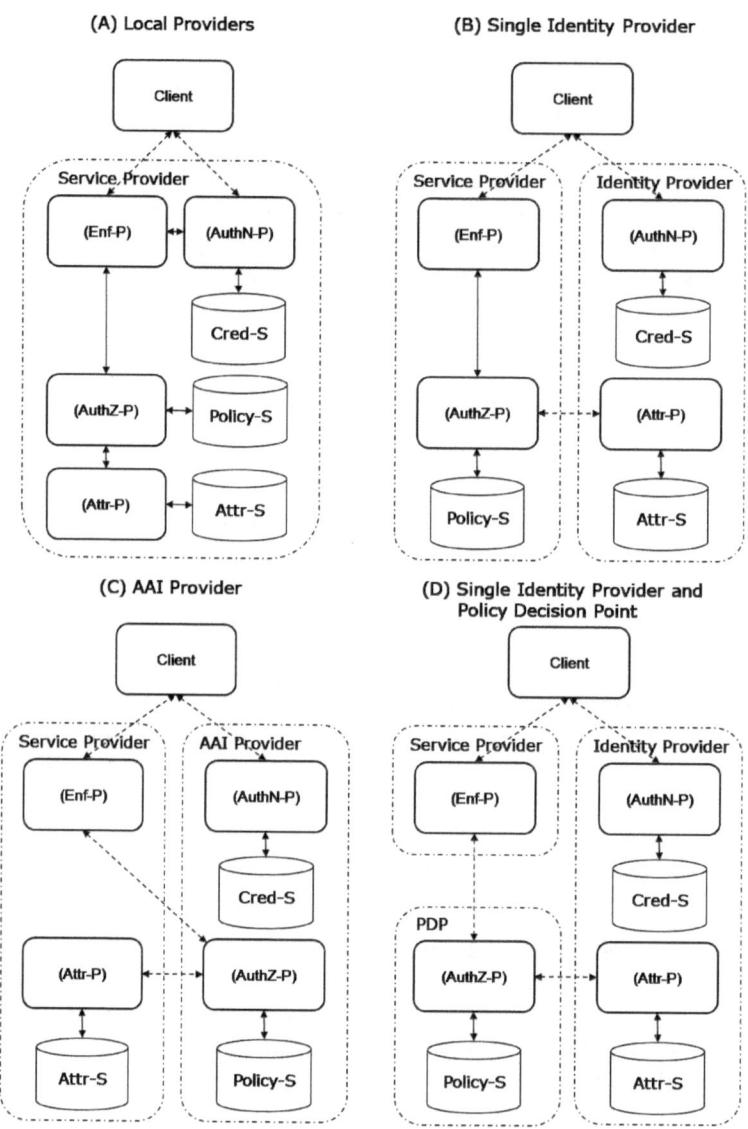

Fig. 3. Simulated Scenarios

service providers are acting as enforcement provider for themselves. There is no need for a Sync-P due to the single, centralized providers. Furthermore the service providers don't need a service repository for storing information about the other service providers, because they don't use capabilities of other service providers.

6.2   Comparison of the Scenarios

We evaluate the aforementioned scenarios regarding performance aspects in particular response times. Figure 4 depicts the cumulative distribution functions (CDF) for different user workloads from 1 to 1000 users in parallel for scenario (D). The x-axis shows the response time for requesting a resource until the authentication and authorization processes successfully granted or denied access in milliseconds from 0.1ms to 10000ms in a logarithmic scale. A value on the y-axis represents the probability of the IAM system to respond in this or less time.

A first glance at this figure shows that the probability for a longer response time increases with the number of users trying to gain access to resources provided by the service providers as expected. The maximum response times for the different workloads are as follows. 1 single user gets a result at the latest after 2ms, 10 users in parallel in 15ms, 100 users in 167ms and 1000 users in 1671ms. A ten times higher user workload leads to a 10 times higher latest response time. So the number of users correlates with the response time of the IAM system in this case. The load is dispersed in scenario (D) to the identity provider and the policy decision point leading to a distributed computation of the various IAM tasks.

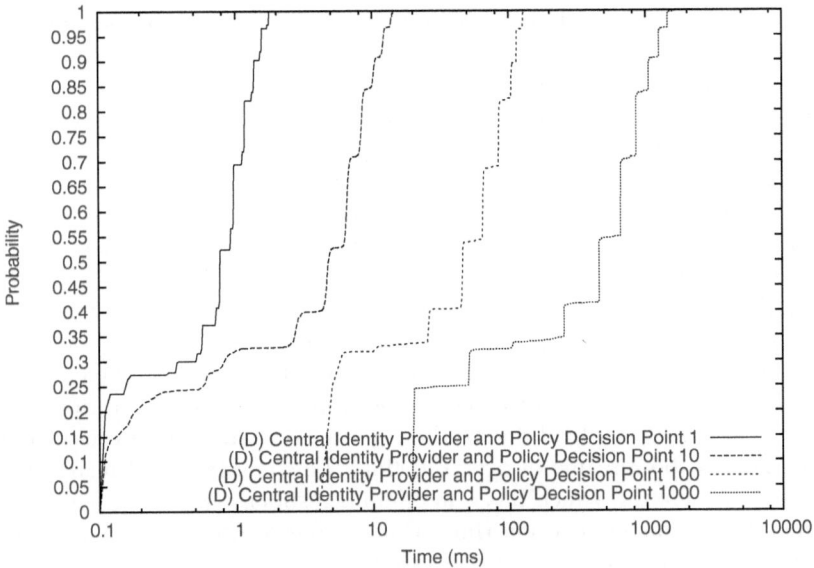

Fig. 4. Scenario (D): Probability of Response Time for 1 up to 1000 Users in Parallel as Cumulative Distribution Functions (Logarithmic Scale)

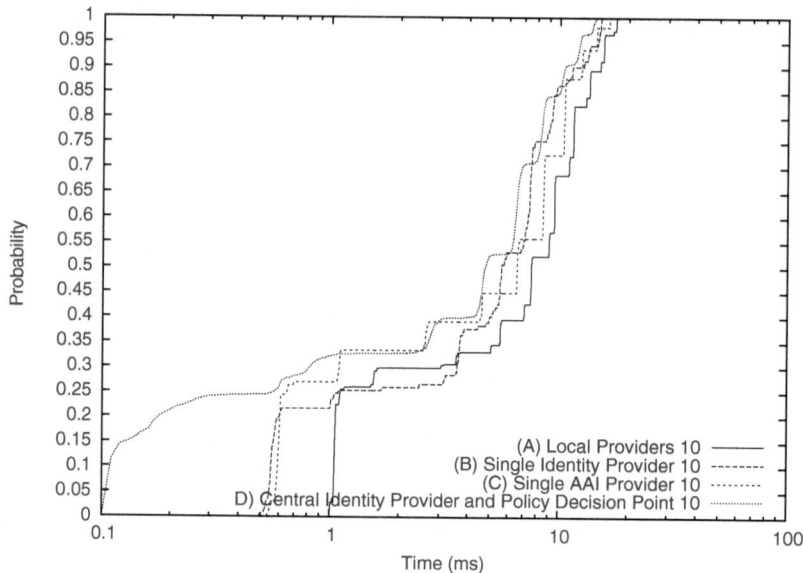

Fig. 5. All Scenarios: Probability of Response Times with Workload of 10 Users in Parallel as Cumulative Distribution Functions (Logarithmic Scale)

If we compare the different simulated scenarios we see distinct response times. Figure 5 shows the CDFs for the response time for 10 users in parallel trying to access resources. The different systems nearly have the same behavior for this user load. 50% of the requests for a single user are served in less than 10ms and the maximum response time is under 20ms in each case.

If we increase the number of users to 100 as depicted in Fig. 6 we can see that scenario (A) has the worst response times of all simulated scenarios. The maximum response time 219ms is nearly twice as high as the response time of scenario (D) with 128ms. The response times of both scenario (B) and scenario (C) are nearly similar under these circumstances, 40% of the access requests can be satisfied in 10ms or less.

Figure 7 shows the scenarios with a workload of 1000 users trying to gain access to the resources in parallel. Between 30% and 35% all scenarios are reacting nearly similarly, but as we can see clearly in higher percentages there is a gap between the local provider scenario and the other scenarios. The local providers are on heavy load due to the resource demands of all providers having a maximum response time of over 15000ms. This is a factor of nearly 10 to the central AAI scenario, which has a maximum response time of 1706ms. Scenario (B) has slightly faster reaction times than scenario (C) with a maximum of approximately 90ms. Best scenario regarding the response time is scenario (D), due to the distribution of resource demands to outsourced servers.

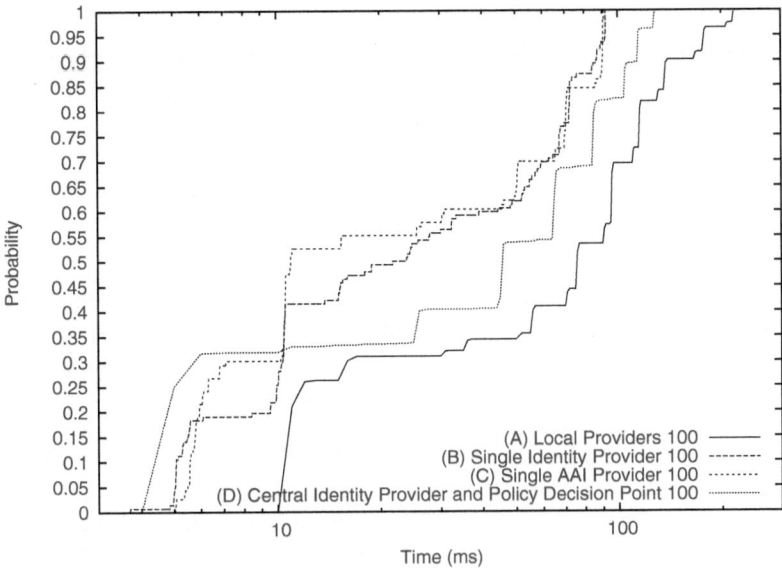

Fig. 6. All Scenarios: Probability of Response Time with Workload of 100 Users in Parallel as Cumulative Distribution Functions (Logarithmic Scale)

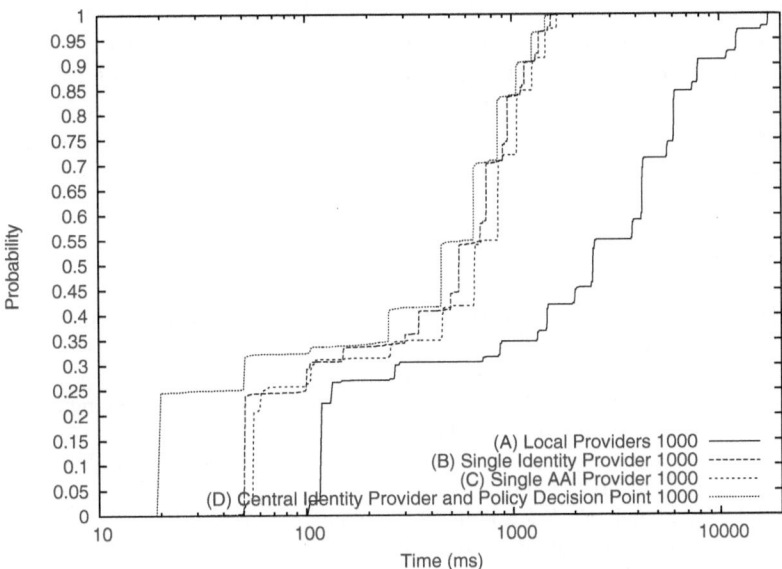

Fig. 7. All Scenarios: Probability of Response Time with Workload of 1000 Users in Parallel as Cumulative Distribution Functions (Logarithmic Scale)

Reviewing the CDFs of all simulated scenarios we can state that scenario (A), where all service providers act as enforcement, authentication, authorization and attribute providers for themselves, is not as efficient as the other simulated scenarios. Scenario (B) and (C) are reacting nearly the same under different user loads. If we take no other metric than response time into account, scenario (D) would fit our requirements the best.

7 Conclusions and Future Work

In this contribution we proposed a methodology and a system model for the evaluation of identity and access management architectures, which assure authorized access to services in distributed environments. This helps system architects of such systems in making the right design decisions, in particular the arrangement of the involved components. The position has significant impact on the properties like performance and scalability of the overall system. We extended existing qualitative evaluations by using the system model to derive criteria and metrics that show qualitative differences of IAM approaches in simulations.

Next steps include the simulation of the remaining metrics and the refinement of the IAM system model, e.g., detailed authentication protocols, fine-grained sync policies or authentication policies, varying user behavior, etc. to achieve more realistic results. This can be achieved by either adapting the Palladio Component Model to be able to determine more identity-specific metrics or by using a more generic simulator. Furthermore, we will further elaborate on the assumptions of the simulated scenarios that will also lead to more realistic results of the simulations. Another aspect that has to be addressed is the simulation of mixed scenarios. For example, some service providers sharing their providers, some using central providers, some only using their local providers, etc. altogether mixed in one simulated scenario.

References

1. Becker, S., Koziolek, H., Reussner, R.: Model-based performance prediction with the palladio component model. In: Proceedings of the 6th international workshop on Software and performance, pp. 54–65. ACM, New York (2007)
2. Benantar, M.: Access control systems: security, identity management and trust models. Springer, Heidelberg (2006)
3. Djordjevic, I., Dimitrakos, T.: A note on the anatomy of federation. BT Technology Journal 23(4), 89–106 (2005)
4. Höllrigl, T., Schell, F., Suelmann, S., Hartenstein, H.: Towards systematic engineering of Service-Oriented access control in federated environments. In: IEEE Congress on Services Part II, SERVICES-2., pp. 104–111 (2008)
5. Jøsang, A., Pope, S.: User centric identity management. In: Proceedings of AusCERT Asia Pacific Information Technology Security Conference, pp. 77–89 (2005)
6. Kormann, D., Rubin, A.: Risks of the passport single signon protocol. Computer Networks 33, 51–58 (2000)

7. Liberty alliance project (2009), http://www.projectliberty.org/
8. Lopez, J., Oppliger, R., Pernul, G.: Authentication and authorization infrastructures (AAIs): a comparative survey. Computers & Security 23(7), 578–590 (2004)
9. Maler, E., Reed, D.: The venn of identity: Options and issues in federated identity management. IEEE Security & Privacy 6(2), 16–23 (2008)
10. Mont, M., Baldwin, A., Griffin, J., Shiu, S.: Towards Identity Analytics in Enterprises. To Appear: Proceeding of the 24th IFIP International Information Security Conference (2009)
11. Passport (2009), https://accountservices.passport.net/ppnetworkhome.srf
12. Pfitzmann, B., Waidner, M.: Federated identity-management protocols. In: Christianson, B., Crispo, B., Malcolm, J.A., Roe, M. (eds.) Security Protocols 2003. LNCS, vol. 3364, pp. 153–174. Springer, Heidelberg (2005)
13. Ping Identity. Federated Provisioning: The Synergy of Identity Federation and User Provisioning,
http://www.pingidentity.com/information-library/
resource-details.cfm?customel_datapageid_1296=7587
14. Sandhu, R., Coyne, E., Feinstein, H., Youman, C.: Role-based access control models. Computer 29(2), 38–47 (1996)
15. Schell, F., Höllrigl, T., Hartenstein, H.: Federated Identity Management as a Basis for Integrated Information Management. it-Information Technology 51(1), 14–23 (2009)
16. Schläger, C., Ganslmayer, M.: Effects of Architectural Decisions in Authentication and Authorisation Infrastructures. In: The Second International Conference on Availability, Reliability and Security, ARES 2007, pp. 230–237 (2007)
17. Schläger, C., Nowey, T., Montenegro, J.: A Reference Model for Authentication and Authorisation Infrastructures Respecting Privacy and Flexibility in b2c eCommerce. In: Proceedings of the First International Conference on Availability, Reliability and Security, pp. 709–716 (2006)
18. Schläger, C., Pernul, G.: Authentication and Authorisation Infrastructures in b2c eCommerce. In: Bauknecht, K., Pröll, B., Werthner, H. (eds.) EC-Web 2005. LNCS, vol. 3590, pp. 306–315. Springer, Heidelberg (2005)
19. Shen, H., Hong, F.: An attribute-based access control model for web services. In: Seventh International Conference on Parallel and Distributed Computing, Applications and Technologies, PDCAT 2006, pp. 74–79 (2006)
20. Shibboleth (2009), http://shibboleth.internet2.edu/
21. Smith, J.: Inside microsoft windows communication foundation. Microsoft Press, Redmond (2007)
22. Wilson, E.: An introduction to scientific research. Courier Dover Publications (1990)
23. OASIS eXtensible Access Control Markup Language, XACML (2009), http://www.oasis-open.org/committees/tc_home.php?wg_abbrev=xacml
24. Yavatkar, R., Pendarakis, D., Guerin, R.: A Framework for Policy-based Admission Control. RFC 2753, Informational (2000)
25. Yuan, E., Tong, J., Inc, B., McLean, V.: Attributed based access control (ABAC) for Web services. In: 2005 IEEE International Conference on Web Services, ICWS 2005. Proceedings, pp. 561–569 (2005)

Power Consumption Optimization of MPI Programs on Multi-core Clusters

Yen-Jun Chen[1], Ching-Hsien Hsu[1], Kuan-Ching Li[2], Hsi-Ya Chang[3],
and Shuen-Tai Wang[3]

[1] Department of Computer Science and Information Engineering
Chung Hua University, Hsinchu, Taiwan 300, R.O.C.
{Patrick,robert}@grid.chu.edu.tw
[2] Department of Computer Science and Information Engineering
Providence University, Taichung 43301, Taiwan
kuancli@pu.edu.tw
[3] National Center for High-Performance Computing
Hsinchu 30076, Taiwan
{jerry,stwang}@nchc.org.tw

Abstract. While the energy crisis and the environmental pollution become important global issues, the power consumption researching brings to computer sciences world. In this generation, high speed CPU structures include multi-core CPU have been provided to bring more computational cycles yet efficiently managing power the system needs. Cluster of SMPs and Multi-core CPUs are designed to bring more computational cycles in a sole computing platform, unavoidable extra energy consumption in loading jobs is incurred.

Data exchange among nodes is essential and needed during the execution of parallel applications in cluster environments. Popular networking technologies used are Fast Ethernet or Gigabit Ethernet, which are cheaper and much slower when compared to Infiniband or 10G Ethernet. Two questions on data exchange among nodes arise in multi-core CPU cluster environments. The former one is, if data are sent between two nodes, the network latency takes longer than system bus inside of a multi-core CPU, and thus, wait-for-sending data are blocked in cache. And the latter is, if a core keeps in waiting state, the unpredicted waiting time brings to cores higher load. These two situations consume extra power and no additional contribution for increasing overall speed. In this paper, we present a novel approach to tackle the congestion problem and taking into consideration energy in general network environments, by combining hardware power saving function, maintaining the transmission unchanged while saving more energy than any general and previous cases.

Keywords: Power Consumption, multi-core processor, cluster Computing, MPI.

1 Introduction

Reduction on power consumption of computer systems is a hot issue recently, since many CPUs and computer-related hardware has been produced and under operation

P. Mueller, J.-N. Cao, and C.-L. Wang (Eds.): Infoscale 2009, LNICST 18, pp. 108–120, 2009.
© Institute for Computer Science, Social-Informatics and Telecommunications Engineering 2009

everywhere. As the number of single-core CPU has reached to physical limitation on current semi-conductor technology, the computing performance has met the bottle-neck. Multi-core CPUs become a simple yet efficient solution to increase perform-ance and speed since that concept SMP in a single chip, that is, making up a small cluster to be executed inside a host. Additionally, it reduces the amount of context switching while in single-core CPUs, increases straight forwardly the overall per-formance.

Figure 1 illustrates the architecture of Intel quad-core CPU, which looks like a combination of two dual-core CPUs. It has four individual execution engines, where each two cores share one set of L2 cache and system bus interface, and con-nect to the fixed system bus. The advantages of this architecture are twofold. The former one is that each core can fully utilize L2 cache as each core needs larger memory, while the latter is that each core accesses L2 cache through individual hub [7] simplifying system bus and cache memory structures. Intel CPU supports "SpeedStep" [3] frequency / voltage control, the technology that changes all cores' frequency at the same.

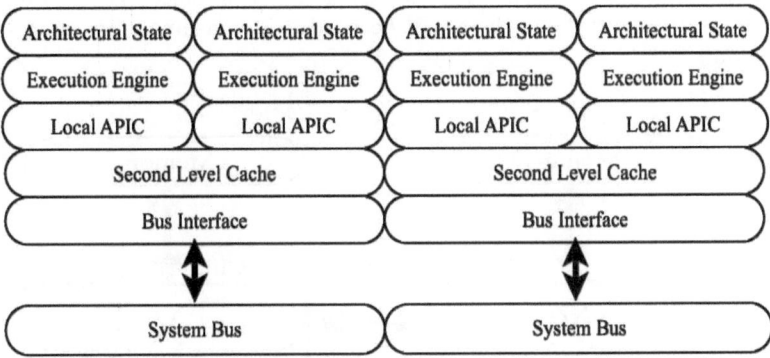

Fig. 1. Intel Quad-Core CPU system structure [11]

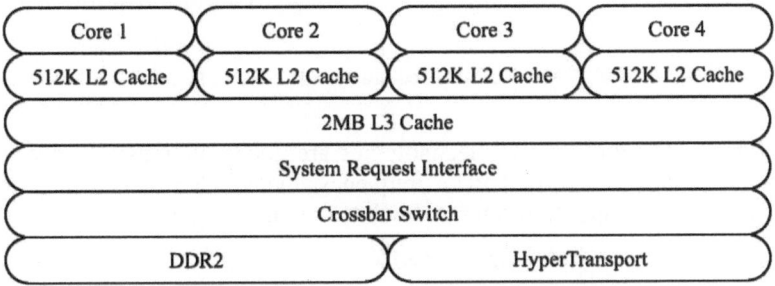

Fig. 2. AMD Quad-Core CPU system structure [12]

AMD quad-core CPU, as shown in Figure 2, has individual L2 cache in each core and share L3 cache, (a special design), and then integrated to DDR2 memory controller into CPU, helping to increase memory access speed. Each core has individual channel to access system bus, and L3 cache and peripheral chips from crossbar switch. AMD provides "PowerNow!" [4] technology to adjust each core's working frequency / voltage.

A cluster platform is built up by interconnecting a number of single-core CPU, and a message passing library, such as MPI is needed for data exchange among computing nodes in this distribution computing environment. In addition, high speed network as Infiniband is needed to interconnect the computing nodes. As multi-core CPUs are introduced and built in cluster environments, the architecture of this newly proposed cluster is as presented in Figure 3. The main advantages of data exchanges between cores inside of a CPU is much faster than passing by a network and South / North bridge chip.

Infiniband networking technology is a good and fast enough solution to connect all computing nodes of a cluster platform, but expensive. Gigabit Ethernet is cheaper solution and widely built in general network environment, though slower in transmission speed and definitely drop down data exchange performance. To send data to a core that is inside of a different host will be needed to consume extra energy when waiting for data.

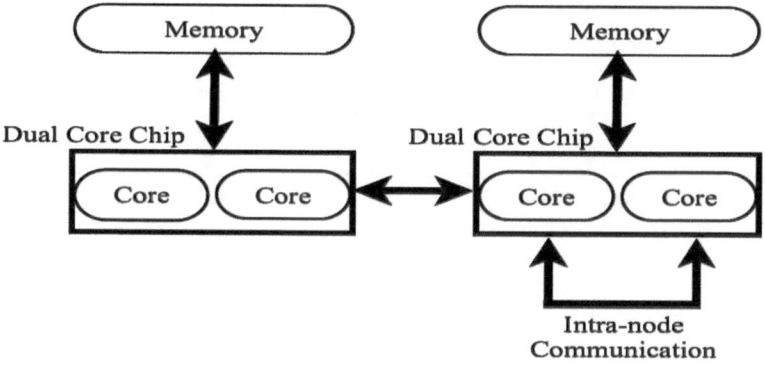

Fig. 3. Multi-core based cluster structure [13]

"SpeedStep" and "PowerNow!" technologies are good solutions to reduce power consumption, since they adjust CPU's frequency and voltage dynamically to save energy. The power consumption can be calculated by the function:

$$P=IV=V^2f=J/s. \tag{1}$$

where P is Watt, V is voltage, I is current, f is working frequency of CPU, J is joule and s is time in seconds. It means that lower voltage in the same current condition saves more energy. How and when to reduce voltage and frequency become an important issue, since one of main targets of clustering computing computers is to increase the performance, while slowing down CPU's frequency is conflict with performance. Considering data latency of network, and CPU load in current CPU technologies, we would like to create a low energy cost cluster platform based on general network architecture, that keeps almost the same data transmission time though lower in energy consumption when CPU in full speed.

The remainder of this paper is organized as follows. Some related works discussed in Section 2, and some challenges we found in our experiment is listed in Section 3. In Section 4, the proposed approach about reducing energy consumption is presented; while the testing environment and performance results in Section 5. Finally the conclusion and future works are discussed in Section 6.

2 Related Works

Based on the concept about reducing computing time, the job scheduling methodology as introduced in [8] was designed targeting for a faster complete data transmission; otherwise, adjust cache block size to find the fastest speed that transmits data using MPI between MPI nodes in situations as listed in [13] was studied, and similar implementation of the method using OpenMP was also observed in [14]. Another investigation focused on compiler that analyze program's semantics, and insert special hardware control command that automatically adjusts simulation board's working frequency and voltage, [10] research needs to be combined both hardware and software resources.

Base on a simulation board, researchers have designed routing path algorithm that tries to find a shortest path to transmit data in Networks-on-Chip [15], in order to reduce data transmission time between CPUs, as also to have opportunities to realistically port and implement it to a cluster environment.

Others, researches have applied Genetic Algorithms to make a dynamically and continuous improvement on power saving methodology [9]. Through a software based methodology, routing paths are modified, link speed and working voltage are monitored at the same time to reduce power consumption, while the voltage detection information required hardware support.

Modern Operating Systems as Linux and Windows provides hardware power saving function as introduced in [1] and [2], where they can drive "SpeedStep" [3] and "PowerNow!" [4] utilizing special driver to control CPU voltage and frequency. Of course hardware support is necessary, since depending on the CPU loading, CPU is automatically selected with lower frequency and voltage automatically.

3 Challenges of Power Saving in Multi-core CPU Cluster Platform

We have built a cluster platform that combines all technologies as listed above for experiment purposes. These advantages bring higher speed for data broadcasting, yet only between cores inside a CPU, a CPU core is maintained with high load means the CPU speed cannot be decreased. Analysis and reasoning on these situations are discussed next.

3.1 CPU Power Control Structure

The "SpeedStep" and "PowerNow!" were not show in Figure 1 and 2. The "Speed-Step" provides solely full CPU frequency and voltage adjustment. The design makes power control easier, though consumes extra energy. If only one core works with high load, power control mechanism cannot reduce other cores' frequency / voltage, nor dropping down the performance of a busy core. Inefficient energy consumption brings temperature increasing, since low loading core generates the same heat as high load one, and brings the CPU's temperature up at the same time.

AMD "PowerNow!" shows advantage in this issue, since we can reduce frequency when core works in lower loading without need to consider other cores' situation, and heat reduction is also another benefit.

3.2 Network Bandwidth and Cache Structure

As shown in Figure 1, Intel's CPU architecture shares L2 cache using individual hub, and it has two advantages and two problems:

A. Advantages

- **Flexible Cache Allocation**

Every core was allowed to use whole L2 cache from cache hub, the hub provides single memory access channel for each core, and simplifies internal cache access structure.

- **Decrease Cache Missing Rate**

When each core has massive cache request, cache memory decreases page swapping from main memory.

B. Problems

- **Cache Hub Congestion**

If huge amount of data request or sending commands happen suddenly, individual cache hub blocks data frames in cache memory or stops commands in queue. All cores and hub keep in busy state and thus consume extra energy.

- **Network Bandwidth Condition**

Lower network bandwidth makes previous situation more seriously in many nodes' cluster, since network speed cannot be as fast as internal CPU bus, if cross-node data frames appear, the delivering time is longer than intra-node data switch.

Compared with Intel, while data frame flood sends to CPU, AMD structure has no enough cache to save them, yet individual bus / memory access channel of each core provides isolated bandwidth, L2 cache built in core reduces data flow interference. Different CPU structure provides their advantages, and weakness appears while they are compared to each other.

3.3 MPI Environment Support

In a general situation, each computing node executed under a given core / host randomly indicated by cluster software, signifies that programmer cannot obtain additional core loading from node's code section. Following our purpose, finding system information about thread / node location works, but it is a hard method since the program would spend large amount of time in device I/O, includes open system state file, analysis information and obtaining node's location. Another alternative method is easier, where we make cluster platform that fixes node location in indicated core or host, and the function helps to get core loading from node's code. OpenMPI is selected for this issue.

4 The Proposed Approach

Upon with CPU specification, CPU power control interface and network structure, we provide a data broadcasting strategy that combines data flow limitation and core frequency controlling as shown below.

4.1 Drop Down Data Transmission Speed

It is not a good method to keep performance. In fact, we add 1μs delay between two packets, in a real environment, and the total transmission time is added as:

$$(N - 1) \times T \tag{2}$$

where N is total number of nodes and T is delay time between packets. We found that the total time has just been added less than one to five seconds in average, when is transmitted 100K data frames across two hosts that are connected via Gigabit Ethernet. Additionally, the advantage is that the loading of a central node that sends data to other nodes is decreased by almost 50%, although the method solves problems as cache hub and CPU internal bus congestion. On the other hand, data receiving core load is decreased by 15% in average when we added 10μs delay in these nodes, yet total transmission time is increased by less than 0.5s.

4.2 Data Broadcasting According to Core Loading

Following the previous result, we provide a Loading-Aware Broadcasting method (LAB). Based on the "PowerNow!" hardware structure, and keeping the same load on all cores is necessary for efficient energy consumption, thus sending data from central node to lowest loading node makes sense. If the load can be reduced on a core, then reducing CPU frequency is permitted for saving energy.

Still in LAB algorithm, as indicated in Figure 4, data frames are sent sequentially from Host 1-Core 0 to other cores. This method is often used to distribute wait-for-calculate data blocks in complex math parallel calculations. MPI provides broadcast command to distribute data block and reduce command to receive result. In order to changing data frame transmission path dynamically, we use point-to-point command to switch data, since this type of command can indicate sending and receiving node.

4.3 Slow Down Lower Loading CPU / Core

Although the challenge presented in subsection 3.1 exists, as for power saving issue, we use AMD system and "PowerNow!" to slow down lowering loading core frequency. The given CPU supports 2 steps frequency, and therefore they work in different voltage and current. Thus we focus on frequency adjustment, and calculating power consumption of each core as below:

$$P = V_{max} \times I_{max} \times T \tag{3}$$

where V_{max} and I_{max} are found from AMD CPU technology specification [6], and T is program execution time. Since "Time" joins the function, the unit of P is Joule.

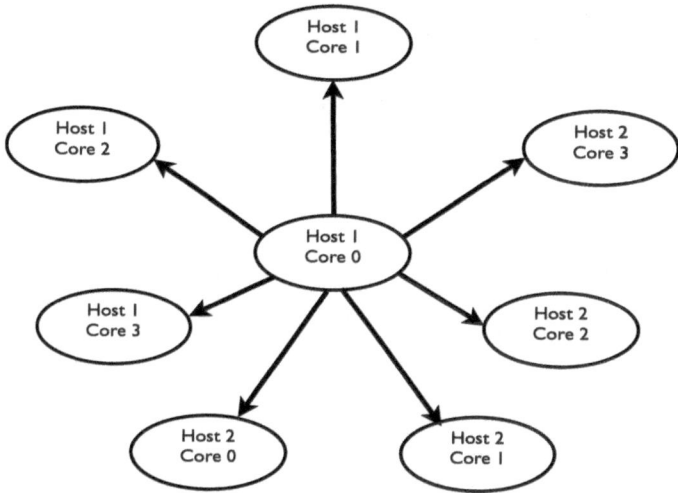

Fig. 4. LAB Algorithm structure diagram

The data distribution algorithm is given as below.

Loading-Aware Broadcasting (LAB)Algorithm

```
generating wait-for-send data frame
if (node 0)
{
   //detect nodes' loading from system information and
     save in TargetNode
   OpenCPUState;
   CalculateCPULoading;
   //sort TargetNode from low to high
   CPULoadingSorting;
   //send data follow sorting result
   while(!DataSendingFinish)
```

```
{
  for(i=1; i<NodeNumber; i++)
    SendData(TargetNode[i]);
}
//send finish message to receiving nodes
for(i=1; i<NodeNumber; i++)
  SendData(i);
}
if (other nodes)
{
  //receive data from node 0
  ReceiveData(0);
  usleep();
}
```

5 Performance Evaluation

In this section, experimental results on proposed power-saving strategy are presented. The cluster platform includes two computing nodes and connected via Gigabit Ethernet, and each node is installed with Ubuntu Linux 8.10 / kernel 2.6.27-9, Open-MPI message passing library is selected for thread execution affinity function, the hardware specification is listed as next:

Table 1. Host specification

CPU	AMD Phenom X4 9650 Quad-Core 2.3GHz
Layer 1 Cache	64K Instruction Cache and 64K Data Cache Per Core
Layer 2 Cache	512K Per Core
Layer 3 Cache	Share 2M for 4 Cores
Main Memory	DDR2-800 4GB

Three different sizes of data frames are transmitted between nodes: 1 byte, 1460 bytes and 8000 bytes. 1 byte frame is not only the smallest one in MPI data frame, but also in network, for complete data transmission in shortest time, source node generates huge amount of 1 byte frame, these packets congest CPU internal bus and network. 1518 bytes frame is the largest one in network, but considering that network header should be inserted into network packet, we select 1460 bytes frame for testing, and then, this size of packet brings largest amount of data in a single packet, and trigger fewest interrupt to CPU. Finally 8000 bytes frame is set for large data frame testing, since it needs to be separated to several other packets by network driver for transmission, and thus need the longest time for data transmission. While the experiment is executed, we send 100K data frames between two nodes, and calculate the power consumption.

Each figure that follows next has four blocks. The first one is executed in Performance Mode (PM, CPU works in 2.3GHz), the second one is PowerSave Mode (PS, 1.15GHz), the third one is OnDemand Mode (OD, slows down frequency while CPU loading lower than 80%), and last one is LAB algorithm. Each block has four delay time configurations, the first one contains no delay between each data frame, the second delays 5μs, the third one delays 10μs, and last one delay 20μs. Still in figures that follows next, TD stands for Transmission Delay, Transmission Time as TT, and PC for Power Consumption.

The "Rank Number" in each figure means the number of nodes / cores join data broadcasting. For example, rank 2 means rank 0 broadcasts data to rank 1, and rank 4 means rank 0 broad-casts data to rank 1, 2, and 3. Since each host has four cores, the rank number 2~4 are internal node data transmission, and rank 5~8 are cross node data transmission. Although only 4 cores join work in rank number 2~4 other cores consume energy at the same time, and we still need to add the energy consumed.

Figure 5 shows the TT for one byte frame, and Figure 6 the PC. Comparing PM, PS and OD mode, we find that TD increases the TT over 3 seconds in rank 2~4 in every frequency level, but increases less than 1 second in 5~8. Figure 6 displayed one byte frame PC. Clearly, the PS mode spends the longest time to transmit data, though consumes the lowest energy. OD mode has none remarkable performance in power saving in rank 7~8, but it uses average 100J less than PM mode in rank 2~6, and keeps TT increasing less than 0.4s in cross-node situation. LAB algorithm displays advantage in no delay situation, less than 1s TT increasing yet consumes almost the same energy in rank 7~8. In other situations, LAB spends maximum 4s longer than OD mode, and saves 250J.

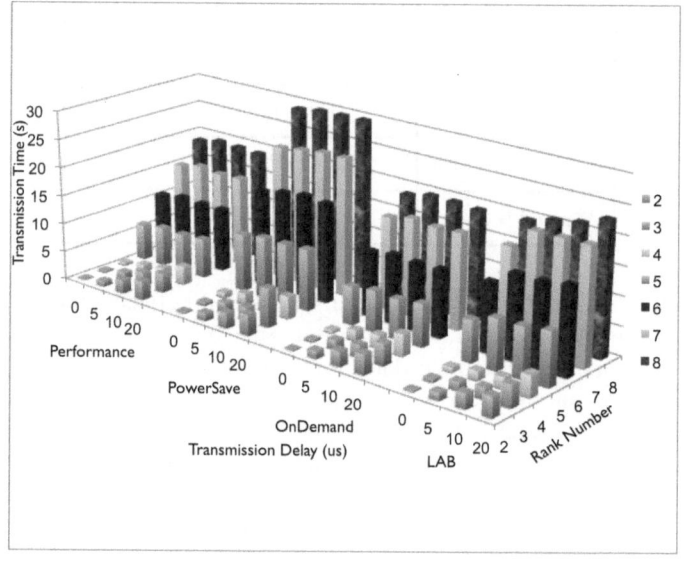

Fig. 5. Time Effect of TD on TT (Frame = 1 Byte)

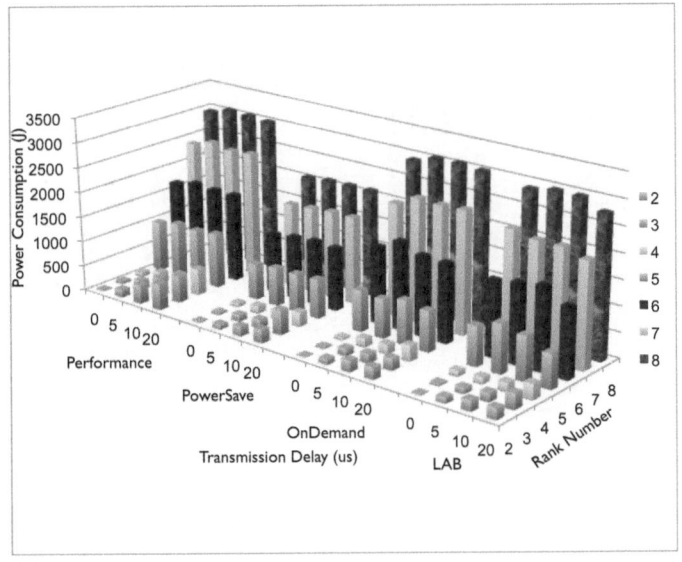

Fig. 6. Power Effect of TD on PC (Frame = 1 Byte)

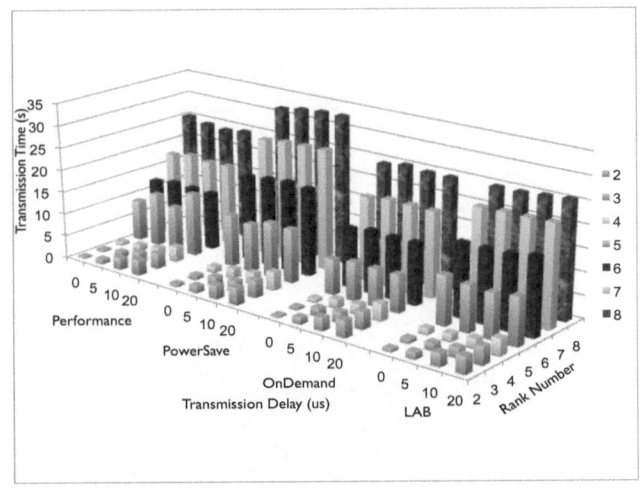

Fig. 7. Time Effect of TD on TT (Frame = 1460 Byte)

Figure 7 shows 1460 bytes frame TT. By comparing PM mode and OD mode, the completed time is longer than 1 byte frame in all situations. In Figure 8, OD mode uses in average over 200J less than PM mode. Our LAB algorithm made uses of 24~25s to complete data transmission as OD mode, yet consumes less than OD mode 200~600J in 8 ranks. In other situations, LAB keeps nearly the same performance, spending 4s longer than OD mode and consuming 200~400J less than OD mode.

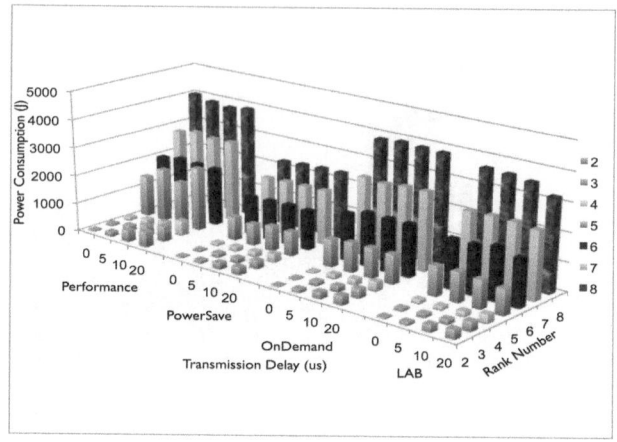

Fig. 8. Power Effect of TD on PC (Frame = 1460 Byte)

Although 8000 byte frame is the longest one, PS mode TT keeps 6s longer than other frames' size, as in Figure 9. Comparing OD and PM Mode, OD mode spends less than 1s longer than PM Mode, yet saves 200~400J in other cases. Comparing LAB algorithm and OD mode, LAB algorithm still keeps its advantages in the longest frame size, spends almost the same TT in 8 ranks and average 2~3s longer in other cross-node situations, consuming 100~ 400J less than OD mode.

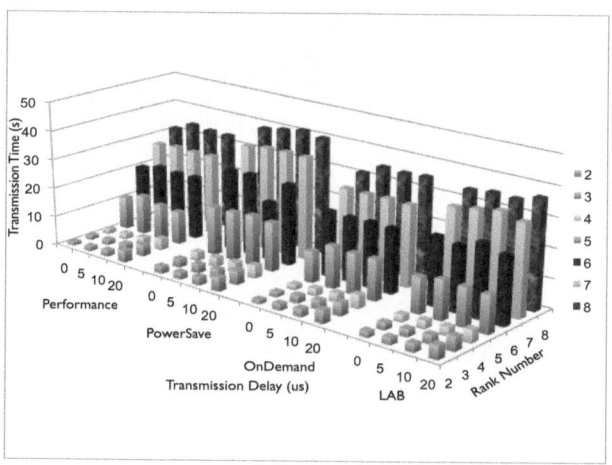

Fig. 9. Time Effect of TD on TT (Frame = 8000 Byte)

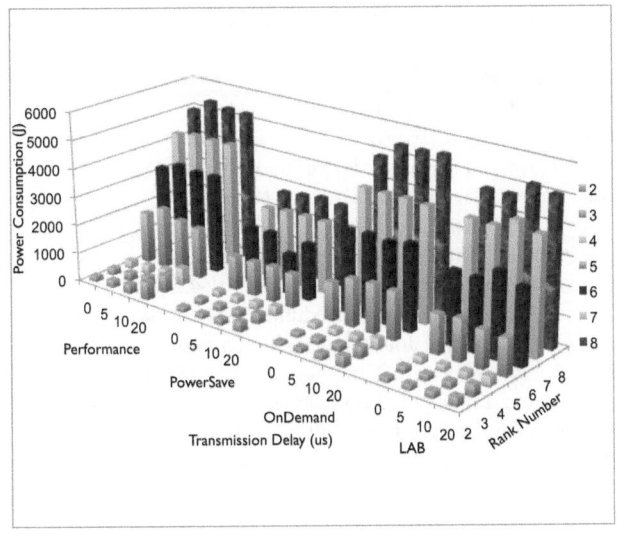

Fig. 10. Power Effect of TD on PC (Frame = 8000 Byte)

6   Conclusion and Future Works

In this proposed research, LAB algorithm keeps in average 4s TT increasing, yet saves 200~600J that compares with OD mode in cross-node situation. Limited by only 2 steps experimental cases of CPU frequencies (2.3GHz and 1.15GHz), we cannot keep CPU loading in a smooth curve. In desktop and server CPU, they do not keep in high loading work longer time, while they complete a concurrent job and next one does not be started. Power saving technology helps to decrease host energy consumption, and decreasing energy cost and carbon dioxide emissions can be reduced.

There are many directions to continue this investigation, to develop methods to save energy. If hardware and software provides functions about voltage or speed control, motherboard or any other type of peripheral device, then a hardware driver, power-aware job scheduling and data distribution algorithms can be combined and implemented, targeting in the construction of a low energy cost cluster computing platform in future.

References

1. Power Management Guide,
   http://www.gentoo.com/doc/en/power-management-guide.xml
2. Enabling CPU Frequency Scaling,
   http://ubuntu.wordpress.com/2005/11/04/
   enabling-cpu-frequency-scaling/
3. Enhanced Intel SpeedStep Technology for the Intel Pentium M Processor,
   ftp://download.intel.com/design/network/papers/30117401.pdf

4. AMD PowerNow! Technology Platform Design Guide for Embedded Processors,
   `http://www.amd.com/epd/processors/6.32bitproc/8.amdk6fami/`
   `x24267/24267a.pdf`
5. AMD / Intel CPU voltage control driver down load,
   `http://www.linux-phc.org/viewtopic.php?f=13&t=2`
6. AMD Family 10h Desktop Processor Power and Thermal Data Sheet,
   `http://www.amd.com/us-en/assets/content_type/`
   `white_papers_and_tech_docs/GH_43375_10h_DT_PTDS_PUB_3.14.pdf`
7. AMD Opteron Processor with Direct Connect Architecture,
   `http://enterprise.amd.com/downloads/4P_Power_PID_41498.pdf`
8. Lan, C.-Y., Hsu, C.-H., Chen, S.-C.: Scheduling Contention-Free Irregular Redistributions in Parallelizing Compilers. The Journal of Supercomputing 40(3), 229–247 (2007)
9. Shin, D., Kim, J.: Power-Aware Communication Optimization for Networks-on-Chips with Voltage Scalable Links. In: Proceeding of the International Conference on Hardware/Software Code sign and System Synthesis, pp. 170–175 (2004)
10. Chen, G., Li, F., Kandemir, M.: Reducing Energy Consumption of On-Chip Networks Through a Hybrid Compiler-Runtime Approach. In: 16th International Conference on Parallel Architecture and Compilation Techniques (PACT 2007), pp. 163–174 (2007)
11. Intel 64 And IA-32 Architectures Software Developers Manual, vol.1,
    `http://download.intel.com/design/processor/manuals/`
    `253665.pdf`
12. Key Architectural Features of AMD Phenom X4 Quad-Core Processors,
    `http://www.amd.com/us-en/Processors/ProductInformation/`
    `0,30_118_15331_15332%5E15334,00.html`
13. Chia, L., Hartono, A., Panda, D.K.: Designing High Performance and Scalable MPI Internode Communication Support for Clusters. In: 2006 IEEE International Conference on Cluster Computing, September 25-28, pp. 1–10 (2006)
14. Noronha, R., Panda, D.K.: Improving Scalability of OpenMP Applications on Multi-core Systems Using Large Page Support. In: 2007 IEEE International Parallel and Distributed Processing Symposium, March 26-30, pp. 1–8 (2007)
15. Ogras, U.Y., Marculescu, R., Lee, H.G., Chang, N.E.: Communication Architecture Optimization: Making the Shortest Path Shorter in Regular Networks-on-Chip. In: 2006 Proceedings of the conference on Design, Automation and Test in Europe, Munich, Germany, March 2006, vol. 1, pp. 712–717 (2006)

Scalable Workload Adaptation for Mixed Workload

Baoning Niu and Jian Shi

Taiyuan University of Technology
79 West Yingze Street
Taiyuan, Shanxi, China
niubaoning@tyut.edu.cn, shijianzhengzhou@126.com

Abstract. Workload adaptation is a performance management process in which an autonomic database management system (DBMS) efficiently makes use of its resources by filtering or controlling the workload presented to it in order to meet its Service Level Objectives (SLOs). The overhead incurred by filtering or controlling the workload is an important factor affecting the effectiveness of workload adaptation. This paper investigates the overhead of AWMF, a framework for workload adaptation and proposes a scalable approach for adapting mixed workload under the framework. The proposed approach allows Query Scheduler, the prototype implementation of AWMF, manage both OLAP and OLTP classes of queries to meet their performance goals by allocating DBMS resources through admission control in the presence of workload fluctuation. Experiments with IBM® DB2® Universal Database™ are conducted to show the proposed approach is scalable and effective.

Keywords: Workload adaptation, Performance management, DBMSs.

1 Introduction

One of the challenging problems that contemporary database management systems (DBMSs) are facing is to guarantee the service level objectives (SLOs) for their complex workloads. The emerging trend of server consolidation results in a workload with diverse and dynamic resource demands with competing performance objectives for different applications. Web-based applications introduce a need for flexible and guaranteed application service levels [1]. In order to meet the SLOs, DBMSs must be able to aware the workload changes and allocate resources accordingly.

Workload adaptation is such a technique to solve the problem. It can be defined as a performance management process in which an autonomic DBMS efficiently makes use of its resources by filtering or controlling the workload presented to it in order to meet its SLOs [6]. A general framework for workload adaptation in autonomic DBMSs, called AWMF, has been proposed in [6]. The framework consists of a workload detection process and a workload control process, involving four functional components, namely workload characterization, performance modeling, workload control and system monitoring. The prototype implementation of the framework, called Query Scheduler, using cost-based workload control is proven to be effective for OLAP workload. Workload control based on multiprogramming levels (MPL) for

P. Mueller, J.-N. Cao, and C.-L. Wang (Eds.): Infoscale 2009, LNICST 18, pp. 121–134, 2009.
© Institute for Computer Science, Social-Informatics and Telecommunications Engineering 2009

OLTP workload under similar framework was discussed in [8]. The performance controller sits at the front of DBMSs, intercepts queries and makes admission control.

Mixed workloads with both OLAP and OLTP queries are common. Controlling mixed workloads is more complex than homogenous workloads. Control of OLAP workloads based on cost is appropriate because the size of OLAP queries varies widely. Since OLTP queries are small, control of OLTP workloads based on MPLs can eliminate the overhead to acquire costs of queries. However, the overhead from a separate controller is still significant to the OLTP queries with sub-second execution time. Usually a transaction consists of several dozens of queries. The accumulative delay from the controller could be several times more than its execution time.

This paper investigates the overhead incurred by controlling workloads in AWMF and explores the techniques can be used under AWMF for a mixed workload using cost-based workload control. The rest of the paper is structured as follows. Section 2 briefly describes AWMF and its prototype implementation – Query Scheduler, for workload adaptation in autonomic DBMSs. Section 3 analyzes the overhead of Query Scheduler and related scalable issues. Section 4 discusses the scalable approach for handling mixed workload in Query Scheduler. The evaluation of the proposed approach for mixed workload is outlined in Section 5. We conclude and suggest future work in Section 6.

2 AWMF and Its Prototype Implementantion

In this section, we briefly introduce AWMF and its prototype implementation for subsequent discussion. For detailed description, please refer to [6].

2.1 AWMF

Workload adaptation is a process of optimizing resource usage by controlling the workload presented to the system. As shown in Fig. 1, the framework for workload adaptation consists of two processes, namely workload detection and workload control, involving four functional components: workload characterization, performance modeling, workload control, and system monitoring.

Workload characterization is concerned with measuring and modeling production workloads [4, 5]. The purpose of characterizing a workload is to understand and determine the resource usage and performance behavior for subsequent workload control. Performance modeling tries to predict the performance of the target system through a model that describes the features of the target system [5]. Workload control components find and enforce an optimal workload control plan to meet the performance objectives when fluctuation in the workload causes the system performance to degrade. System monitoring, or feedback, indicates how well the system is performing by continuously acquiring the execution information of the workload and the resource usage of the system.

Workload detection identifies workload changes by monitoring and characterizing current workloads and predicting future workload trends. As shown in Fig. 1, two functional components, workload characterization and system monitoring, are involved in the workload detection process.

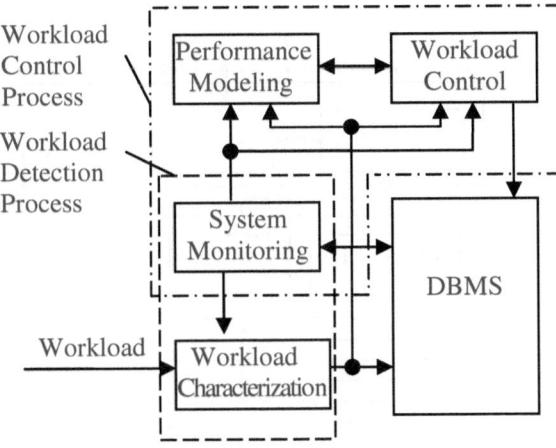

Fig. 1. AWMF

Workload control involves system management via efficient allocation of resources. One of the main issues regarding workload control is how to determine the appropriate amount of control. Under the framework, when workload changes are detected, the workload control component determines whether or not an adjustment is needed. In the positive case, it generates workload control plans and submits them to the performance modeling component for evaluation. It then chooses the optimal plan to exert control over the workload. Three functional components, the workload control, the performance modeling and the system monitoring, are involved in the workload control process.

2.2 Query Scheduler

The Query Scheduler shown in Fig. 2 is a prototype implementation of the workload adaptation framework with IBM® DB2® Universal Database system (DB2 UDB).

Query Scheduler uses Query Patroller [3] (DB2 QP), the workload controller in DB2 UDB, to intercept queries and acquire query information and, via direct commands to DB2 QP, release queries. In this implementation, DB2 QP is configured to automatically intercept all queries, record detailed query information, block the DB2 agent responsible for executing the query until an explicit operator command is received. Finally, DB2 QP was modified to inform Query Scheduler each time a query was intercepted. The Monitor then collects the information about the query from the DB2 QP control tables, including query identification information, query cost, query execution information etc. The Monitor passes the query information to the classifier and the scheduling planner. The Classifier assigns the query to an appropriate service class based on its performance goal and places the query in the associated queue manipulated by the dispatcher. The Dispatcher receives a scheduling plan from the Scheduling Planner and releases the queries in the class queues according to the plan.

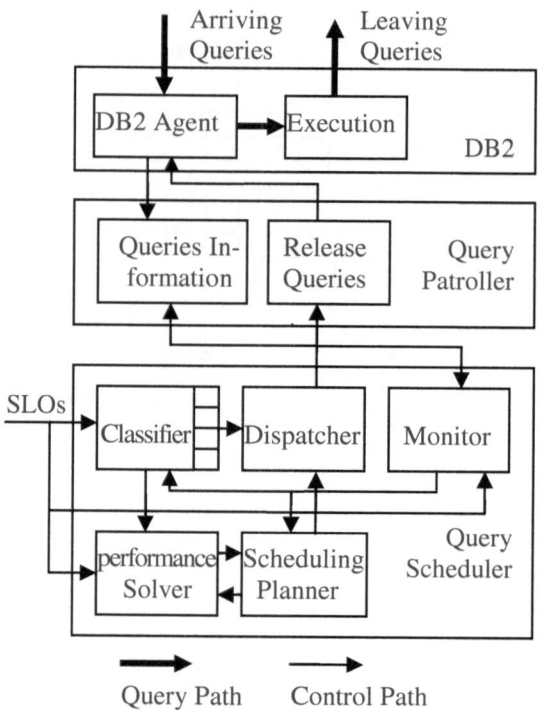

Fig. 2. Query Scheduler

Since workload control is cost-based, a scheduling plan is a set of class cost limits. Each service class is assigned a class cost limit expressed in *timerons*, which is a generic cost measure used by the DB2 UDB optimizer to express the combined resource cost to execute a query. This limit is the maximum allowable total cost of all concurrent queries belonging to a service class. The Dispatcher releases a query for execution by calling the unblocking API provided by DB2 QP, which releases the blocked agents. The Scheduling Planner consults with the Performance Solver at regular intervals to determine an optimal scheduling plan, and passes this plan to the Dispatcher.

3 Overhead of Query Scheduler

The overhead incurred by Query Scheduler includes query interception, acquisition of query information, control logic, and query release as shown in Fig. 3. DB2 provides query information to DB2 QP through TCP/IP connections at the points where a query arrives or terminates. DB2 QP maintains the TRACK_QUERY_ INFORMA-TION table [3] to store the query information. When DB2 QP writes to the table, a trigger on the table is activated and sets up a TCP socket to inform Query Scheduler a query is intercepted or terminated. In either case, Query Scheduler requests the query information through the socket. There are four times of TCP / IP communication, two writes and two reads for DB2 QP. Query Scheduler acquires query information, makes a control decision to release a query at the two points where a query is intercepted and terminated. As we can see the overhead for Query Scheduler is mainly from DB2 QP, especially the two writes and two reads when compared to the other activities.

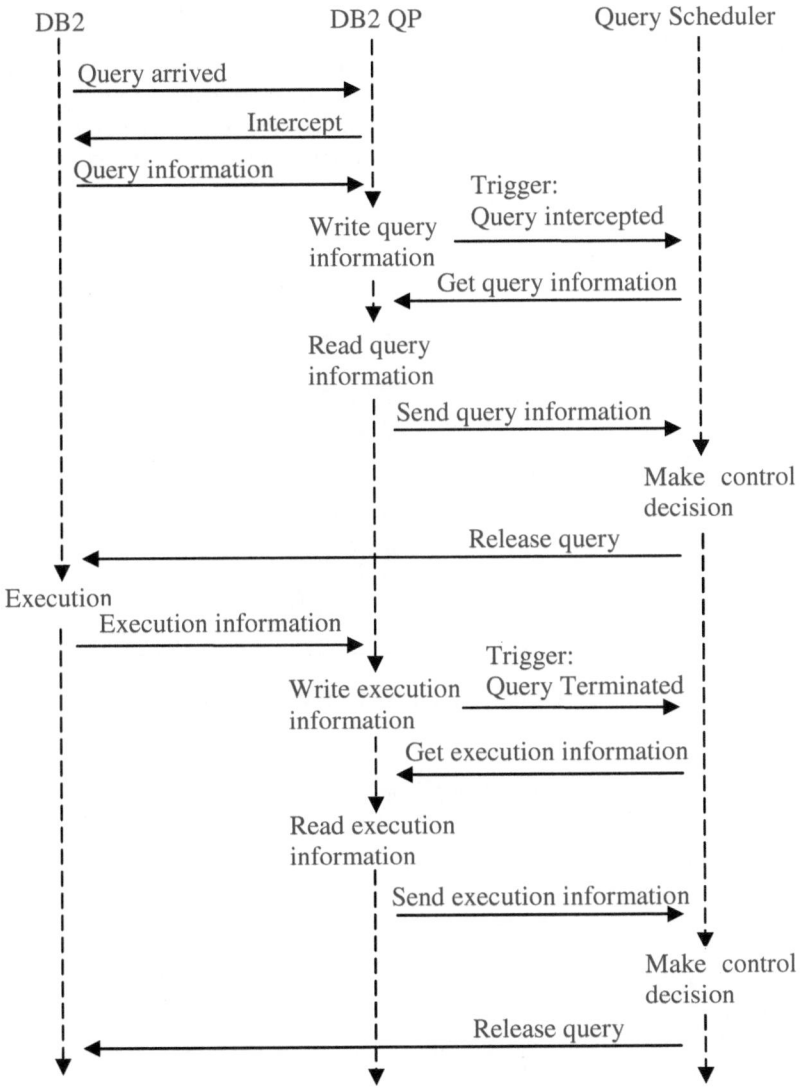

Fig. 3. Overhead of Query Scheduler

We measured the throughputs for OLAP and OLTP workloads with DB2 QP turned on and off. When DB2 QP is turned on, a predetermined total cost limit is set to keep the system from overloading. The OLAP workload is composed of 22 TPC-H [9] queries and the OLTP workload consists of 5 types of transactions from TPC-C [9] benchmark. As shown in Fig. 4, when DB2 QP is turned off, the throughput of the OLAP workload is smaller than when DB2 QP is turned on. This is because the benefit from DB2 QP protecting the system from overload is much bigger than the delay from DB2 QP. Besides, the delay is negligible compared with the long execution time of the OLAP queries.

On the other hand, as shown in Fig. 5, when DB2 QP is turned off, the throughput of the OLTP workload is much higher than when DB2 QP is turned on. This suggests that the delay from DB2 QP is significant to the OLTP queries. The delay from DB2 QP is inherent unless the Query Scheduler is implemented in the kernel of DBMSs, which would eliminate the overhead shown in Fig. 3.

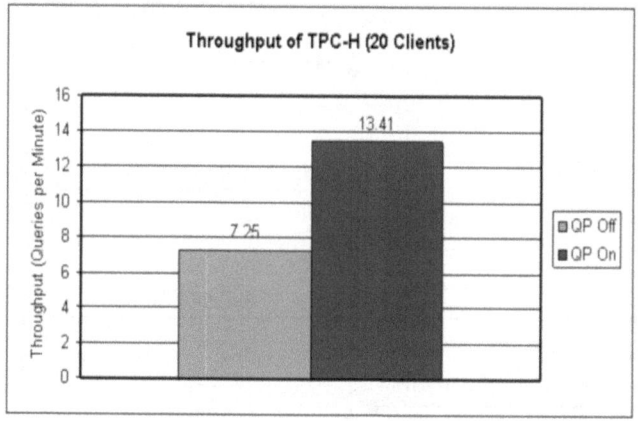

Fig. 4. The overhead of Controlling OLAP Workload with DB2 QP

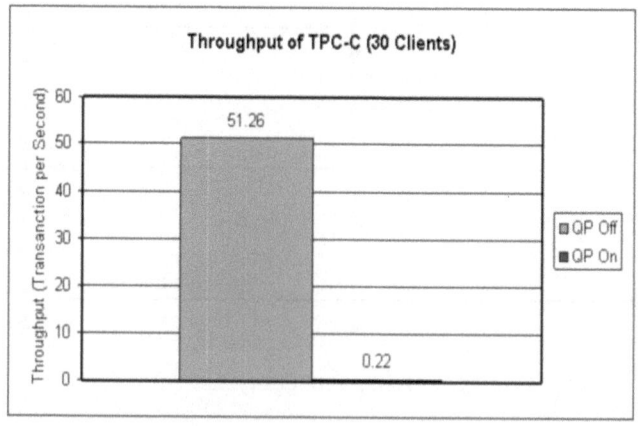

Fig. 5. The overhead of Controlling OLTP Workload with DB2 QP

4   The Scalable Approach

Given the overhead significantly outweighs the sub-second execution time of the OLTP queries, we need to find approaches, besides direct DB2 QP control, to adapt the OLTP queries. With a mixed workload, if we assume that OLTP queries are assigned the highest importance level, which is generally the case in production workloads, then we can indirectly control OLTP queries by controlling the competing OLAP classes. Query Scheduler can allocate more resources to OLTP queries by lowering the cost limit of competing OLAP class and can decrease resources allocated to OLTP queries by raising the cost limit of the competing OLAP class. To do so, we configure DB2 QP to intercept OLAP queries and bypass OLTP queries.

The rest of this section discusses the detailed implementation issues of the scalable approach for the mixed workload with Query Scheduler.

4.1   Choosing Performance Metrics

The most widely used performance metrics are response time, throughput, and execution velocity [2]. Response time and throughput are appropriate when the queries are similar in size. For workloads with widely varying response times, execution velocity, which is a measure of the time a query spends executing compared to its total time in the system, is a better choice. In this implementation, we choose the average response time for OLTP workload and query velocity for OLAP workload. Query Velocity is defined as

$$Query\_Velocity = Execution\_Time / Response\_Time . \tag{1}$$

For average response time goals, a smaller value means better performance. For query velocity goals, a larger value indicates better performance.

4.2   Performance Modeling

For the OLAP workload class, the performance model is [6]:

$$V^k = V^{k-1} C^k / C^{k-1} , \tag{2}$$

where V^{k-1} and V^k are the performance of the OLAP class at the $(k-1)^{th}$ and k^{th} control interval respectively. C^{k-1} and C^k are the class cost limit of the OLAP class at the $(k-1)^{th}$ and k^{th} control interval respectively.

For the OLTP class, we cannot simply use this model. First, the performance metric is different. The OLAP class use query velocity, while the OLTP class uses average response time. Second, the system cannot control the OLTP class directly and the total cost of OLTP queries in the system is unknown. Third, OLAP queries tend to be I/O intensive and OLTP queries are CPU intensive. The cost limit for the OLAP class is not directly usable for the OLTP class. We measured the average response time of the OLTP class relative to the cost limit of the OLAP class (Fig. 6). The number pairs in the legend are (number of OLTP clients, number of OLAP clients). The average response time of the OLTP class is almost linear increases with the increase of the cost limit of the OLAP class when the system is not overloaded (system total cost limit less than 300K timerons). Based on this knowledge, we use a linear model to model the performance of the OLTP workload.

$$t^k = t^{k-1} + s(C^k - C^{k-1}),$$ (3)

where t^{k-1} and t^k are the average response time of the OLTP class at the $(k-1)^{th}$ and k^{th} control interval respectively. C^{k-1} and C^k are the class cost limit of the OLAP class at the $(k-1)^{th}$ and k^{th} control interval respectively. s is a constant and can be obtained by using linear regression.

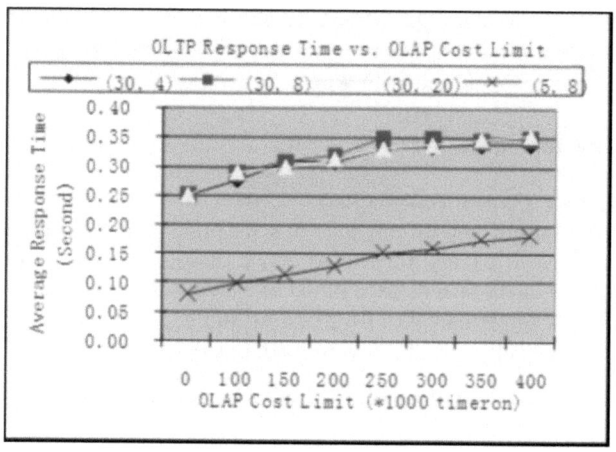

Fig. 6. OLTP performance vs. OLAP cost limit

4.3 Utility Functions

Utility functions are the key to encapsulating multiple SLOs into an objective function and play an important role in allocating resources among workload classes. There is no single ways to choose utility functions. The principles to choose utility functions are:

- The utility should be larger when the performance experienced by a service class is better than the performance goal and smaller when the performance is worse;
- The utility should increase as the performance experienced by a service class increases and decrease otherwise;
- The speed of utility increase should be getting slower with the increase of performance and the speed of utility decrease should be getting faster with the decrease of performance;
- The size and shape of the utility function should be controlled by one or two parameters that can be adjusted by the platform provider to reflect the importance of one class of traffic over another [7].

Even with these principles, choosing a set of proper utility functions is not easy. Based on our experiments we found a general form of utility functions:

$$u = 1 - e^{al\frac{\overline{g}-g}{g-g_w}},$$
(4)

where $\overline{g}$ is the performance goal of the service class to be achieved. I is the importance level of the service class. g_w is the worst performance allowed. g is the real performance. a is a constant that can be assigned by users to reflect the extent of difference between two adjacent importance levels.

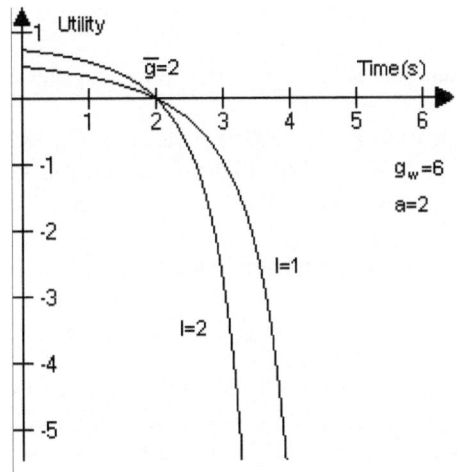

Fig. 7. Utility Function for Response Time Goals

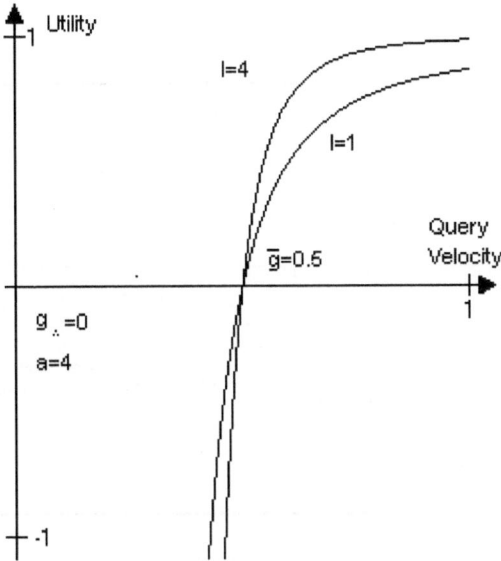

Fig. 8. Utility Function for Query Velocity Goals

The utility function not only complies with the principles and encapsulates both the performance goal and the importance level, but also has good properties (the second derivative exists) allow mathematic methods to be used to optimize the objective functions. Besides, it can be applied to both response time and execution velocity. Fig. 7 shows the utility function applied to response time goals and Fig. 8 for query velocity goals.

5 Experiments

In this section we evaluate the proposed approach to adapting mixed workload with a set of experiments.

The computer system used as the database server is an IBM xSe-ries® 240 machine with dual 1 GHZ CPUs, four PCI/ISA control-lers, and 17 Seagate ST 318436LC SCSI disks. We use IBM DB2 UDB Version 8.2 and Query Patroller as supporting components.

The system cost threshold is determined in the same way in [6].

5.1 Workload

We use the TPC-H benchmark as our OLAP workload and TPC-C benchmark as our OLTP workload. The mixed workload consists of a class of TPC-H and a class of TPC-C queries submitted by interactive clients, each class having a performance goal. Each client submits queries one after another with zero think time. The TPC-H database consists of 500MB of data. Four very large queries (queries 16, 19, 20 and 21) are excluded from the workload. The TPC-C database contains 50 warehouses. Workload intensity is controlled by the number of clients for each class (see Fig. 9). Each test ran for 12 hours and consists of 9 80-minute periods.

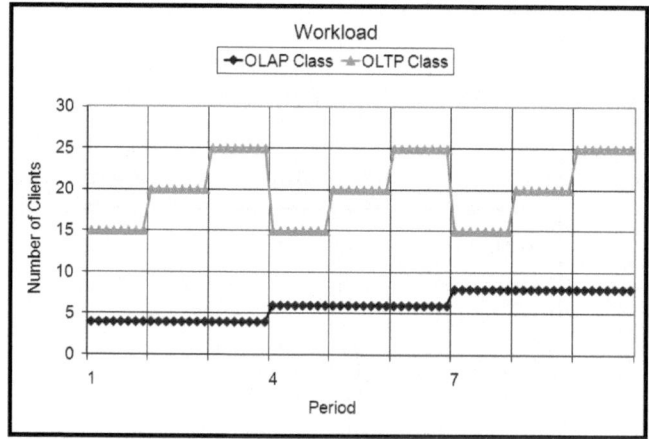

Fig. 9. Workload

The OLAP class is assigned with a lower importance level, for example 1. The OLTP class is assigned a higher importance level, for example 2. The heaviest workload is in period 9 where 8 clients from the OLAP Class and 25 clients from the OLTP class are issuing queries simultaneously.

5.2 Experimental Results

The set of experiments show the proposed approach in dealing with mixed workload relative to that of DB2 QP. The analysis of the results is discussed in Section 5.3. In all experiments, we use the workload shown in Fig. 9.

No Class Control. In this experiment, no control is exerted over the workload except for the total cost limit. This experiment serves as our baseline measure to observe how the performance changes with the changes of workload. The result is shown in Fig. 10.

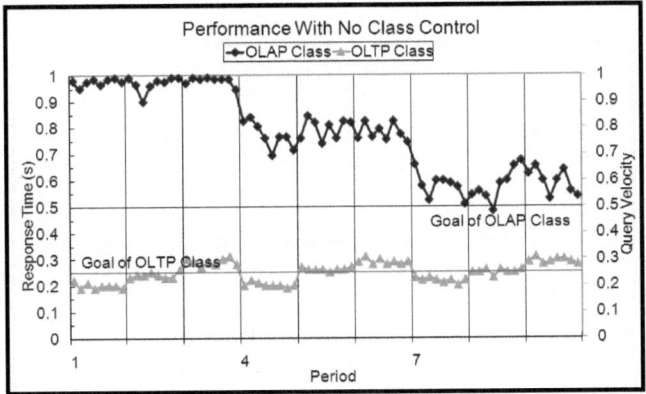

Fig. 10. Performance with No Class Control

Class Control with DB2 QP. In this experiment, we use DB2 QP as the performance controller. Because the DB2 QP imposes significant overhead on the OLTP class, there is no control over the OLTP class. Using the typical query control strategy of DB2 QP, the OLAP queries are partitioned into three groups based on the cost of the queries: large, medium and small. Queries whose cost is in the top 5% of the workload are placed in the large group; queries whose cost is in the next 15% are placed in the medium group and the remaining queries are placed in the small query group. The result is shown in Fig. 11.

Class Control with Query Scheduler. This experiment uses Query Scheduler to control performance. The performance goals for OLAP Class and OLTP Class are set as 0.5 (velocity) and 0.25 seconds (average response time) respectively. The total cost limit is 300000 timerons. Class control is performed by setting the cost limit for OLAP class, which is calculated during execution according to the performance of each workload class and predefined utility functions. In other words, the cost limit for OLAP class is calculated by optimizing the objective function. The results are shown in Fig. 12 for the performance and in Fig. 13 for the adjustment of the cost limit for both classes.

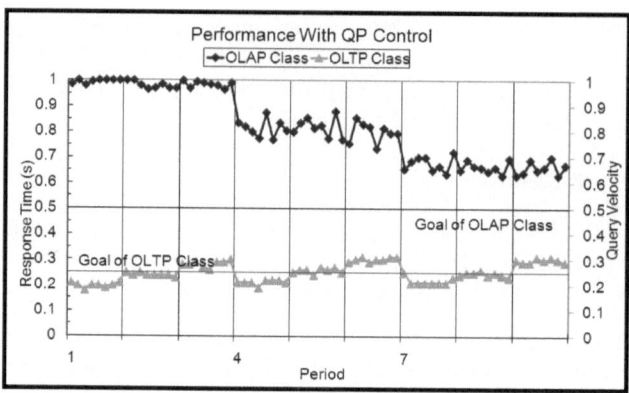

Fig. 11. Performance with DB2 QP Control

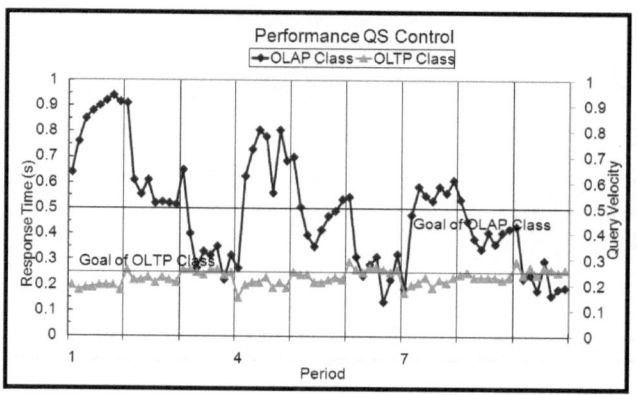

Fig. 12. Performance with Query Scheduler Control

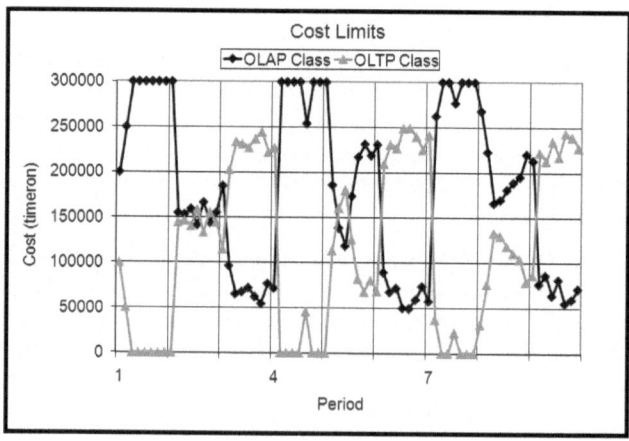

Fig. 13. Adjustment of Class Cost Limits with Query Scheduler Control

5.3 Analysis of the Experimental Results

Scalability of the New Approach. Although DB2 QP can directly control OLTP class, the heavy overhead incurred by directly controlling OLTP class makes it unscalable. Both DB2 QP and Query Scheduler can control OLTP class indirectly through directly control OLAP class. This provides a scalable approach for controlling OLTP class. DB2 QP can only set a static cost limit for OLAP class, while Query Scheduler can adjust cost limits for both classes dynamically (Fig. 13) to reflect the workload changes.

Differentiated Services. Query Scheduler with the proposed scalable approach can deliver differentiated service and DB2 QP can only provide limited differentiated service, while no-class-control can not. As shown in Fig. 12 for Query Scheduler, the OLTP class can better meet its performance goals than the OLAP class because the OLTP class is more important than the OLAP class. Since DB2 QP cannot dynamically adjust the cost limit for the OLAP class, the differentiated service that DB2 QP can provide is to set a static cost limit for the OLAP class, ignoring any fluctuations of both workload classes. For periods 3, 6 and 9 in Fig. 11, the cost limit for the OLAP class is set too high, because the important class, the OLTP class cannot meet its performance goal.

Adaptability. Query Scheduler with the proposed scalable approach can adapt to the workload changes to provide better differentiate service than DB2 QP. DB2 QP sets a static cost limit on the OLAP class to control its resource consumption and reserve resources for the OLTP class. However DB2 QP cannot adjust the limit to reflect resource requirements of the importance class - the OLTP class. As shown in Fig. 11, the performance goal of the OLTP class is always missed during the periods 3, 6 and 9 when the intensity of OLTP workload is high. Query Scheduler can detect workload changes for both classes and adjusts the cost limits for each workload class by maximizing the system utility. As shown in Fig. 12, the important class, the OLTP class, meets its performance goal almost all the time.

Dynamic Resource Allocation. From Fig. 13, we observe that Query Scheduler adjusts the class cost limits according to the workload changes. A higher class cost limit means more resources are allocated to the class. The amount of resources allocated to a class is based on its need to meet its performance goal and trade off with the other class. In the case of DB2 QP control, both classes are given a fixed amount of resources.

To conclude, the proposed approach can avoid the high overhead related to controlling the OLTP class and is effective for adapting mixed workload. It is able to respond to the workload changes using admission control to give preference to the important class.

6 Conclusions and Future Work

In this paper we briefly introduce AWMF, a general framework for workload adaptation, and its prototype implementation – Query Scheduler. We then investigate the overhead incurred by controlling workloads and propose a scalable approach for adapting mixed workload for Query Scheduler. The proposed approach indirectly controls OLTP workload by directly control OLAP workload. A general form of utility functions is proposed to reduce the pain to find the proper utility functions. Through a set of experiments we have shown that the proposed approach can avoid the high overhead related to controlling the OLTP class and is effective for adapting mixed workload.

In the future, we plan to study the possibility to implement the control mechanism inside the DBMSs, since this is the most effective way to control workload. We need to further investigate the overhead incurred by directly controlling workload and the approaches to avoid the overhead. Performance modeling for cost-based resource allocation is another issue need to be addressed. The accuracy of the performance models is the centre concern.

Acknowledgments. This research is supported by the IBM Centre for Advanced Studies (CAS), Toronto, the Natural Sciences and Engineering Re-search Council of Canada, the Centre for Communication and Information Technology, a division of Ontario Centres of Excel-lence Inc., and Shanxi Scholarship Council of China.

References

1. D.H. Brown Associate Inc.: HP Raises the Bar for UNIX Workload Management, http://whitepapers.silicon.com/ 0,39024759,60104905p-39000654q,00.htm
2. IBM Corporation: MVS Planning: Workload Management, 7th edn. (2003)
3. IBM Corporation: DB2 Query Patroller Guide: Installation, Administration, and Usage (2003)
4. Lo, T., Douglas, M.: The Evolution of Workload Management in Data Processing Industry: A Survey. In: Proceedings of 1986 Fall Joint Computer Conference, Dallas, TX, USA, pp. 768–777 (1986)
5. Menascé, D.A., Almeida, V.A.F.: Capacity Planning for Web Performance: Metrics, Models, and Methods. Prentice Hall, Upper Saddle River (1998)
6. Niu, B., Martin, P., Powley, W.: Towards Autonomic Workload Management in DBMSs. Journal of Database Management 20(3), 1–17 (2009)
7. Pacifici, G., Spreitzer, M., Tantawi, A., Youssef, A.: Performance Management for Cluster Based Web Services. IEEE Journal on Selected Areas in Communications 23(12), 2333–2343 (2005)
8. Schroeder, B., Harchol-Balter, M., Iyengar, A., Nahum, E.: Achieving Class-based QoS for Transactional Workloads. In: Proceedings of the 22nd International Conference on Data Engineering, p. 153 (2006)
9. Transaction Processing Performance Council, http://www.tpc.org

Tuning Performance of P2P Mesh Streaming System Using a Network Evolution Approach[*]

Rui Wang, Depei Qian, Danfeng Zhu, Qinglin Zhu, and Zhongzhi Luan

Beihang University,
Xueyuan Road. 37, 100191 Beijing, China
{rui.wang,depei.qian,danfeng.zhu,qinglin.zhu,
zhongzhi.luan}@jsi.buaa.edu.cn

Abstract. Resilience and startup delay are the most important performance metrics to evaluate the P2P streaming systems. To simultaneously improve the two metrics, we propose several mechanisms at different system evolution stages. At the first stage, media server encodes the stream into multiple substreams of the same length. Redundancy is introduced by using Reed-Solomon (RS) coding before distributing the sub-streams to different successors. Each peer in the network establishes a cooperative relationship with others to obtain all required sub-streams. At the stage of new peer arrival, a parent selection algorithm with relatively lower complexity is proposed which takes full advantage of redundant coding. After the peer builds up streaming transmission, it replaces some parents with a latency-based decision mechanism. In case of node failure, a swap-in-turn repairing algorithm between different sub-stream sources is proposed to ensure the high continuity of steaming transmission. Simulation results show that 1) the redundant coding and the parent replace algorithm in case of node failure can effectively reduce interruption of data streams; 2) the codes with higher redundant degree can adapt to more dynamic scenario. Meanwhile, the codes with redundancy does not significantly decrease the effective transmission ratio when network is dynamic; 3) transmission achieves higher performance when the number of substreams is between 8 and 16; and 4) the parent switching mechanism can significantly decrease the startup latency for a big proportion of peers.

Keywords: P2P, Streaming, Mesh, Redundant Coding, Churn.

1 Introduction

Streaming service on the Internet has drawn significant attentions recently for its more interesting content than texts and pictures in web pages. As the participating peers contribute their upload bandwidth capacities to serve the others, P2P streaming system can sustain much more users than that with traditional Client/Server mode under

[*] This work was supported in part by a grant from NSFC under the contract 60673180 and 90612004, and by grants from National High- Tech Program of China (863 program) under the contracts 2006AA01A106 and 2006AA01A118.

P. Mueller, J.-N. Cao, and C.-L. Wang (Eds.): Infoscale 2009, LNICST 18, pp. 135–151, 2009.
© Institute for Computer Science, Social-Informatics and Telecommunications Engineering 2009

the constraint of server's outgoing bandwidth. Among the several types of P2P streaming systems, pull-based random mesh gains dramatic success due to its simplicity and robustness[1]. Many successful commercial systems such as PPLive [2]and UUSee [3] use this mechanism.

In some systems, streaming server splits data into multiple blocks, and delivers them to the participating peers. Each peer queries missing blocks from its neighbors. This block routing introduces great overhead and uncertainty to the transmission of peers.

Instead of using data block as the routing unit, some systems like CoolStreaming[4] uses sub-stream as the routing unit. The streaming server splits data into multiple sub-streams of equal length, and distributes them to different peers. Peers build neighborhood relationship with each other to obtain the complete set of sub-streams. Once the connection is built, the packets belonging to the same sub-stream will be delivered continuously. In this pattern, each peer needs to receive data from several relay peers. When a peer is disabled, the playback in its successor will be interrupted until another parent peer is determined. In a highly dynamic network, peers suffer greatly from the unpredictable user join/quit action.

Since the peer has to receive all the sub-streams before it can playback the streaming, the startup delay is determined by the slowest one. As both the P2P network organization and the neighbor selection are random, the arrival time of different sub-streams may vary significantly, and the slower ones will slow down the playback and increase the startup time.

According to the conclusion of CoolStreaming[4], the system dynamics is the most critical factor that affects the overall performance, and the critical performance problem in a P2P streaming system is the excessive startup time. Through the measurement and analysis to some commercial P2P streaming system, [5] found that in these systems a lot of important decisions, such as how to pick a parent, seem to follow a randomized greedy algorithm.

This paper uses a network evolution approach to optimize the system performance. We propose several mechanisms at the different stages of the system evolution in order to cope with the node dynamics and to decrease the startup delay.

The rest of this paper is organized as follows: Section 2 presents a concise review of solutions for the nodes dynamics and startup delay in P2P streaming networks. Section 3 models the system. Section 4 gives the algorithms for parent selection and adjustment, and node failure handling. Our simulation methodology and results are described in Section 5. Finally, section 6 gives the conclusion of the paper.

2 Related Works

To solve the problem of transmission interruption caused by nodes departure, PRIME [6] used the ratio of bandwidth and peer degree as a metric named bandwidth-degree condition, to evaluate the system performance. Once the ratio value changes, system can immediately detect the bottleneck and relocate the bandwidth.

Feng [7] and Zimu [8] found that some stable nodes in P2P streaming networks affect the performance greatly though their amount is few. So they tried to identify the stable nodes and enable them to play more important roles in the system.

Redundant Coding such as Reed-Solomon [9] is another solution to avoid transmission interruption. Encoded to multiple sub-streams redundantly, the data could be recovered at peers which received any subset containing a certain number of sub-streams of the streaming.

Damiano[10] analyzed the mesh streaming system with a stochastic graph theory and drew the relations between delay and the number of sub-streams. It demonstrated that the transmission with multiple sub-streams is necessary to the system performance. However, it does not improve the system stability with redundancy of coding, and does not concern the influence of nodes failure on the successors.

Kumar[11] used buffer to alleviate the interruption when nodes are disabled. Through the stochastic fluid analysis to the mesh streaming system, it showed that buffer can dramatically improve the stability of the system, since peers with more buffered data will have longer time to find a substitute data source when a parent is disabled. But large buffer will significantly increase the startup delay.

Zhou [12] studied the greedy strategy and the rare first strategy used in data searching using stochastic model, and proposed a mixed strategy that can be used to achieve a good balance between the continuity and startup latency. It has similar intent with this paper, while it is in different approach, and does not make use of the redundancy of the coding.

S. Liu[13] derived the performance bounds for minimum server load, maximum streaming rate, and minimum tree depth under different peer selection constraints in P2P streaming networks. Though this work provides excellent insights, it ignores the dynamics of the network.

3 System Model and Assumption

In this system, following assumptions are taken:

Assumption 1: streaming server splits the data into S' sub-streams of the same length, and then encodes it with $RS(S, S')$ coding to S sub-streams, $S > S'$. Peers that have received any S' sub-stream can recover the data, as shown in Fig. 1.

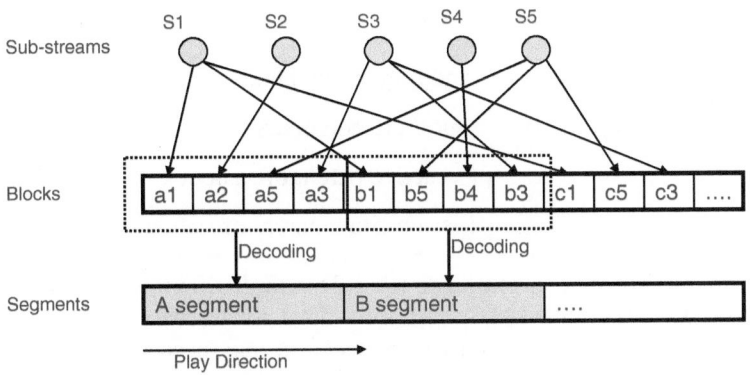

Fig. 1. Buffer filling in redundant sub-stream pattern (S'=4,S=5)

A set of existing peers will be presented to the new peer joining in the system randomly. The new peer selects a subset of this peer set as its neighbors, and requires the sub-streams from them. Once a peer gets a sub-stream, it can provide the sub-stream for other peers. Constrained by the limitation of outgoing bandwidth, it only provides sub-streams with lower latency.

Assumption 2: each node downloads a specific sub-stream from a single node, and each node downloads only a single stripe from a given parent, even if the parent could provide multiple sub-streams.

Assumption 3: each peer has B neighbors. Peer selects S neighbors as the data providers named as active parents, and selects D neighbors as substitutes which will be used in case of active parent failure.

We define the relationship of peers in the system:

Definition 1. Two peers are *neighbors* if they are connected with each other.

Definition 2. Peer i is an *active parent* of peer j about sub-stream k if peer i provides sub-stream k for peer j, and j is an offspring of peer i.

Definition 3. If peer i could provide sub-stream k for peer j but not really provide it at the moment, peer i is a *substitute parent* of peer j about sub-stream k, and j is an offspring of peer i.

In this paper, we assume that a substitute parent does not reserve bandwidth for its offspring.

We abstract the network as a graph, the vertices of the graph represent the peers, and edges connecting vertices represent the connections between peers.

We use a $n \times n$ connectivity matrix C to describe the relationship of peers in the network. The value of element c_{ij} in C represents the relationship of peer i and j. The definition of c_{ij} is as follows:

$$c_{ij} = \begin{cases} 0 & i = j \\ 0 & i \text{ and } j \text{ are not neighbors} \\ \eta & i \text{ and } j \text{ are neighbors} \\ \alpha_k & i \text{ is active parent of } j \text{ about } k \\ \beta_k & i \text{ is substitute parent of } j \text{ about } k \end{cases}$$

Note that the parent relationship is directed. Due to the limitation of outgoing bandwidth, each peer has limited offspring peers. This connectivity matrix maintains the global information, while for an arbitrary peer i, it only needs to maintain the information about the i th line, $L_i = [c_{i0}, c_{i1}, \cdots, c_{in}]$, which contains all the offspring of

i, and the i th column, $V_i = (c_{0i}, c_{1i} \cdots, c_{ni})^T$, which contains all the parents of i. In each of the vector the peer maintains, it omits the element whose value is 0, i.e., the peer does not maintain the disconnected peers. So this matrix is a distributed description structure that allows the peers to maintain its local information.

4 System Evolution

From the evolution's point of view, the state transfer of the network is driven by the change of relationship among nodes. In this section, we describe the processing of peer arrival and departure.

4.1 Peer Arrival

At any time t, the instantaneous state of network could be represented by the connectivity matrix C. When a new peer b arrives, it contacts one existing node, and initializes its neighbor list. The matrix C will be added with a new row and a new column and turns to a $(n+1)\times(n+1)$ matrix with the value of each element of the new row and new column filled with η. The peer b asks its neighbors for available sub-streams, and gets a vector $V_{i,b}$ from each neighbor containing the sub-streams that the neighbor can provide. Each vector has S elements, each of them represents a sub-stream. The value of the k th element is a_k if the k th sub-stream is available in this neighbor, else it is 0. Within the set of all the vectors $\{V_{0,b}, V_{1,b}, \cdots V_{x,b}\}$, peer b selects the source for each sub-stream. So for arbitrary sub-stream k, b selects a neighbor as its active parent if in the vector the value of k th element is α_k. Besides the active parents, the peer b also needs to select a roughly equal number of substitute parents for each sub-stream. That is, in the connectivity matrix, we need to fill in the column vector $V_b = (c_{0b}, c_{1b} \cdots, c_{nb})^T$ of peer b, ensure that the V_b at least contains all elements in the set $\{\alpha_1, \alpha_2, \cdots, \alpha_n\}$, and contains the elements in $\{\beta_1, \beta_2, \cdots, \beta_n\}$ as uniformly as possible.

The parent selection problem above could be transferred to a bipartite graph matching problem and solved by Hungarian Algorithm [14] with complexity of $O(n^3)$. With the redundancy of the coding, we do not need a complete matching. The description of parent selection algorithm is as follows:

1) Let N be the neighbor set, here we set $|N| = n$. Let S_{substr} denote the sub-stream set. The set of sub-stream set which could be provided by each neighbor is denoted by $\Gamma = \{S_0, \cdots S_n\}$;

2) Sort the neighbors decreasingly according to the numbers of sub-streams they can provide, and then get the neighbor vector N_s;

3) Search the provider for each sub-stream in N_s. When all the sub-streams get their provider, stop searching and record the position. Then we get a sub vector N' of vector N_s;

4) Sort the sub-stream identifies increasingly to form a vector of Str;

5) For each sub-stream in Str, we select the node as its parent that can provide fewer sub-streams than other node . Once the node is selected as a parent, it is deleted from the neighbor set;

6) Search more substitute parents for each sub-stream in Str that does not have average number of providers until the numbers of its providers reaches the average value, or all the neighbors are checked.

The complexity of this algorithm is $O(n^2)$ which is better than the Hungarian Algorithm. The pseudo code is shown as follows:

Algorithm 1. Parent Selection Algorithm

```
Input: neighbor set N; sub-stream set S, sub-streams of
 each neighbor {S1,S2,…Sn}.
Output: active parents set Vact, substitute set Vsub.
N=SortBySubStreams(N);
foreach n in N do // count the providers of sub-stream
  if (Marked(S) and |Ns|>=|S|) break;
    foreach s in Sn { Mark(s, S); add n to SRCs} // SRCs
     represents the set of neighbor that can provide sub-
     stream s.
    add n to Ns;
end foreach
Str= SortSubstreamBySourceNumber(S);
foreach s in Str do //select parent
  foreach n in SRCs do
     vi = the last n;
     add vi to Vact;
     delete vi from Ns;
  end foreach
end foreach
foreach s in S do // add sub parents
   if (|SRCs|<Mean{|SRC0,SRC1,…,SRCs|})
      foreach n in N do
        if ((s in Sn) and (n notin Ns))   add n to Vsub;
      end foreach
   endif
end foreach
```

Following is a simple example for the peer arrival processing. We assume that the number of sub-streams $S = 3, S' = 2$, so the possible value of α_k is in $\{\alpha_1, \alpha_2, \alpha_3\}$. There are 5 peers in the network besides the source server. The network connectivity is shown in Fig. 2(a).

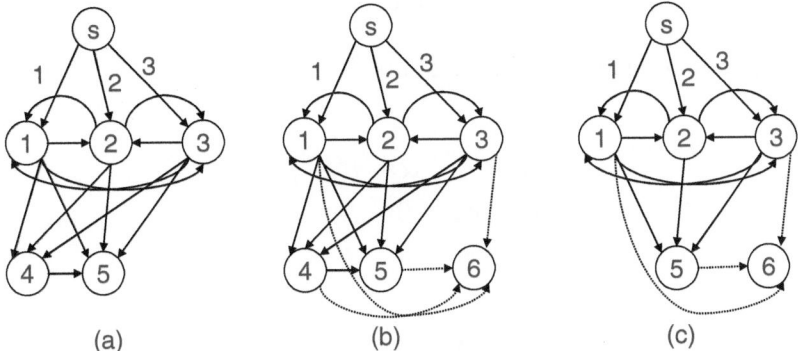

(a)   (b)   (c)

Fig. 2. Peer arrival and departure (a) Original network (b) peer 6 arrival (c) peer 4 quit

We assume that the connectivity matrix of Fig. 2 (a) is:

$$C = \begin{bmatrix} 0 & \alpha_1 & \alpha_1 & \alpha_1 & \alpha_1 \\ \alpha_2 & 0 & \alpha_2 & \alpha_2 & \beta_2 \\ \alpha_3 & \alpha_3 & 0 & \alpha_3 & \alpha_3 \\ \eta & \eta & \eta & 0 & \alpha_2 \\ \eta & \eta & \eta & \eta & 0 \end{bmatrix}$$

Note that for a given network connections, the connectivity matrix is not unique. Assuming that a new peer 6 arrives and builds the connection relationship as Fig. 2 (b), the matrix C turns to be

$$C = \begin{bmatrix} 0 & \alpha_1 & \alpha_1 & \alpha_1 & \alpha_1 & \eta \\ \alpha_2 & 0 & \alpha_2 & \alpha_2 & \beta_2 & 0 \\ \alpha_3 & \alpha_2 & 0 & \alpha_3 & \alpha_3 & \eta \\ \eta & \eta & \eta & 0 & \alpha_2 & \eta \\ \eta & \eta & \eta & \eta & 0 & \eta \\ \eta & 0 & \eta & \eta & \eta & 0 \end{bmatrix}$$

Among the matrix, the sixth row represents all the offspring of peer 6, and the sixth column represents all the parents of peer 6. Then peer 6 asks its neighbors what resource they can provide. Let's assume that peer 6 receives the following resource vectors:

$$V_{1,6} = [\alpha_1, \alpha_2, 0]$$
$$V_{3,6} = [0, \alpha_2, \alpha_3]$$
$$V_{4,6} = [0, 0, \alpha_3]$$
$$V_{5,6} = [\alpha_1, 0, 0]$$

After the selection algorithm, the matrix turns to

$$C = \begin{bmatrix} 0 & \alpha_1 & \alpha_1 & \alpha_1 & \alpha_1 & \alpha_1 \\ \alpha_2 & 0 & \alpha_2 & \alpha_2 & \beta_2 & 0 \\ \alpha_3 & \alpha_2 & 0 & \alpha_3 & \alpha_3 & \alpha_2 \\ \eta & \eta & \eta & 0 & \alpha_2 & \alpha_3 \\ \eta & \eta & \eta & \eta & 0 & \beta_1 \\ \eta & 0 & \eta & \eta & \eta & 0 \end{bmatrix}$$

We can see that there is no α_k or β_k in the last row of C. When a new peer joins in the system, the row corresponding to the contribution of the new peer will be formed this way, which means, the new peer has not contributed its bandwidth to the existing nodes in the network yet. So we apply a feedback process in the network. New peers send the sub-stream identities that it can provide to some of the originally existing peers, so that the new peers could be the substitute parents of the existing ones. Peers with not enough substitute parents will make use of the feedback periodically. The procedure is similar to the parent selection illustrated above. The following matrix is a possible result of the feedback action.

$$C = \begin{bmatrix} 0 & \alpha_1 & \alpha_1 & \alpha_1 & \alpha_1 & \alpha_1 \\ \alpha_2 & 0 & \alpha_2 & \alpha_2 & \beta_2 & 0 \\ \alpha_3 & \alpha_2 & 0 & \alpha_3 & \alpha_3 & \alpha_2 \\ \beta_2 & \eta & \beta_2 & 0 & \alpha_2 & \alpha_3 \\ \beta_3 & \beta_1 & \eta & \eta & 0 & \beta_1 \\ \eta & 0 & \eta & \beta_2 & \beta_3 & 0 \end{bmatrix}$$

4.2 Parent Adjustment

A peer needs to receive at least S' sub-streams of one streaming segment before the segment can be decoded and played. So the playback delay of each segment depends on the S'th received sub-stream. Due to the random neighbor assignment, peers select the parents without considering the delays of the corresponding sub-streams. The delays of sub-streams in one segment will be out-of-order. In this way, the last (S'th) required sub-stream is very likely the transmission bottleneck. In order to decrease the startup delay, we propose a parent adjustment mechanism to replace the parent of the bottleneck sub-stream. Our approach is focused on checking closeness of the arrival time of each sub-stream which belongs to the same segment.

Let $d_j(i)$ denote the delay of data block belonging to sub-stream j in segment i. We give the definition of the delay of sub-stream in a segment as follows:

Definition 4. Within each segment, the delay of the first arrived data block is 0; the delays of following blocks are represented in the difference of arrival time; the delay of a sub-stream equals to the delay of corresponding data blocks in each segment.

Then we get the delay vector of arbitrary segment i as follows:

$$L(i) = \{d_0(i), \cdots, d_{S'}(i)\}^T$$

According to the definition 4, we compute the variance $D(d)$ of delays of sub-streams in each segment. With the value of $D(d)$, we can judge that whether or not the sub-streams in each segment have similar delays. We introduce a variance threshold δ which could be used as the criterion to determine whether or not a peer needs to adjust its parents. The decision is made following the rules below:

1) When $D(d) > \delta$, the peer needs to adjust some of the sub-streams. Let s' denote the identity of the S'th arrival sub-stream, let $\overline{d}$ represent the mean delay of the first S' sub-streams of all, and let $\Delta\overline{d}_i$ denote the difference between the delay of each sub-stream and the mean delay $\overline{d}$.

2) If the peer only has S' active parents, calculate the mean value of this difference $E(\Delta\overline{d}_i)$. If $\Delta\overline{d}_{s'} > E(\Delta\overline{d}_i)$, it implies that the sub-stream s' becomes the bottleneck of this peer, so we replace the parent providing s' with an randomly selected neighbor.

3) If the peer has more than S' active parents, not only the parent for sub-stream s' needs to be replaced as mentioned in 2), but also the parents whose sub-stream slower than s' need to be replaced.

4.3 Peer Failure

When a peer d quits, the connections related with it are canceled. So in the connectivity matrix, the d th column and d th row is filled with 0. If peer d is the substitute parent of another peer, that peer does not need to react immediately. The node needs to add a new substitute parent in the next feedback process. If peer d is the active parent of some node, that peer needs to find a new active parent from the substitute parent nodes as soon as possible.

Normally, the system search only the backup peers for the missing sub-stream, the backup peers probably fails to recover the transmission. If the peer does not have any available backup parents or the backup parent does not provide the required sub-stream in time, the peer will encounter data missing, and the successors of this peer will also suffer the same problem consequently.

When the backup parent can not provide the required resource directly, we propose to search the available resource in the current active parents, and find an adaptable match in all the available neighbors with a swap-in-turn pattern. The algorithm is shown as follows:

Algorithm 2. Peer Failure Handling Algorithm

```
input: active parents collection Vi, the failed stripe
  id :x; substitute parents collection: Sub.
output: final SubStream collection Vi.
foreach p in Sub do
    subnode= find_Substream(ak, x, p);
    if subnode not null
        add subnode to Vi; return;
    endif
end foreach
foreach ni in Vi do
    add ni to V;
end foreach
Vi=Algorithm1(V);
```

Using the example in Fig. 2, we assume the node 4 fails, and then the connection is as Fig. 2 (c). According to the set of resource vector $\{V_{1,6}, V_{3,6}, V_{4,6}V_{5,6}\}$, peer 6 adjusts the data source for the missing sub-stream. The changing of the sixth column of matrix C is shown in Fig. 3.

$$
\begin{bmatrix} \alpha_1 \\ 0 \\ \alpha_2 \\ \alpha_3 \\ \beta_1 \\ 0 \end{bmatrix} \rightarrow \begin{bmatrix} \alpha_2 \\ 0 \\ \alpha_3 \\ 0 \\ \alpha_1 \\ 0 \end{bmatrix}
$$

Fig. 3. Parents swap-in-turns

In the sixth column, peer 6 loses the source of sub-stream 3, and none of its substitute parents could provide sub-stream 3 at this moment. But peer 3, original source of sub-stream 2, could provide sub-stream 3 also. So we set peer 3 as the source of sub-stream 3, peer 1 as the source of sub-stream 2, and change the state of peer 5 as the active parent for sub-stream 1. This switch mechanism can avoid the situation that the substitute parents can not provide some sub-streams. Then the matrix C becomes

$$C = \begin{bmatrix} 0 & \alpha_1 & \alpha_1 & 0 & \alpha_1 & \alpha_2 \\ \alpha_2 & 0 & \alpha_2 & 0 & \alpha_2 & 0 \\ \alpha_3 & \alpha_2 & 0 & 0 & \alpha_3 & \alpha_3 \\ 0 & 0 & 0 & 0 & 0 & 0 \\ \beta_3 & \beta_1 & \eta & 0 & 0 & \alpha_1 \\ \eta & 0 & \eta & 0 & \beta_3 & 0 \end{bmatrix}$$

Beside peer 6, peer 5 also changes peer 2 to the active parent for sub-stream 2 due to the quit of peer 4.

5 Simulation

In order to evaluate the parent selection and adjusting algorithm, and the peer failure handling algorithm, we developed a simulation with Peersim[15] simulator.

5.1 Methodology and Metrics

We initialize the topology in which nodes degree follows power-law. At the beginning, we insert 1000 overlay nodes to the network, and set the link latency using DS^2 [16] of Rice University. Nodes join in and leave the system randomly. The interval of both action subjects to a Poison process with mean of λ. So both the node arrival and departure actions have an average rate of $\frac{1}{\lambda}$. We can get different average rate by varying the value of λ.

The streaming bit rate is set to 400kbps according to the setup in CoolStreaming4, which must be satisfied at all peers during their streaming playback. Each segment has 50KB data, represents 1 second of playback, and is divided into 400 blocks. The data in each segment is redundantly encoded. For example, $RS(9,8)$ coding splits the data into 8 sub-streams, and encodes them into 9 sub-streams, each with a bit rate of 50kbps.

We define the parameters and performance metrics used in the simulation as follows: (1) Churn rate: the ratio of the number of node joining in or left to the average number of nodes in the system. Bigger churn rate means nodes change more frequently. For instance, in a system with churn rate of 2, the value of λ is 0.05, the average rates of both nodes arrival and nodes leaving are 20 per second. So in 100 seconds, the number of nodes leave the system is about 2000, which is about twice of average number of nodes in system. (2) Transmission interruption: we check every offspring node of the peer when it leaves the system. For each offspring that fails to find the substitution for the missing sub-stream in the current neighbors, we count a transmission interruption. (3) Steady degree: the ratio of the number of peers with no transmission interruption to the number of all its brothers when their active parent failed. (4) Effective transmission ratio: the ratio of the total amount of received and decoded data by all peers to the total amount of data transmitted in the network.

5.2 System Resilience

First we evaluate the resilience of this system. To compare with non-redundant coding, we use $RS(12,8)$ redundant coding. By varying the churn rate, we get the result shown in Fig. 4.

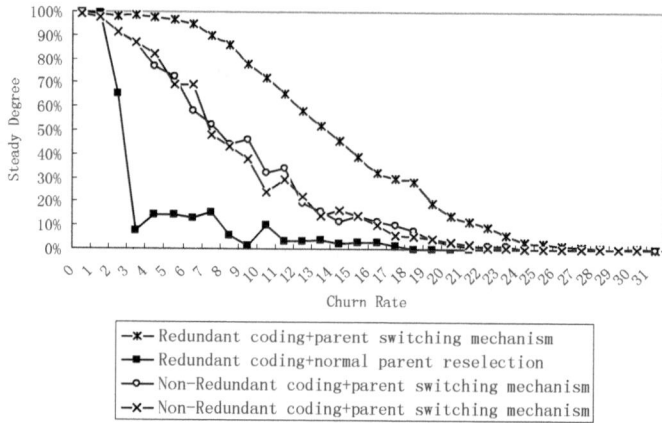

Fig. 4. The effect of redundant coding and parent swap-in-turns algorithm

We can see that both the redundant coding and parent switch algorithm is effective in improving the system resilience. The combinational use of these two mechanisms can ensure high quality for more than 80% users when churn rate is below 10.

In order to observe the sensitivity of the transmission quality to the number of sub-streams (value of S'), we varied the value of S' from 4 to 16, set the neighbor number $N = 30$, and get the result of continuity, startup latency, average hops and bandwidth usage shown in Fig. 5(a) (b) (c) (d), respectively. Here we use a non-redundant coding, that is, $S = S'$. We can see that when the number of sub-streams is between 8-16, the performance is acceptable.

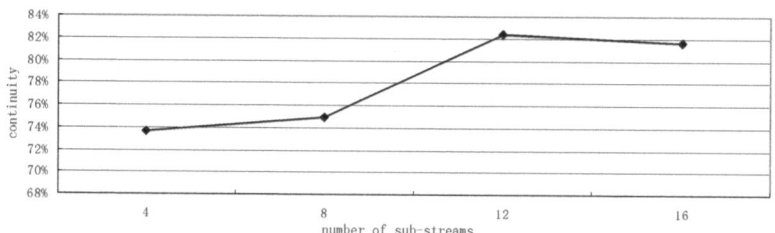

Fig. 5. (a) Continuity on different number of sub-streams

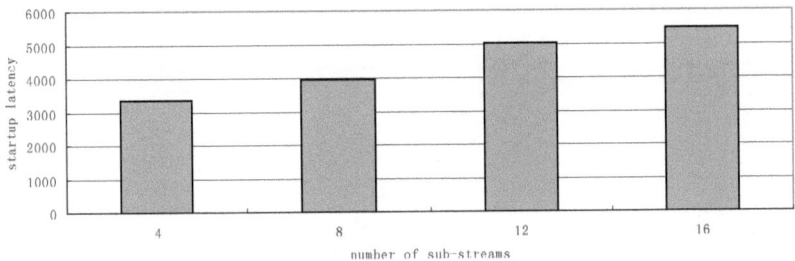

Fig. 5. (b) Startup latency on different number of sub-streams

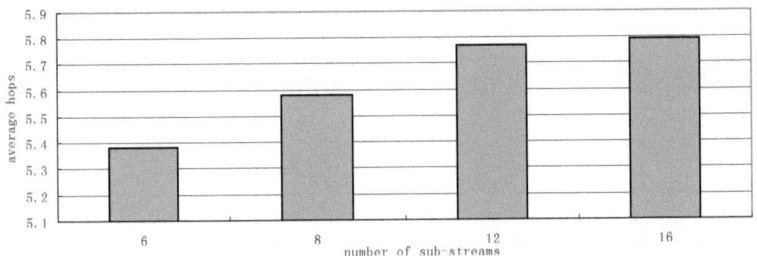

Fig. 5. (c) Average hops on different number of sub-streams

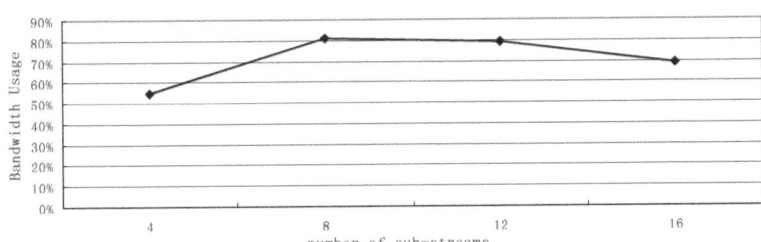

Fig. 5. (d) Bandwidth usages on different number of sub-streams

We then observe the sensitivity of transmission quality to coding redundancy by varying the churn rate and redundancy degree. The result is shown in Fig. 6. As the redundancy increase, the transmission quality becomes better.

Though redundancy improves the transmission quality, we have to answer the following question: Does redundancy cause inefficient transmission? We compared the transmission efficiency of the redundant and non-redundant coding and the result is shown in Fig. 7. When the churn rate is relatively lower, the coding schemes with higher redundancy achieve lower transmission efficiency. While when the churn rate becomes higher (beyond 8), the transmission efficiency of redundant coding is not significantly lower than that of non-redundant coding.

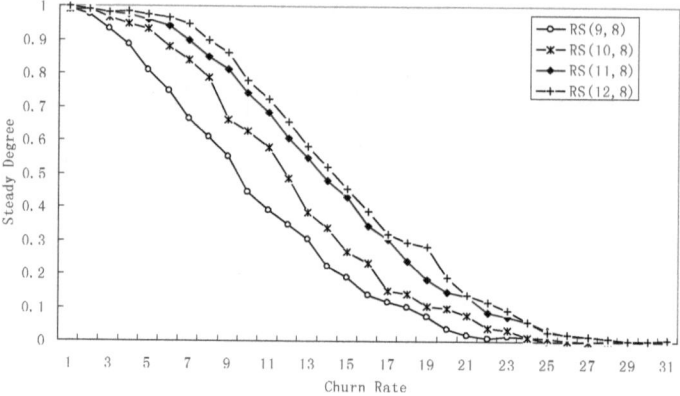

Fig. 6. Comparison of different redundancy of coding on resilience

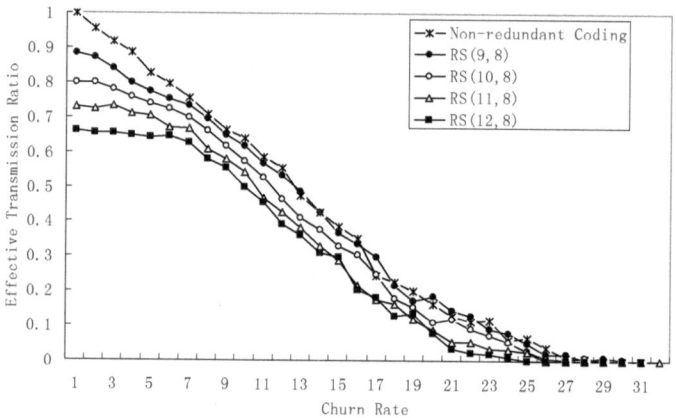

Fig. 7. Comparison of different redundancy of coding on effective transmission ratio

5.3 Startup Latency

In this section, we observe the efficiency of parent switching algorithm. We set $S' = 8$, and get the result shown in Fig. 8 by varying the delay variance threshold.

The best result by adjustment is achieved when the variance threshold is set to a medium value, like 5000ms-9000ms. Most peers that need a adjustment can achieve an improvement in delay performance and the whole network delay is reduced by 30%. When the threshold is beyond 9000ms, some peers that do need an adjustment will be missed.

We set $S' = 16$ and repeat the experiment. The result is shown in Fig. 9. Besides the conclusion drawn when $S' = 8$, we can further conclude that when the number of sub-streams becomes larger, the number of peers that need adjustment decreases, and the appropriate range of variance threshold become narrower. So in this situation, we

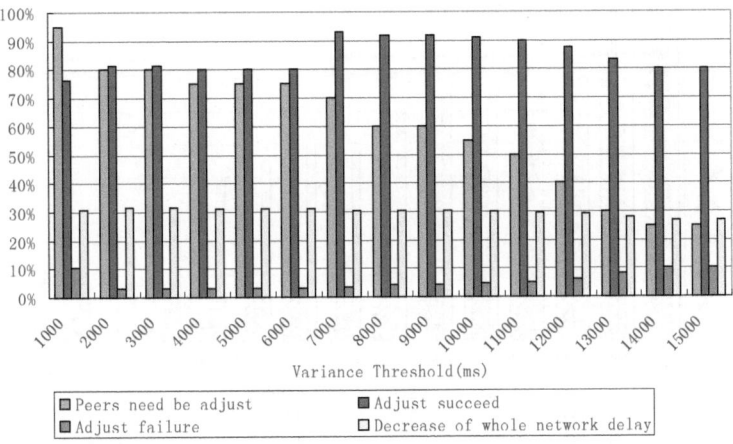

Fig. 8. Adjust effect (S'=8)

should be more cautious in determining the threshold so as to achieve the best result. For example, when the threshold is 5000ms, only 24% of peers need to be adjusted, and we can achieve almost 100% success rate. Note that the link latency parameter used in simulation is the practically measured value from the Internet, so the setup of variance threshold is meaningful in the practical systems.

Fig. 9. Adjust effect (S'=16)

In order to find how many peers still need to be adjusted after the first adjustment, we compare the result between $S'=8$ and $S'=16$ in Fig. 10 and can see that the system with more sub-streams could be adjusted more quickly.

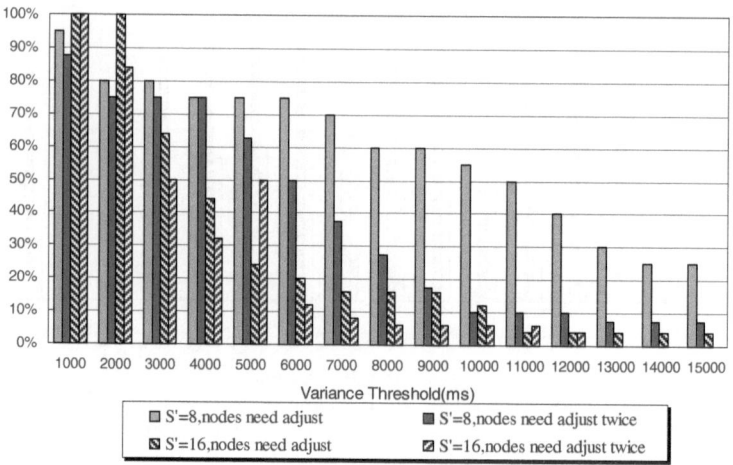

Fig. 10. Comparison of situation after the first adjust between S'=8 and S'=16

6 Conclusion

In this paper, we propose several mechanisms to improve the performance of P2P streaming systems at the different network evolution stages. Our purpose is to alleviate the influence of network dynamics to the system stability, and to decrease the peer startup delay. Simulation results show that 1) the redundant coding and the parent switching algorithm in case of node failure can effectively reduce interruption of data streams; 2) the codes with higher redundant degree can adapt to more dynamic scenario and the codes with redundancy does not significantly decrease the effective transmission ratio when network is dynamic; 3) transmission achieves higher performance when the number of substreams is between 8 and 16; and 4) the parent switching mechanism can significantly decrease the startup latency for a big proportion of peers.

References

1. Magharei, N., Rejaie, R., Guo, Y.: Mesh or Multiple-Tree: A Comparative Study of Live P2P Streaming Approaches. In: Proc. of IEEE INFOCOM (2007)
2. PPLive, http://www.pplive.com/
3. UUSee, http://www.uusee.com/
4. Li, B., Xie, S., Qu, Y., et al.: Inside the New CoolStreaming: Principles, Measurements and Performance Implications. In: Proc. of IEEE INFOCOM (2008)
5. Ali, S., Mathur, A., Zhang, H.: Measurement of commercial peer-to-peer live video streaming. In: Proc. Workshop on Recent Advances in P2P Streaming, Waterloo, ON, Canada (August 2006)
6. Magharei, N., Rejaie, R.: PRIME: Peer-to-Peer Receiver-drIven MEsh-based Streaming. In: Proc. of IEEE INFOCOM 2007 (2007)

7. Wang, F., Liu, J., Xiong, Y.: Stable Peers: Existence, Importance, and Application in Peer-to-Peer Live Video Streaming. In: Proc. of IEEE INFOCOM 2008 (2008)
8. Liu, Z., Wu, C., Li, B., Zhao, S.: Distilling Superior Peers in Large-Scale P2P Streaming Systems. To appear in Proc. of IEEE INFOCOM 2009 (2009)
9. Koetter, R., Vardy, A.: Algebraic soft-decision decoding of Reed-Solomon codes. IEEE Transactions on Information Theory 49(11) (2003)
10. Carra, D., Cigno, R., Biersack, E.: Graph based analysis of mesh overlay streaming systems. IEEE Journal on Selected Areas in Communications 25(9), 1667–1677 (2007)
11. Kumar, R., Liu, Y., Ross, K.: Stochastic Fluid Theory for P2P Streaming Systems. In: Proc. of IEEE INFOCOM 2007 (2007)
12. Zhou, Y., Chiu, D., Lui, J.C.S.: A Simple Model for Analyzing P2P Streaming Protocols. In: Proc. of IEEE ICNP 2007 (2007)
13. Liu, S., Zhang, R., Jiang, W., Rexford, J., Chiang, M.: Performance bounds for peer-assisted live streaming. In: Proceedings of the 2008 ACM SIGMETRICS (2008)
14. Edmonds, J., Karp, R.: Theoretical improvements in algorithmic efficiency for network flow problems. Journal of ACM 19(2), 248–264 (1972)
15. PeerSim, http://peersim.sourceforge.net/
16. DS2, http://www.cs.rice.edu/~bozhang/ds2/

HVS-Based Imperceptibility Evaluation for Steganography

Ma Xiu-ying and Lin Jia-jun

East China University of Science and Technology
Shanghai 200237, China
maxiuyingyuyu@163.com

Abstract. The aim of steganography is to conceal the very existence of hidden communication, so imperceptibility is the primary demand. However there are short of corresponding evaluation methods. Most researchers still use Peak-Signal-to-Noise Ratio (PSNR) for their imperceptibility evaluation, while ignoring the speciality of steganography. In this paper, firstly, we present an objective method of imperceptibility evaluation for gray image, which is based on both characteristics of steganography and human visual systems (HVS).Then, based on the color masking, metric CHPSNR for color image is proposed. CHPSNR relates embedding capacity to steganography, and can reflect the localized distortion of stego images. Extensive experimental results demonstrate that our method is superior to global PSNR, which is consistent with HVS and can effectively evaluate the performance of steganographic algorithm.

Keywords: steganography, HVS, evaluation, imperceptibility, Peak Signal to Noise Ratio.

1 Introduction

Information hiding has become the forefront of information security. As an intersecting subject, it includes mathematics, cryptography, information theory, computer vision and other computer application techniques. Information hiding has become the hot topic for researchers in the world [1-4]. There are many studies on steganography and steganalysis in published literatures. However, there are short of corresponding evaluation methods, which will hinder the development of information hiding [5, 6]. Therefore, it is urgent to establish a benchmark for information hiding.

Establishing a benchmark is to be considered based on performance indices including security, capacity, robustness and perception, etc. These indices are usually conflictive, but imperceptibility is the basic requirement. There are two methods to measure imperceptibility of steganography: (1) subjective evaluation: in designed experiments, some observers are chosen to rate the images by specified rules; (2) objective evaluation: some algorithms are used to evaluate the image degrades. Subjective evaluation is the same as the result judged by human vision, but it is time-consuming and complicated. Furthermore, it is influenced by some subjective factors such as observer's professional background, psychology and motivation. Objective evaluation

P. Mueller, J.-N. Cao, and C.-L. Wang (Eds.): Infoscale 2009, LNICST 18, pp. 152–161, 2009.
© Institute for Computer Science, Social-Informatics and Telecommunications Engineering 2009

has the advantage of convenience and quickness. It is easy to be realized in application systems, but inconsistent with HVS.

PSNR has been widely used as the important and even unique objective evaluation metric by many researchers up until now. But PSNR is unsuitable for evaluation because the nature of information hiding is not merely the relationship between signal and noise. To achieve the result perfectly matches with the quality perceived by human observers, HVS based objective evaluation has become the research emphasis.

In the next section, we introduce the HVS-based imperceptibility evaluation method. Section 3 describes a HVS-based evaluation method for gray image, on the basis of which a new evaluation metric CHPSNR for color stego image is proposed in section 4. Experimental results and conclusions are given in Section 5 and 6 respectively.

2   HVS-Based Imperceptibility Evaluation

HVS-based algorithms simulate some low-level characteristics of HVS, which map the absolute errors between cover images and stego images into JNDs(Just noticeable difference) that can be perceived by human vision. When errors are higher than sensitive threshold, they can be perceived, else be ignored. Through above processing, evaluation results consistent with observer's subjective perception can be achieved.

Details of HVS-based algorithm are as follows: (1) blocking: the image is divided into many regular blocks for the convenience of calculation;(2) the execution of decomposition: image blocks are decomposed by different spatial frequency and orientation, while every composition of spatial frequency and orientation called a channel; (3) comparison: compare cover images with stego images to acquire error images; (4) mask: apply temporal-spatial filter to every channel to simulate low-level characteristics of HVS, calculate errors on the background of reference images; (5) the execution of modeling: calculate and model the average errors of the whole images, relate them to mean opinion score (MOS) of image quality ,then estimate parameters of model on the testing sets[7,8]. This method simulates all the characteristics of HVS comprehensively, which can ensure the coherence of subjective evaluation and objective evaluation.

3   HPSNR Based on HVS for Gray Image

Human eyes process image with encoding the features extracted from spatial, frequency and color, not point-by-point. Human's Visual Perception Characteristics do not match with Statistical distribution of information. HVS sensitivity function in HVS model can be represented as:

$$H^{'}(\omega) = (a + b\omega)\exp(-c\omega) .$$ (1)

where the radial frequency ω is in cycles per degree of visual angle subtended, a, b and c are constants that decide the shape of HVS. When $H^{'}(\omega)$ arrives its peak around 3 cycles/degree, the shape of HVS is represented as

$$H(\omega) = (0.2 + 0.45\omega)\exp(-0.18\omega) \ . \tag{2}$$

When applied DCT transform in image coding system, the original image is symmetrical extended. However, we can't observe this scene that doesn't exist at all. So the following correction function is employed [9]:

$$|A(\omega)| = \left\{ \frac{1}{4} + \frac{1}{\pi^2}\left[\log_e\left(\frac{2\pi\omega}{\alpha} + \sqrt{\frac{4\pi^2\omega^2}{\alpha^2} + 1}\right)\right]^2 \right\}^{\frac{1}{2}} \ . \tag{3}$$

where $\alpha = 11.636/\text{degree}$, hence, HVS sensitivity function can be calculated as:

$$H(\omega) = H'(\omega)|A(\omega)| = \begin{cases} 0.05\exp(\omega^{0.554}) & \omega < 7 \\ \exp[-9(|\lo \ g_{10}\ \omega - \lo \ g_{10}\ 9|^{2.3})] & \omega \geq 7 \end{cases} \ . \tag{4}$$

To convert from the two-dimensional (2-D) DCT variables i and j to ω, the following conversion formula is employed:

$$\omega(cycle\ /\deg ree) = \omega_d\ (cycle\ /\ pixel)*\omega_s\ (pixel\ /\deg ree)\ . \tag{5}$$

where $\omega_d = \dfrac{1}{2N}\sqrt{i^2 + j^2}$, $i, j = 0,1,\ldots\ldots,N-1$, ω_s is the sampling density dependent upon the viewing distance, N is the DCT block size and is chosen to be eight. For a GIF image with a height of 288 pixels and viewed at a distance of four times the image height, ω_s is 20 pixels/degree. In our simulation, we chose ω_s to be the nearest number divisible by2N. i.e., $\omega_s = 32$.

Using HVS sensitivity function as weighted values, HPSNR is calculated as:

$$HPSNR = 10\log_{10}\frac{\max(x)^2}{\|H(\omega)(I'-I)\|^2} \ . \tag{6}$$

It is obvious that the bigger the HPSNR is, the better the quality of the image is.

For the convenience of comparing, we give the global PSNR for gray image:

$$PSNR = 10\log_{10}\left(\frac{\max(x)^2}{EMS}\right) \ . \tag{7}$$

where EMS is the mean square error of image under test.

An experiment is shown in figure 1.For a standard Lena image, we concentrate the noise on one of the copy, while on another copy we add gaussian noise evenly. Here we can distinguish the differences easily, however, they have the same PSNR. Obviously, PSNR is unsuitable for evaluating information hiding performance, but HPSNR matches with human vision perfectly.

(a) concentrated noise   (b) scattered gaussian noise

PSNR=36.01db   PSNR=36.01db

HPSNR=79.84db   HPSNR=80.88db

Fig. 1. HPSNR for images with the same PSNR

In another experiment, we use several typical steganography tools to hide different secret message into 1000 gray images which are select from USC-SIPI Image Database and digital camera. Table1 summarizes HPSNR results with some popular steganography tools.

Table 1. HPSNR for different steganography tools with various embedding capacity

Capacity	S3en	HIP	Ezstego	Stash It	Stools
2%	70.7921	68.9815	30.1018	29.9757	25.8865
5%	62.6225	60.3354	29.3230	29.2640	25.1502
10%	58.8701	56.9818	27.9846	28.2044	24.6170
20%	55.5026	53.9685	27.5806	27.1713	24.2023
30%	55.0575	53.2391	-----	-----	23.5823
40%	53.8178	51.1605	-----	-----	23.1587

From the table 1, we can find that S3en and Hide in Picture have the best imperceptibility, while Ezstego and Stash It are better than Stools, which matches with our direct observation. For S3en and Hide in Picture, modification for original image by LSB is least, therefore, they have the best imperceptibility; Stools is worse than Ezstego and Stash It which modify index value, because Stools reduces the color in color palette. We can draw the conclusion that HPSNR can be use to evaluate imperceptivity of gray image.

4   CHPSNR Based on HVS for Color Image

A color digital image is often represented by the color components(R, G, B). Due to three visual cells each of which is most sensitive to red light, green light and blue light, human have different color sensitivity. When external chromatic light stimulates our eyes, the mixture of different responses to these three cells forms color sensory. Human eyes' sensitivity to color is more complicated than luminance.

There are other color models such as YIQ model besides RGB model. The luminance component Y in YIQ model reflects comprehensive energy of color components (R,G,B),which is monochromatic restoration of the full color image .The luminance component Y cam be calculated as

$$Y = 0.299R + 0.587G + 0.114B .$$ (8)

where every coefficient reflects the sensitivity to each color. Experiments show that when we choose weighted ratio as R: G: B=2:1:4, it is the most beneficial to image quality [10]. We can see from the ratio that when we use luminance which is mixed by color components (R,G,B)as 1 unit, contribution ratio of the red light ,green light and blue light are2/7, 1/7 and 4/7 respectively .Using these ratios, we define CHPSNR as follows:

$$CHPSNR = 10\log_{10} \frac{3*m*n*\{\max(x)\}^2}{\sum_{k}\sum_{i,j} [\| h_{ijk} *(\frac{2}{7}e_{ijkr}) \|^2 + \| h_{ijk} *(\frac{1}{7}e_{ijkg}) \|^2 + \| h_{ijk} *(\frac{4}{7}e_{ijkb}) \|^2]} .$$ (9)

where e_{ijkr} , e_{ijkg} and e_{ijkb} are error images of R, G and B level respectively.

5 Experiment Results

Here, we introduce the peak signal to noise ratio for color image [11]:

$$CPSNR = 10\log_{10} \frac{\max(x)^2}{(EMSr + EMSg + EMSb)/3} .$$ (10)

where EMSr, EMSg and EMSb are mean square error for R, G and B respectively.

5.1 Effect of Color on Stego Image's Quality

Now, we'll give two examples to show the effect of color on stego image's quality.

Example 1: Hiding the same gray image into R, G and B level of Lena as shown in figure2 (a) respectively using LSB algorithm based on spatial domain, through which we acquire three stego images as shown in figure2 (b), figure2(c) and figure2 (d).

Example 2: Hiding the same secret messages into R, G and B level of Pepper as shown in figure3 (a) respectively using LSB algorithm based on spatial domain, through which we acquire three stego images as shown in figure3 (b), figure3(c) and figure3 (d).

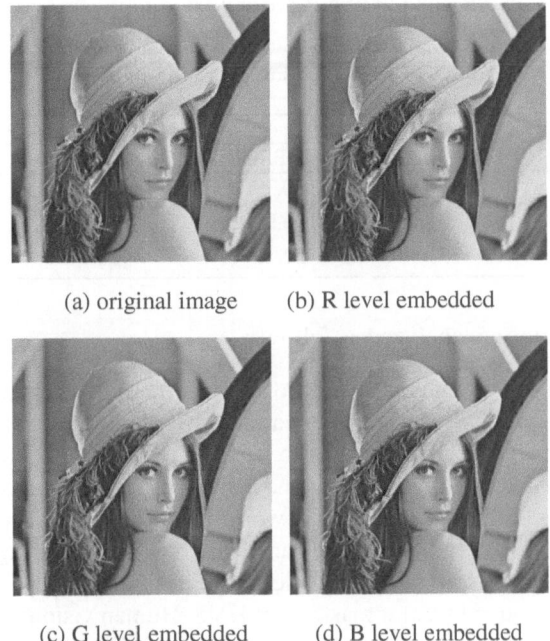

(a) original image   (b) R level embedded

(c) G level embedded   (d) B level embedded

Fig. 2. Images hidden secret image at different level of Lena

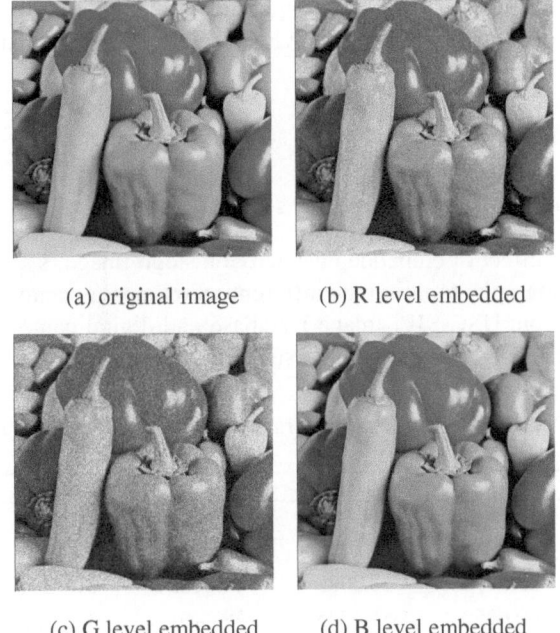

(a) original image   (b) R level embedded

(c) G level embedded   (d) B level embedded

Fig. 3. Images hidden same secret messages at different level of Pepper

The calculated CPSNR and CHPSNR are shown in table 2.

Table 2. CPSNR, CHPSNR for different level

Color	Lena		Pepper	
	CPSNR	CHPSNR	CPSNR	CHPSNR
R	69.5320	110.7907	24.0093	46.1320
G	69.5067	106.9205	24.5865	36.4797
B	69.5331	122.4596	24.6103	49.1335

Experiment results are analyzed as follows:

(1) Results judged by human eyes. Comparing three stego images with original image in figure2, we can see after careful observation that some area on the top of the cap in stego images seems to be reddening, greening and bluing respectively. The image in figure2(d) is most close to the original one, which has the best quality; image in figure2(b) is worse than it; while image in figure2(c) has the worse quality. In figure3, we can clearly see that the image in figure3(d) is most close to the original one, while image in figure3(c) has the worse quality. These are decided by color masking of HVS. Human vision's sensitivity to blue is lowest, while sensitivity to green is highest. Therefore, when message is hidden in blue level, the stego image has the best quality.

(2) Results calculated by global CPSNR. As can be seen from table2, three CPSNRs of Lena and three CPSNRs of Pepper are very similar, which means that the three images have almost the same visual quality. Obviously, this result does not match with the truth.

(3) Results calculated by CHPSNR. Seen from table2, results evaluated by CHPSNR match with human eyes' subjective judgment.

5.2 Effect of Capacity on Stego Image' s Quality

In order to see the effect of embedded capacity on stego image' s quality, we use several typical steganography tools to hide different secret message into 1000 color images which are select from USC-SIPI Image Database and digital camera. Table3 summarizes CHPSNR results with some popular steganography tools.

Table 3. CHPSNR for different steganography tools with varies embedding capacity

Capacity	S3en	HIP	Ezstego	Stash It	Jsteg-Shell
2%	75.8337	73.7605	60.9975	56.3697	49.4933
5%	68.7031	66.2222	49.8717	45.4717	39.7870
10%	63.0196	60.3883	44.0163	39.4814	36.1853
20%	60.6252	57.4525	38.7401	33.0271	-----
30%	58.0634	55.4314	-----	-----	-----
40%	55.4299	53.3794	-----	-----	-----

It can be seen from experiment results that:

(1) S3en and Hide in Picture have the best imperceptibility, while Ezstego and Stash It are better than Jsteg-Shell, which matches with our direct observation.

(2) CHPSNR decreases with the embedding capacity; that is to say, CHPSNR relates capacity to quality evaluation.

5.3 Localized Distortion

In order to observe the local distortions intuitively, perception error of every block is expressed with graphic method. Distribution map for CHPSNR is shown in figure 4, where coordinates represent the position of CHPSNR, the block is 8*8 in our example.

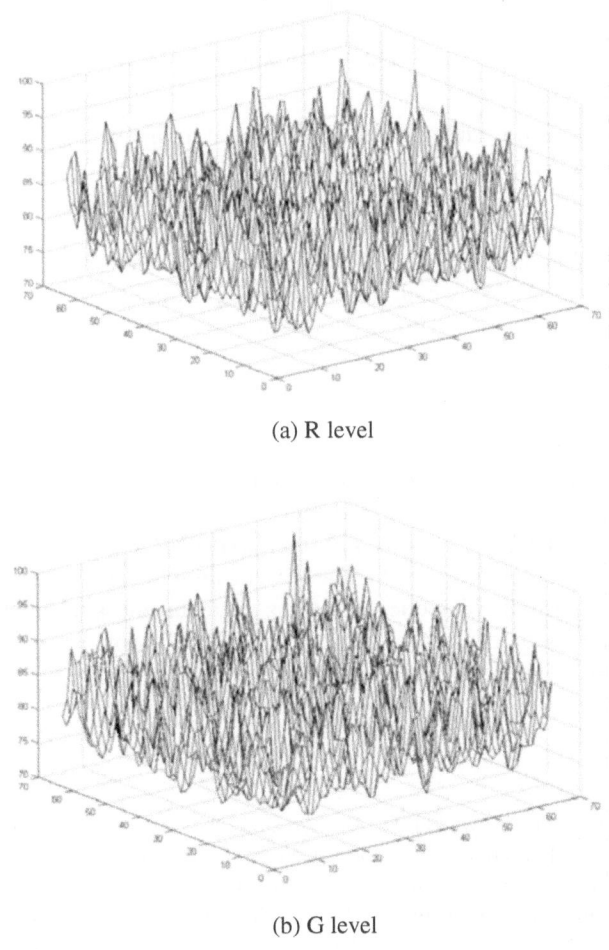

(a) R level

(b) G level

Fig. 4. HPSNR distribution map for each level of color stego image

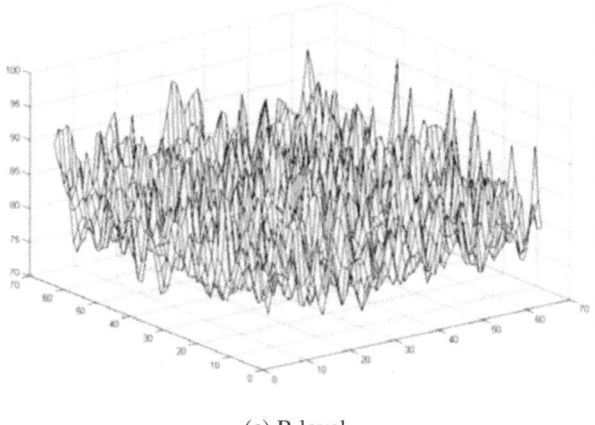

(c) B level

Fig. 4. (*Continued*)

As can be seen from figure 4, local distortions of an image are different. There are differences among R, G and B level even in the same position. Investigating local distortions can help researchers to improve the steganographic algorithm, which will promote the development of steganography and steganalysis.

Therefore, we can draw the conclusion that the evaluation method proposed in this paper matches with HVS, which can effectively evaluate the imperceptibility of steganography.

6   Conclusions

In this paper, we discuss the effect of color on HVS sensitivity, on the basis of which the weighted values are calculated, and then an evaluation metric CHPSNR is proposed. Experimental results demonstrate that CHPSNR can well reflect the image degrades, which is consistent with HVS and can be used to evaluate the performance of steganography algorithm. We believe that this achievement is of great importance to research and application of information hiding, and will promote the development of information hiding algorithm and evaluation method.

References

1. Fridrich, J., Lisonek, P., Soukal, D.: On Steganographic Embedding Efficiency. In: Information Hiding, 8th International Workshop, Alexandria, VA, pp. 282–296 (2008)
2. Ker, A.D.: Steganographic Strategies for a Square Distortion Function. In: Proceedings SPIE, Electronic Imaging, Security, Forensics, Steganography, and Watermarking of Multimedia Contents, San Jose, CA (2008)

3. Parvez, M.T., Gutub, A.A.-A.: RGB Intensity Based Variable-Bits Image Steganography. In: Asia-Pacific Services Computing Conference, APSCC 2008, pp. 1322–1327. IEEE, Los Alamitos (2008)
4. Li, X., Yang, B., Cheng, D., Zeng, T.: A Generalization of LSB Matching. IEEE Signal Processing Letters 16(2), 69–72 (2009)
5. Xiang-wei, K., Ru-feng, C., Xiao-hu, B., Ting, Z., De-li, Y.: A Perception Evaluation Scheme for Steganography. In: Liu, J., Cheung, Y.-m., Yin, H. (eds.) IDEAL 2003. LNCS, vol. 2690, pp. 426–430. Springer, Heidelberg (2003)
6. Ker, A.D.: Quantitative Evaluation of Pairs and RS Steganalysis. In: Proceedings SPIE Electronic Imaging, Security, Steganography, and Watermarking of Multimedia Contents VI, San Jose, pp. 83–97 (2004)
7. van den Branden, Lambrecht, C.J., Verscheure, Q.: Perceptual quality Measure Using a Spatio-Temporal Model of the Human Visual System. In: Proceedings of SPIE, pp. 450–461 (1996)
8. Zhou, W., Bovik, A.C.: A Human Visual System Based Objective Video Distortion Measurement System. In: International Conference on Multimedia Processing and Systems (2001)
9. Tan, S.H., Ngan, K.N.: Classified perceptual coding with adaptive quantization. IEEE Trans. Circuits System for Video Technology, 375–388 (1996)
10. Wang, X.-y., Y ang, H.-y., Chen, L.-k.: New Color Image Watermarking Based on Adaptive Quantization. Mini-Micro Systems, 1525–1529 (2005)
11. Hamad Hassan, M., Gilani, S.A.M.: A fragile watermarking scheme for color image authentication. In: Proceedings of World Academy of Science, Engineering and Technology, pp. 312–316 (2006)

Hasten Dynamic Frame Slotted ALOHA Algorithm for Fast Identification in RFID System

Siti M. Wasikon and Mustafa M. Deris

Faculty of Information Technology and Multimedia,
Universiti Tun Hussein Onn Malaysia
{mahfuzoh,mmustafa}@uthm.edu.my

Abstract. The problems of identifying a set of tagged objects simultaneously in an RFID network have hampered the adoption of RFID universally. When multiple tags transmit their IDs in a single period of time to a single reader over a shared wireless channel, the tag signals may collide. This collision will disturb the reader's identification process. Hence, we proposed a modified version of Accelerated Frame Slotted ALOHA protocol called Hasten Dynamic Frame Slotted ALOHA (HDFSA) to condense a number of retransmission for one tag, thereby reducing the processing time. In HDFSA, the unread tag will be provided with a new slot in the subsequent reading cycle. The simulation conducted revealed that HDFSA outperformed the present Accelerated Frame Slotted ALOHA up to 78 percent in terms of processing time with less complexity, while preserving the accuracy of tag identification.

Keywords: RFID, Tag Anti-Collision, Unread Tag.

1 Introduction

In the early stage of RFID existence, various study have shown that RFID system provides an efficient and inexpensive mechanism for automatically collecting the identity information of an object [1]. This automatic identification (autoID) device operates by transmitting a signal (radio wave) from the reader to the tags. Every command that broadcast by a reader will be processed by all the tags within the range of reader. The reader then will recognize the objects through the ID that given by tags.

A simultaneous data transmission by several tags to a single reader will lead to mutual interference, and therefore to data loss which also known as tag collision [2] occurred. Tag collision makes RFID loss their usefulness as a quick, flexible, and reliable method to electronically detect [3] a variety of objects in one time. This is especially critical for passive tag due to its limitation to detect collisions or to figure out neighboring tags. Therefore, the need for anti-collision protocol is necessary to enable the recognition of multiple tags in a single time.

In general, there are two types of familiar tag anti-collision for passive tags, namely ALOHA based and tree based protocols. Tree-based protocols such as the binary tree protocol [4], [5] and the query tree protocol [6], [7], [8] operate by traversing the node sequentially. Every tag that transmits their ID in the same time will form

P. Mueller, J.-N. Cao, and C.-L. Wang (Eds.): Infoscale 2009, LNICST 18, pp. 162–174, 2009.
© Institute for Computer Science, Social-Informatics and Telecommunications Engineering 2009

a set. A splitting mechanism is applied to the colliding set where it is then will be partitioned into two subsets recursively in turn to be recognized. Thus, the iteration process will relatively cause an identification delay after the splitting procedure from one set until all the tags is being identified. Furthermore, in the worst case of some tree based protocol, the size of tree that the protocol has to traverse might be as equal as the number of bit of serial number inside the tags.

On the other hand, ALOHA based algorithm such as ALOHA [9], slotted ALOHA [10], frame slotted ALOHA [11], [12] and dynamic frame slotted ALOHA [13], [14], [15], [16], [17] is a simple procedure with low complexity. ALOHA based protocol was introduced in order to cut down the number of probability of collision by providing the time slot. The time slot given will allow the tags to transmit their ID in their preferable time which is distinct from each other. Thus, the occurrence of collision will reduce and this offer low complexity and computation [18].

One of dynamic frame slotted ALOHA family, Accelerated Frame Slotted ALOHA (AFSA) algorithm which is proposed in [16], had came out with a good idea of solution to counteract the probability of undetected collision in [14]. AFSA, which based on Enhanced Dynamic Frame Slotted ALOHA (EDFSA) [14], revealed that by reducing the length of bit sequence used in the reservation phase, the average tag reading time had outperformed [14] and [17] more than 40%. However, 'tag starvation problem' as happen to other ALOHA based protocol [19], might caused the unread tags in the first reading cycle not being identified for a long time in the next cycle of reading process.

Hence, we proposed a modified version of AFSA, called Hasten Dynamic Frame Slotted ALOHA (HDFSA) which restrains the unread tag in the first reading cycle from being collided in the next reading cycle. We focus our attention on scheduling of the unread tags in the subsequent reading cycle. By reducing collisions in the subsequent reading cycle, identification process of tags will be faster and tags can be recognized with only a few transmissions of ID. The essential element of HDFSA is a new timeslot that provide specifically for the unread tags in the subsequent reading cycle. HDFSA make use of the new timeslot allocation after the acknowledgement phase. If tags are going not to be acknowledged by the reader, then the unread tags will quickly occupy the exclusive timeslot prepared to allow them send their IDs. The simulations result showed that our proposed algorithm reduced the total delay time for identifying all the tags while preserving the accuracy of tag identification.

The remainder of this paper is organized as follows. Section 2 describes the existing ALOHA based tag anti-collisions protocols and Section 3 introduces the proposed Hasten Dynamic Frame Slotted ALOHA protocol. Section 4 then will present the simulation results and analysis, and finally Section 5 draws conclusions.

2   Aloha Based Tag Anti-collision Protocols

The basic of ALOHA based protocol in RFID system relies on the concept of transmitting the ID randomly whenever reader broadcast the query. If collision occurs, tags will need to wait for random time to retransmit the requested ID.

2.1 Slotted ALOHA (SA) Algorithm

SA is a tag identification method that is introduced to curb the problems of receiving data efficiently in ALOHA protocol. Instead of transmitting data randomly to the reader, the Slotted ALOHA algorithm brings in a number of slots for each tag transmits its serial number [6]. The reader will simply identify the tag when it receives the serial number without collision. However, if the number of tags exceeds the number of slot allocated, the tags are more likely to collide and it cannot guarantee the reasonable response time to identify all the tags [20].

2.2 Frame Slotted ALOHA (FSA) Algorithm

In order to guarantee the response time in SA algorithm, Philips Semiconductor [20] was proposed Basic Frame Slotted ALOHA (BFSA) to schedule the transmission of data. The used of frame in BFSA is advisable to support multiple tags reading by a single reader in a time. A frame was define by [14] as the time interval between requests of reader which consists of a number of slots.

In every tag identification process of BFSA, the fixed frame size and the random number will be broadcasted by a reader to be received by the tags [14]. The random number generated is then used to assign the slot of tags that will be slotted in. If the tag collision occurred, those collided tags have to reply to the next request of reader and this cycle of reading process will be repeated until there is no collision anymore. However, in certain circumstances such as when there are large number of tags involed [14], [15], there is a possibility that no tag is being identified although the read cycle is repetitious. This will reduce the efficiency of identification process. Based on this drawback, a study has proposed a new approach of anti-collision algorithm called Dynamic Frame Slotted ALOHA (DFSA).

2.3 Dynamic Frame Slotted ALOHA (DFSA) Algorithm

DFSA solves the problem in BFSA by dynamically regulating the frame size according to the number of tags. In the tag identification process, DFSA which is introduced by [13] will use information (ie. number of slot, and number of tags collided) from the used slot to determine the frame size in the next reading cycle. This approach indirectly makes the identification process of tags more efficient than existing BFSA. However, the frame sizes indefinitely change according to the number of tag [14], [15], [21], since its have an upper bound that limits the regulation. The performance also could be unsatisfied if the number of tags is higher than the permissible frame size [15] where it will reduce the number of collision [21]. As the technology advance, research on this algorithm is also being actively done to provide better tag allocation.

Enhanced Dynamic Frame Slotted ALOHA (EDFSA) Algorithm. Since that, Enhanced Dynamic Frame Slotted ALOHA (EDFSA) is introduced by [14] with a better adjustment of frame size by grouping the collided tags. By default, if the estimation number of tags is under the threshold, EDFSA does not have to group the unread tags. Otherwise, EDFSA will restrict the number of responding tags by dividing the tags into group nd only one group have to respond to the reader if the number of unread tags is higher than the threshold [15]. EDFSA's new method of grouping the tags offered better performance in reducing the tag collision probability and was improved the system efficiency. Furthermore, this fact has been supported by a few researchers [16], [21] where the system efficiency of EDFSA hovers around 36.8% better than DFSA.

Variant Enhanced Dynamic Frame Slotted ALOHA (VEDFSA) Algorithm. Even though EDFSA offered better performance than DFSA in reducing the tag collision probability, its group solution for unread tags is fixed. This means the group will not change during the whole reading process. Therefore, VEDFSA algorithm is proposed to overcome this problem. VEDFSA restructured the grouping mechanism in EDFSA using dynamic division of tags group. In VEDFSA, the tags in each group are going to give out signal and then being identified by a reader in a different group to achieve the optimal reading. In the next cycle of reading process, the collection of these collided tags will be grouped into a new group and this will decreases the retransmission of unread tags when the numbers of tags are very large [15]. Meanwhile in EDFSA, the unread tags in one group will be recognized repeatedly until its being identified.

Accelerated Frame Slotted ALOHA (AFSA) Algorithm. VEDFSA focused on improvement of retransmissions information but has not improved the inherent problem of tag collision probability in EDFSA. Therefore, V. Sarangan [16] was proposed a new tag anti-collision algorithm called Accelerated Frame Slotted ALOHA (AFSA) which comprised five phases to reduce the number of collision. The five phases are advertisement, reservation, reservation summary, data transmission, and acknowledgement phases respectively as shown in Figure 1 below. AFSA had changed the length of bit sequence in [14] algorithm's into the optimal value and this has resulted a better average tag reading time compared to EDFSA.

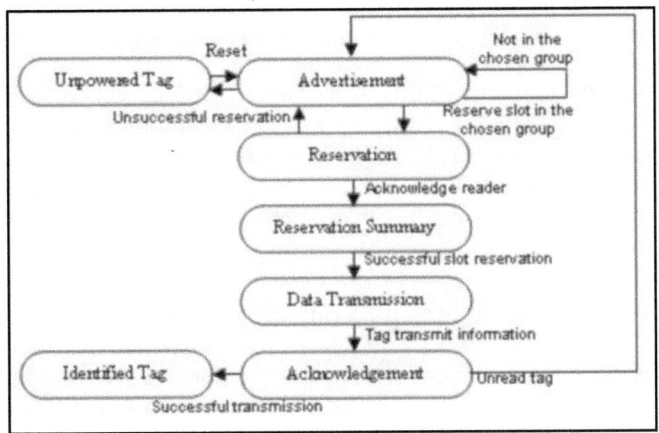

Fig. 1. AFSA framework

Step 1 – Advertisement Phase. For the first read cycle, the number of frame size (N) and number of groups (M) are broadcasted by reader. Upon receiving the values N and M, all tags will generate two random numbers. The first random number plays a role to determine either the tag can participate or not this first round. The tags are only allowed to participate if the remainder of modulo operation on first random number with M is zero. The second random number generated using uniform distribution once the tags allowed participating in first round. This second random number will determine the slot where the tags can transmit their data.

Step 2 – Reservation Phase. In the second phase, tags with the second random number generated in Step 1 will let reader knows which slot they have been chosen. Unlikely, in other slotted ALOHA protocols (FSA, DFSA, and EDFSA), tags will sent their data right away to the chosen slot. While AFSA approached proposed to send n bit sequence in their chosen slot, where n is a protocol parameter. For a given value n, there are 2^n possible n bit sequences. Every tag will randomly pick one of these 2^n sequences and transmits the value to the slot in the reader that has been chosen.

If the slot in the reader is succeeds receives the n bit sequence transmitted by tag, then it implies that the tag has successfully reserved this slot for transmitting its data. Since each tag transmits n bit sequence to the slot, the total duration of this phase will be $N*n$ bit times.

Step 3 – Reservation Summary Phase. During this phase, reader will let the tags know their status of reservation. The reservation status will be advertised through a bitmap of length N. For example, assuming that $N = 4$, and the bitmap is 1001, this 1001 n bit sequences indicate the successful slot that have been reserved by tag is slot number 1 and slot number 4. In other words, occurrence of bit 1 in location i indicates that only one tag had chosen slot i. Meanwhile, during slots 2 and 3, the reader did not receive any n bit sequence. This mean the occurrence of bit 0 in location i indicates two possibilities: (i) collisions – where there might be more than one tag chooses the slot. Thus, when the tags transmitted their random number on n bit sequences, collision occurred and consequently, the reader will not be able to decode the receive signal; or (ii) idle – means that the slot is not choose by any of the tags.

Step 4 – Data Transmission Phase. After step 3, all tags will be aware with their status of reservation. Only for those tags that are successful in their reservation are allowed to transmit their data in the next phase namely data transmission phase. Noted that if S is the total number of '1's in the N bit summary bit string, this means that only S data transmissions are possible. Therefore, there are only S data transmission into the chosen slot during data transmission phase, where $S \leq N$.

Step 5 – Acknowledgement Phase. This is the final phase in a round of reading cycle of tag identification. During this phase, reader wills acknowledges tag about the data that have been transmitted by tags. The acknowledgment is sent in the form of a bit '1' indicates that the transmission was received successfully and '0' indicates that the transmission was not successful.

All tags that received positive acknowledgement from the reader will become muted or killed, and will not participate in the next reading process again. The duration of this phase is S bit times.

Through the simulations and analyses conducted, AFSA had minimized the number of tag collisions and had reduced total wastage of bandwidth owing to unoccupied slots. Thus, AFSA gives better tag reading time over existing models.

Every phase in Figure 1, will perform a specific task within some duration time. Let T_{oc} is the total duration of a round reading cycle in AFSA for five different phases. In the complete process of tag reading, T_{oc} is computed as :

$$T_{oc} = T_p^1 + T_p^2 + T_p^3 + T_p^4 + T_p^5 \tag{1}$$

Where T_p^1 is duration for advertisement phase, T_p^2 is duration time for reservation phase, T_p^3 is duration time for reservation summary phase, T_p^4 is duration time for data transmission phase, and T_p^5 is duration time for acknowledgment phase respectively. This means in the first cycle of reading process contains T_p phases which is equivalent to :

$$T_{oc} = \sum_{i=1}^{RP} T_p^i \tag{2}$$

where RP is number of respective phases involved.

If there were T_{oc} times of reading cycles that the unread tag have been through until it is being identified, then the summation of T_{oc} for n number of cycle AFSA is computed as follow :

$$T_{AFSA} = \sum_{j=1}^{n} T_{oc}^j \tag{3}$$

However, the 'tag starvation' problem that discussed in the foregoing research [4] still suffering AFSA algorithm. An improvement still can be made in order to restrain the unread tag from being collide in the subsequent reading cycle. Therefore, we proposed a modified version called Hasten Dynamic Frame Slotted ALOHA (HDFSA) to handle the identification of unread tags in the subsequent reading cycle.

3 Hasten Dynamic Frame Slotted Aloha (HDFSA)

Hasten Dynamic Frame Slotted ALOHA (HDFSA) was inspired based on AFSA algorithm. The basic idea of HDFSA protocol is to improve the processing time of tag identification process without compromising the accuracy of data transmitted. HDFSA implementation retained the enhancements incorporated into AFSA, but modified the subsequent reading cycle operation to include HDFSA mechanism. The processing time of HDFSA algorithm was measured based on the elapsed time calculated during the identification process. While the time-complexity of HDFSA algorithm only consider on the process of HDFSA in handling the unread tags.

3.1 HDFSA Protocol

Figure 2 below illustrates the proposed framework of HDFSA. HDFSA protocol has prevented the unread tags from going into the same phases as in the first reading cycle in AFSA. As a resulted, HDFSA has condensed the number of retransmission for one tag, thereby reducing the time of tag identification process. It is rule of thumb where the number of collision is reduced when reducing the retransmission of tag. HDFSA improves the subsequent read cycles of unread tags by providing a new mechanism once the tag cannot be read.

In Figure 2, if there is no acknowledgement from the reader to the tag in the fifth phase, then this tag is consider as collided tag or unread tag. HDFSA operates by assuming that each unread tags will be provided with a new slot for them to send their information. Before tags are sending their information, booking number has been given to each unread tag which refers as the slot where the tag will send its information. One tag will be given one booking number which is according to the turn that the tag cannot be read. For example, if Tag 5 is the first tag that can not be identify, then Tag 5 will be given number '1' as its booking number which refer to the slot number 1. It is means that every slot will only contain one tag in one time. Thus, during the subsequent cycle of reading process, HDFSA algorithm allows the unread tags to send their data directly to the certain slot which has already assigned according to the given booking number. It is then reduced the number of retransmission of one tag in order to identify again when it is being collided in the first reading cycle.

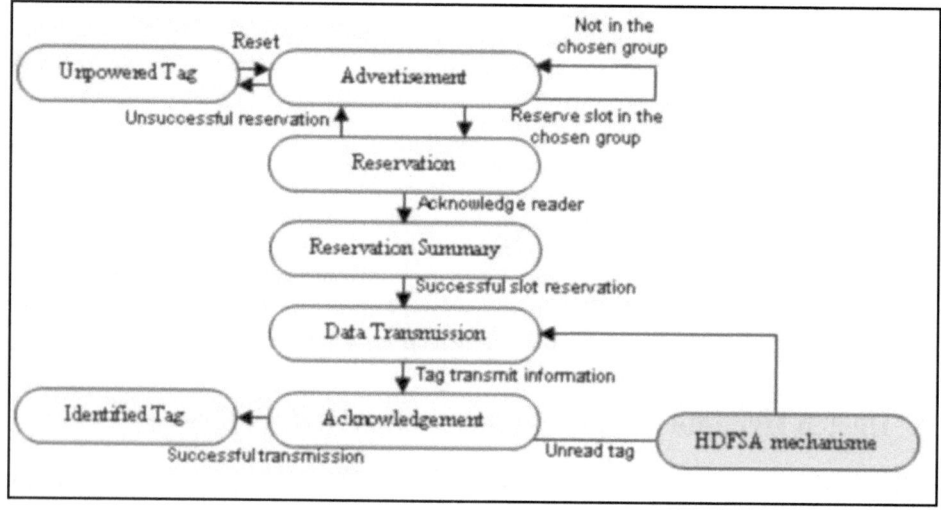

Fig. 2. HDFSA theoretical framework

In HDFSA, when tags are not being identified in the first reading cycle, the reader will prepare a new slot based on the number of unread tags. Every unread tag then will be given with a number called booking number. This booking number is referring to the slot number where the unread tags have to send their information. One tag will be assigned with one booking number. Thus, only one tag will be slotted into the slot and being identified. This will reduce the retransmission of tag and consequently reduce the time used in one identification process.

Let T_{sr} is the total duration of subsequent read cycle, the duration for this cycle should be as follow:

$$T_{sr} = T_p^3 + T_p^4 + T_p^5 \tag{4}$$

Since the unread tag will only through the HDFSA mechanism phase, data transmission and acknowledgement phase in its next reading cycle, the duration of time involves in identifying one tag is reduced as computed in equation 4.

Consider the total duration of first reading cycle like equation 1. Thus, the total duration T_H of one process of HDFSA algorithm   are computed as (5) and (6) equation.

$$T_H = T_{oc} + T_{sr} \tag{5}$$

$$T_H = \sum_{i=1}^{RP} T_p^i + \sum_{i=3}^{RP} T_p^i \tag{6}$$

Thus, for equation (6) and (3) we can say that the total duration of HDFSA is less than total duration of AFSA i.e., $T_H < T_{AFSA}$

Algorithm 1. HDFSA tag anti-collision algorithm operation	
1	BEGIN
2	Step0. Initialization
3	Step 1. Advertisement Phase
4	*for all* tag, tag < TOTALTAGS
5	Reader *r1* broadcast *N* and *M*
	(where *N*=frame size, *M*=group number)
6	Tag generate 2 random number *rnd*
7	*if* first rnd mod *N* = 0
8	TagObject[i] participate in the cycle
9	*if* TagObject[i] participate
10	TagObject[i].2nd *rnd*
	(where second *rnd* refer to number of slot choose)
11	calculate duration time for advertisement phase
12	Step2.Reservation Phase
13	*for all* tag, tag < TOTALTAGS
14	TagObject[i] broadcast the slot number to *r1*
15	TagObject[i] sent *n* bit sequences to the chosen slot
16	*if* slot[i] = *n* bit sequence
17	slot[i] successfully reserved
18	calculate duration time for reservation phase
19	Step 3. Reservation Summary Phase
20	*r1* let tag know reservation status
21	calculate duration time for reservation summary phase
22	Step 4. Data Transmission Phase
23	*for all* tag, tag < TOTALTAGS
24	TagObject[i] transmit data
25	calculate duration time for data transmission phase
26	Step5. Acknowledgment Phase
27	*for all* tag, tag < TOTALTAGS
28	TagObject[i] acknowledge *r1*
29	calculate duration time for acknowledgement phase
30	*if* Ack.TagObject[i] = 1
31	TagObject[i] = sleeping
32	*else*
33	prepare new_slot
34	Nsleep
35	fsize = Nsleep
36	TagObject[i].booking_number
	(where booking number equivalent to slot number)
37	TagObject[i] transmit data
38	TagObject[i] acknowledge reader
39	END

Fig. 3. HDFSA algorithm

3.2 HDFSA Algorithm

From Figure 2, the most important part of HDFSA algorithm is the way this algorithm handle the unread tag once it has been failed to be identify after through the first round of reading cycle. A clear step can be seen in step 33 of HDFSA algorithm that illustrated by Figure 3.

After the last stage of acknowledgement phase in the first reading cycle, a new slot will be prepared by HDFSA to allocate the unread tag. For every tag that has been read, reader will send a positive acknowledgement to the tag and become muted (line 31). Meanwhile, for the tags that are failed to be read, reader will send a negative acknowledgement. Therefore, in HDFSA, a new slot is created for this specific unread tag. The algorithm of HDFSA begins by preparing a new slot in Step 32 once the tag is not being acknowledged by the reader. In Step 33, a new slot is prepared to allocate the unread tag. This unread tag will be given a booking number that represent the number of a slot that they will transmit their data such present in Step 36. The booking number is generated according to the turn that tag being not identified. For example, if tag C is the first tag that cannot be identified then the reader will generate booking number '1' for tag C which means a new slot for tag C is slot number 1. By using this booking number, tag C will then be sent their data directly to the allocating slot as in Step 37. In Step 38 this tag will then be acknowledged by reader that it was being identified.

3.3 Computational Complexity

Based on HDFSA algorithm shows in Figure 3, time complexity is used to evaluate the complexity of algorithm proposed.

Time complexity can be expressed as the number of operations that algorithm have to execute when input has a particular size. We evaluate the complexity of algorithm exclusively on the segment where the tag is started being unread which begins from Step 30 as illustrates in Figure 3 and Figure 4.

In the HDFSA algorithm (see Figure 3), to handle the unread tag, HDFSA has to perform one loop such in Step 30. It is then followed by twenty two operations inside the loop. Thus, $22n+2$ operation is used in HDFSA algorithm and the time complexity is $O(n)$.

In contrast with AFSA algorithm, there are 7 *for* loops to execute as illustrates in Figure 4 below. 5 loops refer to the five phases in AFSA algorithm and the rest of two loops refer to initialization process. AFSA algorithm handles the unread tag inside the *while* loop. Inside the *while* loop there are $14+14n$ operations involved. For first time through the *while* loop, it takes $1 + (14 + 14n)$, which $14n + 15$. Second time through the *while* loop, it takes $14(N - 1) + 15$ operations, $14(N - 2) + 15$ until $14(1) + 15$ the end of operations. The operations performed to handle the unread tag in AFSA can be simplified as below.

$$(14n+15)+(14(n-1)+15)+\ldots\ldots+(14(2)+15)+(14(1)+15) =$$
$$14[n+(n-2)+\ldots..+2+1]+15n=14n(n+1)/2+15n$$
$$= 7n^2+7n+30n$$
$$= 7n^2 + 37n$$

Thus, $7n^2 + 37n$ operation are used to handle the unread tags in AFSA and the time complexity is $O(n^2)$ where it is larger than HDFSA algorithm.

Algorithm 2. AFSA tag anti-collision algorithm operation	
1	BEGIN
2	Step 0. Initialization
3	Step 1. Advertisement Phase
4	*for all tag*, tag < TOTALTAGS
5	Reader *r1* broadcast N and M
	(where N=frame size, M=group number)
6	Tag generate 2 random number *rnd*
7	*if* first rnd mod N = 0
8	TagObject[i] participate in the cycle
9	*if* TagObject[i] participate
10	TagObject[i].2nd *rnd*
	(where second *rnd* refer to number of slot choosed)
11	culculate duration time for advrtisement phase
12	Step 2. Reservation Phase
13	*for all tag*, tag < TOTALTAGS
14	TagObject[i] broadcast the slot number to *r1*
15	TagObject[i] sent *n* bit sequences to the chosen slot
16	*if* slot[i] = *n* bit sequence
17	slot[i] successfully reserved
18	culculate duration time for reservation phase
19	Step 3. Reservation Summary Phase
20	*r1* let tag know reservation status
21	culculate duration time for reservation summary phase
22	Step 4. Data Transmission Phase
23	*for all* tag, tag < TOTALTAGS
24	TagObject[i] transmit data
25	culculate duration time for data transmission phase
26	Step 5. Acknowledgment Phase
27	*for all* tag, tag < TOTALTAGS
28	TagObject[i] acknowledge *r1*
29	culculate duration time for acknowledgement phase
30	*if* Ack.TagObject[i] = 1
31	TagObject[i] = sleeping
32	*while* (!done)
33	Estimate tag count
34	Set frame size
35	Set group
36	Repeat Step 1
37	Repeat Step 2
38	Repeat Step 3
39	Repeat Step 4
40	Repeat Step 5
41	END

Fig. 4. AFSA algorithm

4   Results and Analysis

In this section, we compare the performance of HDFSA with AFSA based on the elapsed time taken by both algorithms.

Table 1 below presents the comparison of the elapsed time in millisecond (msec) between HDFSA and AFSA algorithm. The experiment conducted considered five different input value of number of tags to be identified. From Table 1, Figure 5 illustrates the number of comparison into graph. It is noted that the elapsed time of AFSA algorithm gradually increased when the number of tags is significantly high. This is due to the number of phases that the unread tags have to recursively through once it is failed to be identified in the first reading cycle.

However, HDFSA require less processing time as shows in Table 1 where the elapsed time to complete the identification process is less as compared to AFSA algorithm. Figure 5 illustrated that the elapsed time of AFSA algorithm is gradually increased with the number of tags. Mean while HDFSA's elapsed time is remained stable with the number of tags. For example, from Table 1 and Figure 4, when there are 300 of tags presented in the interrogation area of reader, AFSA algorithm acquire 80,000 millisecond to complete one process to identify all tags, meanwhile in AFSA only 10,000 millisecond required to perform one complete process to identify 300 of tags.

This showed that HDFSA algorithm is more efficient compared to AFSA algorithm up to more than two orders of magnitude. Therefore, HDFSA algorithm outperform AFSA algorithm approximately 85 percent.

Table 1. Comparison of the elapsed time between HDFSA and AFSA

Number of Tag	HDFSA(msec)	AFSA(msec)
100	10,000	40,000
200	10,000	56,000
300	10,000	80,000
400	14,000	118,000
500	18,000	138,000
600	18,000	164,000
700	20,000	192,000

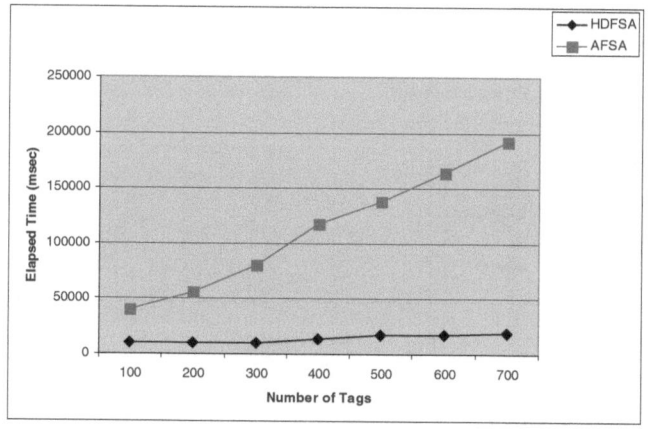

Fig. 5. Simulation results for elapsed time of HDFSA and AFSA

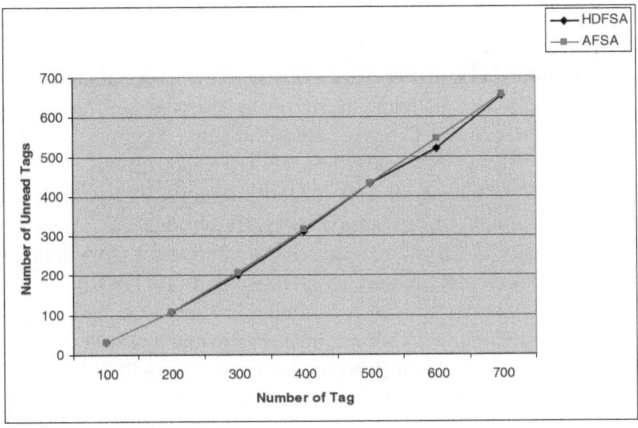

Fig. 6. The number of unread tags in one process

Figure 6 shows the average number of unread tags that obtained in one identification process for HDFSA and AFSA algorithm by increasing the number of tags. It is obviously that HDFSA algorithm performs as well as AFSA algorithm with almost the same average number of unread tags in each process. Thus, the accuracy of HDFSA algorithm is remain as AFSA algorithm.

5   Conclusion

This research was focused on tag collision problem that occurred among the passive tags during identification process in RFID system. A new approached inspired from AFSA algorithm, called HDFSA was proposed. HDFSA is likely reduced the processing time with a new technique introduced in handling the unread tags. HDFSA provide a new slot for the unread tags to allow tags directly transmit their data instead of through the five phases as in AFSA algorithm. The simulation of RFID static reading system developed with HDFSA tag anti-collision revealed that HDFSA outperformed the present AFSA algorithm up to 78% in terms of processing time with less time complexity, while preserving the accuracy of tag identification.

References

1. Finkenzeller, K.: RFID Handbook. John Wiley & Sons, Inc., New York (1999)
2. Shepard, S.: RFID: Radio Frequency Identification. McGraw-Hill, New York (2005)
3. Krebs, D., Liard, M.J.: White Paper: Global Markets and Applications for Radio Frequency Identification (2001)
4. Myung, J., Lee, W.: Adaptive Binary Splitting for Efficient RFID Tag Anti-Collision. IEEE Communications Letters 10, 144–146 (2006)
5. Ho-Seung, Kim, J.-H.: Anti-Collision Algorithm Using Bin Slot in RFID System. In: Proceeding of the TENCON (2005)

6. Seol, J.-M., Kim, S.-W.: Efficient Collision-resilient RFID Tag Identification using Balances Block Design Code. In: Sixth IEEE International Conference on Computer and Information Technology (CIT), p. 220. IEEE Xplore, New York (2006)
7. Law, C., Lee, K., Siu, K.-Y.: Efficient Memoryless Protocol for Tag Identification. In: The 4th International Workshop on Discrete Algorithms and Methods for Mobile Computing and Communications Boston. Massachusetts, United States (2000)
8. Hush, D.R., Wood, C.: Analysis of Tree Algorithms for RFID Arbitration. In: The IEEE International Symposium on Information Theory. Cambridge, MA, USA (1998)
9. Abramson, N.: The ALOHA System: Another Alternative for Computer Communications. In: The AFIPS Joint Computer Conferences, Houston, Texas (1970)
10. Metcalfe, B.: Steady-state Analysis of A Slotted and Controlled Aloha System with Blocking. ACM SIGCOMM Computer Communication Review 5, 24–31 (1975)
11. Vogt, H.: Efficient Object Identification with Passive RFID Tags. In: Mattern, F., Naghshineh, M. (eds.) PERVASIVE 2002. LNCS, vol. 2414, p. 98. Springer, Heidelberg (2002)
12. Schoute, F.C.: Dynamic Frame Length ALOHA. IEEE Transactions on Communications 31(4), 565–568 (1983)
13. Cha, J.-R., Kim., J.-H.: Novel Anti-collision Algorithms for Fast Identification in RFID System. In: The 11th International Conference on Parallel and Distributed Systems, ICPADS 2005 (2005)
14. Lee, S.-R., Joo, S.-D., Lee, C.-W.: An Enhanced Dynamic Frame Slotted ALOHA Algorithm for RFID Tag Identification. In: The Second Annual International Conference on Mobile and Ubiquitous Systems: Networking and Services, MobiQuitous 2005 (2005)
15. Peng, Q., Zhang, M., Wu, W.: Variant Enhanced Dynamic Frame Slotted ALOHA Algorithm for Fast Object Identification in RFID System. In: Proceeding of the IEEE Int. Workshop on Anti-Counterfeiting, Security, Identification (2007)
16. Sarangan, V., Devarapalli, M.R., Radhakrishnan, S.: A Framework for Fast Tag Reading in Static and Mobile Environments. Computer Networks: The International Journal of Computer and Telecommunications Networking 52, 1058–1073 (2008)
17. Khandelwal, G., Lee, K., Yener, A., Serbetli, S.: ASAP: A MAC Protocol for Dense and Time-Constrained RFID Systems. EURASIP Journal on Wireless Communications and Networking 9, 4028–4033 (2007)
18. Klair, D.K., Chin, K.-W., Raad, R.: The Suitability of Framed Slotted Aloha Based RFID Anti-Collision Protocols for Use in RFID-Enhanced WSN's. In: The 16th International Conference on Computer Communications and Networks (ICCCN), Honolulu (2007)
19. Myung, J., Lee, W.: Adaptive Splitting Protocols for RFID Tag Collision Arbitration. In: Proceeding of the MobiHoc 2006, Florence, Italy (2006)
20. Semiconductor, P.: I-Code1 System Design Guide: Technical Report (2002)
21. Bonucelli, M.A., Lonetti, F., Martelli, F.: Tree Slotted ALOHA: A New Protocol for Tag Identification in RFID Networks. In: The International Symposium on World of Wireless, Mobile, and Multimedia Networks, WoWMom 2006 (2006)

A Lightweight Mechanism to Mitigate Application Layer DDoS Attacks

Jie Yu[1,2], Chengfang Fang[2], Liming Lu[2], and Zhoujun Li[3]

[1] Department of Computer Science, National University of Defense Technology, China
[2] Department of Computer Science, National University of Singapore, Singapore
[3] School of Computer Science and Engineering, Beihang University, China
yj@nudt.edu.cn, {c.fang,luliming}@comp.nus.edu.sg, lizj@buaa.edu.cn

Abstract. Application layer DDoS attacks, to which network layer solutions is not applicable as attackers are indistinguishable based on packets or protocols, prevent legitimate users from accessing services. In this paper, we propose Trust Management Helmet (*TMH*) as a partial solution to this problem, which is a lightweight mitigation mechanism that uses *trust* to differentiate legitimate users and attackers. Its key insight is that a server should give priority to protecting the connectivity of good users during application layer DDoS attacks, instead of identifying all the attack requests. The trust to clients is evaluated based on their visiting history, and used to schedule the service to their requests. We introduce *license*, for user identification (even beyond NATs) and storing the trust information at clients. The license is cryptographically secured against forgery or replay attacks. We realize this mitigation mechanism and implement it as a Java package and use it for simulation. Through simulation, we show that *TMH* is effective in mitigating session flooding attack: even with 20 times number of attackers, more than 99% of the sessions from legitimate users are accepted with *TMH*; whereas less than 18% are accepted without it.

Keywords: DDoS Attacks, Trust, Lightweight, Application layer.

1 Introduction

Distributed denial of service (DDoS) attack refers to the attempt to prevent a server from offering services to its legitimate users, typically by sending requests to exhaust the server's resources, e.g. bandwidth or processing power. DDoS attack, which makes a server suffer in having slow responses to clients or even refusing their accesses, may be exploited by one's business competitors expecting to gain an edge in the market or political enemies trying to stir chaos. Since more and more efficient DDoS defense mechanisms and tools are proposed and installed on routers and firewalls, the traditional network layer DDoS attacks, such as SYN flooding, ping of death, Smurf, etc, are much easier to be detected and defended against. Nowadays, they are giving way to sophisticated application layer attacks [15]. Application layer DDoS attack is a DDoS attack that sends

P. Mueller, J.-N. Cao, and C.-L. Wang (Eds.): Infoscale 2009, LNICST 18, pp. 175–191, 2009.
© Institute for Computer Science, Social-Informatics and Telecommunications Engineering 2009

out requests following the communication protocol and thus these requests are indistinguishable from legitimate requests in the network layer. Most application layer protocols, for example, HTTP1.0/1.1, FTP and SOAP, are built on TCP and they communicate with users using sessions which consist of one or many requests. An application layer DDoS attack may be of one or a combination of the following types[15,24]: (1) *session flooding attack* sends session connection requests at a rate higher than legitimate users; (2) *request flooding attack* sends sessions that contain more requests than normal sessions; and (3) *asymmetric attack* sends sessions with more high-workload requests. In this paper, we focus on how to mitigate the session flooding attack.

Constrained by the bandwidth and processing power, application layer servers will set a threshold for the maximum number of simultaneously connected sessions to guarantee the quality of services. Under session flooding attack, a defense mechanism is needed by the server to reject attackers and to allocate the available sessions to legitimate users. The fraction of the rejection of requests from legitimate users over the total number of requests from legitimate users is called the False Rejection Rate (FRR), similarly, False Acceptance Rate (FAR) can be defined. Although a DDoS defense mechanism should reduce both FRR and FAR, reducing FRR is more important for the sake of user experience. That is, a server would rather maximally accommodate the legitimate user sessions, even if a small number of attacker sessions are not detected. Furthermore, the defense mechanism must be lightweight, to prevent itself from being the target of DDoS attacks. It is also preferred that the defense mechanism is independent of the details of the services, as then it can be deployed at any server without modification.

In this paper, we propose a lightweight mechanism, named Trust Management Helmet (*TMH*), that uses trust management to mitigate session flooding DDoS attack. For every established connection it records four aspects of trust to the user: short-term trust, long-term trust, negative trust and misusing trust which are used to compute an overall trust that helps in determining whether to accept a client's next connection request. These values are stored as part of a license at clients and when a client revisits the server, he attaches his license to the session connection request. Based on the license, *TMH* computes the client's overall trust, updates his license, and decides whether to accept his request. The license is designed such that the server can easily identify the client and verify his associated trusts, but license forgery or replay is computationally infeasible. We also extend *TMH* to collaborative trust management among multiple servers. Our mechanism is independent from services deployed on servers and is portable[1]. We have implemented it as a Java package and it can run separately and then redirect scheduled requests to servers protected or be integrated with other open-source application layer servers after slight modification.

As far as we know, our work is the first in applying trust management to application layer DDoS defense. Trust of a client is built up through his visiting history, and used as the criteria in evaluating the likelihood of the client being

---

[1] The mechanism is called as a helmet for this reason as well as its lightweight.

legitimate or not. Most existing schemes use packet rate as the metric to identify attackers. It is potential that intelligent attackers can adjust their packet rate based on server's response to evade detection [7]. In contrast, clients' visiting histories are hard to be modified, because servers keep access logs, and the data used in trust evaluation are secured using cryptography. Hence using trust as the evaluation criteria will be more reliable in application layer DDoS attacks.

The organization of this paper is as follows. In Section 2, we discuss related work. We describe the legitimate user model and attacker model in Section 3. We then propose our *TMH* defense mechanism in Section 4 and in Section 5, we simulate and analyze it. Finally, we extend *TMH* to collaborative trust management in Section 6 and conclude in Section 7.

2   Background and Related Work

There are extensive works on defending against network layer DDoS attacks with different strategies and heuristics, for example, anomaly detection [11], ingress/egress filtering [20], IP trace back [9,18], ISP collaborative defense [3], etc. Recently, the more sophisticated application layer DDoS attack [15] is threatening the security of the Internet content providers, especially web servers. One critical application layer DDoS attack is the index reflection attack [8]. In this attack, attackers declare to be the victim and pretend to share lots of resources in peer-to-peer network, so as to fool a large number of peers into requesting download of resources from the victim. It has been verified on many P2P applications, such as Gnutella [2], Bittorrent, Overnet [13], FastTrack [8], ESM [13], etc. We also verified this attack on Kad [25], which is the first DHT implemented in real applications and has millions of simultaneous users as to date. E. Athanasopoulos *et al.* [2] found that attackers can construct HTTP packets by misusing Gnutella protocol and then build new HTTP connections with victim (web servers) and download high workload resources. In index reflection attack, attackers do not need to control any botnets and thus it is very easy to perform this attack. Since application layer DDoS attacks are non-intrusive and protocol-compliant, attackers are indistinguishable based on packets or protocols and thus these attacks cannot be defended using network layer solutions. Clearly, new defense mechanisms are required for application layer DDoS attacks.

M. Walfish *et al.* [21] proposed a speak-up method, which encourages clients to send more session connection requests. This method is based on the assumption that attackers are already using most of their upload bandwidth so that they cannot react to the encouragement. S. Ranjan *et al.* [15] proposed a counter-mechanism by building legitimate user model for each service and detecting suspicious requests based on the content of the requests. S. Khattab *et al.* [6] proposed living baiting for applications that can be decomposed into several virtual services. It leverages group-testing theory to detect attackers with small state overhead. J. Yu *et al.* [24] introduced a detection and offense mechanism to protect legitimate sessions, but it is too resource consuming to be implemented. M. Srivatsa *et al.* [17] performed admission control to limit the number of concurrent clients served by the online service. Admission control is based on port hiding that renders the online service invisible to unauthorized clients by hiding the port number on which the service accepts incoming requests. This mechanism need a challenge server which can be the new target of DDoS attack. Y. Xie et al. [22,23] proposed a anomaly detector based on hidden semi-Markov model to describe the dynamics of Access Matrix and to detect the attacks. The entropy of document popularity fitting to the model was used to detect the potential application-layer DDoS attacks.

Trust management has been well studied in distributed systems to ensure the fairness in resource sharing or to evaluate the reliability of a resource provider. It has many potential applications in P2P networks. Trust management often uses peers' records, such as their upload and download data amount, or peer reviews, to build up trust information [4,16]. *P2PRep* [4] provided a protocol on top of Gnutella to estimate the trustworthiness of a node. M. Srivatsa et al. [16] identified three vulnerabilities of decentralized reputation management and proposed *TrustGuard* that let reputation grow slowly but drop quickly. In this paper, we apply trust management to defend against application layer DDoS attacks.

3   Legitimate User and Attacker Model

In this section, we build the legitimate user model, and the attacker model with several attack strategies of different complexity. Firstly, we would like to make two assumptions about the server.

Assumption 1. Under session flooding attacks, the bottleneck of a server is the maximal number of simultaneous session connections, called as *MaxConnector*. It depends not only on the bandwidth of the server, but also on other resources of the server, e.g. CPU, memory, maximal database connections.

Assumption 2. Without attacks, the total number of session connections of the server should be much smaller than *MaxConnector*, e.g., smaller than 20% of *MaxConnector*, as a server would set the threshold much higher to tolerate the potential burst of requests, e,g., flash crowds on websites.

3.1   Legitimate User Model

In contrast to attackers, legitimate users are people who request services for their benefit from the content of the services. Therefore, the inter-arrival time of requests from a legitimate user would form a certain density distribution $density(t)$ [5]. With this insight, we build the user model in the following way:

1. Use traces of Internet accesses to build an initial model $density_0(t)$, where t is a inter-arrival time and $density(t)$ is the probability a legitimate user will revisit the service after t seconds. Many traces has been done by researchers, e.g. F. Douglis et al. [5] traced web users to investigate caching technique in World Wide Web, and M. Arlitt et al. [1] presents a workload characterization study for Internet Web servers. Six different data sets are traced in this study: three from academic (i.e., university) environments, two

from scientific research organizations, and one from a commercial Internet provider.

2. Rebuild user model $density_{i+1}(t)$ with the newly collected inter-arrival times of all legitimate users after *TMH* runs d days under model $density_i(t)$, where d is randomly chosen from $[d_{min}, d_{max}]$. Note that we build the new density distribution using the data of legitimate users, whose requests are accepted by *TMH*. It means that $density_{i+1}(t)$ is tightly derived from $density_i(t)$ and hence is difficult to be fooled by attackers.

As a practical legitimate user model, it should satisfy the following properties: firstly, it should converge fast to the users' accesses interval distribution; secondly, it should be dynamic as the distribution may change from time to time; and most importantly, it should be lightweight to be easily implemented and monitored in the defense mechanism. The user model we proposed in this section can satisfy the first two requirements as the density function is updated regularly; and it is lightweight as the update to density distribution is incremental and it does not try to capture the complicated reasons for the changes reflected.

In our implementation, we employ the traces collected at AT&T Labs-Research and Digital Equipment Corporation by F. Douglis *et al.* [5] to build $density_0(t)$. In this initial density distribution model, there are a number of peaks in the user request arrival intervals, with the most prominent ones corresponding to intervals of one minute, one hour and one day. The mean inter-arrival time was 25.4 hours with a median of 1.9 hours and a standard deviation of 49.6 hours.

3.2 Attacker Model

The goal of session flooding DDoS attack is to keep the number of simultaneous session connections of the server as large as possible to stop new connection requests from legitimate users being accepted. Therefore, an attacker may consider using the following strategies when he controls a lot of zombie machines or can misuse P2P network as an attack platform as introduced in section 2:

1. Send session connection requests at a fixed rate, without considering the response or the service ability of victim.
2. Send session connection requests at a random rate, without considering the response or the service ability of victim.
3. Send session connection requests at a random rate and consider the response or the service ability of victim by adjusting request rate according to the proportion of accepted session connection requests by the server.
4. First send session connection requests at a rate similar to legitimate users to gain trust from server, then start attacking with one of the above attacking strategies.

The tradeoff of these strategies is between cost and ability to avoid the detection. Strategy 1 and 2 are easy to implement, but they are also easier to be detected; strategy 3 and 4 are more complicated as they consider the server responses or modeling legitimate users. Strategy 4 requires long-term preparation of attackers in order to gain a high trust level. This strategy needs attackers being more "patient". In session flooding attacks, attackers cannot spoof their IPs or change them within a session, because a session is set up on TCP connection which requires a three-way handshake. Since attackers cannot hide themselves through modifying IPs, they would prefer using strategy 3 and 4 to mimic behavior of legitimate users, to evade detection. We will simulate each strategy in Section 5.

4   Mitigation by Trust Management

We have considered the following properties in designing our mitigation mechanism: (1) It should be deployed at the server for incentive and performance reasons [14]. (2) It should be lightweight, to reduce the processing delay and to avoid being a new target of attacks. (3) It should be easy to deploy and independent to the details of servers. The defense mechanism need not know what services the server runs or what configuration it uses. (4) It should be adaptive to the server's resource consumption and differentiate between concurrent requests.

To evaluate the visiting history of clients[2] effectively, we use *trust*. The client who behaves better in history will obtain higher degree of trust. Here we define several components of it before defining trust.

Definition 1. Short-term trust T_s, estimating the recent behavior of a client. It is used to identify those clients who send session connection requests at a high rate when the server is under session flooding attacks.

Definition 2. Long-term trust T_l, estimating the long-term behavior of a client. It is used to distinguish clients with normal visiting history and those with abnormal visiting history.

Definition 3. Negative trust T_n, cumulating the distrust to a client, each time the client's overall trust falls below the initial value T_0. It is used to penalize a client if he is less trustworthy than a new client.

Definition 4. Misusing trust T_m, cumulating the suspicious behavior of a client who misuses its cumulated reputation. It is used to prevent vibrational attacks by repeatedly cheating for high trust.

Definition 5. Trust T, representing the overall trustworthiness of a client, which takes into account all of his short-term trust, long-term trust, negative trust and misusing trust.

To reduce the processing overhead brought by *TMH*, a short-term blacklist should be implemented. The blacklist records the list of clients whose trust values are too low. When a client's trust T drops below some threshold, he is recorded

---

[2] Clients are used to represent both legitimate users and malicious attackers in this paper.

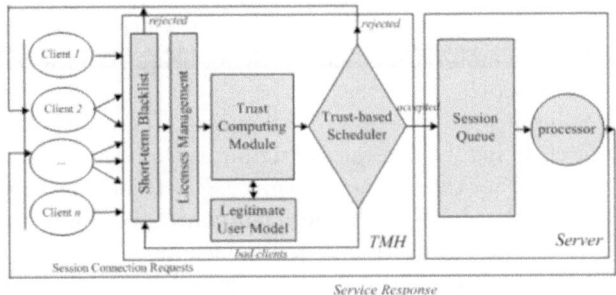

Fig. 1. The components of *TMH* and its communication with other modules

into the blacklist with an expiration time. He is then banned from accessing the server until his blacklist record expires.

The *TMH* mitigation mechanism is deployed at the server. A session connection request first reaches *TMH* and it checks whether the client is blacklisted; if not, it computes the trust to the client and use trust-based scheduling to schedule the connection request for the server. The architecture of *TMH* is shown in Fig.1. We will introduce the components of it in the rest of this section.

4.1   License Management

Because of mobile technology, users can make connections at different network segments. It is difficult to identify mobile users with dynamic IPs. Users connected from a proxy (e.g. HTTP proxy) are also difficult to be identified. Therefore, one way to mitigate session flooding attacks is to give priority in serving a subset of the good users, who we can identify and trust. The identification information and trust states can be stored at clients and verified by the server.

We call the information stored at clients as *license*. It contains the following: 64-bit identifer ID, IP address of client IP, the overall trust T to the client, negative trust T_n, misusing trust T_m, last access time LT, average access interval AT, the total number of accesses AN, and a keyed hash H of the concatenation of all the above, with a 128-bit server password SP as the key. SP is private to the server. Note that we identify a client by his public IP and the server assigned identifier. If IP address alone is used, clients behind NATs cannot be distinguished, because they share the same public IP address. Including the identifier ID enables uniquely identifying a client even if he is hidden behind NATs.

A license serves two functionality: for user identification and trust computation. The identification information, such as ID and IP, must be stored at the client license. The state variables for trust computation can be stored at the client or at the server. Each has its advantages and drawbacks. Keeping licenses at a server largely prevents attackers from tempering them, but it is a single point of data failure. Issuing licenses to users distributes the storage, making *TMH* more scalable in supporting clients, but the server needs to verify the authenticity of a license. It trades off between a server's storage and computation resources. We use client-based license for distributing the data and better scalability. The license can be dispensed to clients using cookies or by additional application layer protocols.

Client provides his license whenever he requests a connection. *TMH* verifies the license by first checking if the request originates from the IP address included in the license[3] and whether the last access time LT matches the server's log, then validating if the hash H agrees with the hash computed using the license and the server password SP. Connection request without a license will be treated as from new users and a new license will be issued if *TMH* decides to accept it. Note that an attacker can not change its IP address during a single session since a session must be set up according a full-TCP connection which needs three-handshake. Even in different sessions, an attacker is only able to change its IP address in a limited range, such as in a small network segment; otherwise, ISPs can not route handshake packets to the attacker.

Correctness. If the hash is one way and weak-collision resistant (e.g., MD5 or SHA-1), then a user is not able to create a valid license without the server password, except with negligible probability. The proof follows from the definition of weak-collision resistance and one way function.

Implementation. We mainly consider the protection of the most important application layer server on Internet, i.e. web server, which is also the most favourite target of known DDoS attacks. Cookies (RFC 2965, 2109) are small bits of textual information that a web server sends to a browser and that the browser returns unchanged when visiting the same web site or domain later. They are widespread used for convenient purposes, e.g. identifying a user during an e-commerce session, avoiding username and password, customizing a site, and so on. The default setting of most operation systems and browsers allow cookies. Hence, we employ them to keep the license information of the client. In our implantation, we use Java Servlet Cookie API to manage licenses. Table 1 shows the license set and get functions in our implantation of *TMH*. These functions are very lightweight and need little process power. Note that although each cookie is limited to 4KB, it is enough for us since each license needs only 544 bits.

4.2 Adaptive Trust Computing

The computation of trust T' employs T, T_n, T_m, LT, AT and AN in license, current time *now*, and *usedRate* (i.e., the percentage of connected sessions over *MaxConnector*) of the server. Based on Assumption 2 in Section 3, $usedRate \ll 1$ normally. As we explained, a server should give priority to protecting the connectivity of good users during session flooding attacks, instead of identifying all the attack requests. Since a higher trust value means a request is more likely to be accepted, it is desired to satisfy: $T_{legitimate\ user} > T_{new\ client} > T_{attacker}$.

---

[3] It is suggested that we only compare the class prefixes of IPs to support DHCP users.

Table 1. License management functions

```
void setLicense(String license, long maxAge){
   Cookie cookie = new Cookie("TMH.license", license);
   cookie.setMaxAge(maxAge);
   response.addCookie(cookie);
}

String getLicense(){
   Cookie[] cookies = request.getCookies();
   String license = ServletUtilities.getCookieValue(
                      cookies, "TMH.license", null);
   return license;
}
```

Short term trust is very important in distinguishing attackers, as almost all DDoS attacks are carried out in a relatively short period. For short-term trust, we consider both the interval of latest two accesses of the client and the current process ability of the server. Considering two different session connection requests with the same access interval at different arrival time, for the client when it arrives the server is relatively busy, it has a higher possibility to be an attacker and thus the short-term trust of it will be relatively lower. We give the formula of short-term trust as follows:

$$T_s' = \frac{density(now - LT)}{e^{\alpha \times usedRate}} \tag{1}$$

where α is a weight factor deciding the influence of $usedRate$. It is a positive real number with default value 1 and can be modified by servers as needed. When $\alpha \approx 0$, the short-term trust mainly relies on the interval of the latest two accesses of the client.

Long term trust is the most important factor when a legitimate user builds up his credit. For long-term trust, the negative trust, average access interval and the total number of accesses should all be taken into account. They can represent the long-term behavior of a client. The formula of long-term trust is:

$$T_l' = \frac{lg(AN) \times density(AT)}{e^{T_n}} \tag{2}$$

Using the short-term trust and long-term trust computed above and the misusing trust provided in license, we can then compute trust T' as follows:

$$T' = min(2 \times \frac{\beta \times T_s' + (1 - \beta) \times T_l'}{e^{T_m}}, \ 1) \tag{3}$$

where $\beta \in [0, 1]$ with default value 0.5, it decides the weight of short-term trust and long term trust in the overall trust computation.

Negative trust is used to penalize users that have carried out attack, or carried out abnormal requests during periods that the server is busy. It cumulates the difference of trust T' to the initial value T_0 each time T' is smaller than T_0. The formula is as follows:

$$T_n' = max(T_n + \gamma \times (T_0 - T'),\ T_n) \tag{4}$$

Misusing Trust prevents vibrational attacks that repeatedly cheat for high trust by checking whether a user's trust is decreasing. It cumulates the difference in trust values if trust T' is smaller than the last time. The formula is as follows:

$$T_m' = max(T_m + \gamma \times (T - T'),\ T_m) \tag{5}$$

where $\gamma \in (0, 1]$, which is a weight factor deciding the degree of cumulation. It can be assigned by servers according to their demands with default value 1.

Recall that in above four formulas, T_n and T_m are the negative trust and misuse trust provided by the license respectively. For a client accessing the server for the first time, its initial value of the overall trust is 0.1, and its initial value of negative trust and misusing trust are both 0, i.e. $T_0 = 0.1$, $T_{n0} = T_{m0} = 0$.

Computation overhead. As can be seen from the formulas, the computation in updating a trust value is minimal. The major factor of computation overhead is in generating the cryptographic hash of a license. Yet each hash input is only 544 bits, and MD5 can compute more than 120,000 such hashes per second (measured in software using Java 5.0 and a PC with 2.13GHz CPU and 2GB memory). Even if using an off-the-shelf PC as a server, the server is capable of verifying more licenses than the normal network bandwidth can transmit. Besides, servers usually have more computational resources.

4.3   Trust-Based Scheduler

When a session connection request reaches *TMH*, it firstly validates the license the client provides. If passed, it will compute the client's new overall trust, negative trust and misusing trust and then update this information into the license. Afterwards, the scheduler in *TMH* decides whether to redirect it to the server based on the trust values.

TMH schedules session connection requests once every time slot. If the total number of the on-going sessions and the sessions waiting to be connected is not larger than the *MaxConnector* of the server, the scheduler will redirect all requests to the server. Otherwise, suppose there are N session connection requests waiting to be connected and the percentage of requests should be dropped is θ, we propose following the scheduling policies to drop suspicious requests:

1. *Foot-n*: sort all requests in current time slot by the clients' trusts in the decreasing order. For clients that have the same overall trust, sort them by their misusing trusts in the increasing order. We then drop the last $n = \theta \times N$ requests.

2. *Probability-n*: give each client i a probability p^i

$$p^i = min(\frac{T^i \times (1 - \theta) \times N}{\sum_{j=1}^{N} T^j}, 1)$$ (6)

to denote the probability at which his session connection request will be accepted. Thus we drop his request with probability $1 - p^i$.

4.4 Possible Attacks

We discuss some possible attacks to *TMH* in this subsection.

Index reflection attack. In Section 2, we described the index reflection attack. The peers manipulated into flooding session connection requests are either new users to the server or behave as attackers with strategy 4. During attack, *TMH* gives priority in serving the known users with high trusts. As the attacking peers frequently request for session connections, the trust of them drops till they are blacklisted. Thus they are penalized.

License forgery, replay and deletion attacks. Clients might not follow the protocol of *TMH* exactly, they might try to cheat about the license, for example, forging a new one, sharing a license, using an old license, or refuse to store a license.

As mentioned, the license is hashed with a server password, thus, it is computationally infeasible for a forgery to be valid. If attackers send random licenses to make *TMH* verify, *TMH* risks exhausting its computation power. However, the computation performed by *TMH* is lightweight, it can verify as many licenses in time as the network can transmit. And as the license stores the IP address, sharing a license is only possible for clients within the same subnet or NAT. Furthermore, since the last access time is included in the license, *THM* can detect if a client reuses an old license, by cross-checking the last access information the server logs, i.e. 64-bit identifer ID and last access time LT.

If an attacker discards his license of low trust to pretend to be a new user, he will still be assigned lower priority than the known users with high trusts. Additional efforts can be made to distinguish a benign new user and an apparent new user but who is actually a zombie attacker having discarded his license. For example, *TMH* can issue a request on the server's behalf, asking the new users to send their connection requests to another IP which is also under the server's control. If a user responds to the request and redirects his connections correctly, the user is not a zombie machine [19]. Graphical turing test [12] is another possible solution to tell apart zombies from benign new users.

5 Simulation

We implement *TMH* as a package, which consists of about 500 lines of Java source code. This package can run separately and then redirect scheduled requests to web servers or be integrated with other open source web servers after slight modification, such as Tomcat or JBoss. In this section, we present the simulation results to analyze the performance of *TMH* against different attack strategies and to compare the effect of different scheduling policies.

5.1   Simulation Setup

The simulation is set up in a local area network with 100Mbps links. We simulated 100 legitimate users, varying number of attackers and a server protected by *TMH*. Clients request the server for HTTP sessions. The server directly responds to them if they pass the verification and get scheduled by *TMH*.

Constrained by the server's memory and other resources, *MaxConnector* is set to 1000. That is, the server can serve maximally 1000 concurrent sessions; beyond that, the session requests will be dropped. In our simulation, legitimate users follow the model described in Section 3.1, we set $d_{min}=15$ and $d_{max}=20$; while attackers attack with different strategies described in Section 3.2. The life time of a session follows an exponential distribution with mean equals to 20 seconds.

TMH uses default values of α, β and γ in the computation of trust. It issues license to new users with $density(now - LT)$ and $density(AT)$ set to be 0.1. After it verifies a license and updates the trust, it schedules the requests using the policies described in Section 4.3. For comparison, we also implemented two simple scheduling policies: (1) *Tail-n*: drop the $n = \theta \times N$ requests that arrive last in a time slot. (2) *Random-n*: randomly drop $n = \theta \times N$ requests in a time slot. A time slot is one second.

5.2   Results and Analysis

Fig.2 shows the change of overall trusts of legitimate users and attackers. Its result is obtained using *Probability-n* as the scheduling policy. For Fig.2(a), there are 100 legitimate users and no attacker; for Fig.2(b) to Fig.2(f), there are 500 attackers, besides the 100 legitimate users. All the users and attackers are started sequentially. In each simulation, the change of overall trusts of each legitimate user is very similar to each other. To illustrate this, we keep track of three representative users, that is, users started at the beginning, in the middle and at the end. Following the same argument, we select three attackers based on the starting sequence.

Fig.2(a) plots the trusts of three selected users when there is no attacker. All requests are accepted. It shows that the trusts of legitimate users quickly increase from 0.1 to 0.3 in the first few sessions. After 50 sessions, their trust values are over 0.5.

For Fig.2(b), attackers use strategy 1. They send session connection requests with a fixed rate at one request per 5 seconds. Fig.2(b) shows the trusts of legitimate users increase slower than in Fig.2(a). That is due to the high used rate of server's session connections under attacks. After 50 sessions, the trusts of legitimate users are around 0.4. However, the trusts of attackers decrease to around 0.01 in the first few sessions due to their high request rate, and they keep reducing slowly in the following sessions.

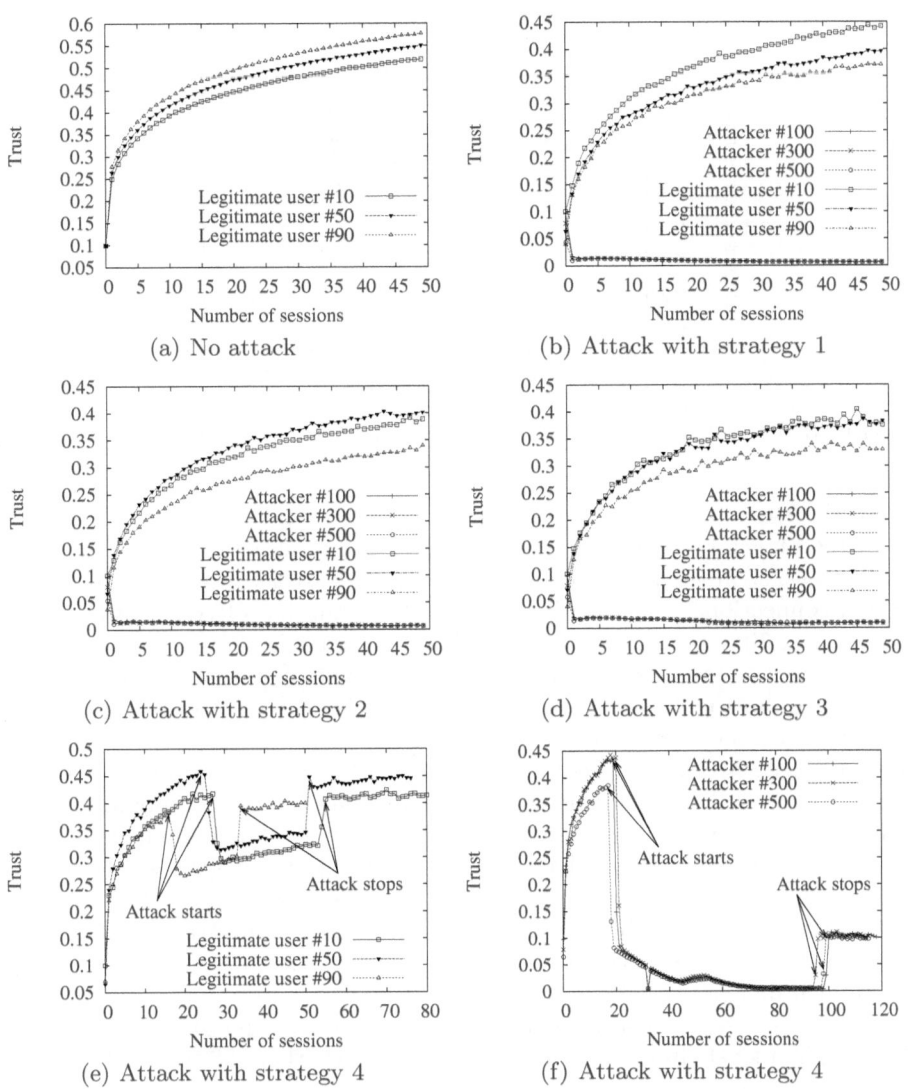

Fig. 2. Global trusts over the number of sessions

For Fig.2(c), attackers use strategy 2. They send session connection requests with varying rate at one request in every 5 to 10 seconds uniformly. The randomness in attack rate causes the server to experience some burst of session requests. This decreases the misusing trust of legitimate users, which results in the fluctuation of their trust values, as shown in the figure. After 50 sessions, the trusts of the legitimate users are about 0.38.

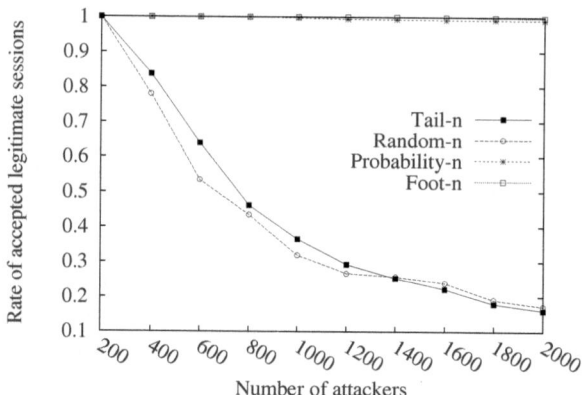

Fig. 3. The rate of accepted legitimate sessions over the number of attackers

For Fig.2(d), attackers use strategy 3. They adjust their sending rate between 5 to 10 seconds for a request, according to the rate of accepted requests by *TMH*. This attack strategy brings in more randomness to the used rate of server's session connections, and thus increasing the fluctuation of trusts of legitimate users. After 50 session requests, the trusts of legitimate users are about 0.35. Notice that the trust of attackers in Fig.2(b) is smaller than the trust of the same session in Fig.2(c) which is then smaller than the trust in Fig.2(d).

When attackers use strategy 4, the change of the overall trusts of three legitimate users are plotted in Fig.2(e) and that of three attackers are plotted in Fig.2(f). Attackers first send session connection requests complying with the legitimate user model; then attack using strategy 1 for a period; finally they follow the legitimate user model again. When attack starts or stops, the number of sessions requested by clients differs because the access interval in the legitimate user model is probabilistic. Fig.2(e) shows that the trusts of legitimate users decrease by 30% in three sessions after the attack starts. This is because of the sudden increase of used rate of server's session connections. However, they slowly increase even when the attack is carrying on and almost recover to about their original level after attack stops. Fig.2(f) shows that the trusts of attackers decrease to a much lower level and is at around 0.1 even they stop attacking. Note that we have removed some middle results under attacks in Fig.2(f) so that it is convenient to compare with Fig.2(e).

We compare different scheduling policies by plotting the acceptance rate of legitimate sessions, i.e. $1 - FRR$, in Fig.3. The number of legitimate users is 100 and the proportion of each kind of attackers who adopt one of the four attack strategies is 25%. We can see that under trust-based scheduling strategies, the acceptance rate of legitimate sessions keeps at a high level and is insensitive to the number of attackers. Even when the number of attackers is 2000, the acceptance rate of legitimate user sessions is still 99.1% and 99.7% with *Probability-n* and *Foot-n* scheduling policies respectively. However, it is only 16.0% using *Tail-n* policy and 17.2% using *Random-n* policy.

6   Collaborative Trust Management

Many services are related but provided by different servers, e.g., online auction and PayPal, or e-newspaper and its advertisements. The related servers probably share a large group of clients. For the common good or economic incentives, *TMH*s deployed at these servers can collaborate with one another by sharing trust information of clients. We say these *TMH*s form a collaboration group. The trust information shared is particularly useful in distinguishing legitimate users. The collaborating *TMH*s can take either or both actions below:

1. *Exchange blacklist*: a *TMH* exchanges its blacklist (including client ID and its expiration time) with other *TMH*s periodically. When a *TMH* receives a blacklist, it merges the received blacklist into its own.
2. *Exchange the trust values of clients*: a *TMH* sends its overall trust of clients to other *TMH*s periodically. A client may visit the same server multiple times within a period. Only the latest overall trust logged by *TMH* is exchanged. When client j requests a new session, *TMH* i uses following formula to recompute the overall trust T_G^j of the client, which considers both the local trust T^j computed by *TMH* i and the recommended trust T_r^j from other *TMH*s:

$$T_G^j = \tau \times T^j + (1 - \tau) \times \sum_{r \in I(i)} \frac{C_{ir} \times T_r^j}{\sum_{r \in I(i)} C_{ir}} \tag{7}$$

where $I(i)$ is the collaboration group of *TMH* i, C_{ir} is the confidence level that *TMH* i has for the recommended trust from *TMH* r, and $\tau \in [0, 1]$ is the confidence level of *TMH* i itself, 1 means the most confident and 0 the least.

The collaboration of *TMH*s can reduce the false negatives of a single *TMH* and accelerate the identification of attackers.

7   Conclusion

To defend against application DDoS attacks is a pressing problem of the Internet. Motivated by the fact that it is more important for service provider to accommodate good users when there is a scarcity in resources, we present a lightweight mechanism *TMH* to mitigate session flooding attack using trust evaluated from users' visiting history. We verify its effectiveness with simulations under different attack strategies. Comparing to other defense mechanism, *TMH* is lightweight, independent to the service details, adaptive to the server's resource consumption and extendable to allow collaboration among servers. In future work we will investigate how to apply *TMH* into real-world applications and how to defend against other types of application layer DDoS attacks, including request flooding attack and asymmetric attack.

References

1. Arlitt, M., Williamson, C.: Web Server Workload Characterization: The Search for Invariants. In: Proceedings of ACM SIGMETRICS 1996 (1996)
2. Athanasopoulos, E., Anagnostakis, K., Markatos, E.: Misusing Unstructured P2P systems to Perform DoS Attacks: The Network That Never Forgets. In: Zhou, J., Yung, M., Bao, F. (eds.) ACNS 2006. LNCS, vol. 3989, pp. 130–145. Springer, Heidelberg (2006)
3. Chen, Y., Hwang, K., Ku, W.: Collaborative Detection of DDoS Attacks over Multiple Network Domains. IEEE Transations on Parallel and Distributed Systems (2007)
4. Cornelli, F., Damiani, E., Vimercati, S., Paraboschi, S., Samarati, P.: Choosing reputable servents in a p2p network. In: Proceedings of WWW 2002 (2002)
5. Douglis, F., Feldmannz, A., Krishnamurthy, B.: Rate of change and other metrics: a live study of the World Wide Web. In: Proceedings of USENIX Symposium on Internetworking Technologies and Systems (1997)
6. Khattab, S., Gobriel, S., Melhem, R., Mossäe, D.: Live Baiting for Service-level DoS Attackers. In: Proceedings of INFOCOM 2008 (2008)
7. Li, Q., Chang, E., Chan, M.: On the Effectiveness of DDoS Attacks on Statistical Filtering. In: Proceedings of INFOCOM 2005 (2005)
8. Liang, J., Naoumov, N., Ross, K.W.: The Index Poisoning Attack in P2P File Sharing Systems. In: Proceedings of INFOCOM 2006 (2006)
9. Lu, L., Chan, M., Chang, E.: Analysis of a General Probabilistic Packet Marking Model for IP traceback. In: Proceedings of ASIACCS 2008 (2008)
10. Mirkovic, J., Dietrich, S., Dittrich, D., Reiher, P.: Internet Denial of Service: Attack and Defense Mechanisms. Prentice Hall PTR, Englewood Cliffs (2004)
11. Mirkovic, J., Prier, G.: Attacking DDoS at the source. In: Proceedings of ICNP 2002 (2002)
12. Morein, W.G., Stavrou, A., Cook, D.L., Keromytis, A.D., Misra, V., Rubenstein, D.: Using graphical turing tests to counter automated DDoS attacks against web servers. In: Proceedings of ACM CCS 2003 (2003)
13. Naoumov, N., Ross, K.: Exploiting P2P Systems for DDoS Attacks. In: Proceedings of INFOSCALE 2006 (2006)
14. Natu, M., Mirkovic, J.: Fine-Grained Capabilities for Flooding DDoS Defense Using Client Reputations. In: Proceedings of LSAD 2007 (2007)
15. Ranjan, S., Swaminathan, R., Uysal, M., Knightly, E.: DDoS-Resilient Scheduling to Counter Application Layer Attacks under Imperfect Detection. In: Proceedings of INFOCOM 2006 (2006)
16. Srivatsa, M., Xiong, L., Liu, L.: TrustGuard: Countering Vulnerabilities in Reputation Management for Decentralized Overlay Networks. In: Proceedings of WWW 2005 (2005)
17. Srivatsa, M., Iyengar, A., Yin, J., Liu, L.: Mitigating application-level denial of service attacks on Web servers: A client-transparent approach. ACM Transactions on the Web (2008)
18. Stone, R.: CenterTrack: An IP Overlay Network for Tracking DoS Floods. In: Proceeding of 9th Usenix Security Symposium (2002)
19. Thing, V.L.L., Lee, H.C.J., Sloman, M.: Traffic Redirection Attack Protection System (TRAPS). In: Proceedings of IFIP SEC 2005 (2005)
20. Tupakula, U., Varadharajan, V.: A Practical Method to Counteract Denial of Service Attacks. In: Proceedings of ACSC 2003 (2003)

21. Walfish, M., Vutukuru, M., Balakrishnan, H., Karger, D., Shenker, S.: DDoS Defense by Offense. In: Proceedings of SIGCOMM 2006 (2006)
22. Xie, Y., Yu, S.: Monitoring the Application-Layer DDoS Attacks for Popular Websites. IEEE/ACM Transactions on Networking (2009)
23. Xie, Y., Yu, S.: A large-scale hidden semi-Markov model for anomaly detection on user browsing behaviors. IEEE/ACM Transactions on Networking (2009)
24. Yu, J., Li, Z., Chen, H., Chen, X.: A Detection and Offense Mechanism to Defend Against Application Layer DDoS Attacks. In: Proceedings of ICNS 2007 (2007)
25. Yu, J., Li, Z., Chen, X.: Misusing Kademlia protocol to perform DDoS attacks. In: Proceedings of ISPA 2008 (2008)

A Multidimensional Mapping Mechanism Based Secure Routing Method for DHT

Zhixin Sun[1,2], Kai Bu[1], and Ke Ding[1]

[1] Nanjing University of Posts and Telecommunications, College of Computer
Xin Mofan Road. 66, 210003 Nanjing, P.R. China
[2] State Key Laboratory for Novel Software Technology,
Nanjing University, 210093 Nanjing, China
sunzx@njupt.edu.cn, bukai521@yahoo.com

Abstract. For improving the routing security of traditional DHT, in this paper, a Multidimensional Mapping Mechanism and a secure routing method based on it are proposed against various routing attacks. The proposed mechanism, which maps the resource search and related peers to a smaller space following the same topology with current DHT protocol to simplify the routing operation and decrease the coupling degree between security mechanisms and routing geometry, lays a solid foundation for applying to diversified DHT protocols. The subsequently proposed security measures based on Multidimensional Mapping Mechanism for DHT routing still keeps independent of certain DHT protocol. It pervades throughout the whole routing process, and peers could correct the malicious routing under its security rules. The theoretical analysis and simulation experiment result show that the secure routing method proposed in this paper can improve the average success ratio of lookup through effectively inhibiting malicious behavior.

Keywords: Multidimensional Mapping Mechanism, DHT (Distributed Hash Table), Routing Attack, Secure Routing.

1 Introduction

DHT (Distributed Hash Table) [5] is the key technology of research and realization of structured P2P (Peer-to-Peer) network, which employs distributed hash algorithm of DHT protocol to solve the structured distributed storage problems. In P2P network over DHT based topology, each peer and resource have a unique identifier which generated by hash computing, the most obvious characteristic is that peer does not need to record all other peers' information, but only maintains a relatively smaller routing table including certain peers. Then lookup message is effectively routed based on this simple routing table and related storing rule of resource's distribution information and this can abolish flooding algorithm in unstructured P2Pnetwork and improve the routing efficiency and lower the routing overhead. Due to its distribution, self-organizing and high scalability, designing routing algorithm with high efficiency for DHT is becoming a hotspot in international research on structured P2P. The representative DHT protocols prototype include the MIT's

P. Mueller, J.-N. Cao, and C.-L. Wang (Eds.): Infoscale 2009, LNICST 18, pp. 192–205, 2009.
© Institute for Computer Science, Social-Informatics and Telecommunications Engineering 2009

(Massachusetts Institute of Technology) Chord [8], Microsoft Research Institute's Pastry [1], as well as UC Berkeley's CAN [16] and Tapestry [2] etc.

However, an important prerequisite to running DHT mechanism effectively is that peers are fully trusted in P2P system, which means peer security is highly required. But compared with the traditional C/S network, P2P network drastically increase the probability of peers implementing malicious behavior due to its characteristics of self-governing and dynamic, which make it hard to assure the security of DHT routing algorithm. [3,6] analyzed the routing algorithms of typical DHT and summed up potential malicious behaviors of peers. Malicious peer may forward lookup message incorrectly or broadcast incorrect routing updating information which may prevent the attacked peers from using P2P service normally. Also, following the regular routing algorithm, malicious peer may deny that it does store the searched data or declare its storage state but refuse to provide them. Besides, inconsistent behavior performed by malicious peer usually makes it harder to identify and preclude the malicious one when choosing appropriate peer to forward lookup message to.

For improving the routing security of traditional DHT protocols and overcoming the disadvantages of current security mechanisms, this paper proposes a Multidimensional Mapping Mechanism and a secure routing method for DHT based on it. The Multidimensional Mapping Mechanism maps the resource search and related peers to a smaller space topologized under the same routing geometry with current DHT protocol to simplify the routing operation and decrease the coupling degree between security mechanism and topology, and this lays a solid foundation for applying to diversified DHT protocols.

The rest of this paper is organized as follows. Section 2 gives an overview and analysis of currently related research work. Section 3 presents the Multidimensional Mapping Mechanism and a series security measures for DHT routing algorithm based on it. Section 4 analyzes the theoretical performance of the security method proposed in this paper and reports on the simulation experiment. Finally, conclusion with a brief discussion is provided in Section 5.

2 Related Work

Currently, the research methods of secure DHT routing mainly focus on the following directions.

2.1 Improving the Routing Algorithm

Castro et al suggested restoring optimized routing table for fast routing and constrained table for secure routing for each peer [10]. While executing the data search, the peer forwards the lookup message according to the optimized routing table and verifies the lookup result through collaborating with some neighbors. However, the overhead introduced by communication with neighbor peers in each verification process, recursive query according to the constrained table after verification failed, and broadcast operation followed by identifying unreliable peers during queries, will effect the method's performance to some extend.

Paper [9] added an additional table storing information of some neighbors to each peer and introduced a wide path lookup mechanism. Several routing paths are constructed according to neighbors' information for lookup message. Only when peers at the same level fail in all paths will cause the resource search failure. It makes the structured P2P system more robust to malicious routing attacks. But this method require a $O(\log^2 N)$ connections for each peer and increase the complexity of routing operation to $\Omega(\log^2 N)$.

2.2 Trust Model

Papers [14,17] concluded and analyzed typical trust models based on P2P environment, and pointed out that the recommendation based trust relationship from social society is a reasonable research method. The global trust model is just based on this idea; it calculates peer's global trust value through iterative of satisfactory value amongst peers.

Literature [13] distributes a unique global reputation value according to the upload logs of document, when peer i wants to know peer k's global reputation value, it firstly gets the reputation information which have traded with peer k, then generalizes peer k's reputation from its trade partner's reputation value. However, this proposed model does not provide punishment mechanism to peers which cause service failure. The reputation value of malicious peers will not decrease immediately and this will result that the model can not reflect peers reputation value in that period of time. In addition, the iterative messages in the whole network caused by each trade process will also affect the performance of the network.

2.3 Employing Certificate Authority

Myrmic model [12] introduced an on-line CA (Certificate Authority) named NA (Neighborhood Authority) based on the off-line CA. NA participates in the structured P2P network management by issuing Neighborhood Certificate to certain peers when peers join or leave. Then peer can verify the lookup result through querying neighborhood certificate copies stored on neighbors of the peer which returns the result. This verification costs $2l$ (the number of neighborhood certificate copies) communication messages. During NA failure, newly coming peers can search resource via the peers which have neighborhood certificate but can not join the network until any on-line NA available. This rule further delays the overall routing table update, and the introduction of NA itself is not a reasonable choice due to against the essential characteristics of P2P network, namely distributed or non-centralized, to some extend.

Besides, current security mechanism usually aims at specific DHT protocol, which leads to a limitation of generality and scalability when applying to multiform DHT routing geometries or new-style P2P applications. Report mechanism introduced by Trust Model may also be used by malicious peer to slander other peers by deliberately sending malicious reports. And the inconsistent routing table update amongst peers will also cause a mistake to judge a legitimate peer as malicious one.

Therefore, it is important to find a more reasonable research method with higher generality and scalability but less influence to routing performance of the traditional DHT protocol compared with current secure mechanisms. In fact, if the ideal state that each peer can acquire information of all other peers within P2Pnetwork could be achieved, then all malicious routing attack could be detected and the routing security issues figured out. But this can hardly be realized for structured P2P network including numerous peers with frequent join and leave. In this paper, we propose a Multi-dimensional Mapping Mechanism to map routing operation of lookup message and related peers into a smaller space aiming at relatively strengthening information sharing amongst peers and simplifying implementation of secure routing measures.

3 Multidimensional Mapping Mechanism Based Secure DHT Routing Method

In this section, we firstly enumerate and analyze several typical routing attack behaviors of malicious peers and then introduce the Multidimensional Mapping Mechanism and secure DHT routing method based on it.

3.1 Analysis of Typical Routing Attacks

In order to meet the demand of scalability, maintainability and the resource discovery algorithm's efficiency for structured P2P, DHT protocol stipulates that each peer can only store a small number of network peers' information, which makes peers vulnerable to malicious routing attacks due to lack of enough information of other peers. Fig. 1 demonstrates several possible routing attacks malicious peer may commit. Peer Q sends lookup message to search resource k with identifier *key* of which the distribution information is stored on peer B. Peer A is peer B's predecessor in the correct routing path, when receiving the lookup message A forwarded, if peer B is malicious it may ① deny that it stores the information related to k or discard this inquery message, and return lookup failure to Q; ② deny that it stores the information related to k and forward the lookup message to certain next hop peer C, then C or other sub sequent peers returns the failed message. But if A itself is a malicious peer, it might

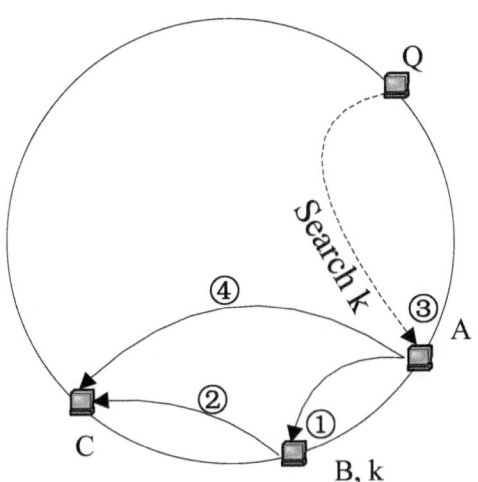

Fig. 1. DHT routing attacks examples

③ discard the lookup message and return a failure result; ④ wrongly route the lookup message to peers which are not supposed target peers, and the peers that receive messaged forwarded by A would return search failed message to Q.

Through analyzing the possible routing attacks mentioned above, we find that one of the fundamental reasons is that each node can only acquire a few peers' information which makes peers not transparency to each other. If peers Q, C, A can obtain the information of keys that are stored on peer B, then B can not successfully commit malicious behaviors like ①, ②; if peers Q, C can obtain the information of keys stored on A, the routing attacks like ③ or ④ can not be implemented. Next we will introduce the Multidimensional Mapping Mechanism and how it work against DHT routing attacks through strengthening information sharing amongst peers.

3.2 Overview of Multidimensional Mapping Mechanism

Rule 1. Multidimensional Mapping Mechanism: When requirement of space conversion met, peers related to the remainder routing operation with identifiers distribute in $p_{1i} \in \{p_{1a}, p_{1(a+1)},\ldots, p_{1b}\}$ in current space S_1 (peer identifier $p_{1i} \in \{p_{10}, p_{11},\ldots, p_{1(n-1)}\}$, where n represents the maximum number of peers S_1 can hold) will be mapped into a smaller space S_2 with identifiers $p_{2i} \in \{p_{20}, p_{21},\ldots, p_{2(m-1)}\}$. The maximum number of peers of S_2 can be expressed as $m = 2\exp\|\log_2(b-a+1)\|$.

Rule 1 depicts the principle of Multidimensional Mapping Mechanism. As shown in Fig. 2, peer $Q1$ in current space S_1 sends a lookup message which is forwarded to peer $P1$. $P1$ starts space conversion operation as required condition met and maps itself and other peer related to remainder routing operation into a smaller space S_2 retopologizing under the same geometry with S_1. When $P3$ receiving the forwarded lookup message, space conversion requirement is met again and routing operation is going on after being mapped into the new space S_3. Fig. 2 explicitly demonstrates that

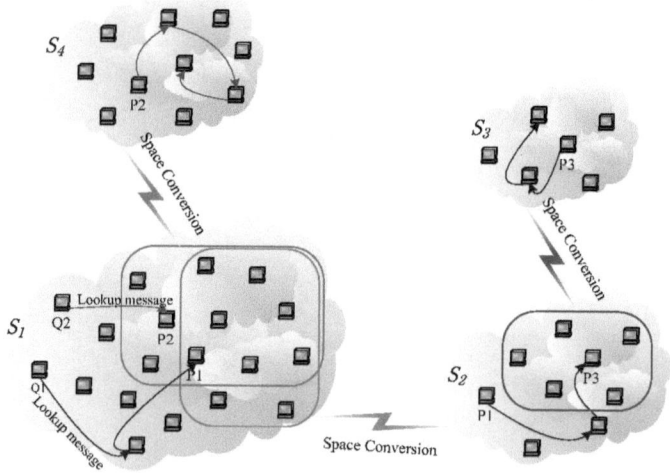

Fig. 2. Demonstration of Multidimensional Mapping Mechanism

each success implementation of space conversion can simplify the security assurance through continuing the remainder routing operation in a smaller space. S_4 represents the space converted by peer $P2$ when space conversion condition is met during the routing process of another lookup message started by peer $Q2$.

As to the requirement that space conversion needed, mapping method, and maintenance of routing information in new space, we will clarify them detailedly along the following sections.

3.3 Multidimensional Space Division

In structured P2P network, each peer (or resource) is assigned an unique identifier which is an integer generated by hash calculation. All identifiers distribute within the same value range [11]. For most DHT protocols, distribution information of resource whose identifier is *key* is stored on peer of which the identifier is equal to or larger than but nearest to *key*. Successful resource search comes after that lookup message is correctly routed to related peer and distribution information of searched *key* is returned [4]. In this paper, we realize Multidimensional Mapping Mechanism through identifier division (rule 2) and mapping multidimensional space according to divided identifier groups (rule 3).

Rule 2. Identifiers Division: Let n be the identifier length, divide it into m groups, and each group's length p_i is constrained by expression $\sum_{i=1}^{m} p_i = n$. ($1 \leq i \leq m$).

Rule 3. Multidimensional Space Mapping: The ith dimension space corresponds to identifier groups $[p_i, p_{i+1}, p_{i+2},...,p_m]$, and the number of peers it includes is

$$s_i \leq 2^{n-\sum_{j=1}^{i-1} p_j} \ (1 \leq j \leq i-1, 1 \leq i \leq m), \text{ or } s_i \leq 2^{\sum_{j=i}^{m} p_j} \ (1 \leq i \leq j \leq m).$$

Rule 2, rule 3 can be explained in company with Fig. 3. In order to map peers to a smaller field, thus to simplify the DHT security mechanism, we divide the identifiers into certain groups. Let $p_i$bits denote the length of identifier group I ($i \in [1,m]$, where m is the total number of divided groups). Then aiming to the target of reducing the space that routing operation works in, we assign certain number of identifier groups to one space. The ith dimension space related identifier length is $n - \sum_{j=1}^{i-1} p_j$ ($1 \leq j \leq i-1, 1 \leq i \leq m$) or $\sum_{j=i}^{m} p_j$ ($1 \leq i \leq j \leq m$).

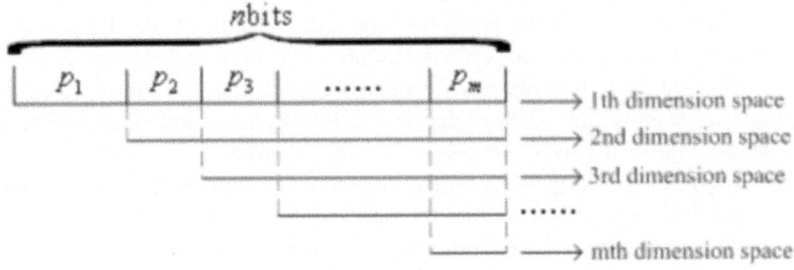

Fig. 3. Space mapping through identifier division

Thus the domain of the ith dimension space's identifier is ($currentID$, $curren$-

$tID+ 2^{n-\sum_{j=1}^{i-1}p_j}$] ($1\leq i\leq i-1$, $1\leq i\leq m$) or ($currentID$, $currentID+ 2^{\sum_{j=i}^{m}p_j}$] ($1\leq i\leq j\leq m$), here $currentID$ is identifier of the peer which is responsible for starting space mapping). In addition, the 1st ($i=1$) dimension space corresponds to the complete identifier, that is, the initial P2P topological space. The mth dimension space is the final dimensional space. When $m=1$, it means that the identifier have not been divided, and the related topology is just equal to traditional DHT.

3.4 Quick Location and Initial Security Check

In order to control the routing overhead introduced by Multidimensional Mapping Mechanism, the 1st dimension space still uses traditional DHT routing mechanism. For instance, if it uses Chord's routing algorithm [8], routing table of the 1st dimension space will divide the one-dimensional circle into n parts. Here n is equal to the length of identifier and should meet the constraint $n=\lceil\log N\rceil$ with network scale N. The ith field corresponds to the identifier [($nodeID+2^{i-1}$)/mod2^n, ($nodeID+2^i$)/mod2^n) ($1\leq i\leq n$), and chooses the first online peer in this field as the next hop peer of related table entry. Distribution information of sharing resource with identifier key is stored by the first peer which meets $nodeID\geq key$.

On this basis, we propose initial security check measure to avoid security issues in traditional DHT routing process. Peers use the initial security check measure to verify the lookup message they received and consider it as the evidence to judge whether the previous hop peer is malicious or not. Below is detailed procedures for algorithm 1 which define principle of initial security check measure.

1) If peer stores information corresponding to key in lookup message, then search successes and send key related information to the querier peer. Otherwise, go to 2);

2) If $nodeID$ is smaller than key, then the peer forwards lookup message. Otherwise, go to 3) If $nodeID$ is smaller than key, then the peer forwards lookup message. Otherwise, go to 3);

3) If $nodeID$ is larger or equal to key, traditional DHT will consider it as lookup failure, but this consideration is usually not reasonable. For instance, if there already exists peers responsible for information related to key in a peer and its previous hop peer, but the previous hop peer's routing table did not update in time, this is why we do not directly judge it as failure when $nodeID$ is equal to key and peer does not store key related information. We make a rule in such situation, peers search whether peer exists between key and $nodeID$ according to its routing table, if exists, go to 4); otherwise, go to 5);

4) Peer searches the largest identifier between key and $nodeID$ according to its routing table, then routes the lookup message to this identifier related peer;

5) Run space conversion mechanism, and continue to search in the mapped space.

Algorithm 1: Algorithm for initial security check measure
1: if (*store_info(key)* is TRUE)
2: *info = get_info(key)*;
3: *send_info(info,quefierID)*;
4: *return success*;
5: else
6: if (*nodeID<key*)
7:   *forward(key)*; //*continue routing the lookup mesage*
8: else
9:   if (*has_peer_in(nodeID,routing_table)* is TRUE)
10:    *pre_peer = the peer with the largest peer identifier between key and nodeID*;
11:    *reroute(key,pre_peer)*;
12:   else
13:    *startup space conversion mechanism*;

3.5 Space Conversion Mechanism

On the basis of multidimensional mapping mechanism and initial security check measure, space conversion mechanism is introduced to judge on what condition the multidimensional mapping mechanism will be called (Rule 4) to proceed the remainder routing operation in a relatively smaller field (Rule 5).

Rule 4. Space Conversion Condition: When $|nodeID - key| \leq \delta$, the inquery information will be routed to higher dimensional space to continue resource lookup.

Here δ, calculated by formula $\delta = 2\exp(sum(p_{i+1}, p_{i+2}, p_{i+3}, \ldots p_m))$, is the threshold which determines whether to run space conversion mechanism. It is defined by current dimension i and the length of identifier related to space with neighboring dimension. According to rule 4, if the difference between two identifiers of current peer and searched resource falls into the range of current space and the neighboring higher dimension space, space conversion will be start by current peer. The following rule 5 and rule 6 give the calculation conditions about the dimension of newly converted space.

Rule 5. The dimension i of the new mapped space should meet

$$2^{\sum_{j+1}^{m} p_j} \leq |currentID - key| \leq 2^{\sum_{j=i}^{m} p_j}.$$

Rule 6. $currentID = \begin{cases} nodeID. & nodeID \leq key \\ nodeID'. & nodeID > key \end{cases}$

The *currentID* is identifier of the peer which starts space convert mechanism when rule 4 works. Otherwise, the first peer with smaller identifier (*nodeID'*) but nearest to peer *key* recorded in routing table will be delegated to run space conversion mechanism.

Algorithm briefly generalizes the procedures of space conversion method.

Algorithm 2: Algorithm for space conversion mechanism
1: if (*|nodeID-key|<=δ*)
2: if (*nodeID<=key*)
3:   *currentID=nodeID*;
4:   *convert_space(currentID,i)*;

5: else
6:    *reroute the lookup message with key to the largest nodeID' that is less or*
       equal than key;
7:    *currentID=nodeID';*
8:    *convert_space(currentID,i);*
      //convert_space(currentID,i) converts the space to the ith
      //dimension by peer with nodeID equal to currentID
9: *convert_space(currentID,i)*
10:   *|currentID-key| should be in the nodeID range of i+1th and ith space;*

3.6 Routing in Final Dimension Space

During the space conversion process, if the dimension of the new space is m calculated under rule 5, the lookup message would be transferred to the final dimension space. According to space mapping mechanism, the final dimension space has the smallest area scale compared with space of other dimensions. Recurring to the neighbor set maintains by each peer, we rule that all the peers which are mapped to the area share routing information among each other. Then one step routing mechanism and final security check mechanism are proposed based on it, we will explain the two mechanisms along with the expatiation of the routing procedures in final dimension space.

Algorithm 3: Algorithm for routing operation in final dimension space
 1: direct_routing(*currentID, init_resultID*)
 2: if (*share(key, nodeIDs)* is TURE)
 3:   if (*nodeIDs* ==1)
 4:    *init_resultID=the nodeID of the peer found by share();*
 5:   else
 6:    *init_resultID=the nodeID of the peer with the updated info.;*
        //final security check mechanism by init_resultID
 7: if (*store_info(key)* is TRUE)
 8:   *resulted=init_resultID;*
 9:   *send_info(info, querierID);*
10:   *return success;*
11: else
12:   *resulted=the nodeID of the peer with nodeID that is larger than and nearest*
             to key;
13:   if (*store_info(key)* on *resulted* is TRUE)
14:    *send_info(info, querierID);*
15:    *return success;*
16: else
17:    *send_fail(key, querierID);*
18:    *return false;*

Algorithm 3 illustrates the main procedures of routing operation in final dimension space. Peer with identifier *currentID* is responsible for mapping remainder routing operation into the final dimension space. Firstly, peer *currentID* checks that if there is peer storing information inquired by lookup message according to the share information of other peers and routes the lookup message to the most appropriate peer (with identifier *nodeID*) if any. We called this procedure as one step routing mechanism.

As the routing table update will take a certain period of time, there may exists more than one suitable peer that stores the distribution information of searched resource with identifier *key*. So we do not return this peer (with identifier *init-resultID*) as the final lookup result (with identifier *resultID*), but employ it to run the final security check mechanism. If peer *init-resultID* does exactly store the searched resource information, lookup succeeds and *init-resultID* returns the information of *key* to querier (with identifier *requerierID*); else, peer *init-resultID* runs one step routing operation again and choose another appropriate peer as *resultID*. The final result of lookup message will be returned by peer *resultID* according to whether it stores *key* related information or not.

4   Performance Evaluation

To satisfy routing information requested by the multidimensional mapping mechanism proposed in this paper, peer mapped into new space needs to get some additional information except the current routing table. Suppose that all the other dimension spaces, except the final dimension space, follow the same routing table structures with current DHT protocol (take Chord for example here), then after comparing with table entries [5,7,8] and according to multidimensional space mapping (rule3), it can be concluded that the first dimension space is just corresponding with the entire previous structured P2P network, and the routing table needs no extra information. The maximum number of peers in space with dimension from 2 to m-1 is decreasing gradually, so as the entries of routing table. And the routing table of the i+1th dimension space just partially tallies with the ith dimension space's. Besides, the initial security check measure guarantees that only when difference between *nodeID* and *key* is relatively small the space conversion mechanism is called, i.e., the times of space conversion operation will be relatively few and this also further limits costs of routing table update introduced by secure routing method proposed in this paper.

As to the routing overhead, 1) if no malicious exists in the whole routing path, the routing path will be same with traditional DHT before falling into the final dimension space. According to the one step routing mechanism, the routing operation for lookup message only takes one step. But to the traditional DHT routing algorithm, it will need at least one routing operation when most related peers are online. Thus, routing overhead of secure routing method by this paper will not exceed the traditional DHT ($O(\log N)$); 2) if malicious does commit routing attacks during routing operation, lookup message will be routed to the relatively closest peer to *key* according to initial security check mechanism. This will effectively control the increase of routing overhead before mapping routing operation into the final dimension space not more than m-2 (here m represents the highest dimension of rule 2). Thus, routing overhead for this security method is no more than $O(\log N+m-2)$. Let p be the probability that a peer shows malicious behavior when routing lookup message, then the maximum routing cost of security method proposed in this paper is $(1-p)O(\log N)+pO(\log N+m-2)$, which also could be expressed as $O(\log N)+p[O(\log N+m-2)-O(\log N)]$. This value will gradually approach to $O(\log N)$ as network scale increases.

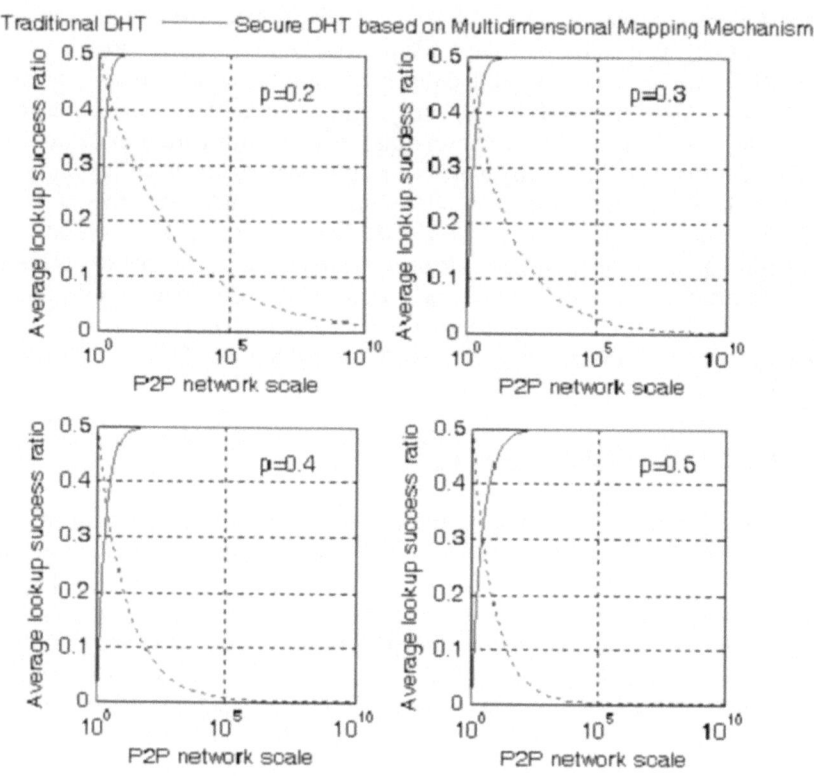

Fig. 4. Comparison of average lookup success ratio under various network environments

The probability p we introduced above ranges from 0 to 1. If taking $0.5\log N$ as the average routing hops for traditional DHT protocol [12], and supposing that resource *key* being searched has equal probability of really exists in current network or not, then average lookup success ratio of traditional DHT will be $F_1(p)=0.5*(1-p)^{0.5\log N}$, which means that only when the searched resource exists and no malicious peer commits routing attack along whole routing path will the lookup be success. For secure routing mechanism proposed in this paper, the average lookup success ratio turns to be $F_2(p)=0.5*(1-p^{0.5\log N+\lambda})> F_3(p)=0.5*(1-p^{0.5\log N})$, i.e., if resource required by lookup message does exactly exist, our proposed security method will fail the resource lookup only when all the peers involved in routing path commit routing attack (here λ represents routing costs introduced by space conversion). Fig. 4 illustrates comparison of average lookup success ratio when $p=0.2$, 0.3, 0.4, 0.5, respectively. With increasing of the network scale, DHT hiring secure routing mechanism proposed in this paper can achieve relatively higher success ratio comparing with traditional DHT.

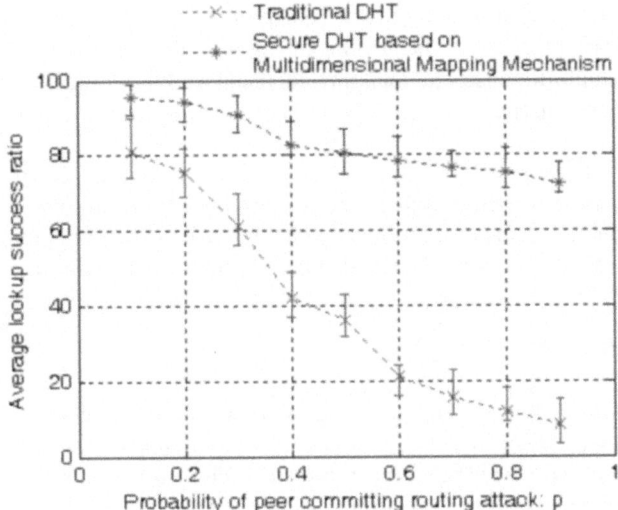

Fig. 5. Simulation results of average lookup success ratio

We also verify the analysis above through experiments in a simulated P2P network including 1000 online peers with 10bits (2^{10}=1024>1000) identifiers. We set 3bits for the identifiers group corresponding to final dimension space. For each routing experiment, a random $key \in [0, 1023]$ is firstly generated and store its information on right peer according to the routing algorithm, and then randomly generate a peer identifier $lookup\_nodeID$ which starts the lookup message to search resource key. Lookup success message will be returned if no malicious routing behavior took place during whole routing process. For experiments of traditional DHT, we suppose that probability of peer committing malicious routing behavior directly proportional to lookup failure caused by this. To compare traditional DHT and secure DHT based on multidimensional mapping mechanism, we repeat 10 groups experiments under each $p \in$ [0.1, 0.2, 0.3, 0.4, 0.5, 0.6, 0.7, 0.8, 0.9] and 100 times for each group for two kinds of DHT protocols. Fig. 5 shows the statistical result of traditional DHT and secure DHT. Lookup success ratio of both kinds of DHT protocol will decrease as probability p increases, but compared with traditional DHT, multidimensional mapping mechanism based secure routing method proposed in this paper can keep strong defense ability to malicious routing attacks and relative high average lookup success ratio as well.

5   Conclusion

In this paper, we propose a novel multidimensional mapping mechanism and secure DHT routing measures based on it against the routing security issues of structured P2P and limitations of current research methods. Multidimensional Mapping Mechanism simplifies the design and implementation through mapping routing operation into a smaller space topologized under the same geometry with current DHT topology. And this also guarantees the nice generality of our proposed method for applying to multiple types of DHT protocols. The results of simulation experiments show that after employing the multidimensional mapping mechanism based secure routing method, DHT can achieve a higher average lookup success ratio with limited cost of routing overhead.

For future work, more effort will be made to improve routing information update in newly mapped space to better control the routing overhead introduced by space conversion mechanism. Besides, final security check mechanism and determination of the lookup result in final dimension space also need further investigation.

Acknowledgments

This research work acknowledges the supports by the National Natural Science Foundation of China (60973140), the National Natural Science Foundation of Jiangsu Province of China (BK2009425), the Innovation Fund for Technology Based Firms (08C26213200495), the Key Technologies R&D Program of Jiangsu Province of China(BE2007058),the National Natural Science Research Program of Colleges of Jiangsu Province of China (08KJB520005).

References

1. Rowstron, A., Druschel, P.: Pastry: Scalable, Decentralized Object Location, and Routing for Large-Scale Peer-to-Peer Systems. In: Guerraoui, R. (ed.) Middleware 2001. LNCS, vol. 2218, pp. 329–350. Springer, Heidelberg (2001)
2. Zhao, B.Y., Huang, L., Stribling, J., Rhea, S.C., Joseph, A.D., Kubiatowica, J.D.: Tapestry: A Resilient Global-scale Overlay for Service Deployment. J. IEEE Journal on Selected Areas in Communications 22, 41–53 (2004)
3. Wallach, D.S.: A Survey of Peer-to-Peer Security Issues. In: International Symposium on Software Security, pp. 31–338. Springer, Heidelberg (2003)
4. Lua, E.K., Crowcroft, J., Pias, M., Sharma, R., Lim, S.: A Survey and Comparison of Peer-to-Peer Overlay Network Schemes. J. IEEE Communications Survey and Tutorial 7, 72–93 (2005)
5. Rescorla, E.: Introduction to Distributed Hash Tables. Technical report, IAB Plenary, IETF-65 (2006)
6. Sit, E., Morris, R.: Security Considerations for Peer-to-Peer Distributed Hash Tables. In: Druschel, P., Kaashoek, M.F., Rowstron, A. (eds.) IPTPS 2002. LNCS, vol. 2429, pp. 261–269. Springer, Heidelberg (2002)
7. Klemm, F., Girdzijauskas, S., Le Boudec, J.-Y., Aberer, K.: On Routing in Distributed Hash Tables. In: 7th IEEE International Conference on Peer-to-Peer Computing, pp. 113–122. Springer, Berlin (2007)
8. Stoica, I., Morris, R., Karger, D., Kaashoek, F., Baladrishnan, H.: Chord: A Scalable Peer-to-Peer Lookup Service for Internet Applications. In: Annual Conference of the Special Interest Group on Data Communication, pp. 149–160. ACM Press, New York (2001)
9. Hildrum, K., Kubiatowicz, J.: Asymptotically Efficient Approaches to Fault-tolerance in Peer-to-Peer Networks. In: Fich, F.E. (ed.) DISC 2003. LNCS, vol. 2848, pp. 321–336. Springer, Heidelberg (2003)

10. Castro M., Druschel P., Ganesh A., Powstron A., Wallach D. S.: Secure Routing for Structured Peer-to-Peer Overlay Networks. In: 5th Symposium on Operating Systems Design and Implementation (2002)
11. Castro, M., Druschel, P., Charlie Hu, Y., Rowstron, A.: Topology-aware Routing in Structured Peer-to-Peer Overlay Networks. Technical report, Microsoft Research (2002)
12. Wang, P., Hopper, N., Osipkiv, I., Kim, Y.: Myrmic: Secure and Robust DHT Routing. Technical report, DTC Research Report (2006)
13. Kamvar, S.D., Schlosser, M.T.: EigenRep: Reputation Management in P2P Networks. In: 12th International World Wide Web Conference, pp. 123–134. ACM Press, New York (2003)
14. Marti, S., Ganesan, P., Garcia-Molina, H.: DHT Routing Using Social Links. In: Voelker, G.M., Shenker, S. (eds.) IPTPS 2004. LNCS, vol. 3279, pp. 100–111. Springer, Heidelberg (2005)
15. Singh, M.G.: Routing Networks for Distributed Hash Tables. In: 22nd Annual Symposium on Principles of Distributed Computing, pp. 133–142. ACM Press, New York (2003)
16. Rarnasamy, S., Francis, P., Handley, M., Karp, R., Shenker, S.: A Scalable Content-Addressable Network. In: Annual Conference of the Special Interest Group on Data Communications, pp. 161–172. ACM Press, New York (2001)
17. Yu, Z.H.: Analysis of Malicious Behaviors in Peer-to-Peer Trust Model. J. Computer Engineering and Applications 43, 18–21 (2007)

A Practical OpenMP Implementation of Bit-Reversal for Fast Fourier Transform

Tien-Hsiung Weng[1], Sheng-Wei Huang[1], Ruey-Kuen Perng[1], Ching-Hsien Hsu[2], and Kuan-Ching Li[1]

[1] Department of Computer Science and Information Engineering Providence University
Shalu, Taichung 43301 Taiwan
{thweng,rkperng,kuancli}@pu.edu.tw
[2] Department of Computer Science and Information Engineering Chung Hua University
Hsinchu 300 Taiwan
robert@grid.chu.edu.tw

Abstract. In this paper, we describe our experience of creating an OpenMP implementation of Bit-reversal for Fast Fourier Transform programs from the existing un-parallelizable sequential algorithm. The aim of this work is to present an analysis of a case study showing the development of a shared memory parallel Bit-reversal for the FFT parallel code with practical and efficient use of multi-core machines. We present our implementation and discuss the results of the case study in terms of program improvement that may be needed to help parallel application developers with similar high performance goals. Our preliminary studies, results and experiments based on FFT code running on a four 4-cores Intel Xeon64 CPUs /Dell 6850 platform. The experimental results show that the performance of our new parallel code on 16 cores shared-memory machine are promising.

Keywords: Shared-memory parallel programming, OpenMP, Bit-reversal, FFT.

1 Introduction

The Fast Fourier Transform (FFT) is one of the most important algorithms used in many fields of science and engineering, especially in signal processing and computational fluid dynamics for solving PDEs. The FFT [2] uses a divide and conquer strategy to evaluate a polynomial of degree n at the n complex nth roots of unity. FFT is easier to parallelize and many parallel FFT algorithms on shared memory machines have been well studied and developed. But practical implementation of The FFT programs consist of two main parts. First, data reordering in the Fast Fourier Transform by permuting the element of the data array using Bit-reversing of the array index. This first stage involves finding the DFT of the individual values, and it simply passes the values along. Next, each remaining stages the computation of a polynomial of degree n at the n complex nth roots of unity is used to compute a new value depends on the values of the previous stage; this process, we called butterfly operation. A Bit-reversal is an operation for an exchange data between A[i] and A[bit-reversal[i]], where the value of i is from 0 to n-1 and value of n is usually 2 to the power of b.

P. Mueller, J.-N. Cao, and C.-L. Wang (Eds.): Infoscale 2009, LNICST 18, pp. 206–216, 2009.
© Institute for Computer Science, Social-Informatics and Telecommunications Engineering 2009

Then bit-reverse[i] = j, the value of j is obtained from reversing b bits from value of i. When the Bit-reversal is not properly designed, it can take a substantial fraction of total execution time to perform the FFT [4].

Our aim in this work was to realize an OpenMP implementation of the Bit-reversal for FFT from un-parallelizable sequential one. Our approach relies on performing single program multiple data (SPMD) style by adding the OpenMP parallel directives. We first discuss the related works. Later, we discuss the important design of our algorithm and compared with the original sequential algorithm. Then, we present the results of our evaluation of this parallel version of Bit-reversal on a four 4-cores Intel Xeon64 CPUs / Dell 6850 platform. We also discuss the possibilities for and challenges of further improvement of the parallel program in Section 5. Finally, we give our conclusions and future plans.

2 Related Work

Our aim in this work was to realize an OpenMP implementation of the Bit-reversal for FFT from un-parallelizable sequential one. Our approach relies on performing single program multiple data (SPMD) style by adding the OpenMP parallel directives. We first discuss the related works. Later, we discuss the important design of our algorithm and compared with the original sequential algorithm. Then, we present the results of our evaluation of this parallel version of Bit-reversal on a four 4-cores Intel Xeon64 CPUs / Dell 6850 platform. We also discuss the possibilities for and challenges of further improvement of the parallel program in Section 5. Finally, we give our conclusions and future plans.

The data reordering in the FFT program using Bit-reversing of array index has been well studied [3][4][6][8][9][10][12]. Most of the algorithms proposed are mainly for the uniprocessor [4][6][8][9]. The optimal Bit-reversal using vector permutations have been proposed by Lokhmotov [6]; their experiments have been run on single processor, but they claimed that their algorithm can be parallelized as well. Takahashi [13] implemented an OpenMP parallel FFT on IA-64 processors. Their code is a recursive FFT algorithm written in Fortran 90, but their bit-reversal algorithm is not presented. An algebraic framework for FFT permutation algorithm using Sisal, a functional language , an performance measurement was done on a Cray C-90 and SUN Sparc 5 machines [3][10]. Bit-reversal program must be carefully designed because it may take about 10-30% of the overall FFT computational time [6]. Not only that, it also can produce significant cache misses when its input data size is very large. This is due to the exchange between two data elements of an array that located in the distance far apart during the permutation of the data element using Bit-reversal of the array index. In addition, some of Bit-reverse sequential algorithms are non-trivial to be parallelized.

Our work is based on the sequential Bit-reversal algorithm proposed by Rodriguez [8], in which they designed an improved Bit-reversal algorithm for FFT. Even though their sequential algorithm appeared to be the best, it is not parallelizable without completely rewriting of its algorithm into a parallel one.

In this paper, we proposed our OpenMP implementation of Bit-reversal for the FFT using the so-called SPMD (Single Program Multiple Data) style of OpenMP, in which reducing number of cache misses and data locality are the main concern in the design of our code. The SPMD style of OpenMP code is distinct from ordinary OpenMP code. In most ordinary OpenMP program, shared arrays are declared and parallel for directives are used to distribute work among threads via explicit loop scheduling. In the SPMD style, systematic array privatizations by creating private instances of sub-arrays gives opportunities to spread computation among threads in the manner that ensures data locality [5]. An in depth study about SPMD style of OpenMP can be found in [5]. Programs written in SPMD style of OpenMP has been shown to provide scalable performance that is superior to a straightforward parallelization of loop for ccNUMA systems [6][11]. More advantages of using OpenMP to parallelize our code are portability, easy to use, easy to maintain as well as incremental parallelization. OpenMP [7] is an industry standard for shared memory parallel programming agreed on by a consortium of software and hardware vendors. It consists of a collection of compiler directives, library routines, and environment variables that can be easily inserted into a sequential program to create a portable program that will run in parallel on shared-memory architectures. It is considerably easier for a non-expert programmer to develop a parallel application under OpenMP than under either Pthreads or the de facto message passing standard MPI. OpenMP also permits the incremental development of parallel code. Thus it is not surprising that OpenMP has quickly become widely accepted for shared-memory parallel programming.

3   OpenMP Implemention

In this section, we give an overview of original un-parallelizable sequential Bit-reversal programs developed by Rodriguez [8]. Next, in Section 3.2 we present and discuss our OpenMP implementation. We describe the steps taken to create the OpenMP program as well as how we rewrote the program from the un-parallelizable one. We also explain our development of parallel Bit-reversal implementation using OpenMP SPMD style by examples.

3.1   Brief Overview of Sequential Bit-Reversal

Our work is based on an improved bit-reversal algorithm for the FFT by Rodriguez [8]. In their original algorithm, computation of the bit-reversal of index for data reordering calculates only the required bit-reversal of indices, which also eliminates the number of unnecessary bit-reversal and swaps. The bit-reversal is computed as bi-

trev= $\sum_{p=0}^{k} b_{p-1-k} 2^{k}$; this corresponds to the sequential pseudo-code as shown in Figure 1.

It uses only array A to store its input data and final results. When the algorithm uses only array A, the data reordering must perform the exchange between elements of A. Even though the swapping is only a simple exchange between the two elements of an array, it actually involves three assignment statements or copies actions. For instances, the swap(A[1],A[2]) produces the copy A[1] to Temp, then A[2] to A[1], and then Temp to A[1].

In this original sequential code as shown in Figure 1, it computes the index upper bound for the variable last = $(N - 1 - N_2)$ where N_2 is $\sqrt{N}$ when number of bits is even and is $\sqrt{2N}$ when number of bits is odd. This eliminates the unnecessary computation of bit-reversal, which reduces number of swaps. In term of the number of moves, it is actually takes $3*(N-N_2)/2$ moves, which is $1.5*(N-N_2)$.

```
0  Bit-reverse(N,p) {
1      NV2 = N >>1;
2      last = (N-1)-(1<<((p+1)>>1));
3      j=0;
4      for(i=1;i<=last; i++)
5      {  for(k=NV2; k<=j; k>>=1) j -=k;
6         j += k;
7         if (i < j) Swap(A[i],A[j]);
8  }
```

Fig. 1. An Improve Bit-reversal function by Rodriguez

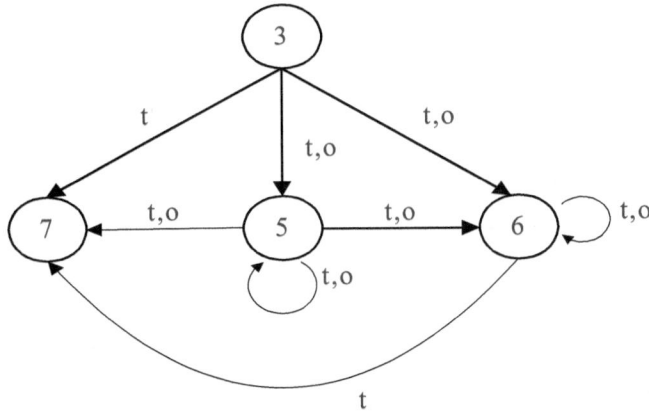

Fig. 2. Data dependence graph of Figure 1

In Figure 1, the program code is not parallelizable due to true and output data dependences between loop iterations of statements j = j - k, j = j + k, and if (i<j). Its data dependence graph is shown in Figure 2; there are true and output dependences between the statements labeled on each edge as t and o respectively. For instance, there are true dependence between statement 3 and 7; true and output dependences between statements 5 and 6, between 5 and 7; the loop on node 6 means there is true and output dependence between statement 6 itself on different iteration of the for loop. As the result, the value of variable j is accumulated for the entire nested for loop, this means that the computation for value of j is depend on the previous value of j. Hence, in order to parallelize this code, modification of this code is mandatory.

3.2 Our OpenMP Version of Bit-Reversal

We implemented our parallel code in this paper; it is quite similar to the one developed by Rodriguez, but with modification as shown in Figure 3 and 4. The original program designed by Rodriguez was not parallelizable because there are true data dependences, and therefore it is impossible to directly add the parallel OpenMP directive to this original for loop.

Figure 3 shows part of the FFT code that only computes data reordering performed by permuting the element of the data array A into M_f using Bit-reversing of the array index. That is $M_f[i]=A[Bit-reverse[i]]$. Instead of putting the result in A, we store the result into M_f. Both arrays have size of n, where n is 2 to power of k, where k is the number of bit to be reversed. In our program, we use more memory spaces in order to parallelize the code, reduce the total number of data copy; so we trade the space for shorter execution time.

In order to write a Bit-reversal parallel code using the SPMD style of OpenMP from the existing un-parallelizable sequential code, we first remove the true data

```
FFT(*A,n,nthreads) {
struct COMPLEX Mf[n],Nth[n/2],Tmp[n/2];
chunksize = n / nthreads;
int offset[nthreads];
  for(i=0;i<nthreads;i++) {
  if(i==0) j=0;
  else {
          k=nthreads/2;
          while(k<=j) {
               j=j-k; k=k/2;
          } //end while
          j=j+k;
  } //end else
offset[i]=j;
  } // end for
#pragma omp parallel private(threadid, address)
   { threadid = omp_get_thread_num();
     address = chunksize * threadid;
     Bit_reverse(A,Mf+address,
                 n,chunksize,offset[threadid]);
}
 . . .
 . . .
}
```

Fig. 3. Main function of the OpenMP FFT

dependence between iteration of variable j, in this case, by the pre-computation of the accumulated value of j for each starting chunk of iteration that will be executed in parallel by a thread. These accumulated starting values of j for each chunk of iteration are stored in the array offset. During the parallel execution of each threads, master thread or thread 0 will access the j from offset[0], thread 1 will access the accumulated starting value of j from offset[1], thread 2 will access accumulated starting value of j from offset[2], and so on. At the first glimpse on this observation,, it seems more pre-computation for accumulated value of j to be done, in reality, it actually only compute k number of elements for array offset, where k is number of threads.

Depends on nthreads (the number of threads), we compute chunk size by dividing the input size by the number of threads. Inside the parallel region where we added the *pragma omp parallel* directive, each thread will compute its address by multiplying the chunk size with its thread id (where master thread is 0, thread 1 is 1, etc.); the two variables (treadid and address) are declared to be private to thread using *private* clause. Next, each thread will call Bit-reversal function with five parameters as shown in Figure 4. First parameter is the first location of array A. Second is address or location of the M_f (M_f+address). Third, n is the size of input, then chunk size, and finally, the offset that have computed earlier.

In each thread, the Bit-reversal function is executed to compute different chunk of element $M_f[i]$, which is correspond to different part data element of M_f that is passed from M_f+address. For example, with n equals to 16, and number of threads equals to 2, master thread (or thread 0) will handle the $M_f[0]$ corresponds to M_f +0; thread 1 will process $M_f[0]$ corresponds to M_f +8, this means $M_f[0]$ is the pointer to actual location 8 of M_f, $M_f[1]$ is location 9 of M_f, and so on.

To better illustrate our OpenMP implementation of parallel code shown in Figure 3, we use a call to FFT(A, 32, 4) as an example, that is we call FFT with size of 32 and 4 number of threads. The chunk size of 8 is calculated. We then allocate array of size

```
Bit_reverse(*A, *Mf, n, chunksize, offset) {
   for(i=0;i<chunksize;i++) {
      if(i==0) j=0;
      else {
         k=n/2;
         while(k<=j) {
            j=j-k; k=k/2;
         }//end while
         j=j+k;
}//end else
      Mf[i]=A[j+offset];
   }
}
```

Fig. 4. Bit-reversal function

equal to number threads for offset, in this case, int offset[4]. Before we perform the Bit-reversal in parallel using OpenMP SPMD style to perform the permutation, we compute only four values to store in four elements of the offset, in this examples, we obtain 0, 2, 1, and 3 for offset[0], offset[1], offset[2], and offset[3] respectively. Inside the OpenMP parallel region where the pragma omp parallel directive is added, four threads will be created; each thread executes Bit-reversal function in Figure 4 with parameters to perform different part of data computation. In this case, thread 0, 1, 2, and 3 will call Bit-reverse with parameters ($M_f+(0*8)$ and value of offset[0] is 0), ($M_f+(1*8)$ and the value of offset[1] is 2), ($M_f+(2*8)$ and offset[2] is 1), ($M_f+(3*8)$ and the value of offset[3] is 3) respectively.

Hence, as shown in Figure 5, master thread(or thread 0) will handle the $M_f[0]$ corresponds to M_f+0; then it computes M_f [i]=A[j+offset]   for i from 0 to number of chunk size; where the offset[0] is 0, then $M_f[0]$=A[0+0], $M_f[1]$=A[16+0], $M_f[2]$= A[8+0], $M_f[3]$=A[24+0], up to $M_f[7]$=A[28+0].

Thread 1 will process $M_f[0]$ corresponds to Mf+8, is the pointer to actual location 8 of M_f, M_f [1] is location 9 of Mf, and so on. The offset[1] is 2. So, $M_f[0]$=A[0+2], $M_f[1]$=A[16+2], M_f [2]=A[8+2], $M_f[3]$=A[24+2], up to $M_f[7]$=A[28+2]. Note that $M_f[0]$ is actually the $M_f[8]$, $M_f[1]$ is $M_f[9]$, $M_f[2]$ is $M_f[10]$, etc. Other threads are also performed in similar manner

Thread ID	Starting address	Value of offset	Mapping							
0	0	0	0	16	8	24	4	20	12	28
1	8	2	2	18	10	26	6	22	14	30
2	16	1	1	17	9	25	5	21	13	29
3	24	3	3	19	11	27	7	23	15	31

Fig. 5. The result of mapping computed by threads

Note that in Figure 5, the variables n, chunksize, offset, i, j, and k are private variables, only array A and M_f are shared variables. Private data is usually stored locally to thread, which promote data locality.

As the results, each of the four threads will call Bit-reverse function that is shown in Figure 5 and they are run in parallel. Thread 0 computes the mapping of 0-0, 1-16, 2-8, 3-24, 4-4, 5-20, 6-12, 7-28. During the generation of this mapping i-j, it copy $M_f[i]$=A[j]. Thread 1 computes 8-2, 9-18, 10-10, 11-26, 12-6, 13-22, 14-14, 15-30, and so on. The complete computation of the mapping of the data reordering is shown in Figure 5.

4 Experiments

Our experimental results based on data reordering by Bit-reversal are performed on a four 4-cores CPUs 2.6Ghz Intel Xeon64 / Dell 6850 platform with 4 GB of main memory, 16KB L1 cache, 1MB L2 cache, and 4 MB L3 cache. We compile the parallel version of our program shown in Figure 3 with icc Intel OpenMP compiler with flag −O2 −openmp and run on Linux Cent OS.   We run this program with size of 2 to the power of 24, 25, 26, and 27 respectively. Each of this was run in parallel using 1, 2, 4, 8, 16 threads (one thread per core). Most of the related works have been run with data size of less than 2^{23}. Our experiment with data size of 2^{27}, the program approximately allocates total of 1 GB main memory.

To explain the shortcoming about the performance of our design algorithm on a uniprocessor machine, we also wrote a version of sequential algorithm, compiled with gcc with −O2 flag, and then run with different size of input data to compare with the original sequential code designed by Rodriguez. The experimental result is shown in Figure 6.

Our version of sequential code labels Wen and original sequential version by Rodriguez label Rod. Both run with input data size of 2^{20}, 2^{21}, up to 2^{27}. The results show that the performance of our sequential code is around 50% percent slower than the original sequential code as the input size grows larger. In the original program, Rod, there are approximately only N/2 number of swap; even though each swap involves 3 copies or moves, so with total of 1.5N number of copies or moves, but only one cache miss on each swap will occurred, so the total of misses is N/2 times. Our sequential code involves only N copies or moves, but each move will cause cache miss, hence there will be approximately the total of N cache misses.

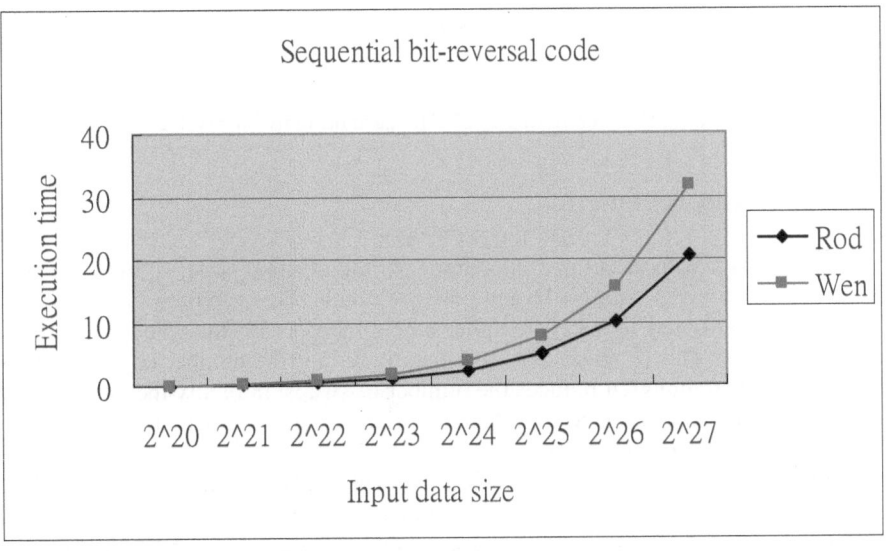

Fig. 6. Sequential codes run on uniprocessor

Figure 7 shows the performance of our OpenMP Bit-reversal. Our experiment is performed base on our SPMD style of OpenMP parallel code with different input sizes starting from 2^{24} up to 2^{27}. The performance results of our parallel SPMD style of OpenMP code shows scalable as the number of processors increases. With number of thread equals to one, the large number of cache misses overhead occurred, this lead to longer execution time, which is twice as much as the number of size increases. This overhead is amortized by the increasing number of threads. With increased number of threads, the total number of cache misses is reduced to as the number of chunk size. For instance, with n equals to 2^{24}, with one thread, the number of cache miss will be 2^{24} times, and with 16 threads, the cache misses will reduce to $2^{24}/16$ times.

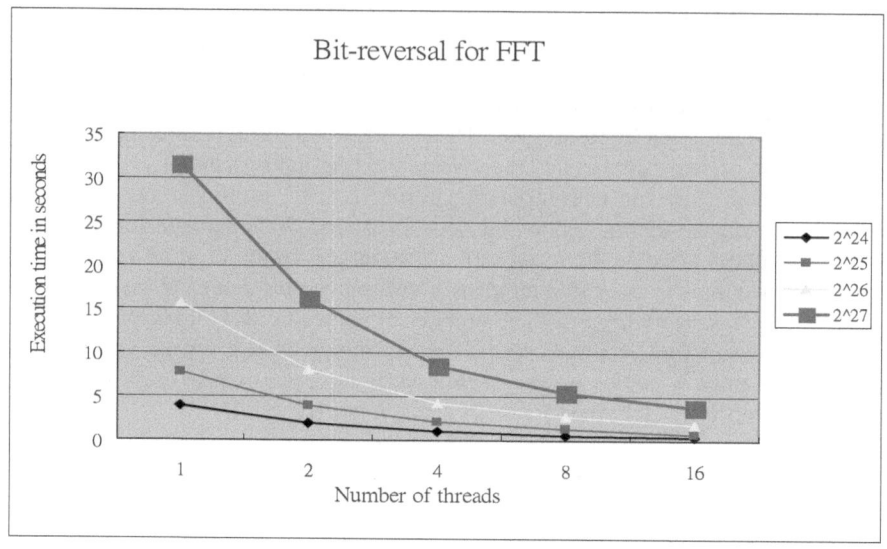

Fig. 7. Data reordering in FFT by permuting by bit-reversal

5   Possible Improvement

First we discuss the short coming encounter for the original code. In Figure 1, when we call this Bit-reverse with N=16 and p=4, we obtain the swap of A between 1-8, 2-4, 3-12, 5-10, 7-14, and 11-13. The upper bound index is 11, the value calculated for the variable, last. This program can significantly reduce the number of swaps from N to $(N-N_2)/2$. Even though it reduces the number of swaps, in reality the swap involves three copy actions. But, since the algorithm reduces the number of swap, there are only N/2 numbers of cache misses.

In our sequential code, the problem will occur when N is significantly large. Then, the swap between the two array elements involved exchange of the far distant element which causes large number of cache misses. For example, when N=2^{26}, then there are assignment statements as the following: $M_f[1] = A[33554432]$, $M_f [2] = A[16777216]$, and $M_f [3] = A[50331648]$, and so on. The copy of $M_f[1]$ from A[33554432], cause the first cache miss from reading from location 33554432, this causes it to load a consecutive block of array from location 33554432 into the cache probably up to the cache size. Then second assignment also cause the cache miss from reading A[16777216], which also load consecutive block of array from location 33554432 into the cache probably up to the cache size. Similar situations occur for the next iteration.

In our sequential code, it encounters more cache misses for very large input size, moreover, since we only run our code in shared-memory platform that has large (4MB) L3 cache and lower latency of memory access, the impact maybe minor. But to run on ccNUMA machines that have greater latency of remove memory access, the consequence is significant. Therefore, good data locality is needed to overcome these problems.

The possible improvement may be to use Bit-reversal data reordering by vector permutations proposed by Lokhmotov [6], They improved the cache optimal methods for Bit-reversal proposed earlier by Zhang [12], where it is designed to be cache optimal; the input source is copied into the buffer to form the tile. Finally, it copies the data from the buffer tile into the target tile. Its practicality, efficiency, and performance are still under our study and are currently our ongoing works.

6   Conclusions and Future Work

We have developed a practical OpenMP SPMD style Bit-Reversal for parallel FFT program from the existing un-parallelizable sequential code. It is a practical, easy to develop and maintain, as well as required only less programming effort. In our algorithm, we design to reduce the number of copy to variable and cache miss as possible when the number of threads getting large enough. Our experimental results are promising in this respect despite more memory spaces are used. Still, there may be more improvements are possible; especially the performance on ccNUMA machines where the memory latency is more significantly larger; therefore, the reduction of the number of cache misses, even for small number of threads is necessary, however, they do require more programming effort. We will continue to work to implement Bit-reversal code into the whole parallel FFT program, either iterative or parallel recursive one using Intel task queuing construct of OpenMP. We will also implement this algorithm using Cilk [14], and then compared them with other implementations.

Acknowledgements

This paper is based upon work supported in part by Taiwan National Science Council (NSC) Grants no. NSC95-2221-E-126-006-MY3 and NSC96-2221-E-126-004-MY3. Any opinions, findings, and conclusions or recommendations expressed in this material are those of the authors and do not necessarily reflect the views of the NSC.

References

1. Chapman, B., Bregier, F., Patil, A., Prabhakar, A.: Achieving High Performance under OpenMP on ccNUMA and Software Distributed Shared Memory Systems. Concurrency and Computation Practice and Experience 14, 1–17 (2002)
2. Cooley, J.W., Tukey, J.W.: An algorithm for the machine calculation of complex Fourier series. Math. Comput 19, 297–301 (1965)
3. Bollman, D., Seguel, J., Feo, J.: Fast Digit-Index Permutations. Scientific Progress 5(2), 137–146 (1996)

4. Karp, A.H.: Bit Reversal on Uniprocessors. SIAM Review 38, 289–307 (1996)
5. Liu, Z., Chapman, B., Wen, Y., Huang, L., Weng, T.H., Hernandez, O.: Analyses for the Translation of OpenMP Codes into SPMD Style with Array Privatization. In: Voss, M.J. (ed.) WOMPAT 2003. LNCS, vol. 2716, pp. 26–41. Springer, Heidelberg (2003)
6. Lokhmotov, A., Mycroft, A.: Optimal bit-reversal using vector permutations. In: Proceedings of ACM Symposium on the 19th Parallel Algorithms and Architectures, pp. 198–199 (2007)
7. OpenMP Architecture Review Board. Fortran 2.0 and C/C++ 2.0 Specifications, http://www.openmp.org
8. Rodriguez, J.J.: An improved Bit-reversal algorithm for the fast Fourier transform. In: Proceedings of International Conference on Acoustics, Speech, and Signal Processing, vol. 3, pp. 1407–1410 (1988)
9. Rubio, M., Gómez, P., Drouiche, K.: A new superfast bit reversal algorithm. International Journal of Adaptive Control and Signal Processing 16(10), 703–707 (2002)
10. Seguel, J., Bollman, D., Feo, J.: A Framework for the Design and Implementation of FFT Permutation Algorithms. IEEE Transactions on Parallel and Distributed Systems 11(7), 625–635 (2000)
11. Wallcraft, A.J.: SPMD OpenMP vs. MPI for Ocean Models. In: Proceedings of First European Workshops on OpenMP (EWOMP 1999), Lund, Sweden (1999)
12. Zhang, Z., Zhang, X.: Fast Bit-Reversals on Uniprocessors and Shared-Memory Multiprocessors. SIAM Journal on Scientific Computing 22(6), 2113–2134 (2000)
13. Takahashi, D., Sato, M., Boku, T.: An OpenMP Implementation of Parallel FFT and Its Performance on IA-64 Processors. In: Voss, M.J. (ed.) WOMPAT 2003. LNCS, vol. 2716, pp. 99–108. Springer, Heidelberg (2003)
14. Frigo, M., Leiserson, C.E., Randall, K.H.: The Implementation of the Cilk-5 Multithreaded Language. In: ACM SIGPLAN 1998 Conference on Programming Language Design and Implementation, pp. 212–223 (1998)

A Scalable, Vulnerability Modeling and Correlating Method for Network Security

Xuejiao Liu[1], Debao Xiao[1], Nian Ma[1], and Jie Yu[2]

[1] Institute of Computer Network and Communication, HuaZhong Normal University, China
[2] Department of Computer Science, National University of Defense Technology, China
liuxuejiao@gmail.com

Abstract. Nowadays attacks are becoming increasingly frequent and sophisticated, and they are also becoming increasingly interconnected. Recent works in network security have demostrated the fact that combinations of vulnerability exploits are the typical means by which an attacker can break into a network. It is therefore in great need of performing vulnerability analysis to do security analysis first and take the initiative to find hidden safety problems, then plan effective security measures. In this paper, we propose an analysis model, which derives vulnerability analysis functionality from the interaction of three distinct processes: scanning, modeling and correlating. Scanning is served as a significant issue for identifying vulnerabilities. Modeling provides a concise representation for expressing fact base such as host configuration, vulnerability information, and network topology. Moreover, correlating is used to provide a perspective into correlating isolated vulnerabilities in order to construct layered attack graph. Transition rule is presented in scalable design, which enables highly efficient methods of vulnerability correlation algorithm. Finally, a real case study has been described to demonstrate the capability of our model.

Keywords: Network security, scalable, modeling, vulnerability correlation.

1 Introduction

Today, with the enhancement of interconnection network and availability of network service, the new means of attack which are direct to the vulnerabilities of system and software are constantly emerging, there has be a growing trend toward vulnerability exploitation in combination. The network is facing increasingly serious security risks. In order to ensure the confidentiality, integrity and availability of computer systems and network, the network administrator needs to do the security analysis first for the system, take the initiative to find hidden safety problems and then plan effective security measures.

There are many potential interactions among multiple hosts and components in a network, such that the configuration and vulnerabilities of one machine will affect the security of others in the network [1]. Generally speaking, many services are perfectly secure when offered in isolation, but when combined with other services they tend to be exploited by attackers to badly compromise the network. There are numerous examples of such chains. A simple example has been illustrated in [6], that is file transfer

P. Mueller, J.-N. Cao, and C.-L. Wang (Eds.): Infoscale 2009, LNICST 18, pp. 217–227, 2009.
© Institute for Computer Science, Social-Informatics and Telecommunications Engineering 2009

protocol (ftp) services and hypertext transfer protocol (http) services hosted on the same machine. If an attacker can use the ftp service to write data to a directory that the web server can read, it may be possible for the attacker to cause the web server to execute a program written by the attacker. For this reason, configuring an enterprise network securely is becoming a daunting task for network administrator.

Even well administered networks are vulnerable to attacks due to the security ramifications of offering a variety of combined services. It is therefore necessary to consider security-related information to protect the network as a whole, including specific vulnerabilities on various hosts in the network, host configuration and connectivity between hosts. More importantly, a significant issue is to design automatic tools that can analyse the configuration of an enterprise network and find potential security vulnerabilities.

Currently, in the field of network security analysis, existing vulnerability techniques are quite effective to scan the single or multiple host vulnerabilities among the target network. However, these tools check all security holes only from isolated perspective, even if a single vulnerability may not appear to pose a significant treat, a combination of such vulnerabilities may allow attackers to reach critical network resources [2]. Our assumption is to model these information after scanning as a general representation of fact, and then based on the scalable transition rule as well as vulnerability correlation algorithm, layered attack graph with probability is construct to identify the critical node of a most possible successful attack.

When analyzing the security of an enterprise network, it is important to consider multi-stage, multi-host attacks. According to *monotonicity property* in [2], where an attacker does not decrease his ability by launching attacks, and hence does not need to relinquish privileges he already gained. That is to say, a determined attacker is not likely to stop at the machine he first compromises, but can be expected to try to penetrate deeper into the network by jumping from one machine to another. Under this assumption, our transition rule is designed based on the consequence of higher privilege escalated and additional connection established.

The remainder of the paper is organized as follows. In the next section, we summarize the principle of security design goals. An analysis model is then proposed in Section 3. Consequently, in Section 4, we discuss formal definition of fact, transition rules, layered attack graph, and give a detailed case study to illustrate the proposed model. Related work are reviewed in Section 5. Finally, Section 6 concludes the paper.

2 Security Design Goals

Network vulnerability is impossible to be entirely eliminate [6]. This is due to two factors. Firstly, a network to be useful it should offer some services. These services are based on various protocols and implemented in softwares which have not designed perfectly and possibly have some shortcomings of their own. Secondly, a network may likely contain hosts that are misconfigured which can be easily exploited by an attacker.

Just as the saying says "there is no absolute thing in the world", there is no absolute security in the network. Even a seemingly well guarded network is often infiltrated by a multi-step network intrusion. For security sake, it is therefore important to protect network assets while still allowing the normal functioning to ensure confidentiality, integrity and availability of the network. Thus, network security analysis must achieve the following goals.

Survivability in Service. Nowadays it is difficult to guarantee that any complex piece of software does not contain some flaws [3]. Network security analysis tries to limit vulnerability while still allowing the network to fulfill its purpose and doesn't effect its performance.

Proactive against Attack. Attacks have become more complex than previously and now attempt to exploit multiple vulnerabilities simultaneously while deploying sophisticated mechanisms to hide their malicious payload. Securing the network has never been more challenging than now. Preventing attacks is better than detecting successful attacks. The real problem facing today is not much how to defend against this divers array of attacks - they are emerging in astonishing speed - but how to defend against them in a proactive manner.

Therefore, the motto of security design is pro-action. It is an impending necessity for proactive and survivable architectures that provide fast recovery and convergence stability for networks susceptible to programmed attacks and faults [4]. That is, our main belief is that security risk(and for that matter vulnerabilities) should be handled at an early stage. The goal of network security analysis is to link up individual vulnerabilities using host configuration information in conjunction with network topology, then find the most vulnerable one to take timely measures.

3   Analysis Model

An accurate network security analysis requires a deep understanding of vulnerabilities and their effects on the network components and the knowledge of how these components are inter-related at which point to be exploited by an attacker in a networked system. Existing analysis models have the problems of inadequate capacity of quantitative analysis and lacking for vulnerabilities correlation.

To address these problems, a network security analysis model is proposed here, which can be described in terms of three steps: scanning, modeling and correlating. Each of these three parts is described briefly in the following sections.

In order to analyze the network vulnerabilities, analysis tools should be able to automatically establish the systematic attack scenarios based on the target network vulnerabilities, network services, connection relations and access authorization [5]. Fig.1 demonstrates the analysis model to construct layered attack graph for network security, benefiting from formal modeling and vulnerability correlation.

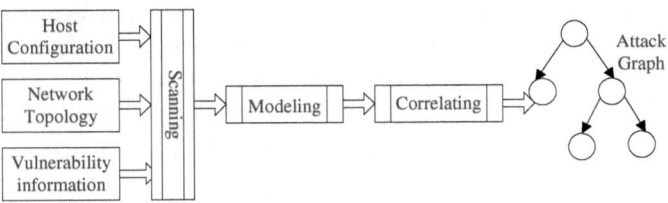

Fig. 1. Network security analysis model

Scanning: Scanning tools and techniques are used in scanning process, determining vulnerabilities of individual host as well as host configuration. Furthermore, understanding network topology (eg. Star, Ring, Fully connected or Partitioned) to specify network accessibility between pair of hosts is critical in considering security analysis.

Modeling: After scanning the network, it may generate a large volume of seemingly disparate information. Modeling process is then used to synthesis and convert these information into a unified representation. In this step we provide a standard representation called fact base for identifying and describing not only network topology but also host and vulnerability attributes.

Correlating: A network vulnerability considered in isolation may not appear to pose a significant threat. But the interdependency of vulnerabilities and the connectivity of a network make such analysis incomplete. To measure the overall security of a network one must first understand the vulnerabilities and how they can be combined to construct an attack.

In this step we perform vulnerability correlation based on the fact base using transition rules. Then an attack graph is produced showing the most vulnerable paths within network. The advantage of static modeling is that system administrators can take advantage of data provided by vulnerability scanners used on their systems and combine it with other known attributes of the network to provide a more complete view of the vulnerability status [7]. While vulnerability correlation algorithm then applies transition rules to static modeling, finding correlation relationship between them. These two approaches can benefit from each other when used together.

4   Vulnerability Correlation

4.1   Fact Modeling

Definition 1. A *fact F* is a triple (h, v, n), where (1) h is a set of attribute names about host configuration, each with an associated domain of values, (2) v is a list of vulnerability information about h, (3) n is an array of connection matrix used to identify all of the connection relations connected to h.

Each fact encodes the knowledge about the hosts within the network and it can be instantiated with any concrete term during modeling process.

4.2   Transition Rule

In order to integrate fact base modeled after scanning process into layered attack graph, a unified representation form is of great need for different types of information in F. Thus we design a XML-based rule for regulating the unified pattern representation. We derive transition rule to define logical relations between different facts. Fact information is static and isolated in nature, additional specification is supposed to give more consideration because dynamic connectivity between the hosts.

Definition 2. A *transition rule R* is defined using XML. Fig. 2 illustrates an example of the transition rule, where it has two XML tags: *fact* and *consequence*. Fact is a starting rule that begins to match the rule if the cve lists on specific host are matched. Consequence refers to the possible impact that vulnerability may result in.

```
<rule id="2" name="WS-FTP Buffer Overflow" probability="0.3">
  <fact cve="CVE-2001-1021,CVE-2007-2213"  host="ANY"
      from="ANY" to="ANY" privilege="ANY">

<consequence>
  <rule from="1:SRC_IP" to="1:DST_IP" privilege="user"
      addcon="1:SRC_IP;n(1:DST_IP)">
  </rule>
</consequence>

</fact>
</rule>
```

Fig. 2. An example of transition rule

The definition of the rule about every attribute is described in Table 1.

Table 1. The attributes of the rule

Attribute	Value	Description
id	decimal	the rule id
name	string	the rule name
probability	<1	the probability of the whole rule
from to	ANY	default value
	IPv4 (x.x.x.x)	IP address
	1:SRC_IP	IP address referenced within the previous rule of SRC_IP
	1:DST_IP	IP address referenced within the previous rule of DST_IP
	n(1:DST_IP)	any host connected to 1:DST_IP
host	h	host configuration information
cve	cve number	a list of vulnerabilities
privilege	none<user<root	privilege access

According to the example of the transition rule, we can see once the cve list is matched, host is padded with h in fact, a set of variables such as from, to and privilege are created for that particular vulnerability using n in fact. After exploiting the WS-FTP Buffer Overflow, the possible consequence may be that access from 1:SRC_IP to 1:DST_IP will escalate to user and there is another connection relationship from 1:SRC_IP to n(1:DST_IP). Finally probability is assigned to evaluate the reliability of this specific transition rule. The definition of probability is based on how difficult it is to exploit that vulnerability by the attacker, which depends on empirical knowledge.

4.3 Vulnerability Correlation Algorithm

Definition 3. Given a set of facts F, a set of consequents C, a transition relation $R_t \subseteq F \times C$, then the consequence may be the fact for another consequence, we called a subsequence relation $R_s \subseteq C \times F$, an *layered attack graph* G is the directed graph $G(F \cup C, Rt \cup Rs)$, $F \cup C$ is the vertex set and $R_t \cup R_s$ is the edge set. Figure 3 shows the vulnerability algorithm to construct layered attack graph.

Vulnerability interactions must be considered to ensure a thorough network security analysis, and that interactions produce sequences of events, called attack chains [1].

Definition 4. A layered attack graph may contain several paths from an initial fact to a successful state. For an attack path exploiting the transition rules $r_1 \rightarrow r_2 \rightarrow \ldots \rightarrow r_n$, suppose the probability for every rule is p_i, $i=1,2,\ldots n$, then the *attach chain probability* is $A=\{ p_1 p_2 \ldots p_n \mid 0 < p_i < 1 \}$

$$A = \prod_{i=1}^{n} p_i$$

What vulnerability correlation do is to generate attack graph. Furthermore, understanding how attackers exploit these vulnerabilities to accrue further capabilities is critical in considering security countermeasures. Fig. 3 illustrates vulnerability correlation algorithm.

INPUT: A set of fact base FB

OUTPUT: Layered attack graph G
1. $C, F, R_t, R_s \leftarrow \varnothing$
2.   for each $f \in FB$ {
3.   if f matches one of the rule
4.   create a consequence node c
            $C \leftarrow C \cup \{c\}$
            $F \leftarrow F \cup \{f\}$
            $R_t \leftarrow R_t \cup \{f \xrightarrow{\text{probability}} c\}$
5.   look up $f' \in FB$ such that there is rule(c) =fact f' {
            $R_s \leftarrow R_s \cup \{c \xrightarrow{\text{probability}} f' \xrightarrow{\text{probability}} c'\}$
            $F \leftarrow F \cup \{f'\}$
            $C \leftarrow C \cup \{c'\}$
6.   generate an layered attack graph G initialed with f
            }
        }
7.   compute every attack chain probability Ai
8.   output G with the max probability of attack chain

Fig. 3. Vulnerability correlation algorithm

As is shown in Fig. 3, in the correlating process, it first reads all the transition rules on startup in order to match individual rules. It functionality ressembles a logical tree cconsisting of "if" and "or" statements, joined together to provide reliable means of identifying attacks or network misbehaviour.

Attack graphs allow the security analyst to assess the true vulnerability of critical network resources, and to understand how vulnerabilities in individual network services contribute to overall vulnerability[14]. The probability index can be used as an indicator to trigger proactive and survivable methodologies to aid fast recovery at the earliest possible stages.

Such attack graphs allow one to see, step by step, the various ways an attacker can incrementally penetrate hosts within a network. Also, it is a layered graph constructed as a result of the relationship between the exploitation of vulnerabilities in different hosts that an attacker may likely carry out in order to reach his final goal.

4.4   A Case Study

In order to validate the effectiveness of the vulnerability correlation algorithm, we construct an experimental environment. Its topology is shown as Fig.4.

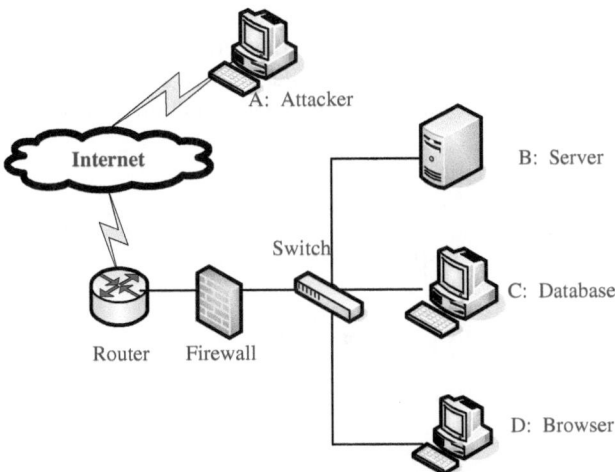

Fig. 4. Experimental network topology

The experimental environment is a switch network, including three host: B, C and D. Host B refers to server running IIS and SSH service. Host C is an important Oracle database running on Linux. Host D is a general browser which can access C. The firewall only allows the exterior hosts to access host B' s via WWW service. The attacker's goal was assigned to gain root privilege of the server.

After scanning and modeling process, the fact information (h and v) of each host is shown as Table 2 and connection modeling is illustrated in Table 3.

There are IIS buffer overflow and sshd buffer overflow existing in host B, which may lead to denial of service or the execution of arbitrary node. Due to another buffer overflow of Oracle in host C, successfully exploiting it an attacker can achieve privilege escalation.

Table 2. Fact (h and v) modeling of the experimental network

H	h	v	Description	Probability
B	122.204.142.1,*	CVE-2002-0150	IIS buffer overflow	0.3
		CVE-2002-0640	Sshd buffer overflow	0.6
C	122.204.142.2, Linux	CVE-2002-1767	Tnslsnr buffer overflow	0.3
D	122.204.142.3, Windows	CVE-2006-2373	SMB Privilege Elevation	0.7

Table 3. Connection relatiship modeling of the experimental network

n	A: Attacker	B: Server	C: Database	D: Browser
A: Attacker	y	80	n	n
B: Server	y	y	y	y
C: Database	y	80	y	y
D: Browser	y	80	y	y

According to vulnerability correlation algorithm as well as transition rule, the layered attack graph is automatically generated as Fig. 5. Each transition in the attack graph represents a specific exploit that an attacker can carry out. Because C trusts D, then D can access C without authenticate and the probability reaches to 0.9 high.

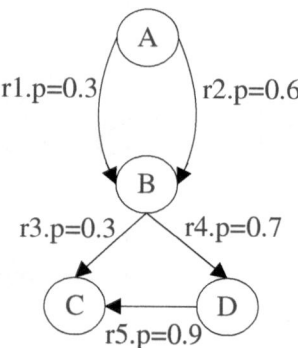

Fig. 5. The layered attack graph

Through analyzing Fig. 5, all the attack chains and their successful probability are shown as Table 4. From that, we can know that A→r2→B→r4→D→r5→C is the most dangerous path than others. So it is necessary to patch for the vulnerability of Tnslsnr buffer overflow in Oracle (CVE-2002-1767) as well as SMB Privilege Elevation (CVE-2006-2373). In addition, strengthening the authenticate relationship from browser D to Database C is also important.

Table 4. Analysis results of attack chain probability

attack chain	probability
A→r1→B→r3→C	0.09
A→r2→B→r3→C	0.18
A→r1→B→r4→D→r5→C	0.189
A→r2→B→r4→D→r5→C	0.378

5 Related Work

Recent works in network security have demostrated the fact that combinations of exploits are the typical means by which an attacker breaks into a network. Analyzing vulnerability for network security is still a new topic in security area, and currently it is rising more and more attentions.

Vulnerability Analysis: Vulnerability analysis techniques perform rigorous examinations to identify system vulnerabilities. There are quite a few vulnerability scanners that are quite effective at what they do - namely identifying vulnerabilities in specific hosts of a target network. Some of the tools are: Nessus [11], System Scanner [10], Retina [12] and etc. However, they do not attempt to identify how combinations of the vulnerabilities on the same host or between hosts on the same network can contribute to the exploitation of a network. Under such circumstances, vulnerability modeling and correlating method is proposed in this paper to improve the operation and efficiency of vulnerability analysis by creating abstract representation conducive to further analysis, chaining together the vulnerabilities uncovered by such tools and thus discover combinations of the exposed vulnerabilities.

Recent advances in vulnerability analysis have yielded the representation of organizing the chains of exploits in the form of graph-based analysis and model checking. While attack graph provides a visual means to represent attack scenarios, and its weakness lies in their construction, as the process is typically accomplished manually. Model checker is served as a powerful inference engine for chaining together network exploits, and suffers from scalability problems. In this paper we revisit the work of graph-based analysis.

Graph-based Analyis: Graph analysis is a common computer science technique to capture steps of a successful system compromise. Researcher have proposed a variety of graph-based approach to represent and generate attack graph (tree, petri net) for analyzing network security [1, 2, 5, 7, 8, 13, 14, 15], including logical attack graph [1], privilege graph [13], exploitation graph[7]and etc. Some of them has addressed scalability [1, 8] and automation [9] problems. Although the precise definitions of attack graph vary by author, there is little attention paid to quantitative analysis in the representation of attack graphs, which results in the attack graph being difficult to use and understand by human beings. Unlike existing approaches whose solutions requires removing the unnecessary nodes and decreasing the scale of the graph, our attack graph is constructed initially with max probability in the attack chain.

6 Conclusion

This paper has proposed a network security analysis model which aims to achieve security design goals, that is to provide proactive against attack and survivability in service. The layered attack graph is generated method based on transition rule. The scale problem of attack graph is solved by limiting attack steps and max successful probability of attack paths.

Layered attack graph directly illustrate casual relationship among vulnerabilities and therefore have the significant advantage of identifying the critical node by probability attached to the transition rule. Our analysis model will complement the available tools for a comprehensive analysis of the exposed network. The case study has shown that our vulnerability correlation algorithm is very efficient.

References

1. Ou, X., Boyer, W.F., McQueen, M.A.: A Scalable Approach to Attack Graph Generation. In: Proceedings of the 13th ACM conference on Computer and Communications Security (CCS 2006), Alexandria, Virginia, USA, October 30-November 3, pp. 336–345 (2006)
2. Jajodia, S., Noel, S., O'Berry, B.: Topological Analysis of Network Attack Vulnerability. In: Kumar, V., Srivastava, J., Lazarevic, A. (eds.) Managing Cyber Threats: Issues, Approaches and Challanges. Kluwer Academic Publisher, Dordrecht (2003)
3. Andrews, J., Moss, T.: Reliability and Risk Assessment. The American Society of Mechanical Engineers (2002)
4. Qu, G., JayaPrakash, R., Hariri, S.: A Framework for Network Vulnerability Analysis. In: Proceedings of IASTED International Conference Communications, Internet and Information Technology (CIIT 2002), St. Thoams, Virgin Islands, pp. 289–298 (2002)
5. Man, D., Zhang, B., Yang, W., et al.: A Method for Global Attack Graph Generation. In: IEEE International Conference on Networking, Sensing and Control (ICNSC 2008), China, April 6-8, pp. 236–241 (2008)
6. Ritchey, R.W., Ammann, P.: Using Model Checking to Analyze Network Vulnerabilities. In: Proceedings of the IEEE Symposium on Security and Privacy, Washington, May 2001, pp. 156–165 (2001)
7. Li, W., Vaughn, R.B.: Cluster Security Research Involving the Modeling of Network Exploitations Using Exploitation Graphs. In: Proceedings of the Sixth IEEE International Symposium on Cluster Computing and the Grid Workshops, CCGRIDW 2006 (2006)
8. Ammann, P., Wijesekera, D., Kaushik, S.: Scalable, Graph-based Network Vulnerability Analysis. In: Proceedings of the 9th ACM Conference on Computer and Communications Security, Washington, DC, USA, pp. 217–224 (2002)
9. Sheyner, O., Haines, J., Jha, S., Lippmann, R., Wing, J.M.: Automated generation and analysis of attack graphs. In: Proceedings of the 2002 IEEE Symposium on Security and Privacy (S&P 2002), pp. 273–284 (2002)
10. Internet Security Systems, SystemScanner, http://www.iss.net
11. Tenable Network Security, Nessus, http://www.nessus.org
12. eEye Digital Security, Retina Network Security Scanner, http://www.eeye.com/html/index.html

13. Dacier, M.: Towards Quantitative Evaluation of Computer Security. Ph.D Thesis, Institut National Polytechnique de Toulouse (Decemeber 1994)
14. Noel, S., Jacobs, M., Kalapa, P., Jajodia, S.: Multiple Coordinated Views for Network Attack Graphs. In: Workshop on Visualization for Computer Security, USA, pp. 99–106 (2005)
15. Zhang, S.J., Li, J.H., Chen, X.Z., Fan, L.: Building network attack graph for alert causal correlation. Computer & Security, 1–9 (2008)

A Self-adaptive Fault-Tolerant Mechanism in Wireless Sensor Networks

Wei Xiao[1,2,*], Ming Xu[1], and Yingwen Chen[1]

[1] School of Computer, National University of Defense Technology, Chang sha, China
[2] Hunan Normal University, Chang sha, China
{xiaowei}@hunnu.edu.cn

Abstract. This work was motivated by the idea of getting admirable fault-tolerant and efficient performance in application when smart sensors are engaged in 'in-network' computing in wireless sensor networks. In such applications, the objective of the sensor network is to repeatedly compute and then deliver to a server some results based on the values measured at the sensors. It is crucial for the sensors to form an optimal network topology and tune to transmission attempt rates in a way that optimize network throughput. However, we cannot ignore the influence from the fault node occurring in the network when the optimal network topology is constructed, which might decrease reliability of data transmitting using formed topology in some applications. So, in this paper, we proposed a self-adaptive way which identifies the node's confidence rate in accordance with its fault possibility, which in turn figures out the weighted volume between any two adjacent nodes. Moreover, we discussed and tried to solve the problems on FTMAWSS (fault-tolerant maximum average-weighted spanning subgraph) in weighted connected graph initiating from clustering WSNs. Because of the use of the tolerant fault, the correctness and efficiency about sensing values in data processing could be guaranteed in our mechanism. Simulation results confirmed the validity of the proposed algorithm with a high degree of accuracy and demonstrated that our proposed way could be scaled to large networks.

Keywords: Fault-tolerant, self-adaptive, sensor networks.

1 Introduction

The potential range of WSNs applications cover a large number of domains from physiological, habitat and environmental monitoring, condition-based maintenance, smart spaces, military, precision agriculture, transportation and inventory tracking [1,2]. Because sensing devices now combine the functions including sensing, computing, and wireless communication, so this smart sensor may have only modest computing power but the ability to communicate will allow sensors to organize themselves into a network and collaborate to execute tasks more complex than just sensing and

---

* This research was supported by China NSF No.60773017 and the Hunan Province Natural Science Foundation of China under the grant NO.06JJ50107.

P. Mueller, J.-N. Cao, and C.-L. Wang (Eds.): Infoscale 2009, LNICST 18, pp. 228–240, 2009.
© Institute for Computer Science, Social-Informatics and Telecommunications Engineering 2009

forwarding the information. This networks environment is defined as 'in-network' computing.

As we known, a global computation proceeds in step comprising of certain local computations at each sensor. Thus, the faster the sensors complete their share of local computations the higher will the global computation rate be. The more frequently exchange of results among neighboring sensors can occur, the more rapidly the progress of the computation may run. Therefore, when the computing rate of nodes is fixed, the packet transport rate is critical capability for the preferable ability of holistic networks computing in sensor networks [6]. And also in [6], it gives a way to optimize communication throughput and form an optimal network subgraph, which express best certain performance (computing rate or delay) besides the additional complexity. However, the decreasing of practical value in given subgraph for the influence of fault node cannot be considered.

Nodes in WSNs are prone to failure due to energy depletion, hardware failure, communication link errors, malicious attack, and so on. So it is essential to provide fault tolerant techniques for distributed wireless sensor networks. Moreover, there are some desired ways to work out faults in the WSNs. One important approach for dealing with the inherent lack of structure in sensor networks has been dominating set based clustering [3,4]. In this paper, we consider only 'soft fault' which may occur in a system on either a permanent or a transient basis. The fault nodes could be detected with special algorithm using transmitted values at sink or aggregated node. Then we could assign nodes with confident rate (CR) respectively and modify transport attempt probability (TAP) at nodes dynamically. So the self-adaptive of sensor networks can be used to construct an optimal network subgraph with fault tolerant in this paper in order to form an effective, practical subgraph topology.

The remainder of the paper is organized as follows. Section 2 provides briefly some relation work, and then gives our difference work. Section 3 the two main aspects in my work are proposed respectively and the algorithms are given. Section 4 presents the simulation experiments and some analysis. Finally section 5 concludes this study and future directions.

2 Related Works

On the one hand, in recent work, many self-adaptive algorithms and protocols have been developed in ad hoc and sensor networks. Its various aspects, including topology discovery and control, scheduling, localization and energy efficiency, have been addressed in the papers. For example, topology formation and scheduling for communication networks have been discussed in [5].The optimal self-organization topology building , include centralized as well as distributed algorithms, is give in ad hoc wireless sensor networks in [6]. [7] Presents a distributed evolutionary algorithm for reorganizing network communication and a message efficient clustering algorithm for sensor networks. Moreover, various self-adaptive procedures are described in [8].On the other hand; in-network aggregation approaches, such as gossip and hash-based algorithms are used to minimize the energy spent in the aggregation operation. Hybrid algorithms have been proposed that methodically try to optimize the use of efficient tree aggregation in [9].Dasgupta [10] presents a tree-based aggregation algorithm. Heidemann et al. [11]

proposes a directed diffusion mechanism in which a user's queries are forwarded to an application aware sensor node based on a least-cost algorithm.

Our work differs from the previous work in the following aspects. Firstly, different from the normal aggregation approaches in fusion nodes, the infections of fault values from sensor to the final products will be considered in our works. We can alleviate fault sensor effect to final answer in fusion nodes furthest, by means of reducing confidence rate of fault nodes step by step. Secondly, the better networks throughput topology in networks will be studied all together. We achieve a FTMAWSS (fault-tolerant maximum average-weighted spanning subgraph) in the connected graph, which is modified from MAWSS (maximum average-weighted spanning subgraph) in [6].

3   Self-adaptive Fault-Tolerant and Optimal Throughput Topology

We assume that a large number of static sensor nodes are placed in a region. These sensors are not only engaged in collecting-and-delivering task but simple integrating data job. Nevertheless, the uppermost values aggregation is completed in fusion nodes, which have strong computing and transmitting power. Fig.1. shows a traffic model for a sensor node in our computing networks. A simple integrate algorithm running on each sensor uses local values and data packet from the other neighbor sensors. And the data packet to be sent to the neighbors is queued up in a packet queue. The nodes within the transmission range of a sensor are designated as its neighbors.

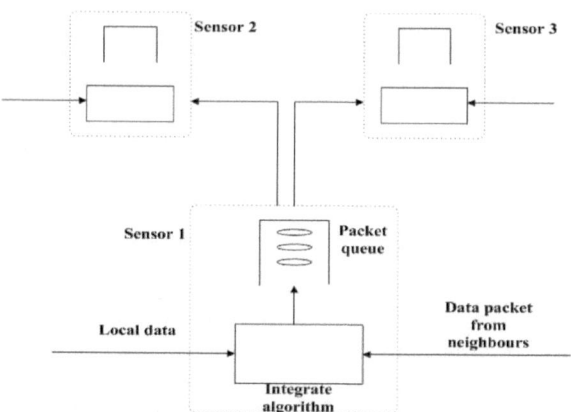

Fig. 1. A traffic model for sensors carrying out values and integrate computation

3.1   Preliminaries

Let $G(V, E)$ denote a connected weighted graph with vertex set V ($|V| = N$), edge set E and weight function $\psi : E \to R^+$. The weight value of an edge $(i, j) \in E$ is denoted by $\psi(i, j)$. Edge weight values generally include link length, skip numbers, and delay times .etc. In our work, the edge weight will be given in following section. We assume all sensors transmit using a fixed transmit power. Without loss of generality, in this paper we assume G is clustering with a fixed sink node and every sensor nodes in G can sense the same event happen in the deploying field. The fusion node has enough computing power and transport ability to achieve data aggregating and information diffusion. A sensor cannot transmit and receive simultaneously.

We assume that time is slotted and channel access is random. In each slot, sensor i decides to transmit packet with probability α_i and decides to receive with probability $(1-\alpha_i)$; α_i is called the ***transport attempt probability (TAP)*** of sensor i, which can be defined as data packet transport throughput and modified based on environment or node state change. When a sensor' TAP is higher, the more data packets are conveyed to other nodes. The more frequently exchanges of results among neighboring sensors can occur, the more rapidly will the overall computation converge. The more rapid the progress of the computation, the more fast the variations of a spatio-temporal process that can be tracked. Thus, we could search a fine way to construct the optimal communication throughput subgraph.

On the other hand, when the sink or aggregated node encounters fault data from fault sensor nodes, detecting it and throwing its impact on the aggregative values in fusion nodes is best choice. So we assign ***confidence rate (CR)*** to each sensor nodes based on deviation between their values with mean values, decrease fault effect on fusion datum, i.e., sensor i will be assigned c_i as confidence rate. Moreover, we give a relational function between CR and TAP, and use it to tie with these two main parameters in my task.

3.2 Modified Self-adaptive Fault-Tolerant Method

In this section, we assume that the sensor graph is multipath routing and can be used with DOI (Duplicate and Order Insensitive) data structure for duplicate elimination [12]. After the value from sensor sensing event and the packet from neighbor are sent to the sink or aggregated node, the detection of data failure and the CR assignment are processed quickly at the sink. In this paper, fusion sensor includes the sink or aggregated node.

Firstly we initialize set $c_i = \dfrac{1}{N}$ and then a weighted averaging process is done at the fusion sensor. The average value is given using formula (1).

$$avg = \frac{\sum_{i=1}^{N} c_i}{N} \tag{1}$$

Where c_i is confidence rate of sensor i which is assigned by fusion sensor, d_i is value from sensor i sense in circumstance. N is the number of nodes in G.

Afterward the maximum distance of the value to the average is computed. Then, this value is used to compute dissimilarity of each node value from the average, see (2). Formula (3) typically used to find distance of two objects [13].

$$m = \max(\{|avg - d_i|, \forall i \in V\}) \qquad (2)$$

$$D(d_i, avg) = \cos([1 - \frac{|avg - d_i|}{m}] \times \frac{\pi}{2}) \qquad (3)$$

The current confidence rate value to each node has an inverse relation to the dissimilarity of node to the average. In other words, if dissimilarity is large, confidence is low and if it is low, the confidence is large. We use (4) and (5) to get current confidence to each node.

$$c_{i-cur} = 1 - D(d_i, avg) \qquad (4)$$

$$c_i = \gamma \times c_{i-old} + (1 - \gamma) \times c_{i-cur} \quad \gamma \in [0,1) \qquad (5)$$

Where c_i is final confidence rate at this round of decision making process is, γ is an empirical parameter. Through this process, nodes that are faulty get less and less weighted so their values get less effective. Fusion sensor assigns confidences rate to detectors; after each round of decision making process, fusion sensor reevaluates these confidences. The confidence rate to sensor will be increased if it has large correlation with final answer in this round and vice versa. As a result of this adaptation process, large weights are assigned to sensors which their history of decisions shows more correlation to the decisions of fusion sensor. Besides above action, the other effect related with transport attempt probability is given in following section.[13]

3.3 The Relational Function between Transport Attempt Probability and Confidence Rate

The relationship between transport attempt probability α_i and confidence rate c_i will be considered in this paper, it is key factor in our proposed tasks. The objective we can achieve higher throughput and best fault-tolerant capacity will be come true, if we find the novel relationship between α_i and c_i. The following formula (6) is given as our selective function.

$$\alpha_i = \begin{cases} \varepsilon_{upper}, & if & c_i \geq \varepsilon_{upper}; \\ c_i^2, & if & \varepsilon_{lower} \leq c_i < \varepsilon_{upper}; \\ 0, & otherwise. \end{cases} \qquad (6)$$

Where ε_{upper} and ε_{lower} are defined as the highest confidence rate and the lowest confidence rate respectively.

In order to calculate transport attempt probability (TAP), bounds on c_i need to be established. We consider that the TAP α_i will increase exponentially with the increase of the CR c_i among bounds. When c_i is under ε_{lower} that mean sensor i is fault with high probability and lost his basic transporting and computing ability with higher probability, so we can assign its TAP is zero. However, when c_i in sensor i exceed ε_{upper} too much, α_i would be assigned much higher fixed value. Nevertheless, the receive rate $(1-\alpha_i)$ is special lower when sensor i is assigned a very higher value, so the small quantity of data packets from neighbors are received. Therefore, we assign a fixed value ε_{upper} as TAP when c_i exceed ε_{upper} . These changes can be seen in fig .2. The best bounds on α_i created from c_i will be investigated carefully in order to gain efficient throughput topology in given sensor networks.

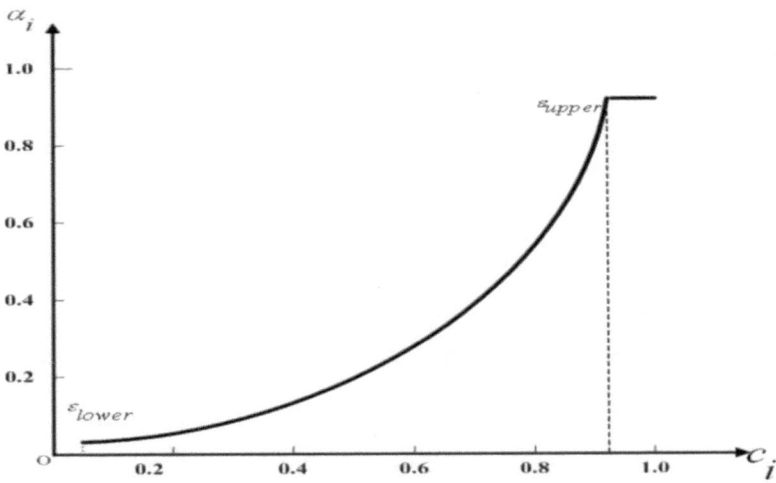

Fig. 2. Function about confidence rate and transport attempt probability

3.4   The Algorithm on Constructing the Fault-Tolerant Optimal Throughput Subgraph

In my applications, the sensors will monitor the environment and collect datum autonomously. Then the sensed values are delivered to sink or fusion sensors. Our work focuses on this paradigm. We consider a random access communication model.

In $G(V,E)$, let $N_i(G$) is the set of neighbors of i and $n_i(G$) is the number of neighbors of i in topology G . Let for every $(i, j)\in E$, p_{ij} , formula (7) give, denote the probability of successful transmission from sensor i to j and also can be defined as weight value in edge (i, j) . $G(V,E)$ With p_{ij} for every edge (i, j) also can be defined as weighted connected graph.

$$p_{ij} = \begin{cases} 0 & , \quad if \alpha_i = 0 \quad or \quad \alpha_j = 0; \\ \alpha_i(1-\alpha_j)P((\dfrac{d_{ij}}{d_0})^{-\eta} \geq \beta), & otherwise. \end{cases} \qquad (7)$$

Where d_{ij} is the distance between i and j, and d_0 is the near-field crossover distance.

The last term in (7) is $P((\frac{d_{ij}}{d_0})^{-\eta} \geq \beta)$ where $(\frac{d_{ij}}{d_0})^{-\eta}$ denotes the path loss with exponent η. β is a given threshold.

Let $G' = (V', E')$ denote a subgraph of a given connected graph G. $N_i(G')$ is the set of neighbors of i in topology G'. $n_i(G')$ is the number of neighbors of i in topology G'.

We can give formula (8) for each i. $M_i(G')$ may be defined as the average throughput of sensor i :

$$M_i(G') = \frac{1}{n_i(G')} \sum_{j \in N_i(G')} P_{ij} \tag{8}$$

$$\xi(G') = \sum_{i \in V'} M_i(G') \tag{9}$$

Define a function ξ on G' as (9), which give the total throughput in G' and also we can define $\hat{G} = \arg\max_{G' \in Gsub} \xi(G')$ where G_{sub} the set of all connected spanning subgraphs of G. Moreover, G_{sub} is nonempty since $G \in G_{sub}$. Otherwise, we recall that TAP α_i is tuned by CR c_i which is adjusted self-adaptive fault-tolerant method. So we call $\hat{G}$ the fault-tolerant maximum average-weighted spanning subgraph (FTMAWSS). Because maximum average-weighted spanning subgraph (MAWSS) for directed and undirected graphs is NP-complete [6], FTMAWSS is NP-complete too.

In the following, we will give centralized FTMAWSS algorithm. The basic idea of constructing the following subgraph comes from [6]. Firstly, we let $\max e(i)$ denotes the heaviest outgoing edge for node i , and $W \max e(i)$ denotes its weight. $E \max e(G) = \{\max e(i) | i \in G\}$ is the set of maximum weight outgoing edges of all the nodes in G. It is clear that FTMAWSS contains $E \max e(G)$. Hence if $(V, E \max e(G))$ is strongly connected, we finished. Otherwise, we consider the $\psi(i, j) = W \max e(i) - \psi(i, j)$, which help us to construct minimum weight outbranching rooted at each i . The minimum weight branch pick out edges with small $\psi(i, j)$ which are the edges with large $\psi(i, j)$. The resulting graph is taken as an approximation to the FTMAWSS. Algorithm is following:

Algorithm 1. Algorithm for finding an approximation $\hat{G}$ to the FTMAWSS of the graph G

Update CR

1. get measures from sensors in graph G, compute average and confidence rate for every sensor nodes using formula (1)-(5).

2. send to all sensors with their updated CR(confidence rate) separately.

3. all sensors determine their TAP(transport attempt probability) separately in accordance with formula (6)

Create FTMAWSS

4. If $(V, E \max e(G))$ is strongly connected then $\hat{G} = (V, E \max e(G))$

5. Else

6. for all $(i, j) \in E$, $\hat{\psi}(i, j) = W \max e(i) - \psi(i, j)$ and set $G_{min} = (V, E, \hat{\psi})$

7. For all $i \in V$, find the minimum weight out-branching of G_{min} rooted at i, be defined as E_{out}^i.

8. $\hat{G} = (V, \bigcup_{i \in V} E_{out}^i)$

We can use this algorithm to create fault-tolerant subgraph from a connected or strongly connected graph. Fig.3. shows topology structure till 300 slots with 100 random sensors deployed in specify area with no fault sensors. Fig.4. shows FTMAWSS constructed from Fig.3 with some fault sensors. In Fig.4, the red dots are the fault nodes, which turn to isolated nodes in FTMAWSS.

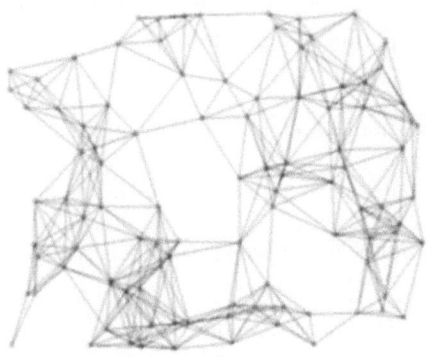

Fig. 3. Topology discovered till 300 slots by 100 sensors with no fault node

Fig. 4. Shows FTMAWSS constructed from Fig.3 with three fault sensors

4 Simulation Results

In this section we provide our simulation results to evaluate its performance using the NS-2 simulator [15]. In this set of simulations, nodes are randomly distributed in a

1000m × 1000m region. We have chose scenarios which consist of several sensors field of different population sizes ranging from 100 to 500 sensor nodes. In the simulation, the propagation model is the two ray ground model, the MAC protocol is IEEE 802.11, and the routing protocol is AODV. The broadcast data packets were sent using CSMA/CA. The sink node will be located on the top of the network. The nodes beside the sink would all be sources in experiment field. Table 1 lists the simulation parameters we have used in our experiments.

Table 1. Simulation parameters

Parameters	value
Simulation time (s)	500
Number of node	100-500
Source data rate (evenMsgs/s)	10
Number of source nodes	100-500
Radio range (m)	20
Transmit energy (mW)	14.88
Receive energy (mW)	10.25
Dissipation in idle (mW)	8.13
Dissipation in sleep (Mw)	0.012

We assume slot synchronization among sensors. We use synopsis diffusion approach and DOI (Duplicate and Order Insensitive) data structure for duplicate elimination [14] to guarantee multi-path routing scheme in networks initially. In each experiment we picked the average of ten runs of our algorithms as the output results. We used ε_{upper} =0.85 and ε_{lower} =0.08 in our experiments and the following metrics to evaluate our mechanism:

- Average delay: average latency from the moment a packet is transmitted to the moment it is received at the sink.
- Average packet loss ratio: number of total packets is lost at nodes to the number of total packets sent at nodes ratio.
- Average effective packet delivery ratio: number of correct packets is received at sink to the number of total packets is received at sink ratio.

Note that, we will also use term FTMAWSS/MAWSS to denote an algorithm for adopting a FTMAWSS/MAWSS topology in the following experiment.

4.1 The Effectiveness of FTMAWSS

Firstly, we consider distinction of networks ability in FTMAWSS comparing with result in MAWSS [6]. Node failures are simulated by injecting especial values to a fixed fraction of the nodes simulated. These nodes were randomly chosen from the sensor field and inject fault values at a random time during the simulation.

Average delay is particularly important in WSNs applications, which demand a fast and dependable response. Generally, when network size is increased, the delay gets higher due to the greater number of hops a packet travel from source to sink. In MAWSS, packets will backdate then cause higher delay when meeting drawback node, because MAWSS don't consider isolating fault node in his construction. As shown in the graph of Fig. 5, for a fixed network size, say 400 nodes, the delay of MAWSS with 20% node failures is 90% higher than FTMAWSS with 20% node failures. We also see that the increasing proportion of delay time in FTMAWSS is lower when the number of failed node is increased.

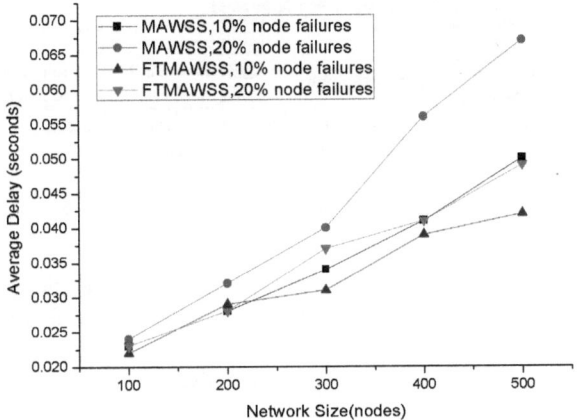

Fig. 5. Average delay with node failures

Sensor network reliability can be measured by its average effective packet delivery ratio, which reflects the correct rate of packets transmissions to the sink. Fig. 6 shows that FTMAWSS is able to maintain a reasonable packet delivery rate even at a high

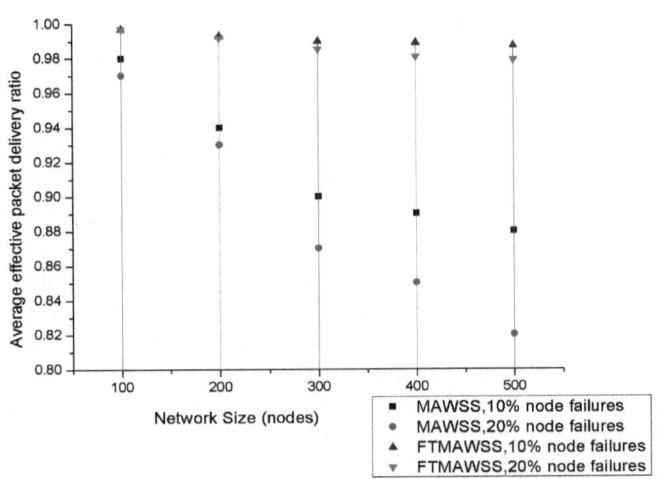

Fig. 6. Average effective packet delivery ratio with node failures

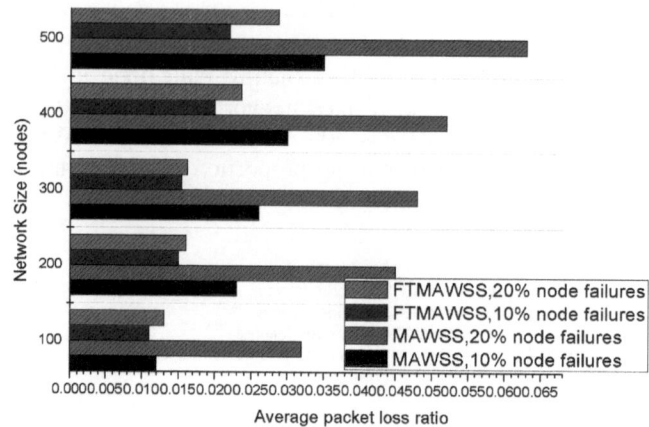

Fig. 7. Average packet loss ratio with node failures

percentage of node failures. This reason is that the failure nodes are detected and isolated by the algorithm which constructed FTMAWSS. However, the effective packet delivery ratio of MAWSS will get lower when network size is increased. Especially as network size is 500 nodes, the effective packet delivery ratio is no more than 0.82. Packet loss ratio is another parameter for sensor networks to ensure reliability and creditability. With the same reason, as shown in the graph of Fig. 7, the packet loss ratio of MAWSS is higher than that of FTMAWSS at every network size.

4.2 The Effectiveness of Different Topologies

In our last set of experiments we add a new topology subgraph building algorithm, which include simply process: in connected or strong connected graph, every node choose two edges connected to its neighbors randomly, till the subgraph is connected or strongly connected. If node has only one neighbor then choose this edge. We call this constructed subgraph topology is RANDOM, certainly which don't be considered with fault tolerant.

Afterward, we fixed the network size, say 500 nodes, and change the fault node percent. Fig.8 shows that FTMAWSS and MAWSS can gain steady average delay till the node failure percent is bigger than 10%. On the other hand, as the node failure is increased, the average delay of RANDOM is raising very quickly. It is clear that the subgraph randomly created can't achieve the whole well transmission capability; despite might choose some edges are the best weighted ones. However, it is surprised for us that the effective packet delivery ratio of RANDOM is higher than that of MAWSS when the failure node percent is bigger than 12%. Fig.9 shows this thing and express the other instance is natural. We think this abnormality might be explained that the probability of packet transmitting through fault nodes is decreasing in RANDOM at high density networks.

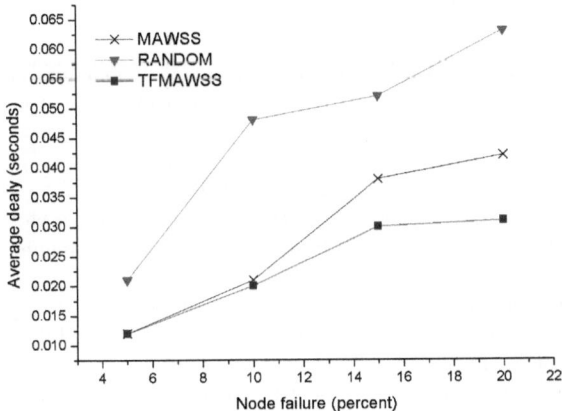

Fig. 8. Average delay with various topologies

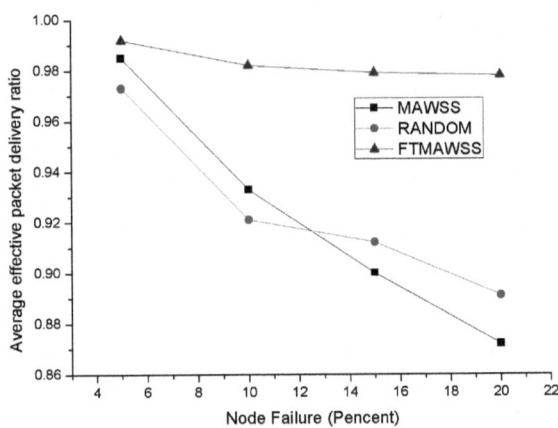

Fig. 9. Average effective packet delivery ratio with various topologies

5 Conclusion

In this paper, we propose a self-adaptive fault-tolerant mechanism in the sensor networks. In "in-network" computing, the sensor nodes are busy with sensing, computing, and transporting combined packets. We use confidence rate, the sink giving, to ascertain and adjust the node transport attempt rate in order to achieve holistic best network throughput. Simulation experiments confirm the validity of our ways and ensure our algorithm is reliability and scalability.

References

[1] Kahn, J., Katz, R., Pister, K.: Next century challenges: mobile networking for smart dust. In: Pro. of ACM/IEEE Intl. conf. on Mobile computing and Networking (Mobicom 1999), Seattle, WA, August 17-19, pp. 271–278 (1999)

[2] Akyildiz, I., Su, W., Sankarasubramaniam, Y., Cayirci, E.: A survey on sensor networks. IEEE Communications Magazine, 102–114 (August 2002)

[3] Baker, D.J., Ephremides, A.: The Architectural Organization of a Mobile Radio Networks via a Distributed Algorithms. IEEE Transactions on Communications COM29(11), 1694–1701 (1981)

[4] Kuhn, F., Moscibroda, T., Wattenhofer, R.: Initializing Newly Deployed Ad Hoc and Sensor Networks. In: Proceedings of the 10th Int. Conf. on Mobile Computing and Networking, MOBICOM (2004)

[5] Krishnan, R., Starobinski, D.: Message-efficient self-organization of wireless sensor networks. In: Proc. IEEE WCNC 2003, pp. 1603–1608 (2003)

[6] Karnik, A., Kumar, A.: Distributed optimal self-organization in ad hoc wireless sensor networks. IEEE/ACM transactions on networking 15(5), 1035–1045 (2007)

[7] Post, M., Kershenbaum, A., Sarachik, P.: A distributed evolutionary algorithm for reorganizing network communications. In: Proc. IEEE MILCOM (1985)

[8] Clare, L., Pottie, G., Agre, J.: Self-organizing distributed sensor networks. In: SPIE-The Int. Sco. for Optical Eng., pp. 229–237 (1999)

[9] Chitnis, L., Dobra, A., Ranka, S.: Aggregation methods for large-scale sensor networks. ACM Transactions on Sensor Networks 4(2), 1–36 (2008)

[10] Kalpakis, K., Dasgupta, K., Namjoshi, P.: An efficient clustering-based heuristic for data gathering and aggregation in sensor networks. In: IEEE WCNC, pp. 1948–1985 (2003)

[11] Heidemann, J.: Building efficient wireless sensor networks with low-level naming. In: 18th.sym. syst. Princ., pp. 146–159 (2001)

[12] Nath, S., Gibbons, P.B., Anederson, Z.R.: Synopsis diffusion for robust aggregation in sensor networks. In: 2nd international conference on embedded networked sensor systems, pp. 250–262 (2004)

[13] Abbasi, A., Ghadimi, E., Khonsari, A.: A distributed clustering algorithm for fault-tolerant event region detection in wireless sensor networks. LNCS, pp. 493–502. Springer, Heidelberg (2007)

[14] Considine, J., Li, F., Kollios, G., Byers, J.: Approximate aggregation techniques for sensor databases. In: 20th international conference on data engineering, pp. 449–460 (2004)

[15] McCanne, S., Floyd, S.: ns Network Simulator, http://www.isi.edu/nsnam/ns/

CAWA: Continuous Approximate Where-About Queries

Alexander Aved, Kien A. Hua, and Antoniya Petkova

School of EECS
4000 Central Florida Blvd
Orlando, Florida, USA
{aaved,kienhua,apetkova}@eecs.ucf.edu

Abstract. With the current proliferation of wireless networks and mobile device technologies, the management of moving object databases to facilitate queries over these domains has been extensively studied. While current systems are concerned with tracing the precise location, or paths, of these objects, in many cases it is sufficient to know that the approximate location or path of a moving object is, with certainty, within known bounds. Thus, we present our work on Continuous Approximate Where-About (CAWA) queries, in which mobile sensors sense the presence of an object (not its precise location) and query servers deduce the object's where-about area from mobile sensor presence updates.

Keywords: Moving object database, continuous query, presence, distributed computing, where-about.

1 Introduction

Given the advances in scaling down the power consumption requirements for and miniaturization of processing devices, and with concurrent gains in processing power, we are becoming a society with massive numbers of mobile devices. Introduce communication mediums, such as the various forms of wireless networks, e.g., Mobile Ad Hoc Networks (MANETS) [1] and MESH networks [2], and it then becomes possible to communicate with and track these mobile devices. Inexpensive GPS receivers facilitate the devices' location awareness in terms of time and location. This mobile, location aware infrastructure provides many exciting applications: military planners are interested in knowing the location of a supply convoy in relation to nearby army tanks and known enemies. Parents waiting for a child to come home would be interested in knowing if she's still in the grocery store, and a courier service might be interested in rerouting vehicles located on a busy highway in which an accident has just been reported. In many instances, the precise location of a Moving Object is extremely relevant: two meters with respect to a car could be the difference between driving on a road and driving into a river beside the road. However, in many applications, an exact location is not required. It is sufficient to know that the location of the queried object is certain to be within a threshold, or more precisely, to know with complete certainty that the exact location of the object is within a known region. Thus, it could be sufficient to know that the convoy is currently contained within a friendly area, that the child is somewhere within the grocery store, or that an RFID-tagged cargo container was detected on a truck when it passed an inspection station [10, 11, 12, 13, 14].

P. Mueller, J.-N. Cao, and C.-L. Wang (Eds.): Infoscale 2009, LNICST 18, pp. 241–257, 2009.
© Institute for Computer Science, Social-Informatics and Telecommunications Engineering 2009

Shipping companies have thousands of delivery vehicles and move millions of packages through their delivery networks. Since it is not feasible to communicate with every object to resolve the location of a single one, we utilize moving object databases to coordinate the querying and location awareness efforts. Generally, queries can be point queries (what is the precise location of cellular telephone X), range queries (which trucks are currently within a certain range of a store), or predication queries (at what intersection will Taxi Z arrive in 15 minutes). Moving object locations can be known to the moving object database through location updates from the object itself, calculated trajectories as a function of time, and other probabilistic methods [15]. However, with current technology, knowing the precise location of a moving object is an extremely difficult problem, because once a location update is broadcast, the object may have already moved or there may be a latency introduced in the propagation of the location update on the physical transmission medium, etc. And if there are millions of tracked objects, the moving object database server(s) must cope with millions of periodic location updates, and must cope with precise location uncertainty and either pass it along in the query result or utilize some probabilistic solution. In this paper we examine a new paradigm for moving object location tracking, which differs from the previously described scenario in two primary ways. First, we point out that in many applications, it is sufficient to know the approximate location of the moving objects within a bound. Second, by utilizing a network of sensors that detect the presence of moving objects (as opposed to receiving location updates from each object), we construct an environment that scales with the number of queries and is robust to the density of the tracked moving objects. Thus, we present our work on *Continuous Approximate Where-About* (CAWA) queries, which are based on mobile sensors that can detect the **presence** (but not the exact locations) of target moving objects as detected by mobile sensors. We present a system design that is both cost effective and scalable. Current design approaches are expensive because the system cost is proportional to the number of moving objects, as each moving object must include GPS and communication hardware to locate and report its locations. Our goal is to design a system whose cost is not dependent on the number of mobile objects, and to therefore substantially reduce the cost of implementation. To have a system that is both simple and scalable, we avoid using spatial indexing techniques, which have a logarithmic computation complexity with respect to the number of moving objects, and instead utilize a design based upon sequential data scans.

The remainder of this paper is organized as follows. We discuss related work in Section 2. The proposed query processing technique for CAWA queries is introduced in Section 3, with the distributed design presented in Section 4. In Section 5, we describe the simulation setting and examine the simulation results. Finally, we offer our conclusions in Section 6.

2 Related Work

The construction of databases for tracking moving objects is a widely researched topic. [16, 18, 19, 20, 21, 22] Due to the continuous movement intrinsic to the problem, the exact locations of the objects can only be known when they are sampled, and by the time that update becomes known to the server the moving objects have likely moved [3]. There are a great diversity of approaches to cope with this problem, for example, by restricting the type of queries that can be resolved by (1) utilizing logic to approximate and cope with error [4], or (2) restricting the movement of the moving objects themselves (e.g., some approaches limit the moving objects to a fixed topology, such as roads, to make the objects' movement easier to predict [5] with lower error or to reduce location updates).

Various architectures for moving object databases have been proposed over the years (e.g., [6]). Even with various indexing schemes (e.g., [7, 8, 9]), most designs are centralized in nature, and do not scale well as the number of moving objects increase. The way data is stored on the server, and the types of queries they can process effects their scalability. Other approaches are well suited for robotics applications (e.g., capable of handling less than 100 moving objects and sensors), but don't appear to be intended for database applications that could scale to millions of moving objects and sensors. [31]

2.1 Spatio-Temporal Queries

We identify two primary types of spatio-temporal queries: point queries (also called coordinate-based queries) and trajectory-based queries [16, 17]. Point queries return all relevant moving objects that satisfy a spatial relationship, e.g., the current location of all city busses. Trajectory queries refer to the trajectory of a single (or multiple) moving object for a time interval specified in the query, and provide results such as the area in which the moving object has traversed, how far it has traveled (a segment length), or just the set of moving objects that satisfy the query (e.g., which trucks traveled on Highway 99 in the past 2 hours).

2.2 Probabilistic Approaches

Due to the continuously moving and possible random nature of moving objects, it is not possible to precisely and continuously monitor and record their location due to the discreteness of measurement instruments. Thus, the query result returned by a moving object database may not be completely consistent with the real-world situation [23, 24]. The goal of probabilistic approaches is to extend the query language with semantics for dealing with this uncertainty. For example, "Which whales have been in Region 1 with probability 90%." [29]

There are two primary approaches for dealing with the representations of movement information: uncertainty about future behavior [24, 25, 26] and uncertainty about previous behavior [23, 27]. Approaches in the first category make use of speed and trajectory information to model the movement of the tracked moving objects in the database, in order to reduce the number of location updates. Examples abound, such as virtual digital battlefields, fleet management, etc. The second approach concerns historical movements, compensating for uncertainty in the precise location of the moving object at a particular time. This has applications in data mining, pattern classification and recognition, and so forth.

3   CAWA Query Processing

A CAWA query is a continuous query that tracks the locations of a moving object to determine its whereabouts in the past t time units, where t is referred to as the *tracking window*. In this paper, the whereabouts of the object are represented by a *minimum bounding rectangle* that encompasses the locations of the query object in the past t time units. At any moment in time, this minimum bounding rectangle is the result of the query; and this result continues to change in size and shape over the course of the continuous query. In this section, we discuss a technique for processing CAWA queries in a single-server environment. We will present a distributed design in Section 4.

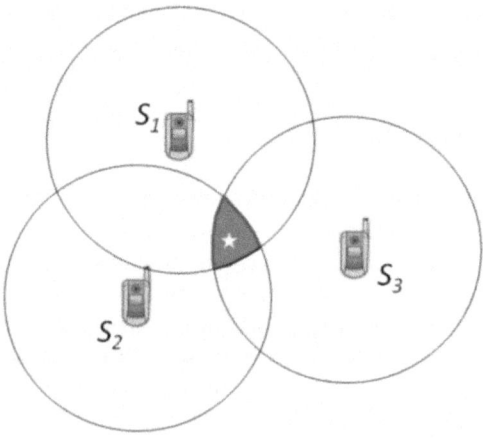

Fig. 1. A moving object (denoted as a star) is detected by three nearby mobile sensors. The solid area can be deducted as the where-about of this moving object at this moment.

There are two kinds of moving objects in the proposed environment: regular moving objects and mobile sensors. We assume that each mobile sensor is equipped with a GPS (*global positioning system*), and always knows its location. A mobile sensor continuously senses the presence of moving objects currently within its sensing range, and reports their identifiers (ID's) to the Query Server, along with the location of the sensor. As an example, a phone company can recruit cellular phones with integrated RFID (*Radio Frequency Identification*) readers to detect objects tagged with RFIDs, within the sensing range of the reader. In our environment, a mobile sensor can detect the identifiers (ID's) of the moving objects within its sensing range. However, the sensor does not know the exact locations of these moving objects. Nevertheless, the query server can fuse information from multiple sensors to deduct the where-about of a moving object. As illustrated in Figure 1, the sensing range of each of the three mobile sensors S_1, S_2, and S_3, is a circular area; and the moving object is shown as a star at the center of the figure. If S_1 is the only sensor that detects this moving object, the best we can say is that the object is somewhere within the circular sensing range of S_1. However, since all three sensors S_1, S_2, and S_3, detect this moving object, the

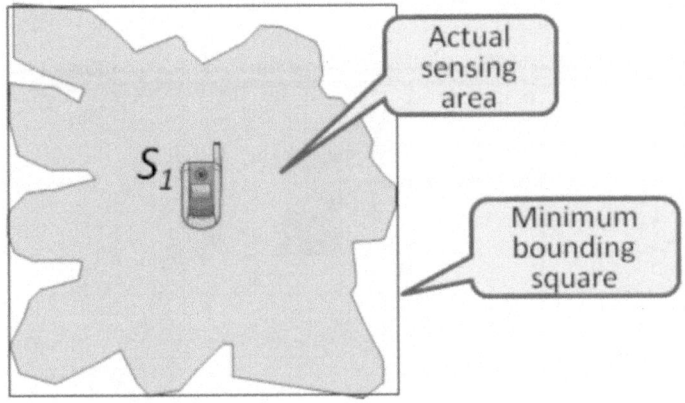

Fig. 2. Approximating the sensing area with a minimum bounding square

query server can safely deduce the where about of the moving object to the overlap area of the three sensing ranges (i.e., the shaded area in Figure 1). Unlike existing techniques that can process queries based on the locations of moving objects, we must rely on the location deduction mechanism in the CAWA environment.

One major advantage of the CAWA approach is the significant reduction in communication cost since only the mobile sensors (not every moving object) need to communicate with the query server. We will observe in the simulation results, presented in Section 5.2, that the number of mobile sensors required to achieve good performance is proportional to the area of the terrain, not the number of moving objects. This implies that the CAWA approach can be very economical to support a very large user community (i.e., a very large number of moving objects). In order to keep the computation cost low, we approximate the sensing range of each mobile sensor as the *minimum-bounding square* (MBS) of its sensing area. We note that the actual sensing area might have an irregular shape depending on the broadcast pattern of the antennas (see Figure 2). Using an MBS as the approximation is also a natural fit for computing the result of a CAWA query, which has a rectangular shape. Using MBS's as the sensing ranges, the where-about of a moving object can be approximated as a rectangular area as illustrated in Figure 3.

The user poses a CAWA query Q to the query server by specifying the ID of the target moving object that is to be tracked. We refer to this target object as the *query object*. At any moment in time, the query object is detected by zero or multiple mobile sensors. If no mobile sensor detects the query object, its where-about for this moment in time is the entire terrain. Typically, the query object is detected by multiple mobile sensors; and the where about of the query object can be narrowed down to the spatial intersection of the areas of coverage of these mobile sensors. Let $R(T)$ denotes this overlap areas at time T. Over the course of this continuous query, this overlap area changes in shape and size as the query object moves and it is detected by different mobile sensors at different times. The result of the CAWA query Q at time T can be computed as follows:

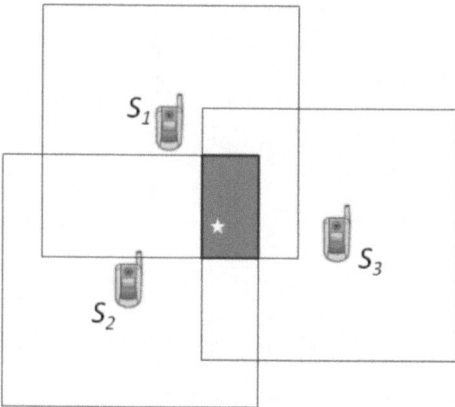

Fig. 3. Sensing range is approximated as a square area. A moving object (denoted as a star) is detected by three mobile sensors. The highlighted overlap area can be deduced as the where-about of the moving object at this moment.

$$Q(T) = \bigcup_{t=T-W}^{T} R(t) \tag{1}$$

where the notation $\cup$ denotes a spatial union of the overlap areas $R(t)$, $T\text{-}W \leq t \leq T$. W is the tracking window. That is, we are interested in the whereabouts of the query object in the last W time units.

To support CAWA queries, the query server maintains the following information:

- **LocTable:** This table maintains the current locations of the mobile sensors. That is, for each *sensorID*, we record its location.
- **QueryTable:** This table maintains the list of query objects (i.e., *objID*'s).
- **DetectedObjTable:** This table maintains the query objects detected by each mobile sensor. Each sensor also reports non-query objects. However, only query objects are recorded in this table.
- **ResultTable:** This table maintains the query results for each of the last T_{max} time units (i.e., the $R(t)$ discussed previously), where T_{max} is the maximum tracking window allowed for any query.

For each iteration, the query server performs the following procedure:

1. Receive data from mobile sensors and update the LocTable.
2. Also use the sensor information and information in the QueryTable to update the DetectedObjTable.
3. Update the ResultTable using information in the DetectedObjTable
4. Compute the result for each query by applying Equation (1) to the entries for each query recorded in the ResultTable.
5. Report the current results to the users.

The above procedure is repeated as long as there is at least one active query in the system. We note that some degree of uncertainty in the locations of the mobile sensors exists due to the iterative nature of the location update process. The validity of the reported locations decreases until the next round of location updates. This issue has been resolved using location estimation techniques (e.g., [28]). Another solution to reduce this effect is to use distributed servers. We present one such solution in the next section.

We discuss the details of the above procedure as follows:

- Step 1: This step can be done on the fly as location information arrives from the mobile sensors.
- Step 2: Since the QueryTable is typically small and fits in the memory, this step can also be done efficiently in parallel with Step 1.
- Step 3: We can scan the table DetectedObjTable, and group the entries according to query objects as follows:

> SELECT   objID, sensorID
> FROM   DetectedObjTable
> GROUP BY objID

  We can then scan the result of the above group-by query, and for each query object (i.e., objID) compute the spatial intersection of the sensors involved. To speed up this process, a hash index on the sensorID attribute of the Loc-Table can be used.
- Step 4: If we sort the ResultTable according to the objID attribute (i.e., query objects), this step can be done in a single scan over this table.

Thus, the query processing technique is quite efficient, such that it involves mostly sequential scans of the data files. Only LocTable needs to be accessed in a random manner in Step 3. However, a hash index can be used to reduce the disk access cost.

4 Distributed Design

In the distributed scenario, the terrain is partitioned into multiple sub-domains, each of which has assigned a query server. Each query server is responsible for moving objects detected within its sub-domain. Each query server is also responsible for the processing of the where-about queries corresponding to the query objects currently within its sub-domain (see Figure 4).

Queries may be poised to any query server on the terrain. Upon receiving a new query from a user, this initial query server examines its local LocTable to determine if the query object is currently within its sub-domain. If this is the case, this query server declares itself the assigned query server for this query; otherwise, this initial query server broadcasts the query to all of the other query servers in the terrain to locate the appropriate query server for this new query. At this time, each of these query servers checks its own local LocTable to verify if it has the query object in its sub-domain. The query server that has the query object in its sub-domain can then take ownership of this particular new query.

The query server, responsible for a given query, processes this query using the technique described in Section 3. As part of this process, the query server tracks the current approximate location of the query object (i.e., its where-about rectangular area). When this approximate location is within a threshold of a neighboring sub-domain, the responsible query server forwards a copy of the query to the query server, say S, of the appropriate neighboring sub-domain. Upon receiving information on this query, the server S activates a countdown counter and anticipates the crossover of this query object before the counter expires. If the query object does cross over and be detected before the timeout, termed *elevation time out* (ETO), S is elevated to be the new responsible query server for this particular query; otherwise, S can discard the expired information on this query when the counter decrements it value to zero.

To support CAWA queries in a distributed environment, the following information is maintained on the query server:

- A queue of CAWA queries the server is actively processing. Each CAWA query consists of (1) the ID of the target object to be tracked (objID), (2) the ID of the user who submitted the query (who can access the query's results) and (3) an *active time span* (ATS) for which the query active (this time span is specified by the user when submitting the query and can be null, in which case the query is valid until explicitly terminated), (4) a unique ID for the query, and (5) the ETO (described previously in this section).
- A queue of the mobile sensors on the terrain, to permit the query server to track the sensors' states: (1) if the mobile sensor can be communicated with (is on-line and the query server has received a message from the mobile sensor within a time threshold) and (2) if it is currently tracking any moving objects that are the target of any queries.

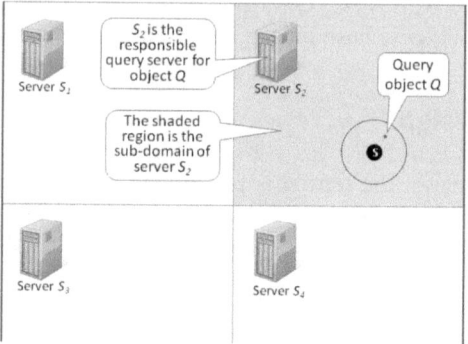

Fig. 4. This figure shows the terrain segmented into four sub-domains. Each sub-domain is assigned a server. Server S_2 is responsible for Query object Q.

5   Performance Study

To assess the performance of CAWA we compare the approximate where-about area for a moving object, the query result returned by the query server, with the ground truth, in terms of precision and recall. The precision metric provides the ratio of the area of the queried mobile node's exact movement (as contained in a minimum bounding rectangle) in terms of the query result (the approximate where about area) returned from the query server, for a window of previous positions. The recall metric provides indication of the area of the true positive area in terms of the false negative and true positive areas (Figure 5, Figure 6, and Table 1).

Table 1. Measurement metrics and corresponding descriptions

Metric	Description
TP, true positive	The overlapping area between the approximate (where-about) area and the exact area (ground truth)
FN, false negative	The area of the exact area (ground truth), that is not a part of the TP area
FP, false positive	The area of the approximate (where-about) area that is not a part of the TP area

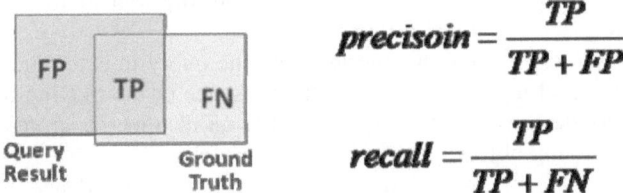

$$precisoin = \frac{TP}{TP + FP}$$

$$recall = \frac{TP}{TP + FN}$$

Fig. 5. Definitions of precision and recall for the performance study, defined in terms of *true positive* (TP), *false positive* (FP), and *false negative* (FN)

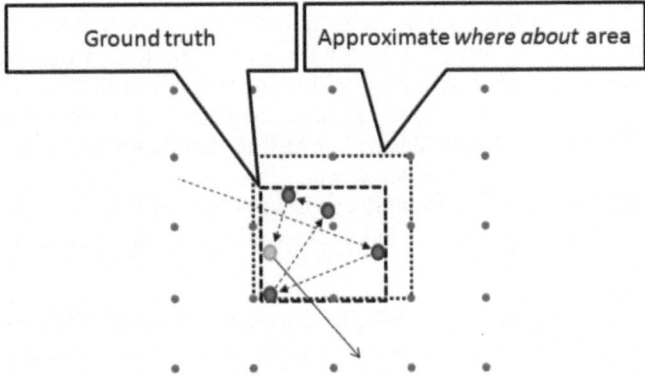

Fig. 6. An example true positive (darker dashes) shown overlaid on the where-about area returned from the query server (dotted rectangle) for a query that tracks the last 4 hops of the moving object

We randomly select a set of 100 queries and average the results. For each query, we randomly choose one moving object and a fixed tracking window size over the past t time units (e.g., the last 50 seconds). (We use the same tracking window size for all the queries that are grouped together.) For example, refer to Figure 6 for an example query with a tracking window of 4 time units.

5.1 Simulation Environment

The performance studies for this research have been conducted with the CAWA simulator, CAWASim. CAWASim is a discrete simulator employing the Random Waypoint model (RWP) to provide for the movement patterns of moving objects [30]. CAWASim simulates the injection of queries over randomly selected moving objects, of the query servers broadcasting and handing off queries to other query servers, mobile sensor to query server communication, the computation of where-about areas (the CAWA query result), and the calculation of ground truth and other metrics. CAWASim is implemented in C# on the .NET 3.5 architecture.

CAWASim simulates the interaction of the following objects:

- The query injector receives the query from the user and broadcasts it to all the query servers in the terrain.
- Query servers receive the queries from the query injector and maintain them in an internal list structure. Once the presence of the moving object is sensed by a mobile sensor, the query server has an idea of the approximate location of the moving object.
- Moving objects move through the terrain in accordance with the RWP model. Once the moving object reaches its destination it pauses for a randomly determined time, and then selects a new destination and speed and begins to move towards it; and on its way moves in and out of the sensing range of mobile sensors.
- Mobile sensors are either fixed at a particular location, or can move in accordance with the RWP model, depending upon the simulation settings. Each mobile sensor maintains a sensing window about it, which can sense the presence of all moving objects within its range. The mobile sensor only detects the presence, it cannot ascertain the precise coordinates of the moving object that is within its sensing range. For simplicity and to reduce calculation overhead, we model the sensing range of the moving object as a rectangle. We note that the rectangle can always be increased to contain any other sensing shape that may be more consistent with the broadcast pattern of an antenna.

Query servers receive updates from mobile sensors when the mobile sensor senses the presence of one or more moving objects within its detection window. If the query server receives data from multiple mobile sensors sensing the same moving object in an area where their query windows overlap, the query server can find the smaller area of intersection between all relevant mobile sensors sensing windows in order to compute a more precise approximate location.

Users pose queries to the query injector by specifying the ID of the target moving object that is to be tracked. The query server broadcasts the query to all of the other query servers, which are in communication with the query injector. Mobile sensors are equipped with GPS devices, and can sense the presence of moving objects that move within a threshold, or spatial sensing window, around each mobile sensor. However, a mobile sensor by itself cannot detect the exact location of a moving object. When a moving object is detected, the mobile sensor communicates its presence to its corresponding query server. The query server maintains a list of all the active queries it is currently monitoring, and once the presence of the moving object is reported by a mobile sensor, the query server has an approximate location for the moving object. It knows the moving object is bounded within the mobile sensor's sensing window, which is known to the query server. For example, if the mobile sensor has a 5 by 5 window in which it can sense moving objects, the query server knows the tracked moving object is somewhere within that area of 25 meters. However, if the mobile sensors are deployed in a way such that they have overlapping sensor areas, then when the query server finds that the moving object is detected by multiple mobile sensors, the query server can take the spatial intersection of the areas of their coverage, in order to deduce a more precise location for the moving object.

A fixed number of continuous queries are posed to the query server over a randomly selected set of moving objects. A selection of relevant configuration parameters are shown in Table 2.

Table 2. Selected CAWASim configuration variables. A value of [x, y] means that a number is randomly chosen between x and y (inclusive) according to a uniform distribution.

Variable	Description	Example Value
RunCount	The number of simulation runs for a configuration	100
TerrainSize	Size of the simulated terrain in meters	1000x1000
NumMovingObjs	The number of moving objects simulated	500
MovObjSpeedIntvl	Movement speed of mobile objects selected from this interval	[1,100]
MovObjDestIntvl	Destination is randomly selected from the object's current position, in this range	[1,100]
PauseIntvl	Length of time a moving object pauses after its destination reached	[0,3] (seconds)
NumSensors	Number of mobile sensors in the simulation	100000
DetectionWindow	Size of the moving sensor's detection window	E.g., 10x10 represents a 10 meter by 10 meter window
DetectWinIntvl	Allows the detection window to be sized randomly (when the mobile sensor is created)	E.g., 0,20. Permits the default window to be expanded randomly
SensorsMove	Specifies if the mobile sensors move during the simulation	True/False

Scenario 1: Dense coverage of mobile sensors

For the series of simulation runs presented here, we varied the size of the mobile sensor's window from 1 to 10 meters on a 1000 x 1000 meter grid, with each mobile sensor (initially) positioned at each integer coordinate (that is, 1000000 mobile sensors arranged in the terrain in 1000 rows and 1000 columns). Two sets of results are presented: (1) where the mobile sensor locations are fixed (they do not move during the simulation) and (2) where they move in accordance with the RWP model with the same parameters as the moving objects (e.g., similar Pause Intervals, Speed Interval, etc.).

Table 3. Select simulation parameters common to all simulation runs

Variable	Value
RunCount	5 (the results from 5 simulation runs are averaged together)
NumMobileObjects	1000
PauseInterval	[1,5]

For this simulation the simulator was configured with values indicated in Table 4. The size of the query window for the mobile sensors was varied from 1 to 10 meters. Table 5 presents simulation results where the sensors move during the simulation. Notice that good precision is achieved quickly without a significant amount of overlap in mobile sensor's sensing windows.

Table 4. Simulation parameters for scenario 1

Variable	Value
TerrainSize	1000x1000
SpeedInterval	[1,20]m/s: the speed is chosen (each time the moving object reaches its destination) uniformly from the range [1,20]
DestinationInterval	[1,20] meters
PauseInterval	[1,5] (node pauses between 1 and 5 seconds after reaching its destination)
QueryWindowSize	50 (the past 50 time units, or seconds, in the tracking window)

Table 5. Scenario 1 results – sensors stationary

Size	Precision %	Recall %	Where-About Area	Ground Truth
1	75.08	100	2577.7	824.2624
2	95.36	100	2794.1	147.7275
3	95.98	100	2681.6	87.9034
4	96.71	100	3027.5	85.6379
5	95.70	100	2832.6	98.0112
6	95.88	100	2726.9	91.8981
7	95.42	100	2630.8	85.6811
8	96.28	100	3034.2	85.0350
9	95.67	100	2729.7	88.5538
10	95.89	100	3013.1	93.3657

The simulation results for Scenario 1 show that the precision and recall are very good and are robust to whether the mobile sensors are stationary or move during the simulation. Note that when the size of the mobile sensor's window is 1, that there is no overlap in the stationary scenario since the mobile sensors are positioned one unit apart from each other.

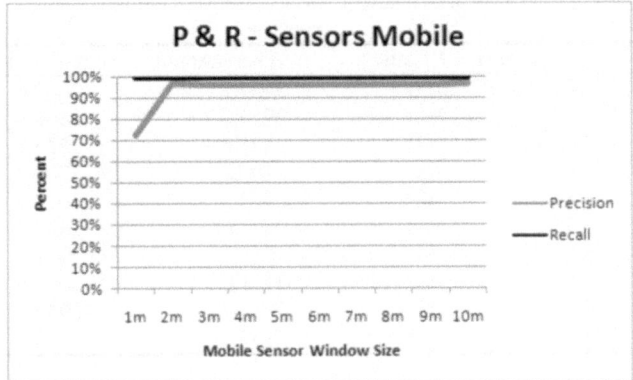

Fig. 7. Precision and Recall – with the mobile sensors moving in the terrain during the simulation, in accordance with the random waypoint model. The terrain size is 1000 x 1000.

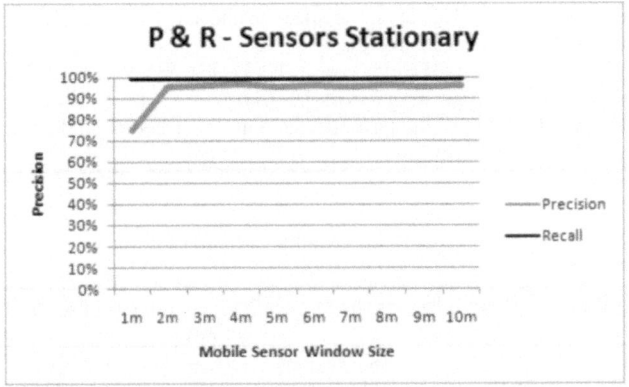

Fig. 8. Precision and Recall shown where the mobile sensors are stationary. The terrain size is 1000 x 1000.

Scenario 2: Sparse Coverage of Mobile Sensors

For the series of simulation results presented here we varied the mobile sensor's window size from 1 to 10 meters on a 500 x 500 meter grid, with a mobile sensor node (initially) positioned in a grid of 250 rows by 250 columns. Two sets of results are presented: (1) where the mobile sensor locations are fixed (they do not move during the simulation) and (2) where they move in accordance with the RWP model with the same parameters as the moving objects (e.g., similar Pause Intervals, Speed Interval, etc.).

For this simulation the simulator was configured with values indicated in Table 7. The size of the query window for the mobile sensors was varied from 1 to 10 meters.

Table 6. Scenario 1 results – sensors mobile

Size	Precision %	Recall %	Where-About Area	Ground Truth
1	72.32	100	3454.7	2642.6
2	96.11	100	2956.2	2866.4
3	95.45	100	2821.6	2735.1
4	95.85	100	2790.7	2703.2
5	95.90	100	2757.3	2670.7
6	95.51	100	2918.6	2829.9
7	95.62	100	3016.5	2911.9
8	95.71	100	3171.0	3067.8
9	95.57	100	3038.7	2940.0
10	96.33	100	3164.7	3072.1

Table 7. Select simulation parameters for scenario 2

Variable	Value
TerrainSize	500x500
SpeedInterval	[1,20]m/s: the speed is chosen
DestinationInterval	[1,20] meters
PauseInterval	[1,5] (node pauses between 1 and 5 seconds after reaching its destination)
QueryWindowSize	50 (the past 50 time units, or seconds, in the tracking window)

Table 8. Scenario 2 results – sensors stationary

Size	Precision %	Recall %	Where-About Area	Ground Truth
1	21.82	100	91747.2	12696.9
2	76.15	100	8924.4	7715.6
3	87.16	100	10954.0	10458.6
4	82.41	100	8970.2	8389.0
5	86.27	100	8800.4	8265.3
6	83.45	100	9019.1	8545.2
7	84.62	100	7762.7	7323.3
8	82.65	100	10337.8	9757.3
9	84.94	100	10645.9	10170.6
10	83.12	100	8881.9	8360.4

Table 9. Scenario 2 results – sensors mobile

Size	Precision %	Recall %	Where-About Area	Ground Truth
1	10.53	100	102957.5	10078.5
2	78.59	100	12025.4	10577.2
3	85.41	100	10650.1	9953.1
4	85.41	100	10650.1	9953.1
5	85.35	100	9985.0	9537.9
6	84.15	100	9291.7	8700.8
7	87.29	100	8786.2	8344.0
8	83.13	100	10474.0	9941.2
9	83.73	100	10025.9	9547.8
10	83.69	100	8096.6	7602.7

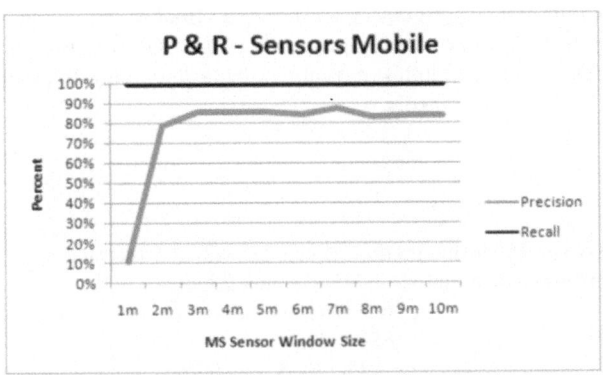

Fig. 9. Precision and Recall – sensors deployed in 250 rows and 250 columns in a 500x500 terrain, and the mobile sensors move in accordance with the RWP model

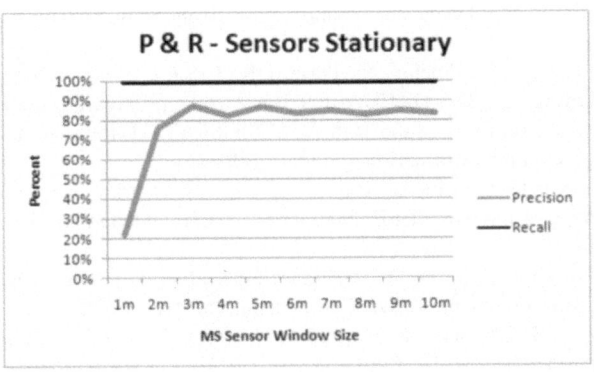

Fig. 10. Precision and Recall – stationary sensors, 250x250

6 Conclusions

We present our research on Continuous Approximate Where-About queries, the first work, to our knowledge, on moving object databases that utilize mobile sensors that sense the presence of an object to deduct its approximate (where-about) location. Mobile sensors detect the presence of a moving object (not its exact location) and report presence updates to a query server, which knows the location and sensing area of each mobile sensor. When a moving object is detected by multiple mobile sensors, the query server takes the spatial intersection of the mobile sensors' sensing windows, as the approximate where-about area of the moving object. In many applications it is sufficient to know the approximate bounded location of a moving object, and in this research we show that even with a sparse population of mobile sensors the query server can deduce a fairly accurate approximation for the moving object, with a tracking window of t time units (e.g., the moving object's last t positions). Furthermore, we designed a system that is both cost effective and scalable.

To facilitate the evaluation of the proposed technique, we created the CAWASim, a discrete simulator that simulates moving objects and their interaction with queries, query servers and mobile sensors.

References

1. Ding, S.: A survey on integrating MANETs with the Internet: Challenges and designs. Computer Communications 31(14) (September 2008)
2. Akyildiz, I., Wang, X., Wang, W.: Wireless mesh networks: a survey. Computer Networks and ISDN Systems 47(4), 445–487 (2005)
3. Pfoser, D., Jensen, C.: Indexing of network constrained moving-object representations. In: Proc. of Advances of Spatial Databases, 6th Intl. Symp. (SSD), pp. 111–132 (1999)
4. Leonhardi, A., Rothermel, K.A.: Comparison of Protocols for Updating Location Information. Cluster Computing 6(4) (2001)
5. Lee, K., Lee, W.-C., Zheng, B.: Fast object search on road networks. In: Proc. of the Int'l Conf. on Extending Database Technology: Advances in Database Technology, EDBT 2009 (2009)
6. Ortale, R., Ritacco, E., Pelekis, N., Trasarti, R., Cosa, G., Giannotti, F., Manco, G., Renso, C., Theodoridis, Y.: The DAEDALUS framework: progressive querying and mining of movement data. In: Proc. of the 16th ACM SIGSPATIAL international conference on Advances in geographic information systems (2008)
7. Gedik, B., Wu, K.-L., Liu, L.: Processing Moving Queries over Moving Objects Using Motion-Adaptive Indexes. IEEE Transactions on Knowledge and Data Engineering 18(5) (May 2006)
8. Chen, S., Jensen, C., Lin, D.: A benchmark for evaluating moving object indexes. In: Proc. of the VLDB Endowment. VLDB Endowment, vol. 1(2) (2008)
9. Hernandez, C., Rodriguez, M., Marin, M.: Complex Queries for Moving Object Databases in DHT-Based Systems. In: Luque, E., Margalef, T., Benítez, D. (eds.) Euro-Par 2008. LNCS, vol. 5168, pp. 424–433. Springer, Heidelberg (2008)
10. Brundick, F., Hartwig, G.: Model-based situational awareness. In: Proc. of the Joint Service Combat Identification Systems Conf., CISC 1997 (1997)

11. Hightower, J., Borrielo, G.: Location systems for ubiquitous computing. IEEE Computer Magazine 34(8) (August 2001)
12. Chamberlain, S.: Model-based battle command: A paradigm whose time has come. In: Proc. of the Symposium on C2 Research and Technology, NDU (1995)
13. Want, R., Schilit, B.: Expanding the horizons of location aware computing. IEEE Computer Magazine 34(8), 31–34 (2001)
14. Pitoura, E., Samaras, G.: Locating objects in mobile computing. IEEE Transactions on Knowledge Data Engineering 13(4), 571–592 (2001)
15. Abdessalem, T., Decreusefond, L., Moreira, J.: Evaluation of Probabilistic Queries in Moving Objects Databases. In: Proc. of International ACM Workshop on Data Engineering for Wireless and Mobile Access (MobiDE 2006), Chicago, Illinois (2006)
16. Guting, R., Schneider, M.: Moving Objects Databases. Morgan Kaufmann Publishers, San Francisco (2005)
17. Cai, Y., Hua, K., Cao, G., Xu, T.: Real-Time Processing of Range-Monitoring Queries in Heterogeneous Mobile Databases. IEEE Transactions on Mobile Computing 5(7) (2006)
18. Hadjieleftheriou, M., Kollios, G., Tostras, V., Gunopulos, D.: Indexing Spatiotemporal archives. VLDB Journal 15(2), 143–164 (2006)
19. Mokbel, M., Ghanem, T., Aref, W.: Spatio-Temporal Access Methods. IEEE Data Engineering Bulletin 26(2), 40–49 (2003)
20. Pelanis, M., Saltenis, S., Jensen, C.: Indexing the past, present, and anticipated future positions of moving objects. ACM Trans. on Database Systems 31(1), 255–298 (2006)
21. Ni, J., Ravishankar, C.: Indexing spatio-temporal trajectories with efficient polynomial approximations. IEEE Trans. on Knowledge Data Engineering 19(5), 663–678 (2007)
22. Pfoser, D., Jensen, C., Theodoridis, Y.: Novel Approaches to the Indexing of Moving Object Trajectories. In: Proc. of Very Large Databases, VLDB (2006)
23. Pfoser, D., Jensen, C.: Capturing the uncertainty of moving-object representations. In: Güting, R.H., Papadias, D., Lochovsky, F.H. (eds.) SSD 1999. LNCS, vol. 1651, p. 111. Springer, Heidelberg (1999)
24. Trajcevski, G., Wolfson, O., Zhang, F., Chamberlain, S.: The geometry of uncertainty in moving object databases. In: Proc. of the ACM International Workshop on Data Engineering for Wireless and Mobile Access, MobiDE (2003)
25. Sistla, A., Wolfson, O., Chamberlain, S., Dao, S.: Querying the Uncertain Position of Moving Objects. In: Etzion, O., Jajodia, S., Sripada, S. (eds.) Dagstuhl Seminar 1997. LNCS, vol. 1399, pp. 310–337. Springer, Heidelberg (1998)
26. Wolfson, O., Sistla, A., Xu, B., Zhou, J., Chamberlain, S., Yesha, Y., Rishe, N.: Tracking moving objects using database technology in DOMINO. In: Tsur, S. (ed.) NGITS 1999. LNCS, vol. 1649, pp. 112–119. Springer, Heidelberg (1999)
27. Moreira, J., Ribeiro, C., Abdessalem, T.: Query Operations for Moving Objects Database Systems. In: Proc. of ACMGIS, pp. 108–114 (2000)
28. Cheng, R., Prabhakar, K.-Y., Liang, B.: An efficient location update mechanism for continuous queries over moving objects. Information Systems 32(4), 593–620 (2007)
29. Abdessalem, T., Decreusefond, L., Moreira, J.: Evaluation of Probabilistic Queries in Moving Objects Databases. In: Proc. of the ACM International Workshop on Data Engineering for Wireless and Mobile Access, MobiDE (2006)
30. Bettsetter, C., Harenstein, H., Perez-Costa, X.: Stochastic properties of the random waypoint mobility model. Wireless Networks 10(5) (2004)
31. Chen, X., Schonfeld, D., Khokhar, A.: Localization and Trajectory Estimation of Mobile Objects with a Single Sensor. In: Proc. of the IEEE/SP 14th Workshop on Statistical Signal Processing, pp. 363–367 (2007)

Chemical Compounds with Path Frequency Using Multi-Core Technology

Kun-Ming Yu[1], Yi-Yan Chang[2], Jiayi Zhou[3], Chun-Yuan Huang[1],
Whei-meih Chang[1], Chun-Yuan Lin[4], and Chuan Yi Tang[5]

[1] Department of Bioinformatics, Chung Hua University
[2] Department of Information Management, Chung Hua University
[3] Institute of Engineering and Science, Chung Hua University
[4] Department of Computer Science and Information Engineering, Chang Gung University
[5] Department of Computer Science, National Tsing Hua University
yu@chu.edu.tw, {frank38,jyzhou}@pdlab.csie.chu.edu.tw,
{chunyuan.huang,wmchang}@chu.edu.tw, cyulin@mail.cgu.edu.tw,
cytang@cs.nthu.edu.tw

Abstract. Drug design is the approach of finding drugs by design using computational tools. When designing a new drug, the structure of the drug molecule can be modeled by classification of potential chemical compounds. Kernel Methods have been successfully used in classifying chemical compounds, within which the most popular one is Support Vector Machine (SVM). In order to classify the characteristics of chemical compounds, methods such as frequency of labeled paths have been proposed to map compounds into feature vectors. In this study, we analyze the path frequencies computed from chemical compounds, and reconstruct all possible compounds that share the same path frequency with the original ones, but differ in their molecular structures. Since the computation time for reconstructing such compounds increase greatly along with the size increase of the compounds, we propose an efficient algorithm based on multi-core processing technology. We report here that our algorithm can infer chemical compounds from path frequency while effectively reduce computation time and obtained high speed up.

Keywords: Chemical compound, feature space, Multi-Core Processing, Branch-and-Bound, OpenMP.

1 Introduction

In recent years, many researchers have worked on the drug design problem in order to develop new drugs based on computation methods. When designing a new drug, the structure of the drug molecule can be modeled by classifying candidate chemical compounds using Kernel Methods [4, 5, 6, 7], within which the most popular one is Support Vector Machine (SVM) [10]. Kernel method is a type of pattern analysis, the task of which is to discover the relationships, such as clusters, rankings, classifications, in the data (such as sequences, vectors, sets of points, images, etc). Kernel methods approach the problem by first mapping the data into a high-dimensional

P. Mueller, J.-N. Cao, and C.-L. Wang (Eds.): Infoscale 2009, LNICST 18, pp. 258–271, 2009.
© Institute for Computer Science, Social-Informatics and Telecommunications Engineering 2009

feature space. Recently, it has also been applied to the classification of chemical compounds [4, 5, 6, 7]. In these approaches, chemical compounds are mapped to feature vectors and then SVMs [9, 10] are employed to learn the rules for classifying these feature vectors. Several mapping methods for feature vectors have been proposed; among them, the mapping of feature vectors based on the *frequency of labeled paths* [6, 7] or the *frequency of small fragments in chemical compounds* [4, 5] are widely used.

In kernel methods, an object in the input space can be mapped into a point (or feature vector) in a space called feature space. Through a suitable function $\varnothing$, a given point y in the feature space can be mapped back into an object in the input space. Such object is called pre-image. The problem exists when mapping a given y in feature space back into an object in the input space such that $y=\varnothing(x)$ is satisfied, as x may not exist.

In [1], a feature vector g is a multiple set of strings of labels with length at most K which represents path frequency. Given a feature vector g, they considered the problem of finding a vertex-labeled graph G that attains a one-to-one correspondence between g and the set of sequences of labels along all paths of length at most K in G.

In previous works [1, 2], a graph can be inferred from the numbers of occurrences of vertex-labeled paths. In [1], they showed that this problem can be solved in polynomial time of the size of an output graph if graphs are trees of bounded degree and the lengths of given paths are bounded, by a constant, whereas this problem is strongly NP-hard even for planar graphs of bounded degree.

In this study, we have taken into account the situation when chemical compounds become increasingly complex, the computation time required to infer pre-images from the feature vectors of these compounds increase at a much faster rate. We resort to parallel computing, in which the computation tasks are assigned to multiple cores appropriately to reduce the overall computation time. We extend the algorithms in [3], and therefore the modified algorithms can support multi-core processing technology.

The rest of this paper is organized as follows. Section 2 introduces the background about problem and definition. Next we describe our proposed algorithms in section 3. In section 4, we show the experimental result. Finally we conclude this paper in section 5.

2   Related Work

For classification of the characteristics of chemical compounds to work, chemical compounds are often mapped into feature vectors. Several methods for converting chemical compounds into feature vectors have been proposed. Among them, methods such as frequency of labeled paths [6, 7] or frequency of small fragments [4, 5] are popular. Recently, the pre-image methods have been proposed. In [4], pre-images were found in a general setting by using Kernel Principal Component Analysis and regression. In [8], stochastic search algorithm is used to find pre-images for graphs. However, these pre-image methods are not derived from a computational viewpoint. In [4], the obtained results and performance of the algorithm was unclear because it was applied only to a few similar cases. Other related pre-image studies include inferring a tree from walks in [12], as well as inferring by graphic reconstruction [13].

In [3], chemical structures are modeled as trees or tree-like structures. They extend algorithms in [1, 2] so that constraints on valences of atoms are taken into account. They proposed an algorithm, *Branch-and-Bound Chemical compound Inference from Path Frequency* (BB-CIPF), which can infer tree from related chemical structures. BB-CIPF works within a few or a few tens of seconds for inferring moderate size of chemical compounds (e.g., the number of carbon atoms are less than 20) with tree or tree-like structures, and can be modified for inferring more general classes of chemical compounds and/or for feature vectors based on frequency of small fragments.

In BB-CIPF, given a tree T^{cur} to be inferred to a target tree T^{target}, T^{cur} is first inserted into a node n to become T^{next}. If the feature vector f^{next} of T^{next} does not comply with the feature vector f^{target} of T^{target}, the T^{next} will be discarded and then the T^{cur} will be re-inserted into another node and be compared to T^{target}.

The advantage of BB-CIPF algorithm is to effectively reduce the computation time, as it terminates the computation process immediately and displays the results once it obtains a solution; this also means that there is only one solution [3]. For example, if there are three objects, a, b and c, which all correspond to the same feature vectors v. Through BB-CIPF algorithm, only one of the objects a, b, c can be inferred from v, so the inferred solution is not necessarily be the most useful one in practice. Therefore, how to produce all possible compounds that are mapped back from the same feature vector but differ in their molecular structures is an important issue in the problem. Moreover, when a compound structure is more complex, it will require more computation time for inference of its solutions.

Parallel computing is a suitable technique in shortening the inference procedure. Parallel computing is a form of computation in which several calculations are carried out simultaneously [11], operated on the principle that large problems can often be divided into smaller ones, and then solved concurrently to provide the solution in a shorter time. While clusters, Massive parallel processing (MPP), and Grids use multiple computers to work on the same task, multi-core and multi-processor computers employ multiple processing elements to work on the same task.

A multi-core processor (or chip-level multiprocessor) combines two or more independent cores (normally a CPU) into a single package that consisted of a single integrated circuit. A dual-core processor contains two cores, and a quad-core processor contains four cores. A multi-core microprocessor implements several processing units in a single physical package. In general, programming is required to orchestrate processes in several cores in order to solve problems.

The OpenMP (Open Multi-Processing) standard allows programmers to take advantage of the new shared-memory, multiprocessor programming systems from vendors like Compaq, Sun, HP, and SGI. Aimed at the researcher working with C/C++ or Fortran programming languages, OpenMP explains both what this standard is and how to use it to create software that takes full advantage of parallel computing. OpenMP support Sun compiler, GNU compiler and Intel compiler.

In this paper, we extend the inference algorithm [3] to obtaining all possible compounds that are mapped back from the same feature vector but differ in their molecular structures. We used the Branch-and-Bound concept to derive the trees or tree-like structures of chemical compounds. Our algorithm is committed to obtain all possible compounds that can be inferred from the same feature vector but differ in their molecular structures. We develop our algorithm based upon the algorithm in [3] so that the computation process will not terminate on the first obtained solution, but will continue to search for all possible solutions. However, in order to output more chemical compounds, it also means that the algorithm will consume more computation time. Therefore, we also propose adopting the multi-core computing technology to reduce the computation time in our proposed algorithm. We hope that by providing more thorough and practical solutions to the inference problem, we can improve on the development of drug design.

3 Multi-Core Chemical Compound Inference from Path Frequency (MC-CIPF)

In the previous section, we have described that when a compound structure is more complex, it will require more computation time for inference of its solutions. That is to say, if the feature vector v in feature space has been mapped from a compound c thought a function $\varnothing$, and we want to find c' where $c' = \varnothing(v)$. If a compound is more complex in structure, its feature vector in feature space is also more complex, and it will require substantially more computation time to map back to c' from v. Therefore, in this paper, we divide computation tasks into several smaller tasks and distribute these tasks appropriately among several processing cores for computation. We propose the Multi-Core Chemical Compound Inference from Path Frequency (MC-CIPF) to obtain all possible compounds.

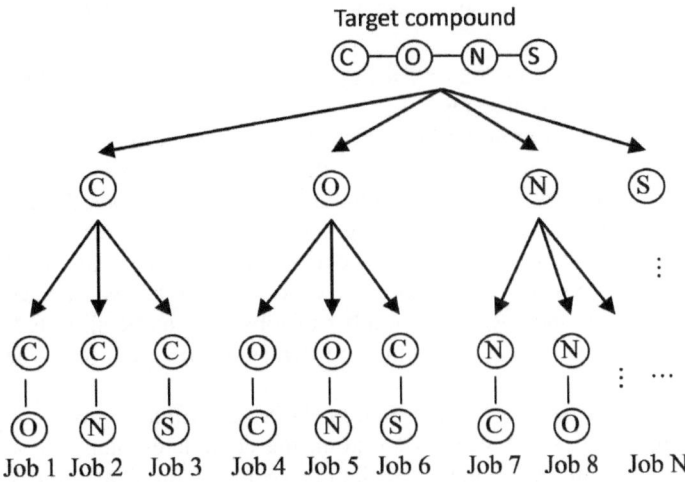

Fig. 1. Each job is initiated based on the atoms that existed in the target compound

In the first step of MC-CIPF, the algorithm loads into the master core a target compound for inference of all other chemical compounds that share the same feature vector. The master core employs the Breadth-First-Search (BFS) algorithm to analyze the target compound and obtain its path frequency for distributing jobs later. Each job is

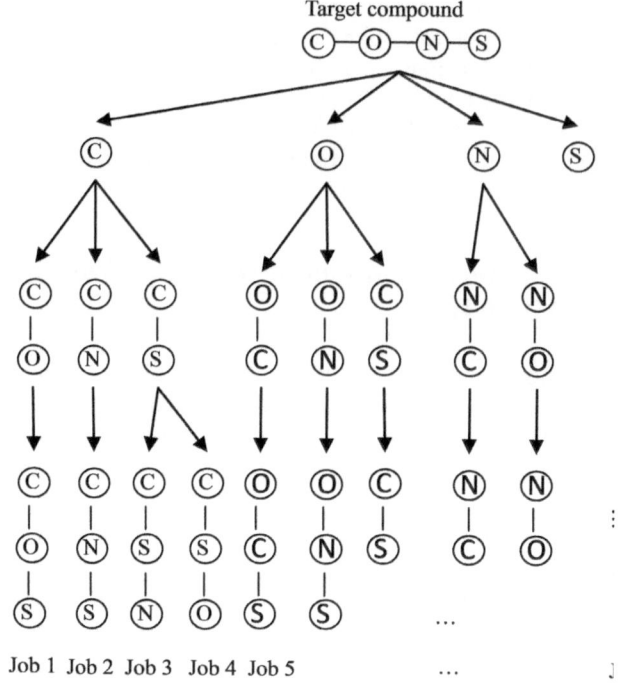

Fig. 2. An example of balancing the load in each core in MC-CIPF

initiated based on the atoms that exist in the target compound (Fig. 1). However, H atoms are not included in this step.

Each job requires different amount of time for computation, and a more complex one will require more time. For example, if there are four cores C_1, C_2, C_3 and C_4, the master core will analyze the target compound, initiate four jobs T_1, T_2, T_3, T_4, and distribute them among four corresponding cores for execution. If T_1, T_2 and T_3 have completed their jobs while T_4 is still in process, T_1, T_2 and T_3 cores will be in idle as there are no more jobs to allocate to these cores. Therefore, we balance the overall computation loads by increasing the number of jobs that can be allocated by the master core and reducing the computation time demanded for each job. The scenario is depicted in Fig. 2.

Each core applies the Depth-First-Search (DFS) algorithm to insert an atom into a candidate compound. After inserted an atom, the candidate compound will be compared with target compound, and if the feature vector of candidate compound has the same structure as parts of target compound structure, the inserted atom will be kept; otherwise, the inserted atom will be dropped, and the algorithm continues on applying DFS to insert the next atom in queue into the candidate compound. If the resulted structure of the candidate compounds is in line with the target structure, it is output as one of the solution. The algorithm iterates until all cores have completed all candidate compounds in their queues.

```
Procedure BFS (T^targe)
  Let T^queue be a queue that stores all candidate compounds;
  for all a ∈ all atoms exist in T^target do
    Let T^temp be a temporary compound
    T^temp ← ∅;
    Insert a into T^temp;
    if T^temp ∈ T^target then
      Add T^temp to T^queue;
    else
      continue (examine the next atom in T^target);
    end
  end
  while T^queue is not empty do
    for each core compute a compound from T^queue per time do
      Compute feature vector f^temp_i from T^temp_i in T^queue;
      if MC-CIPF(T^temp_i, f^temp_i, T^target, f^target)=false then
        output "no solution";
      end
    end

Procedure MC-CIPF(T^temp_i, f^temp_i, T^target, f^target)
  if f^temp_i = f^target then output T^temp_i;
    popup T^temp_i from T^temp;
    return true;
  else
    return false;
  for all a ∈ all atoms exist in T^target do
    L ← ∅;
    if { L(u)|u ∈ V(T^temp)} ∪ {a} ⊈ atomset(f^target) then
      continue;
    for all w ∈ V(T^temp) do
      Let T^next be a tree gotten by connecting new leaf u
with label a to w by bond b;
      if w does not satisfy the valence constraint then
        continue;
      Compute f^next from T^next and f^temp;
      if MC-CIPF(T^next, f^next, T^target, f^target)=true then
        return true;
      end
    end
  return false;
```

4 Experimental Results

For verifying the effectiveness of MC-CIPF, we implemented the proposed algorithm and compared the performance when using single core, dual core and quad

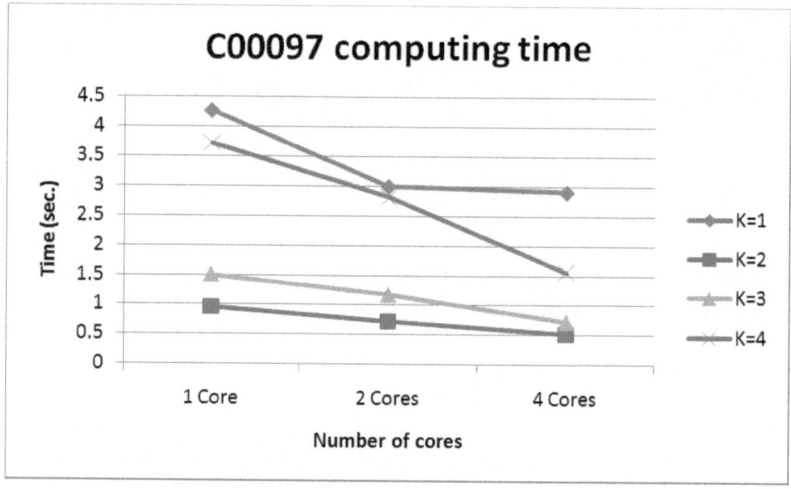

Fig. 3(a). Computing time of C00097

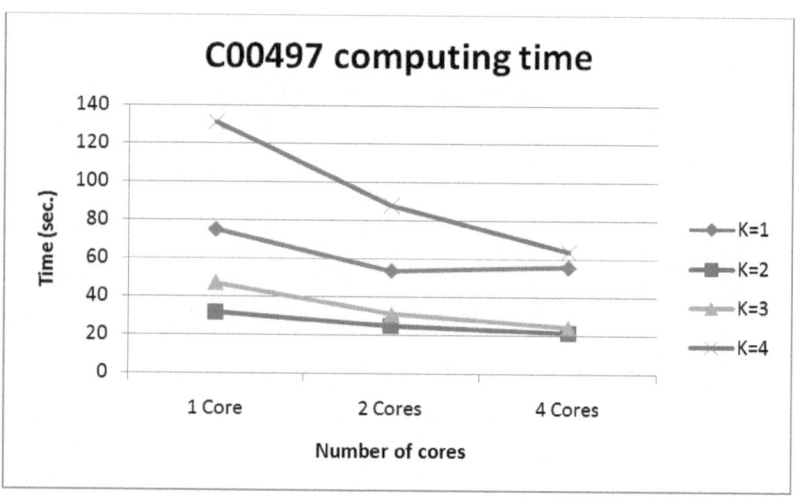

Fig. 3(b). Computing time of C00497

core for computation. The simulation environment is built by using a personal computer equipped with Intel Core 2 Quad Q6600 CPU and 4 GB RAM and installed with the operating system of Windows Vista with Service Pack 1. MC-CIPF was implemented using C language and experimental datasets are retrieved from KEGG LIGAND Database.

In the experiment, we randomly chosen 5 chemical compounds (C00097, C00497, C11109, C14601, and C15987; the number of atoms of compound size with hydrogen are 14, 15, 16, 15 and 19, respectively) from KEGG LIGAND Database and examined them with $K = 1, 2, 3, 4$, where K is the length of sequence label of feature

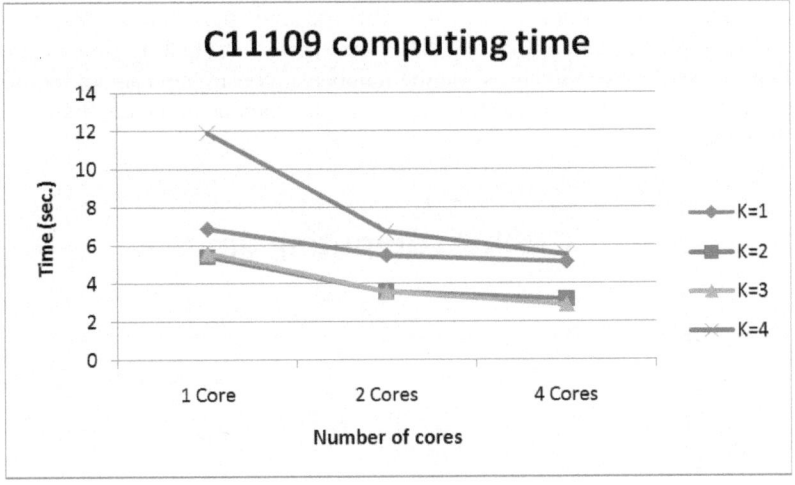

Fig. 3(c). Computing time of C11109

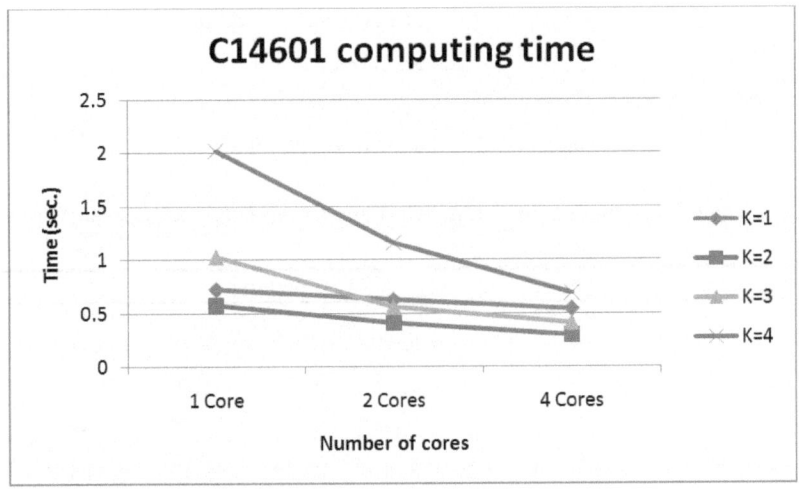

Fig. 3(d). Computing time of C14601

vectors in MC-CIPF. Larger K means more constraints for target compound, which leads to less variation for its molecular structure. Fig. 3(a)-(e) are the computing time for each chemical compound. In each case, we have found that the computing time was reduced as the number of cores was increased. For example, in Fig. 3(c), when K was equal to 4, the computing time was reduced from 11.9337 second with 1 core to 5.542821 second with 4 cores.

When the K value increases, the constraints of the feature vectors increase accordingly. As a result, MC-CIPF spends less computing time in searching for the combinations of target compound, as there is less permitted variations to compute for. However, the path frequency will be longer, so MC-CIPF needs to spend more execution time in re-computing path frequency. Consequently, the shortest computing time occurs when K is equal to 2 in the experiment, since the number of constraints has not increased too much and the length of path frequency is not too long. Details of the computing time are shown in Table 1.

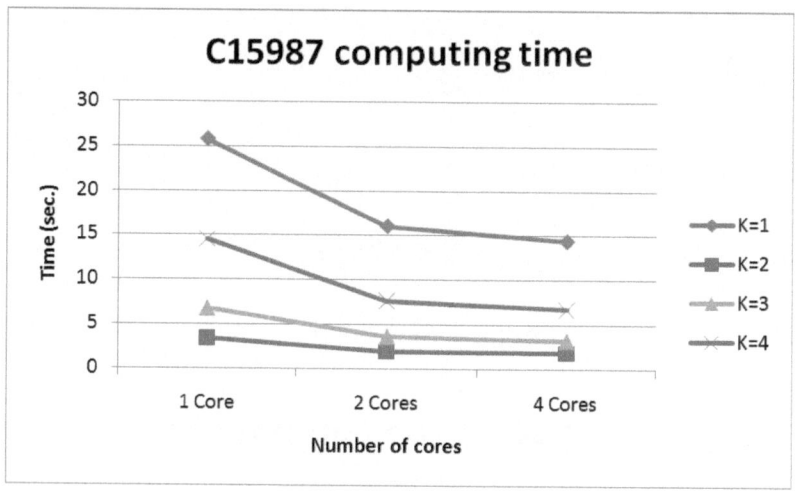

Fig. 3(e). Computing time of C15987

Table 1. Computing time of MC-CIPF for various chemical compounds

Instances	Cores detail		K=1	K=2	K=3	K=4
			CPU time (sec.)			
C00097	1 Core		4.27	0.96	1.49	3.71
	2 Cores	Core 1	2.99	0.26	1.17	2.81
		Core 2	3.00	0.72	1.17	2.81
		Max	3.00	0.72	1.17	2.81
	4 Cores	Core 1	2.91	0.20	0.72	1.56
		Core 2	2.67	0.36	0.46	0.98
		Core 3	0.77	0.35	0.50	0.97
		Core 4	2.91	0.51	0.72	1.56
		Max	2.91	0.51	0.72	1.56
C00497	1 Core		75.44	31.95	47.23	131.42
	2 Cores	Core 1	28.82	8.78	31.26	35.33
		Core 2	54.10	25.12	31.27	88.09

Table 1. (*Continued*)

		Max	54.10	25.12	31.27	88.09
	4 Cores	Core 1	13.76	3.93	24.43	11.05
		Core 2	31.23	7.77	12.25	28.88
		Core 3	12.47	7.88	12.26	30.69
		Core 4	56.14	21.67	24.43	64.10
		Max	56.14	21.67	24.43	64.10
C11109	1 Core		6.88	5.42	5.63	11.93
	2 Cores	Core 1	5.47	3.59	3.55	6.73
		Core 2	5.48	3.59	3.56	6.73
		Max	5.48	3.59	3.561	6.73
	4 Cores	Core 1	5.13	3.18	2.90	5.53
		Core 2	1.83	2.06	1.91	3.53
		Core 3	2.48	2.05	1.18	1.93
		Core 4	5.13	3.18	2.90	5.54
		Max	5.13	3.18	2.90	5.54
C14601	1 Core		0.72	0.57	1.02	2.02
	2 Cores	Core 1	0.62	0.40	0.51	0.83
		Core 2	0.62	0.40	0.55	1.16
		Total	0.62	0.40	0.55	1.16
	4 Cores	Core 1	0.54	0.27	0.40	0.37
		Core 2	0.13	0.23	0.38	0.55
		Core 3	0.21	0.25	0.40	0.68
		Core 4	0.54	0.29	0.35	0.58
		Max	0.54	0.29	0.40	0.68
C15987	1 Core		25.73	3.49	6.77	14.52
	2 Cores	Core 1	16.02	2.00	0.35	4.95
		Core 2	11.43	2.00	3.67	7.67
		Max	16.02	2.00	3.67	7.67
	4 Cores	Core 1	14.41	1.87	1.28	2.03
		Core 2	5.78	1.48	1.65	3.16
		Core 3	12.85	1.87	3.25	6.76
		Core 4	1.42	0.72	0.55	0.68
		Max	14.41	1.87	3.25	6.76

More importantly, we want to compare the speedup ratios of MC-CIPF with respect to the core number used in the experiments. Fig. 4(a)-(e) are the speedup ratios of C00097, C00497, C11109, C14601, and C15987. In these figures, the speedup ratios are increased from 1 core to 4 cores, with the best speedup ratio close to 3 (Fig. 4(c)). Interestingly, when the K value is increased, the speedup ratio is raised accordingly.

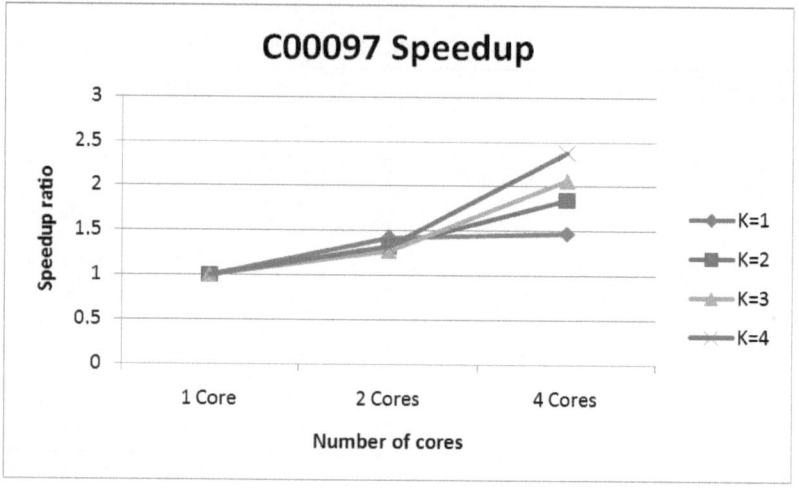

Fig. 4(a). Speedup ratio of C00097

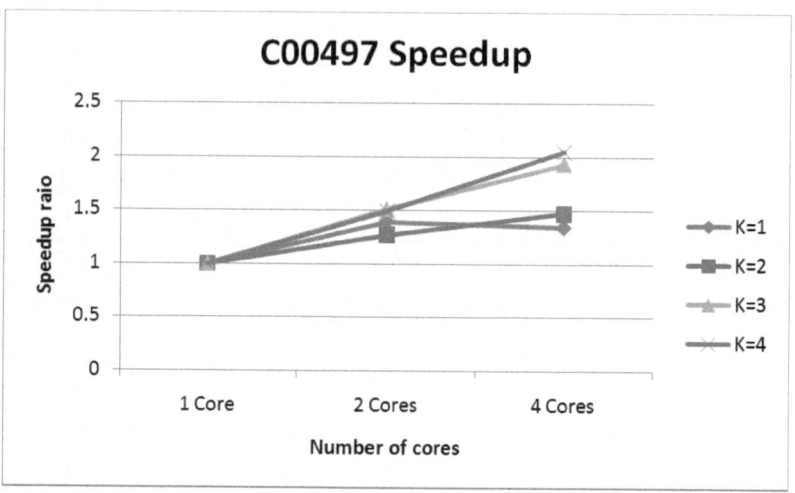

Fig. 4(b). Speedup ratio of C00497

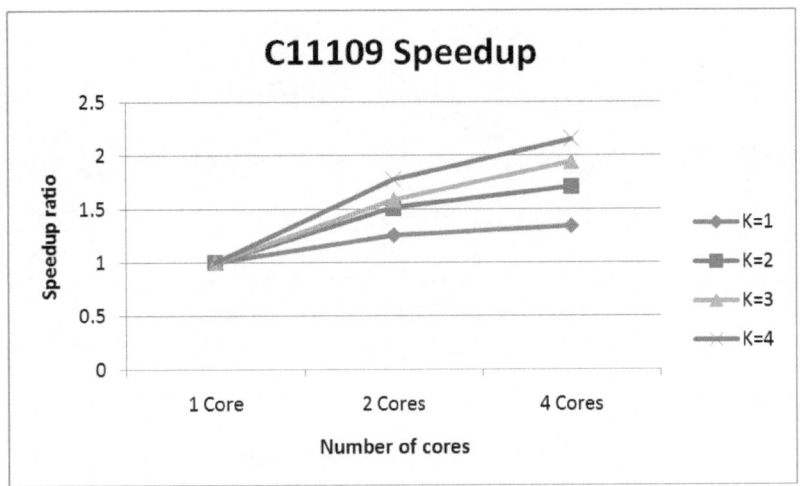

Fig. 4(c). Speedup ratio of C11109

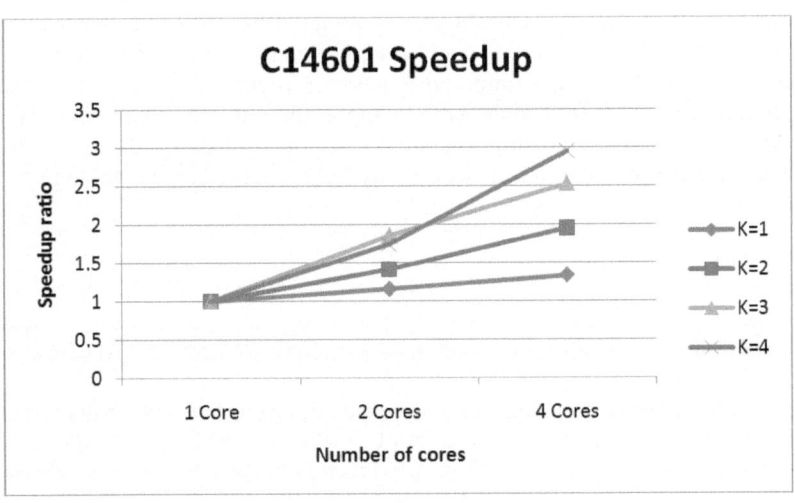

Fig. 4(d). Speedup ratio of C14601

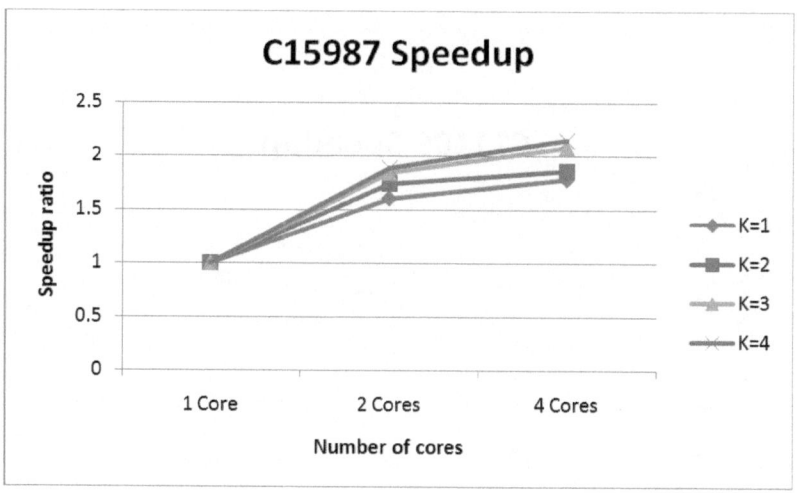

Fig. 4(e). Speedup ratio of C15987

5   Conclusions

In this research, we proposed a multi-core algorithm for solving Chemical Compound Inference from Path Frequency problem. We adopted the Branch-and-Bound concept to evolve the tree-like structures of chemical compounds in the paper. The experimental results show that our algorithm can practically reduce computing time, with the best speedup ratio close to 3 folds while using 4 cores in the experiment. Therefore, our proposed algorithm can infer chemical compounds from path frequency effectively and reduce computation time by employing the multi-core technology.

References

1. Tatsuya, A., Daiji, F.: Inferring a graph from path frequency. In: Garijo, F.J., Riquelme, J.-C., Toro, M. (eds.) IBERAMIA 2002. LNCS (LNAI), vol. 2527, pp. 371–392. Springer, Heidelberg (2002)
2. Tatsuya, A., Daiji, F.: On inference of a chemical structure from path frequency. In: Proc. 2005 International Joint Conference of InCoB, AASBi, and KSBI, pp. 96–100 (2005)
3. Tatsuya, A., Daiji, F.: Inferring a Chemical Structure from a Feature Vector Based on Frequency of Labeled Paths and Small Fragments. In: APBC, pp. 165–174 (2007)
4. Byvatov, E., Fechner, U., Sadowski, J., Schneider, G.: Comparison of support vector machine and artificial neural network systems for drug/nondrug classification. Journal of Chemical Information and Computer Sciences 43, 1882–1889 (2003)
5. Deshpande, M., Kuramochi, M., Wale, N., Karypis, G.: Frequent substructure-based approaches for classifying chemical compounds. IEEE Trans. Knowledge and Data Engineering 17, 1036–1050 (2005)
6. Kashima, H., Tsuda, K., Inokuchi, A.: Marginalized kernels between labeled graphs. In: Proc. 20th Int. Conf. Machine Learning, pp. 321–328 (2003)

7. Mahé, P., Ueda, N., Tatsuya, A., Perret, J.-L., Vert, J.-P.: Graph kernels for molecular structure-activity relationship analysis with support vector machines. Journal of Chemical Information and Modeling 45, 939–951 (2005)
8. Bakir, G.H., Zien, A., Tsuda, K.: Learning to find graph pre-images. In: Rasmussen, C.E., Bülthoff, H.H., Schölkopf, B., Giese, M.A. (eds.) DAGM 2004. LNCS, vol. 3175, pp. 253–261. Springer, Heidelberg (2004)
9. Cortes, C., Vapnik, V.: Support vector networks. Machine Learning 20, 273–297 (1995)
10. Cristianini, N., Shawe-Taylor, J.: An Introduction to Support Vector Machines and Other Kernel-based Learning Methods. Cambridge Univ. Press, Cambridge (2000)
11. Almasi, G.S., Gottlieb, A.: Highly Parallel Computing. Benjamin-Cummings Publishers, Redwood City (1989)
12. Maruyama, O., Miyano, S.: Inferring a tree from walks. Theoretical Computer Science 161, 289–300 (1996)
13. Lauri, J., Scapellato, R.: Topics in Graph Automorphisms and Reconstruction. Cambridge Univ. Press, Cambridge (2003)

Distance Dimension Reduction on QR Factorization for Efficient Clustering Semantic XML Document Using the QR Fuzzy C-Mean (QR-FCM)

Hsu-Kuang Chang[1,2] and I-Chang Jou[1]

[1] Institute of Engineering Science and Technology,
National Kaohsiung First University of Science and Technology, Kaohsiung, Taiwan
[2] Department of Information Engineering, I-Shou University, Kaohsiung, Taiwan
hkchang@isu.edu.tw, icjou@ccms.nkfust.edu.tw

Abstract. The rapid growth of XML adoption has urged for the need of a proper representation for semi-structured documents, where the document semantic structural information has to be taken into account so as to support more precise document analysis. In order to analyze the information represented in XML documents efficiently, researches on XML document clustering are actively in progress. The key issue is how to devise the similarity measure between XML documents to be used for clustering. Since XML documents have hierarchical structure, it is not appropriate to cluster them by using a general document similarity measure. Dimension reduction plays an important role in handling the massive quantity of high dimensional data such as mass semantic structural documents. In this paper, we introduce distance dimension reduction (DDR) based on the QR factorization (DDR/QR) or the Cholesky factorization (DDR/C). DDR generates lower dimensional representations of the high-dimensional XML document, which can exactly preserve Euclidean distances and cosine similarities between any pair of XML documents in the original dimensional space. After projecting XML documents to the lower dimensional space obtained from DDR, our proposed method QR fuzzy c-mean to execute the document-analysis clustering algorithms (we called the QR-FCM). DDR can substantially reduce the computing time and/or memory requirement of a given document-analysis clustering algorithm, especially when we need to run the document analysis algorithm many times for estimating parameters or searching for a better solution.

Keywords: QR factorization, singular value decomposition, distance dimension reduction, PEWF, PEIDF, PESSW, fuzzy C-mean, QR-FCM.

1 Introduction

XML document which is a semi-structured data, have hierarchical structure. Therefore, rather than using the similarity measure of the general document clustering techniques as is, a new similarity measure that considers the semantic and structural information of XML document must be investigated. However, some XML clustering methods used

P. Mueller, J.-N. Cao, and C.-L. Wang (Eds.): Infoscale 2009, LNICST 18, pp. 272–287, 2009.
© Institute for Computer Science, Social-Informatics and Telecommunications Engineering 2009

the similarity measure that takes only the structural information of XML documents into account. Hwang proposed a clustering method that extracts a typical structure of the maximum frequent pattern using *PrefixSpan* algorithm [1] on XML documents [2, 3]. However, since such a typical structure extracted from XML document is not only the structure that represents the XML document itself, but also it cannot be the representative of the whole documents corpus, there is an accuracy issue of similarity. Lian summarized XML documents into *S-graph* which is a structural graph and proposed the calculation method of distance between *S-graphs* to be used for clustering [4]. However, they have no consideration for semantic information on XML documents as they focus on structural information only. Since dimension reduction is one of the fundamental methods for data analysis, there have been a lot of studies on effective and efficient dimension reduction algorithms. There are linear dimension reduction algorithms including principal component analysis (PCA) [5] and multidimensional scaling (MDS) [6]. There are also nonlinear dimensional reduction algorithms (NLDR) including Isomap [7], locally linear embedding (LLE) [8], [9], Hessian LLE [10], Laplacian eigenmaps [11], local tangent space alignment (LTSA) [12] and distance preserving dimension reduction based on the singular value decomposition (DPDR/SVD) [13]. These dimension a variety of areas such as biomedical image recognition, biomedical text data mining, and biological data analysis.

In this paper, we introduce distance dimension reduction (DDR) based on the QR factorization or the Cholesky factorization. DDR can produce t dimensional representations where t is the rank of the original XML data set, which exactly preserve Euclidean L_2-norm distances as well as cosine similarities between any pair of XML documents in the original m-dimensional space when m is much larger than the number of XML documents n, i.e. m > n. It projects the original XML data set into a much lower dimensional space without any loss of the pair-wise Euclidean distance information. Then, other XML documents analysis algorithms can be executed so that we can substantially reduce their computing times and memory requirements without any quality loss of their results.

The rest of this paper is organized as follows. In Section 2, we introduce the preparation XML documents on vector space model. In Section 3, we introduce DDR based on the QR factorization and DDR based on the Cholesky factorization after showing theorems of distance and cosine similarity preserving properties. Section 4 presents experimental results illustrating properties of the proposed DDR methods. Summary is given in Section 5.

2 Preparation for Semantic-Based XML Documents

In this section, we first introduce pre-processing steps for the incorporation of hierarchical information in encoding the XML tree's paths. It is based on the preorder tree representation (PTR) [14] and will be introduced after a brief review of how to generate an XML tree from an XML document. To do so, we have to first go through

Table 1. Preprocessing steps for XML document

Step 1. **Conversion**	Convert the XML document to tree Format. The values of the elements in the tree are not considered here, and only the structural information will be passed on to the subsequent steps.
Step 2. **Path Extraction**	Traverse the elements from the root to each leaf node of the tree. Record the sequence and hierarchical information for each path.
Step 3. **Similar Element Identification and Transformation**	Rename the terms of the paths with unique identifiers. Replace every element with a unique identifier in increasing order.
Step 4. **Nested and Duplicated Path Removal**	Remove any nested and duplicated path. The nested and duplicated paths in the tree are not considered here, and only the unique ones will be passed on to the next step.
Step 5. **Path Elements Encoding**	Based on the structural summary by Step 4, the path elements are encoded.

the following five preprocessing steps for XML documents. They are illustrated in Table 1.

From five steps preprocess, now XML document is modeled as a XML tree $T=(V,E)$. T is connected tree with $V=\{ v_1, v_2, ...\}$ as a set of vertices and $V_1 \in V$, $V_2 \in V$, $(v_1, v_2) \in E$ as a set of edges. One distinguished vertex $r \in V$ is designated the root, and for all $v \in V$, there is a unique path from r to v. As an example, Figure 1 depicts a sample XML tree containing some information about collection of books. The *book* consists of *intro* tags, each comprising *title*, *author* and *date* tags. Each *author* contains *fname* and *lname*, each *date* includes *year* and *month* tags. Figure 1 left shows only the first letter of each tag for the simplicity.

XML document has a hierarchical structure and this structure is organized with tag paths. Each tag path represents document characteristics that can predict the contents of XML document. Strictly speaking, it shows the semantic structural characteristics of XML document. In this paper, we propose a method for calculating the similarity using all tag paths of XML tree representing the semantic structural information of XML document.

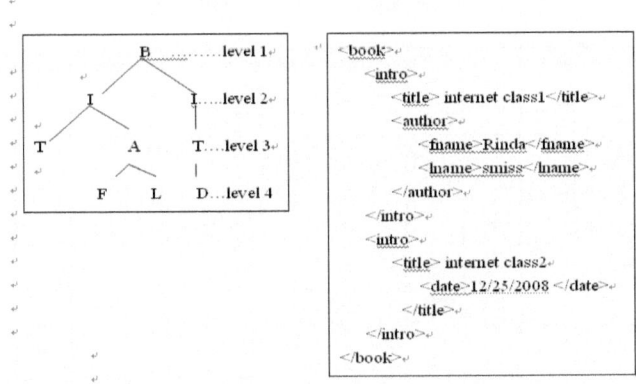

Fig. 1. An example of XML Document

3 Path Element Vector Space Model (PEVSM)

Vector model represents a document as a vector whose elements are the weights of the path elements within a document. In calculating the weight of each path element within a document, Term Frequency and IDF (Inverse Document Frequency) method is used [15]. We define PESSW (Path Element Structural Semantic Weight) that calculate the weight of a path element in a XML document. The PESSW is PEWF (Path Element Weighted Frequency) multiplied by PEIDF (Path Element Inverse Document Frequency). $PESSW_{ij}$ of ith path element in the jth document is shown in equation (1).

$$PESSW_{ij} = PEWF_{ij} \times PEIDF_{ij} \qquad (1)$$

$PEWF_{ij}$ is shown in equation(2).

$$PEWF_{ij} = freq_{ij} \times \frac{1}{x^n} \qquad (2)$$

$PEIDF_{ij}$ is shown in equation (3),

$$PEIDF_{ij} = \log\frac{N}{DF_j} \qquad (3)$$

Table 2 shows PEWF, PEIDF, and PESSW on an example trees in Figure 1.

Table 2. An example of PTWF, PTIDF and PESSW

Path / Element	PEWF			PEIDF			PESSW		
	doc	doc	doc	doc	doc	doc	doc	doc	doc
/B/I/T/D	1.0	0.0	0.0	1.1	0.0	0.0	1.1	0.0	0.0
/B/I/A/F	1.0	1.0	0.0	0.41	0.41	0.0	0.41	0.41	0.0
/B/I/A/L	1.0	1.0	0.0	0.41	0.41	0.0	0.41	0.41	0.0
/M/I/A/L	0.0	0.0	1.0	0.0	0.0	1.1	0.0	0.0	1.1
/B/I/T/	2.0	1.0	0.0	0.41	0.41	0.0	0.81	0.41	0.0
/B/I/A	1.0	1.0	0.0	0.41	0.41	0.0	0.41	0.41	0.0
/B/I/	2.0	1.0	0.0	0.41	0.41	0.0	0.81	0.41	0.0
/B	1.0	1.0	0.0	0.41	0.41	0.0	0.41	0.41	0.0
/M/I/T	0.0	0.0	1.0	0.0	0.0	1.1	0.0	0.0	1.1
/M	0.0	0.0	1.0	0.0	0.0	1.1	0.0	0.0	1.1
/M/I	0.0	0.0	2.0	0.0	0.0	1.1	0.0	0.0	2.2
/I/T/D	0.5	0.0	0.0	1.10	0.0	0.0	0.5	0.0	0.0
/I/A/F	0.5	0.5	0.0	0.41	0.41	0.0	0.21	0.21	0.0
/I/A/L	0.5	0.5	0.5	0.0	0.0	0.0	0.0	0.0	0.0
/I/T	1.0	0.5	0.5	0.0	0.0	0.0	0.0	0.0	0.0
/I/A	0.5	0.5	0.5	0.0	0.0	0.0	0.0	0.0	0.0
/I	1.0	0.5	1.0	0.0	0.0	0.0	0.0	0.0	0.0
/T/D	0.33	0.0	0.0	1.1	0.0	0.0	0.33	0.0	0.0
/A/F	0.33	0.33	0.0	0.41	0.41	0.0	0.14	0.14	0.0
/A/L	0.33	0.33	0.33	0.0	0.0	0.0	0.0	0.0	0.0
/T	0.67	0.33	0.33	0.0	0.0	0.0	0.0	0.0	0.0
/A	0.33	0.33	0.33	0.0	0.0	0.0	0.0	0.0	0.0
D	0.25	0.0	0.0	1.1	0.0	0.0	0.27	0.0	0.0
F	0.25	0.25	0.0	0.41	0.41	0.0	0.1	0.1	0.0
L	0.25	0.25	0.25	0.0	0.0	0.0	0.0	0.0	0.0

Let d_x and d_y be two vectors that represent a XML document doc_x and doc_y. Cosine similarity is defined as the angle between two vectors and quantified by equation (4) and (5).

$$\cos\theta = \frac{d_x \cdot d_y}{|d_x| \cdot |d_y|} \text{ , that is} \tag{4}$$

$$sim(doc_x, doc_y) = \frac{d_x \cdot d_y}{|d_x| \times |d_y|} = \frac{\sum_{k=1}^{t} w_{kx} \times w_{ky}}{\sqrt{\sum_{k=1}^{t} w_{kx}^2} \times \sqrt{\sum_{k=1}^{t} w_{ky}^2}} \tag{5}$$

where $d_x = (w_{1x}, w_{2x}, ..., w_{tx})$ and $d_y = (w_{1y}, w_{2y}, ..., w_{ty})$, t is the total number of path elements in d_x, d_y respectively[16].

3.1   Distance Dimension Reduction (DDR) via the QR Factorization

Let us deal with n XML documents whose dimension is m s.t. $m \succ n$. We compute the QR factorization of the XML document matrix $D \in \Re^{m \times n}$:

$$D = QR = Q\begin{pmatrix} R_1 \\ 0 \end{pmatrix} = (Q_1 \quad Q_2)\begin{pmatrix} R_1 \\ 0 \end{pmatrix} = Q_1 R_1,$$

where $Q \in \Re^{m \times m}$ is an orthogonal matrix and $R_1 \in \Re^{n \times n}$ is an upper triangular matrix. Then, $Q_1 \in \Re^{m \times n}$ can be considered as a dimensionality transformation matrix when m > n and the lower dimensional representation $\hat{x} \in \Re^{n \times 1}$ of a vector $x \in \Re^{m \times 1}$ can be computed as $\hat{x} = Q_1^T x$. Thus, the lower dimensional representation d_i of each XML document $\hat{d}_i = Q_1^T d_i = r_i$, where d_i is the i-th column of D and r_i is the i-th column of R_1.

Theorem 1. QR-Factorization

Let $\left(\vec{d}_1, \vec{d}_2, \ldots, \vec{d}_n\right)$ be a basis of D a subspace of $\Re^m$. For j=2,3,...,n, where we write $\vec{d}_j = \vec{d}_j^{\text{II}} + \vec{d}_j^{\perp}$, with respect to span $\left(\vec{d}_1, \vec{d}_2, \ldots, \vec{d}_{j-1}\right)$.

Then, $\vec{q}_1 = \dfrac{1}{\left\|\vec{d}_1\right\|} \vec{d}_1$

$\vec{d}_2^{\perp} = \vec{d}_2 - \vec{d}_2^{\text{II}} = \vec{d}_2 - (\vec{q}_1 \cdot \vec{d}_2)\vec{q}_1$, and $\vec{q}_2 = \dfrac{1}{\left\|\vec{d}_2^{\perp}\right\|} \vec{d}_2^{\perp}$,

$\vec{d}_3^{\perp} = \vec{d}_3 - \vec{d}_3^{\text{II}} = \vec{d}_3 - (\vec{q}_1 \cdot \vec{d}_3)\vec{q}_1 - (\vec{q}_2 \cdot \vec{d}_3)\vec{q}_2$, and $\vec{q}_3 = \dfrac{1}{\left\|\vec{d}_3^{\perp}\right\|} \vec{d}_3^{\perp}$,

................................,   , and ....

$\vec{d}_j^{\perp} = \vec{d}_j - \vec{d}_j^{\text{II}} = \vec{d}_j - (\vec{q}_1 \cdot \vec{d}_j)\vec{q}_1 - \ldots - (\vec{q}_{j-1} \cdot \vec{d}_j)\vec{q}_{j-1}$, and $\vec{q}_j = \dfrac{1}{\left\|\vec{d}_j^{\perp}\right\|} \vec{d}_j^{\perp}$

................................,   , and ....

$\vec{d}_m^{\perp} = \vec{d}_m - \vec{d}_m^{\text{II}} = \vec{d}_m - (\vec{q}_1 \cdot \vec{d}_m)\vec{q}_1 - \ldots - (\vec{q}_{m-1} \cdot \vec{d}_m)\vec{q}_{m-1}$, and $\vec{q}_m = \dfrac{1}{\left\|\vec{d}_m^{\perp}\right\|} \vec{d}_m^{\perp}$

The Gram-Schmidt process represents a change of basis from the old basis $D = \left(\vec{d}_1, \vec{d}_2, \ldots, \vec{d}_n \right)$ to a new, orthonormal basis $Q = \left(\vec{q}_1, \vec{q}_2, \ldots, \vec{q}_n \right)$ of vector V. If R is the change basis matrix form D to Q, then

$D=QR$

$$\left(\vec{d}_1, \vec{d}_2, \ldots, \vec{d}_n \right) = \left(\vec{q}_1, \vec{q}_2, \ldots, \vec{q}_n \right) \begin{bmatrix} r_{11} & r_{12} & \cdots & \cdots & r_{1n} \\ 0 & r_{22} & \cdots & \cdots & r_{2n} \\ 0 & 0 & r_{33} & \cdots & r_{3n} \\ \cdots & \cdots & \cdots & \cdot\cdot & \cdot\cdot \\ 0 & 0 & 0 & 0 & r_{nn} \end{bmatrix}$$

This equation is called the QR-factorization of the matrix D. Using Gram-Schmidt algorithm, we know that

$$\vec{d}_j = \vec{d}_j^{\,\text{II}} + \vec{d}_j^{\,\perp}$$

$$= (\vec{q}_1 \cdot \vec{d}_1)\vec{q}_1 + \ldots + (\vec{q}_i \cdot \vec{d}_j)\vec{q}_i + \ldots + (\vec{q}_{j-1} \cdot \vec{d}_j)\vec{q}_{j-1} + \left\| \vec{d}_j^{\,\perp} \right\| \vec{q}_j$$

$$= r_{11}\vec{q}_1 + \ldots\ldots\ldots + r_{ij} + \ldots\ldots\ldots\ldots + r_{j-1,j}\vec{q}_{j-1} + r_{jj}\vec{q}_j$$

It follows that $r_{ij} = \vec{q}_i \vec{d}_j$ if $i < j$, $r_{jj} = \left\| \vec{d}_j^{\,\perp} \right\| \geq 0$; and $r_{ij}=0$ if $i > j$. The last equation

implies that R is an upper triangular matrix. The first diagonal entry is $r_{11} = \left\| \vec{d}_1 \right\|$,

since $\vec{d}_1 = \left\| \vec{d}_1 \right\| \vec{q}_1 . (\because \vec{q}_1 = \dfrac{1}{\left\| \vec{d}_1 \right\|} \vec{d}_1)$

3.2 Our Proposed QR-FCM Algorithm

From the QR factorization as the previous section described, we have the originated document vector PESSW, document vector $\bar{r}$ (economic QR factoring), document vector $\hat{r}$ (rank of PESSW), and document vector $\tilde{r}$ (low rank of QR) based on the XML documents, which taken as the QR-FCM input data and then go through the clustering.

$$input \begin{cases} Vector\ PESSW \\ Vector\ \overline{r}_k = \overline{Q}_e^T d \\ Vctor\ \hat{r}_k = \hat{Q}^T d, k = rank(d) \\ Vctor\ \tilde{r}_k = \tilde{Q}^T d, k = lowrank(d) \end{cases} \longrightarrow \boxed{\begin{array}{c} \text{QR-FCM} \\ \\ \text{Clustering} \end{array}} \longrightarrow f_i$$

$F(I) = [f_1, f_2, \ldots, f_c]$, where $f_i = \sum_{j=1}^{N} \mu_{ij} P_j = \dfrac{1}{N} \sum_{j=1}^{N} \mu_{ij}$.

Fuzzy c-means (FCM) is a method of clustering which allows one piece of data to belong to two or more clusters. This method (developed by Dunn in 1973 and improved by Bezdek in 1981) is frequently used in pattern recognition. It is based on minimization of the following objective function:

$$J_m = \sum_{i=1}^{N} \sum_{j=1}^{C} \mu_{ij}^m \left\| d_i - c_j \right\|^2 , 1 \le m \le \infty$$

where m is any real number greater than 1, u_{ij} is the degree of membership of d_i in the cluster j, d_i is the ith of d-dimensional measured data, c_j is the d-dimension center of the cluster, and $\|*\|$ is any norm expressing the similarity between any measured data and the center.

Fuzzy partitioning is carried out through an iterative optimization of the objective function shown above, with the update of membership u_{ij} and the cluster centers c_j by:

$$\mu_{ij} = \frac{1}{\sum_{k=1}^{C} \left(\dfrac{\left\| d_i - c_j \right\|}{\left\| d_i - c_k \right\|} \right)^{\frac{2}{m-1}}} , \quad c_j = \frac{\sum_{i=1}^{N} \mu_{ij}^m . d_i}{\sum_{i=1}^{N} \mu_{ij}^m}$$

This iteration will stop when $\max_{ij} \left\{ \left| \mu_{ij}^{(k+1)} - \mu_{ij}^{(k)} \right| \right\} < \xi$, where ξ is a termination

criterion between 0 and 1, whereas k are the iteration steps. This procedure converges to a local minimum or a saddle point of J_m. The QR-FCM algorithm is composed of the following steps:

1. *Input the number of clusters c, the weighting exponent m, and error tolerance ε.*

2. *Initialize the cluster centers $c = \{c_i\}$, for $1 \le i \le C$.*

3. *Initialize $U=[u_{ij}]$ matrix, $U^{(0)}$*

4. *At k-step: calculate the centers vectors $C^{(k)}=[c_j]$ with $U^{(k)}$*

$$c_j = \frac{\sum_{i=1}^{N} \mu_{ij}^m \cdot d_i}{\sum_{i=1}^{N} \mu_{ij}^m}$$

5. Update $U^{(k)}$, $U^{(k+1)}$

$$\mu_{ij} = \frac{\left(\frac{1}{\|d_j, v_i\|_2}\right)^{\frac{1}{m-1}}}{\sum_{i=1}^{C} \left(\frac{1}{\|d_j, c_i\|_2}\right)^{\frac{1}{m-1}}}, \quad \mu_{ij} = \frac{1}{\sum_{k=1}^{C} \left(\frac{\|d_i - c_j\|}{\|d_i - c_k\|}\right)^{\frac{2}{m-1}}}$$

6. If $\| U^{(k+1)} - U^{(k)} \| < \xi$ then STOP; otherwise return to step 4.

4 Experiment Result

4.1 Within-Group-Variance and Between-Group-Variance Using Membership μ

The purpose of any clustering technique [17], [18], [19], [20], [21] is to evolve a K x n partition matrix (U)=D of a data set D $(D = \{d_1, d_2, ..., d_n\})$ in $\mathfrak{R}^N$, representing its partitioning into a number, say K, of clusters (C_1; C_2; . . . ; C_K). The partition matrix (U) = D may be represented as U=[μ_{kj}], k=1,..,K, and j= 1,..., n, where u_{kj} is the membership of pattern d_j to clusters C_k. In crisp partitioning of the data, the following condition holds: u_{kj}=1 if $d_j \in C_k$; otherwise, u_{kj}=0. Right now, we use the membership u as separation measuring degree to figure out the variance of the within-group-variance and between-group-variance among the XML documents in the different cluster. First, we define the useful definitions as follows.

Definition 1. The closeness (denseness) of the XML documents in the ith cluster (C_i)

$$C_i = \frac{\sum_{j \in S_i} \mu_{ij}}{|S_i|} \quad \text{where} \quad I_{i,j} = \begin{cases} 1 & if \quad \mu_{i,j} = \max_{1 \le k \le C} \mu_{k,j} \\ 0 & if \quad \mu_{i,j} \ne \max_{1 \le k \le C} \mu_{k,j} \end{cases},$$

, μ_{ij} is the membership calculated from the QR-FCM (QR fuzzy C-mean) and

$$S_i = \{ j \mid I_{i,j} = 1 \}.$$

Definition 2. Within-Group-Variance (WGV) of the cluster

$$WGV(\mu, V; D) = \sum_{i=1}^{C} \sum_{j \in S_i} (C_i)^{-1} \| d_j, v_i \|_2 \tag{6}$$

C_i is the denseness within the cluster which is defined as the membership μ_{ij} with the ith cluster. μ_{ij} is calculated from QR-FCM (QR fuzzy C-mean). μ_{ij} represents the membership of the XML document d_j within the cluster i. If the all membership within the ith cluster is large, then each XML document is close to the central document. That means each XML document is close to the central document within the cluster, each close to the central document, high denseness, low variance. C_i is the denseness determined by the μ_{ij} membership. Beside, from the distance of XML document and central document, $\| d_j, v_i \|_2$, defined the XML document diversity within the cluster. We defined the within-group-variance as combine both of these two criteria, the bigger C_i the more dense, and the smaller $\| d_j, v_i \|_2$ the better result for the within-group-variance, so we have $_{min}\{WGV\}$.

Definition 3. The contribution of the separation XML document d_j among λcluster and

m cluster defined as $\mu_{\lambda,j} * \mu_{m,j}$.

Example 1

$$m == \begin{array}{c} C_1 \\ C_2 \end{array} \begin{bmatrix} d_1 & d_2 & d_3 \\ \mu_{11} & \mu_{12} & \mu_{31} \\ \mu_{12} & \mu_{22} & \mu_{32} \end{bmatrix} = \begin{array}{c} C_1 \\ C_2 \end{array} \begin{bmatrix} d_1 & d_2 & d_3 \\ 0.8 & 0.1 & 0.4 \\ 0.2 & 0.9 & 0.6 \end{bmatrix},$$

$$\mu_{11} * \mu_{21} = 0.16, \mu_{12} * \mu_{22} = 0.09, \mu_{13} * \mu_{23} = 0.2$$

From the membership matrix m, the smaller the $\mu_{\lambda,j} * \mu_{m,j}$, the bigger contribution of the separation for the λ cluster and m cluster.

Example 2

$$m=\begin{array}{c} \\ C_1 \\ C_2 \\ C_3 \end{array}\begin{bmatrix} d_1 & d_2 \\ \mu_{11} & \mu_{12} \\ \mu_{21} & \mu_{22} \\ \mu_{31} & \mu_{32} \end{bmatrix}=\begin{array}{c} \\ C_1 \\ C_2 \\ C_3 \end{array}\begin{bmatrix} d_1 & d_2 \\ 0.8 & 0.5 \\ 0.1 & 0.3 \\ 0.1 & 0.2 \end{bmatrix} \quad \mu_1^*\mu_{21}=0.08 \ \mu_{12}^*\mu_{22}=0.15.$$

Shows the separation contribution of the XML document d_1 with cluster 1 and cluster 2 (C_1 and C_2) and the separation contribution of the XML document d_2 with cluster 1 and cluster 2 (C_1 and C_2).

Definition 4. Between-Group-Variance (BGV) among two clusters is defined as the following

$$BGV(\mu,v)=\frac{1}{\binom{C}{2}}\sum_{\lambda=1}^{C-1}\sum_{m=\lambda+1}^{C}\left(\frac{\sum_{j\in S_\lambda\cup S_m}\mu_{\lambda,j}*\mu_{m,j}}{|S_\lambda|+|S_m|}\right)^{-1}\|v_\lambda,v_m\|_2 \tag{7}$$

where $S_\lambda=\{j\,|\,I_{\lambda,j}=1\}$ and $S_m=\{j\,|\,I_{m,j}=1\}$, v_λ,v_m are the vector of the

central document on the λth and the m-th cluster separately.

From the Example 2 on the Definition 3, we know that $\dfrac{\sum_{j\in S_\lambda\cup S_m}\mu_{\lambda,j}*\mu_{m,j}}{|S_\lambda|+|S_m|}$ repre-

sents the separation contribution for all XML documents in the cluster λ and m. Combine the representing separation contribution using membership with be-tween-group distance to define a between-group-variance (BGV), the smaller value of

$\dfrac{\sum_{j\in S_\lambda\cup S_m}\mu_{\lambda,j}*\mu_{m,j}}{|S_\lambda|+|S_m|}$, the more separation and the more separation contribution. The

maximized $\|v_\lambda,v_m\|_2$ is desired. So, $BGV(\mu,v)$ get larger get better. Finally, we

combine $BGV(\mu,\upsilon)$ with $WGV(\mu,\upsilon;D)$ to define a $WB(\mu,\upsilon;D)$ membership cluster validity indicator so called $WB(\mu,\upsilon;D)$ as follows.

$$WB(\mu,\upsilon;D) = \frac{(B)etweeb-(G)roup-(V)ariance(\mu,\upsilon)}{(W)ithin-(G)roup-(V)ariance(\mu,\upsilon;D)} = \frac{BGV(\mu,\upsilon)}{WGV(\mu,\upsilon;D)}$$

$$= \frac{\dfrac{1}{\binom{C}{2}} \displaystyle\sum_{\lambda=1}^{C-1} \sum_{m=\lambda+1}^{C} \left(\dfrac{\displaystyle\sum_{j\in S_\lambda \cup S_m} \mu_{\lambda,j} * \mu_{m,j}}{|S_\lambda|+|S_m|} \right)^{-1} \left\| \upsilon_\lambda, \upsilon_m \right\|_2}{\displaystyle\sum_{i=1}^{C} \sum_{j\in S_i} (C_i)^{-1} \left\| d_j, \upsilon_i \right\|_2}$$

$$= \frac{\dfrac{1}{\binom{C}{2}} \displaystyle\sum_{\lambda=1}^{C-1} \sum_{m=\lambda+1}^{C} \dfrac{\left\| \upsilon_\lambda, \upsilon_m \right\|_2}{\dfrac{\displaystyle\sum_{j\in S_\lambda \cup S_m} \mu_{\lambda,j} * \mu_{m,j}}{|S_\lambda|+|S_m|}}}{\displaystyle\sum_{i=1}^{C} \sum_{j\in S_i} \dfrac{\left\| d_j, \upsilon_i \right\|_2}{C_i}} \tag{8}$$

The maximized $WB(\mu,\upsilon;D)$ is better that means $\max_C WB$ is desired.

Definition 5. Precision, Recall, and F-Measure

Let X represent the set of XML documents and let $C = \{C_1, \ldots, C_k\}$ be a clustering of X.
Moreover, let $C^\Delta = \{C_1^\Delta, \ldots C_\ell^\Delta\}$ designate the human reference classification. Then
the recall of cluster C_i with respect to class C_i^Δ, R_i, is defined as $|C_i \cap C_i^\Delta|/|C_i^\Delta|$.
The precision of cluster C_i with respect to class C_i^Δ, PR_i, is defined as
$|C_i \cap C_i^\Delta|/|C_i|$. The F-Measure combines the precision and recall measures from
information retrieval [22]. The F-Measure combines both values as follows:

$$F - Measure = \frac{2}{\dfrac{1}{PR_i} + \dfrac{1}{R_i}} \tag{9}$$

and uses the formula to evaluate the QR-FCM clustering result on the following section.

4.2 Working on Real Data Sets

We have developed a prototype and performed extended evaluation of our framework
for validity clustering XML documents. We tested the performance as well as the

quality of the clustering results using real data. The prototype testbed is a java-based software that can (a) generate synthetic XML documents or use existing ones, (b) extract feature (structural summaries) from XML documents, (c) norm distance calculate pair-wise structural distances between these summaries, (d) perform the QR-Fuzzy C-mean (QR-FCM). The goal of our work is to find documents with structural similarity, that is, documents generated from a common DTD. For any choice of distance metric, we can evaluate how closely the reported lower rank dimension document matrix corresponding to the actual originated XML. The experiments were conducted as follows. The following five DTDs were downloaded from ACM's SIGMOD Record homepage [23]: OrdinaryIssuePage.dtd(O in short), ProceedingsPage1999.dtd(P-1999 in short), ProceedingsPage2002.dtd(P-2002 in short), IndexTerm1999.dtd (IT in short), Ordinary2002.dtd (Ord-2002 in short) , and Ordinary2005.dtd (Ord-2005 in short). For another real data set we used the documents on ADC/NASA [24]:70 XML documents from adml.dtd (Astronomical Dataset Markup Language DTD). Also we download the nigara data [24]: 150 XML documents from movie.dtd, department.dtd, club.dtd, and personnel.dtd. Based upon these sets of XML documents with similar characteristics, their accuracy of low rank dimension information retrieval were computed, analyzed and reported as follows. Table 1 first shows the results of QR fuzzy C-mean (QR-FCM) on the variant numbers of PESSW XML documents (50, 70, 90, and 120) from originated 3 DTDs, 4 DTDs and 5 DTDs which we called the heterogeneous XML documents, then Table 2 shows the results of QR fuzzy C-mean (QR-FCM) on the variant numbers of economic QR factorization $R = \overline{Q}^T d$ XML documents (50, 70, 90, and 120) from originated 3 DTDs, 4 DTDs and 5 DTDs , and Table 3 shows the results of QR fuzzy C-mean (QR-FCM) on the variant numbers of $\hat{r}_k = Q_k^T d$ (k=rank of PESSW) XML documents (50, 70, 90, and 120) from originated 3 DTDs, 4 DTDs and 5 DTDs and finally Table 4 shows the results of QR fuzzy C-mean (QR-FCM) on the variant numbers of $\tilde{r}_k = Q_k^T d$ (k=low rank of k) XML documents (50, 70, 90, and 120) from originated 3 DTDs, 4 DTDs and 5 DTDs. We also compute the value of F-measure on the clustering quality measure.

Table 3. QR Fuzzy C-mean (QR-FCM) on PESSW XML from variant DTDs

PESSW	3 Origin DTDs				4 Origin DTDs				5 Origin DTDs			
	Q	II	N		Q	II	N	M	Q	II	N	M	D
# XML	50	70	90	120	50	70	90	120	50	70	90	120
Space	125k	397k	484k	619k	144k	427k	564k	713k	142k	497k	518k	689k
WB	0.14	0.31	.21	.025	.09	.029	.021	.022	.08	.023	.02	.015
PR	1.0	1.0	1.0	1.0	1.0	1.0	1.0	1.0	1.0	1.0	1.0	1.0
R	1.0	1.0	1.0	1.0	1.0	1.0	1.0	1.0	1.0	1.0	1.0	1.0
F-Measure	1.0	1.0	1.0	1.0	1.0	1.0	1.0	1.0	1.0	1.0	1.0	1.0

(Q)rdinaryIssuePage.dtd, (I)ndex(T)ermPage.dtd,(N)asa,(M)ove.dtd,(D)ept.dtd

Table 4. QR Fuzzy C-mean (QR-FCM) on $\bar{r}_k = \bar{Q}_k^T d$ XML from variant DTDs

$\bar{r}_k = \bar{Q}_k^T d$ k=economic rank	3 Origin DTDs				4 Origin DTDs				5 Origin DTDs			
	Q	II	N		Q	II	N	M	Q	II	N	M	D
# XML	50	70	90	120	50	70	90	120	50	70	90	120
Space	23k	45k	75k	93k	23k	44k	76k	166k	23k	133k	75k	133k
WB	0.14	.031	.21	.025	.09	.029	.02	.022	.08	.023	.02	.015
PR	1.0	1.0	1.0	1.0	1.0	1.0	1.0	1.0	1.0	1.0	1.0	1.0
R	1.0	1.0	1.0	1.0	1.0	1.0	1.0	1.0	1.0	1.0	1.0	1.0
F-Measure	1.0	1.0	1.0	1.0	1.0	1.0	1.0	1.0	1.0	1.0	1.0	1.0

(Q)rdinaryIssuePage.dtd, (I)ndex(T)ermPage.dtd,(N)asa,(M)ove.dtd,(D)ept.dtd

Table 5. QR Fuzzy C-mean (QR-FCM) on $\hat{r}_k = \hat{Q}_k^T d$ XML from variant DTDs

$\hat{r}_k = \hat{Q}_k^T d$ k= rank(D)	3 Origin DTDs				4 Origin DTDs				5 Origin DTDs			
	Q	II	N		Q	II	N	M	Q	II	N	M	D
# XML	50	70	90	120	50	70	90	120	50	70	90	120
Space	4k	18k	23k	35k	6k	19k	28k	48k	7k	40k	28k	40k
WB	0.14	.031	.21	.025	.09	.029	.02	.022	.08	.023	.02	.015
PR	1.0	1.0	1.0	1.0	1.0	1.0	1.0	1.0	1.0	1.0	1.0	1.0
R	1.0	1.0	1.0	1.0	1.0	1.0	1.0	1.0	1.0	1.0	1.0	1.0
F-Measure	1.0	1.0	1.0	1.0	1.0	1.0	1.0	1.0	1.0	1.0	1.0	1.0

(Q)rdinaryIssuePage.dtd, (I)ndex(T)ermPage.dtd,(N)asa,(M)ove.dtd,(D)ept.dtd

Table 6. QR Fuzzy C-mean (QR-FCM) on $\tilde{r}_k = \tilde{Q}_k^T d$ XML from variant DTDs

$\tilde{r}_k = \tilde{Q}_k^T d$ k= low rank	3 Origin DTDs Ω П N				4 Origin DTDs Ω П N M				5 Origin DTDs Ω П N M D			
# XML	50	70	90	120	50	70	90	120	50	70	90	120
Space	2k	9k	11k	17k	3k	10k	14k	24k	3k	20k	14k	20k
WB	0.14	.031	.21	.025	.09	.029	.02	.022	.08	.023	.02	.015
PR	1.0	1.0	1.0	1.0	1.0	1.0	1.0	1.0	1.0	1.0	1.0	1.0
R	1.0	1.0	1.0	1.0	1.0	1.0	1.0	1.0	1.0	1.0	1.0	1.0
F-Measure	1.0	1.0	1.0	1.0	1.0	1.0	1.0	1.0	1.0	1.0	1.0	1.0

(Ω)rdinaryIssuePage.dtd, (П)ndex(T)ermPage.dtd,(N)asa,(M)ove.dtd,(D)ept.dtd

5 Conclusion and Future Work

The original XML documents $D_N=[d_1,d_2,..,d_N]$ are modeled on the vector space model according to the path element on each document, that is D_N=PESSW, then do QR factorization on the PESSW we derived the PESSW=QR ($D = \overline{Q}_k \overline{R}_k$), or $\overline{Q}_k^T D = \overline{R}_k$, and then take the rank on the $\hat{r}_k = \hat{Q}_k^T d$ with the rank of PESSW, and finally $\tilde{r}_k = \tilde{Q}_k^T d$ with the low-rank of QR on PESSW. We passed the 4 resulting vectors (PESSW, $\overline{R}_k$, $\hat{R}_k$, and $\tilde{R}_k$) into the QR-FCM clustering algorithm to get the clustering result. From the clustering results on the section experiment, we found the same clustering result from the variant PESSW, $\overline{R}_k$, $\hat{R}_k$ and $\tilde{R}_k$ vectors. We conclude that use the low-rank vector $\tilde{R}_k$ instead of PESSW original document, not only saving the space on the input vector but also spending less time to cluster on the documents. Based on the clustering, the next issues will be arisen such as how to index the clustered XML documents for speeding up query response, for example like R-tree and B$^+$-tree, and how to manage the dynamic-updating XML document for adding XML document, adding a path element, and modifying a path element weight.

References

[1] Pei, J., Han, J., Asi, B.M., Pinto, H.: PrefixSpan: Mining Sequenctial Pattern efficiently by Prefix-Projected Pattern Growth. In: Int. Conf. Data Engineering, ICDE (2001)

[2] Hwang, J.H., Ryu, K.H.: XML A New XML clustering for Structural Retrieval. In: International Conference on Conceptual Modeling (2004)

[3] Hwang, J.H., Ryu, K.h.: Clustering and retrieval of XML documents by structure. In: Gervasi, O., Gavrilova, M.L., Kumar, V., Laganá, A., Lee, H.P., Mun, Y., Taniar, D., Tan, C.J.K. (eds.) ICCSA 2005. LNCS, vol. 3481, pp. 925–935. Springer, Heidelberg (2005)

[4] Lian, W., Wai-lok, D.: An Efficient and Scalable Algorithm for Clustering XML Documents by Structure. IEEE Computer Society Technical Committee on Data Engineering (2004)

[5] Massay, W.F.: Principal components regression in exploratorystatistical research. J. Amer Statist. Assoc. 60, 234–246 (1965)

[6] Torgerson, W.S.: Theory & Methods of Scaling. Wiley, New York (1958)

[7] Tenenbaum, J.B., de Silva, V., Langford, J.C.: A global geometric framework for nonlinear dimensionality reduction. Science 290(5500), 2319–2323 (2000)

[8] Roweis, S.T., Saul, L.K.: Nonlinear dimensionality reduction by locally linear embedding. Science 290, 2323–2326 (2000)

[9] Saul, L.K., Roweis, S.T.: Think globally, fit locally: Unsupervised learning of low dimensional manifolds. Journal of Machine Learning Research 4, 119–155 (2003)

[10] Donoho, D.L., Grimes, C.E.: Hessian eigenmaps: locally embedding techniques for high-dimensional data. Proc. Natl. Acad. Sci. USA 100, 5591–5596 (2003)

[11] Belkin, M., Niyogi, P.: Laplacian eigenmaps for dimensionality reduction and data representation. Neural Computation 15(6), 1373–1396 (2003)

[12] Zhang, Z., Zha, H.: Principal manifolds and nonlinear dimension reduction via tangent space alignment. SIAM Journal of Scientific Computing 26(1), 313–338 (2004)

[13] Kim, H., Park, H., Zha, H.: Distance preserving dimension reduction for manifold learning. In: Proceedings of the 2007 SIAM International Conference on Data Mining, SDM 2007 (2007)

[14] Dalamagas, T., Cheng, T., Winkel, K.J., Sellis, T.: A Methodology for Clustering XML Documents by Structure. Information Systems 31(3), 187–228 (2006)

[15] Gao, J., Zhang, J.: Clustered SVD strategies in latent semantic indexing. Inf. Process. Manag. 41(5), 1051–1063 (2005)

[16] Berry, M.W., Shakhina, A.P.: Computing sparse reduced-rank approximation to sparse matrices. ACM Trans. Math. Software 31(2), 252–269 (2005)

[17] Tou, J.T., Gonzalez, R.C.: Pattern Recognition Principles. Addison-Wesley, Reading (1974)

[18] Jain, A.K., Dubes, R.C.: Algorithms for Clustering Data. Prentice Hall, Englewood Cliffs (1988)

[19] Frigui, H., Krishnapuram, R.: A Robust Competitive Clustering Algorithm with Application in Computer Vision. IEEE Trans. Pattern Analysis and Machine Intelligence 21(1), 450–465 (1999)

[20] Everitt, B.S.: Cluster Analysis, 3rd edn. Halsted Press (1993)

[21] Maulik, U., Bandyopadhyay, S.: Genetic Algorithm Based Clustering Technique. Pattern Recognition 33, 1455–1465 (2000)

[22] Ye, Y.Q.: Comparing matrix methods in text-based information retrieval. — Tech. Rep., School of Mathematical Sciences, Peking University (2000)

[23] ACM SIGMOD Record home page, http://www.acm.org/sigmod/record/xml

[24] http://www.cs.wisc.edu/niagara/data/

Efficient Top-k Query Algorithms Using K-Skyband Partition

Zhenqiang Gong, Guang-Zhong Sun*, Jing Yuan, and Yanjing Zhong

MOE-MS Key Laboratory of Multimedia Computing and Communication,
School of Computer Science and Technology,
University of Science and Technology of China, Hefei, 230027, P.R. China
{gzqiang,yuanjing,zhongyj}@mail.ustc.edu.cn, gzsun@ustc.edu.cn

Abstract. Efficient processing of top-k queries has become a classical research area. Fagin et al. proposed the "middleware cost" for a top-k query algorithm. In some scenario, there is no way to perform a random access, and Fagin et al. proposed NRA (No Random Access) algorithm for that. In this paper, we investigate the intrinsic relation between top-k queries and K-skyband queries. Based on that relation, we propose a novel algorithm DNRA (Dominate-NRA). The main idea of DNRA is to partition the original dataset into two sub-datasets depending on whether they belong to K-skyband or not. We prove that DNRA performs no more sorted accesses than NRA on any dataset. Furthermore, we partition the dataset into N sub-datasets (N is the number of objects in the dataset), and then we propose our algorithm ADNRA (Advanced-DNRA). The partition of the dataset is pre-computed, and we discuss two techniques to fulfill it. Extensive experiments show that our algorithms perform several orders of magnitude fewer accesses than NRA and that ADNRA performs significantly fewer accesses than DNRA on some datasets.

Keywords: Top-k Queries, K-skyband Queries, NRA Algorithm, Dominate.

1 Introduction

Assume there are a huge amount of objects and every object has M attributes, for each attribute the object has a local score. These local scores can be aggregated to a total score by an aggregate function, and we want to know which k objects have the largest total scores. This scenario is generalized as "top-k queries".

Top-k queries have attracted considerable attention because of its wide use in many areas such as information retrieval[6][7], network and system monitoring[8][9], P2P systems and sensor networks [10][11], etc. The main reason for such attention is that top-k queries avoid overwhelming the user with large numbers of uninteresting answers which are resource-consuming.

A general and simple model proposed by Fagin et al.[1] is that the dataset consists of M sorted lists with N data items. Each data item can be accessed through *sorted access* or *random access*. However, top-k queries with no random access have received

---

* Corresponding author.

P. Mueller, J.-N. Cao, and C.-L. Wang (Eds.): Infoscale 2009, LNICST 18, pp. 288–305, 2009.
© Institute for Computer Science, Social-Informatics and Telecommunications Engineering 2009

increasing interests because in many applications random access is impossible or it's much more expensive than sorted access [2][3][4]. Fagin et al. proposed NRA (No Random Access) algorithm for this case. In this paper, we focus on the cases with no random access, but our methods can be easily generalized to cases where random access is possible.

K-skyband[14] computation is another kind of query, which returns those objects that are dominated by at most K-1 other objects. An object dominates another object if it is as good or better in all attributes and better in at least one attribute. The essential difference between top-k queries and K-skyband queries is that top-k answers may vary with the different aggregate functions while K-skyband answers do not.

Actually, there exist intrinsic connections between top-k queries and K-skyband queries. Firstly, in this paper, we investigate the relation between top-k queries and K-skyband queries, i.e. top-k answers for any increasingly monotone aggregate function belong to K-skyband, where $k \leq K$. Secondly, based on the investigation, we propose our algorithm DNRA (Domination-NRA). The main idea of DNRA is to partition the original dataset into two sub-datasets depending on whether they belong to the K-skyband or not and it only accesses the K-skyband objects when answering top-k queries. For any dataset instance, we prove that DNRA performs no more sorted accesses than NRA. Thirdly, motivated by the idea of partitioning the dataset, we take a further step to partition the dataset into N sub-datasets (some sub-datasets may be empty) according to the *degree of domination* (see definition 3 in section 3.3) of the objects. Our algorithm ADNRA (Advanced-DNRA) comes into being on the basis of this partition. Fourthly, we discuss two techniques of dataset partition, which is done *offline*. Finally, we do extensive experiments to compare NRA algorithm and our algorithms. The results show that our algorithms perform several orders of magnitude fewer sorted accesses than NRA and that ADNRA performs significantly fewer sorted accesses than DNRA.

The rest of this paper is organized as follows. In section 2, we define the problem formally and review NRA algorithm. In section 3, we describe our algorithm DNRA and its advanced version ADNRA, and we discuss the pre-computation of the dataset partition. In section 4, we show the experimental results. In section 5, we discuss some related works. Finally, in section 6, we conclude this paper and introduce our future works.

2   Problem Definitions and NRA Algorithm

In this section, we describe the model of our problem and review NRA algorithm proposed in [1].

Our model of the dataset can be described as follows: assume the dataset D consists of M sorted lists, which are denoted as $L_1, L_2, ..., L_M$. Each sorted list consists of N data items. Each data item is a pair $(x, s_i(x))$, where x is an object, $s_i(x)$ is x's *ith* local score which is a real number in the interval [0,1]. Sorted list means that objects in each list are sorted in descending orders according to their local scores. Each data item can be accessed only by sorted access, so the middleware cost of an algorithm is $a_s C_S$, where a_s is the number of sorted accesses performed and C_s is the cost of a

Table 1. Meanings of basic symbols used

N	Number of objects	k	Number of objects returned
M	Number of lists	S_x^{ub}	upper bound of S_x
S_x	overall score of x	$s_i(x)$	The *ith* local score of x
S_x^{lb}	lower bound of S_x	s_i	Bottom score of the *ith* list

single sorted access. For any object x, its overall score $S_x = f(s_1(x), s_2(x), \cdots, s_M(x))$, where the aggregate function f is assumed to be monotone in this paper. Our task is to find k objects whose overall scores are the highest k ones.

For this problem, Fagin et al. proposed the algorithm NRA (No Random Access)[1]. The basic idea of NRA is to evaluate an object's overall score using the upper bound and lower bound of the overall score. We rewrite NRA algorithm in Fig.1. In the algorithm, we replace the original notations with ours.

Algorithm NRA

1. Do sorted access in parallel to each of the M sorted lists L_i. At each depth d (when d objects have been accessed under sorted access in each list):

   - Maintain the bottom values $s_i^{(d)}$, $i \in \{1, 2, \cdots, M\}$, encountered in the lists.

   - For every object x with discovered fields $L = L^{(d)}(x) \subseteq \{1, ..., M\}$, compute the values S_x^{lb} and S_x^{ub}. (For object x that has not been seen, these values are virtually computed as $S_x^{lb} = f(0, 0, ..., 0)$ and $S_x^{ub} = f(s_1^{(d)}, s_2^{(d)}, \cdots, s_M^{(d)})$ which is the threshold value.)

   - Let $Y^{(d)}$, the current top-k list, contain the k objects with the largest S_x^{lb} values seen so far (and their scores); if two objects have the same S_x^{lb} value, then ties are broken using the S_x^{ub} values, such that object with the highest S_x^{ub} value wins (and arbitrarily among objects that tie for the highest S_x^{ub} value). Let $t^{(d)} = \min \{ S_x^{lb} \mid x \in Y^{(d)} \}$

2. Halt when (a) at least k distinct objects have been seen and (b) $\tilde{t} \leq t^{(d)}$, where $\tilde{t} = \max\{ S_x^{ub} \mid x \notin Y^{(d)} \}$. Return the objects in $Y^{(d)}$.

Fig. 1. Algorithm NRA

The following example illustrates NRA algorithm.

Example 1. Assume $M=2$, $N=6$, $k = 2$, the aggregation function is summation, and the lists shown in Table 2 of Fig.2 can only be sorted accessed. Call accessing each list once in parallel an *attempt*. In Fig.2, Table 3-6 show how algorithm NRA performs sorted accesses at each attempt on this dataset. Table 7 shows how the top-2 objects and the parameter $\tilde{t}$ updated at each attempt. NRA algorithm halts after 8 sorted accesses

Table 2. Sorted Lists

(X₂,0.95)	(X₃,0.95)
(X₁,0.92)	(X₄,0.90)
(X₅,0.89)	(X₆,0.88)
(X₃,0.88)	(X₂,0.87)
(X₄,0.87)	(X₁,0.87)
(X₆,0.86)	(X₅,0.85)

Table 3. Attempt 1

(X₂,0.95)	(X₃,0.95)
(X₁,0.92)	(X₄,0.90)
(X₅,0.89)	(X₆,0.88)
(X₃,0.88)	(X₂,0.87)
(X₄,0.87)	(X₁,0.87)
(X₆,0.86)	(X₅,0.85)

Table 4. Attempt 2

(X₂,0.95)	(X₃,0.95)
(X₁,0.92)	(X₄,0.90)
(X₅,0.89)	(X₆,0.88)
(X₃,0.88)	(X₂,0.87)
(X₄,0.87)	(X₁,0.87)
(X₆,0.86)	(X₅,0.85)

Table 5. Attempt 3

(X₂,0.95)	(X₃,0.95)
(X₁,0.92)	(X₄,0.90)
(X₅,0.89)	(X₆,0.88)
(X₃,0.88)	(X₂,0.87)
(X₄,0.87)	(X₁,0.87)
(X₆,0.86)	(X₅,0.85)

Table 6. Attempt 4

(X₂,0.95)	(X₃,0.95)
(X₁,0.92)	(X₄,0.90)
(X₅,0.89)	(X₆,0.88)
(X₃,0.88)	(X₂,0.87)
(X₄,0.87)	(X₁,0.87)
(X₆,0.86)	(X₅,0.85)

Table 7. Each attempt of NRA

Objects	Top-2 Lower bounds	$\tilde{t}$
(X₂, X₃)	(0.95,0.95)	1.90
(X₂,X₃)	(0.95,0.95)	1.83
(X₂,X₃)	(0.95,0.95)	1.80
(X₂,X₃)	(1.82,1.83)	1.79

Fig. 2. An example shows how NRA works

3 Dominate-NRA Algorithms

In this section, we first discuss the relation between top-k queries and K-skyband queries (Section 3.1). Thereafter, in Section 3.2, we describe our algorithm DNRA and discuss its performance. Then, in Section 3.3, we introduce ADNRA. Finally, in Section 3.4, we address the process of pre-computation.

3.1 Top-k Queries and K-Skyband Queries

In the following, we first introduce the definition of dominate and propose an observation about it. Then, we define the K-skyband set and discuss its relation to top-k queries.

Definition 1 *dominate*[5]. We say object x *dominates* y or y is *dominated* by x if and only if they satisfy two conditions: (1) for each $i \in \{1,2,\cdots,M\}$, $s_i(x) \geq s_i(y)$. (2) there exists at least one number $j \in \{1,2,\cdots,M\}$ satisfying $s_j(x) > s_j(y)$.

Our definition of dominate is different from that in [5], since we use $\geq$ (or $>$) instead of $\leq$ (or $<$). However, there does not exist essential differences between them.

Observation 1. If object x dominates object y and the aggregate function is increasingly monotone, then we have $s_x > s_y$.

Proof. We can easily get the correctness of the observation according to the definition of dominate. $\square$

Definition 2. *K-skyband* [14]. For a dataset D, its *K-skyband* is a set of objects that are dominated by at most K-1 other objects.

For the dataset in Example 1, the K-skyband for $K=2$ includes objects x_1, x_2, x_3 and x_4. Notice that x_2 and x_3, which are the top-2 objects with f = sum, belongs to the K-skyband for $K=2$.

Observation 2. For any increasingly monotone aggregate function, the top-k objects belong to the K-skyband, where $k \leq K$.

Proof. For any object x that does not belong to the K-skyband, there exists at least K other objects that dominate it. According to observation 1, we know that there exists at least K other objects whose overall scores are strictly larger than x 's, which means that x cannot be top-K. Since $k \leq K$, we have the top-k objects for any increasingly monotone aggregate function belong to the K-skyband. $\square$

Motivated by the fact that the top-k objects for any increasingly monotone aggregate function belong to the K-skyband, where $k \leq K$, we can use the K-skyband query as a pre-computing step to answer top-k queries. After pre-computing the K-skyband off-line, any top-k queries with $k \leq K$ for any increasingly monotone aggregate function can be addressed only accessing the K-skyband objects.

3.2 Dominate-NRA Algorithm(DNRA)

In this section, based on the observations discussed in the above section, we first introduce our algorithm DNRA (Dominate-NRA) and prove its correctness. Then, we evaluate its performance. Specifically, we prove that DNRA performs no more sorted accesses than NRA on any dataset.

The description of DNRA algorithm is shown in Fig.3. Through pre-computation (addressed in section 3.4), it first partitions the original dataset D into two sub-datasets, i.e. D_g and D_b, where D_g contains all the K-skyband objects and D_b contains the rest. Then it runs NRA only on D_g in order to find top-k answerers of the original dataset D.

Algorithm DNRA
1. Through pre-computation, we partition the original dataset D into two sub-datasets, i.e. D_g and D_b, where D_g contains all the K-skyband objects and D_b contains the rest.

2. Run NRA algorithm on D_g to find top-k objects, where $k \le K$.

Fig. 3. Algorithm DNRA

The following theorem provides the correctness of DNRA.

Theorem 1. If the aggregate function is increasingly monotone, then DNRA correctly finds the top-k objects, where k ≤ K.

Proof. According to observation 2, top-k objects belong to the K-skyband, where $k \le K$. Here, D_g and the K-skyband contain the same objects, that is, top-k objects belong to D_g. Since NRA algorithm correctly finds the top-k objects in D_g, DNRA correctly finds the top-k objects of the original dataset.   □

To evaluate the performance of DNRA, we first introduce three lemmas as follows.

Lemma 1. Let $DS_x^{ub}(d)$ be the upper bound of x's overall score in DNRA at depth d. Let $NS_x^{ub}(d)$ be the upper bound of x's overall score in NRA at depth d. Then, for any object $x \in D_g$, we have $DS_x^{ub}(d) \le NS_x^{ub}(d)$.

Proof. The upper bound of object x's overall score is calculated using an increasingly monotone aggregate function by substituting its missing fields with relative bottom values. For any object $x \in D_g$, its fields seen by NRA before depth d are also seen by DNRA before depth d, and its fields seen by DNRA but not seen DNRA before depth d, and its fields seen by DNRA but not seen by NRA before depth d are no larger than the relative bottom values in NRA. Furthermore, bottom values in DNRA are no larger than the relative bottom values in NRA at depth d. So, we have $DS_x^{ub}(d) \le NS_x^{ub}(d)$.   □

Lemma 2. Let $DS_x^{lb}(d)$ be the lower bound of x's overall score in DNRA at depth d. Let $NS_x^{lb}(d)$ be the lower bound of x's overall score in NRA at depth d. Then, for any object $x \in D_g$, we have $DS_x^{lb}(d) \ge NS_x^{lb}(d)$.

Proof. For any object $x \in D_g$, its fields seen by NRA before depth d are also seen by DNRA before depth d. The lower bound of x's overall score is calculated using an increasingly monotone aggregate function by substituting its missing fields with 0. So we have $DS_x^{lb}(d) \ge NS_x^{lb}(d)$.   □

Lemma 3. Let $Y(d)$ contain the current top-k objects in NRA at depth d and $t(d) = \min$ { $NS_x^{lb}(d) \mid x \in Y(d)$ }.Let $Y'(d)$ contain the current top-k objects in DNRA and $t'(d) = \min$ { $DS_x^{lb}(d) \mid x \in Y'(d)$ }. If all the objects in $Y(d)$ belong to D_g , then we have $t'(d) \geq t(d)$.

Proof. At any depth d , assume $x' \in Y'(d)$ satisfying $DS_{x'}^{lb}(d) = t'(d)$. There are two cases depending on whether x' belongs to $Y(d)$.

Case 1: $x' \in Y(d)$. Since $x' \in Y(d)$, we have $NS_{x'}^{lb}(d) \geq t(d)$. And according to lemma 2, we have $DS_{x'}^{lb}(d) \geq NS_{x'}^{lb}(d)$. So, we have $t'(d) = DS_{x'}^{lb}(d) \geq NS_{x'}^{lb}(d) \geq t(d)$, that is, $t'(d) \geq t(d)$, as desired.

Case 2: $x' \notin Y(d)$. In this case, there exists one object $y \in Y(d)$ but $y \notin Y'(d)$. Since $y \in Y(d)$, we have $NS_y^{lb}(d) \geq t(d)$. Since $y \notin Y'(d)$, we have $t'(d) \geq DS_y^{lb}(d)$. And according to lemma 2, we have $DS_y^{lb}(d) \geq NS_y^{lb}(d)$. So, we get $t'(d) \geq DS_y^{lb}(d) \geq NS_y^{lb}(d) \geq t(d)$, that is, $t'(d) \geq t(d)$, as desired. □

Theorem 2. The number of sorted accesses to the lists done by DNRA is always less than or equal to that of NRA.

Proof. For any dataset D, we assume NRA algorithm stops at depth d and DNRA algorithm does not stop before depth d . Let $Y(d)$ contain the top-k objects that outputted by NRA and $t(d) = \min\{ NS_x^{lb}(d) \mid x \in Y(d)$ }. Let $Y'(d)$ contain the current top-k objects in DNRA at depth d and $t'(d) = \min$ { $DS_x^{lb}(d) \mid x \in Y'(d)$ }. The k objects in $Y(d)$ must belong to D_g , so we have, according to lemma 3, $t'(d) \geq t(d)$. Since we assume DNRA does not stop at depth d , there exists an object $x \in D_g$ and $x \notin Y'(d)$ satisfying that $DS_x^{ub}(d) > t'(d)$. We need to generate contradictions. There are two cases depending on whether x belongs to $Y(d)$.

Case 1: $x \notin Y(d)$. Since we have $DS_x^{ub}(d) \leq NS_x^{ub}(d)$ according to lemma 1 and $NS_x^{ub}(d) \leq t(d)$ according to the stopping rule of NRA, we get $DS_x^{ub}(d) \leq NS_x^{ub}(d) \leq t(d) \leq t'(d)$, which contradicts with $DS_x^{ub}(d) > t'(d)$.

Case 2: $x \in Y(d)$. In this case, there exists one object $y \in Y'(d)$ but $y \notin Y(d)$. Since $y \in Y'(d)$ and $x \notin Y'(d)$, we have $DS_y^{lb}(d) \geq t'(d) \geq DS_x^{lb}(d)$. Since $x \in Y(d)$ and $y \notin Y(d)$, we have $NS_x^{lb}(d) \geq t(d) \geq NS_y^{ub}(d)$. Combined with lemma 1 and lemma 2, we get $NS_x^{lb}(d) \geq t(d) \geq NS_y^{ub}(d) \geq DS_y^{ub}(d) \geq DS_y^{lb}(d) \geq t'(d) \geq DS_x^{lb}(d) \geq NS_x^{lb}(d)$. So we have $DS_x^{lb}(d) = DS_y^{lb}(d) = DS_y^{ub}(d) = t'(d)$. Since $DS_x^{lb}(d) = DS_y^{lb}(d)$, we have $DS_x^{ub}(d) \leq DS_y^{ub}(d)$ according to the ties breaking rules of $Y'(d)$. Finally, we get $t'(d) = DS_x^{lb}(d) \leq DS_x^{ub}(d) \leq DS_y^{ub}(d) = t'(d)$, that is, $DS_x^{ub}(d) = t'(d)$, which contradicts with $DS_x^{ub}(d) > t'(d)$.

Hence, the assumption that DNRA does not stop before depth d is unwarranted. In other words, DNRA does stop before depth d .   □

3.3 Optimization

The key idea of DNRA is that it classifies the objects into two categories depending on whether they belong to the K-skyband or not and it only accesses the K-skyband objects when answering top-k queries. One weakness of DNRA is that it cannot address the top-k queries with $k > K$. To cope with top-k queries with $k > K$, we take a further step to classify the objects into N categories. In the following, we begin by proposing a method to classify objects. Then, based on this method, we partition the original dataset N sub-datasets. Our algorithm ADNRA (Advanced-DNRA) comes into being on the basis of this partition.

Definition 3 *degree of domination.* If some object x is dominated by i other objects, we say the degree of domination of x is i, denoted as $dd(x) = i$.

This definition provides us a kind of method to classify objects, i.e. we can classify objects into N categories by their degree of domination. Based on the classification of the objects, we can partition the original dataset D into N sub-datasets, denoted as $D_0, D_1, \cdots, D_{N-1}$ (some sub-datasets may be empty), where $\forall x \in D_i$, satisfying $dd(x) = i$. The partition is done offline. The following theorem reduces our accessing scope to $D_0, D_1, \ldots, D_{k-1}$ when answering top-k queries.

Theorem 3. If the aggregate function is increasingly monotone, then top-k objects must be among sub-datasets $D_0, D_1, \cdots, D_{k-1}$

Proof. Actually, the K-skyband for $K = k$ consists of sub-datasets $D_0, D_1, \cdots, D_{k-1}$. And according to observation 2, top-k objects belong to K-skyband if $k \leq K$. So the top-k objects must be among sub-datasets $D_0, D_1, \cdots, D_{k-1}$.   □

Now, we can describe our algorithm ADNRA. Its description is shown in Fig.4. ADNRA algorithm uses a sequential policy to access $D_0, D_1, \cdots, D_{k-1}$. Specifically, when $candidate_j = \varnothing$ and $t \geq T_j$, ADNRA stops accessing D_j and goes on accessing D_{j+1} (Note: $candidate_j$ may return to be nonempty since some object in Y coming from D_j may become a candidate some time later). After this sequential process, it checks whether there exists some $candidate$ that is nonempty. And if $candidate_l$ is nonempty, it continues performing sorted accesses on D_l .

Actually, we can design another policy to perform sorted accesses on sub-datasets $D_0, D_1, \cdots, D_{k-1}$, i.e. dataset-level-parallel policy. Dataset-level-parallel policy works as follows: firstly, we distribute the sub-datasets $D_0, D_1, \cdots, D_{k-1}$ onto k processors; secondly, let the ith processor computes in parallel the top-$(k-i)$ objects in D_i , and store them in Y_i ; thirdly, we combine $Y_0, Y_1, \ldots, Y_{k-1}$ to get Y ; finally, it checks whether there exists some $candidate$ that is nonempty. And if $candidate_l$ is nonempty, it continues performing sorted accesses on D_l in parallel.

Algorithm ADNRA:

1. Run NRA on D_0 to find top-k objects in D_0 , and store the results in Y . Let $t = \min\{\ S_x^{lb} \mid x \in Y\ \}$

2. $j := 1$

3. For D_j , do sorted accesses in parallel to each of the M sorted lists L_i . Accessing each list once on D_j in parallel is called an *attempt*. After each attempt on D_j , go to up-date_process: update $s_{1j}, s_{2j}, ..., s_{Mj}$ (bottom scores of D_j), T_j (the threshold value of D_j), lower bounds and upper bounds of objects in *candidate$_j$* (*candidate$_j$* is a set of objects whose current upper bounds of their scores are larger than t and that do not be-long to Y) and of objects in Y that come from D_j , Y , t and all the sets of *candidate* . When *candidate$_j$* $= \varnothing$ and $t \geq T_j$, go to step 4.

4. $j := j+1$. If $j < k$, then go to step 3, or go to step 5.

5. For each l , while *candidate$_l$* $\neq \varnothing$, continue performing sorted accesses on D_l in parallel. After each attempt on D_l , go to update_process as described in step 3.

6. Halt when (a) at least k distinct objects have been seen, (b) $t \geq T_j$, for $j = 0, 1, ..., k-1$ and (c) for $j = 0, 1, ..., k-1$, *candidate$_j$* $= \varnothing$. Return the objects in Y .

Fig. 4. Algorithm ADNRA

The following theorem provides the correctness of ADNRA.

Theorem 4. If the aggregate function is increasingly monotone, then ADNRA correctly finds the top-k objects.

Proof. Let $t = \min\{\ S_x^{lb} \mid x \in Y\ \}$. We must show that for any object x , $x \notin Y$ and $x \in D_j$ for some $j \in \{0, 1, ..., k-1\}$, we have $S_x \leq t$. There are two cases, depending on whether x has been seen or not when ADNRA stops.

Case 1: x has been seen when ADNRA stops. Since *candidate$_j$* $= \varnothing$ when ADNRA stops, we have $S_x \leq S_x^{ub} \leq t$, as desired.

Case 2: x hasn't been seen when ADNRA stops. Since $S_x^{ub} = T_j$ and $t \geq T_j$ when AD-NRA stops, we have $S_x \leq S_x^{ub} = T_j \leq t$, as desired.   □

The following example illustrates how ADNRA works.

Example 2. The dataset is the same as that in Example 1. Through pre-computation (addressed in section 3.4), the dataset is partitioned into three sub-datasets, which are illustrated in Table 8. First, ADNRA runs NRA on D_0 to find top-2 objects in D_0 , that is, x_2 and x_3 . Then it continues accessing D_1 . After just an attempt on D_1 ,it stops

Table 8. Sub-datasets

D_0	
(X_2,0.95)	(X_3,0.95)
(X_3,0.88)	(X_2,0.87)
D_1	
(X_1,0.92)	(X_4,0.90)
(X_4,0.87)	(X_1,0.87)
D_2	
(X_5,0.89)	(X_6,0.88)
(X_6,0.86)	(X_5,0.85)

accessing D_1. Then it checks whether there exists some number l satisfying $candidate_l \neq \varnothing$, if there does, it continues accessing D_l. In this example, there does not exist such number l. So ADNRA halts after 6 sorted accesses. ADNRA performs two fewer sorted accesses than NRA on this dataset.

3.4 Pre-computation

Both our algorithms are based on the pre-computation, which is aimed to pre-compute D_b and D_g in DNRA and $D_0, D_1, \cdots, D_{N-1}$ in ADNRA. D_g contains and only contains the K-skyband objects, so any algorithm that can address K-skyband queries, e.g. BBS [14], can be used to pre-compute D_b and D_g in DNRA . For the pre-computation of $D_0, D_1, \cdots, D_{N-1}$ in ADNRA, the key point is to pre-compute the degree of domination of each object. In the rest of this section, we propose an algorithm called BFA (Brute-force algorithm) and introduce an algorithm called bitmap to pre-compute the degree of domination of each object. Bitmap algorithm is proposed in[13] to address skyline queries, but it is also powerful to compute the degree of domination of each object .

3.4.1 Brute-Force Algorithm

Brute-force algorithm (BFA) scans the M sorted lists, and store the objects with their M local scores in an extra list. The data item in the extra list is like ($x, s_1(x), s_2(x), ..., s_M(x)$), where x is an object, $s_i(x)$ is x 's ith local score. The objects in the extra list are sorted in non-increasing orders respect to their first local scores. Then BFA scans the sorted extra list. When an object x is seen, BFA compares it with objects seen before it and objects having not been seen yet but whose first local score is the same as x 's. After the comparisons, we get the degree of domination of x . The time cost of BFA is $O(MN^2)$. And the extra space needed is also $O(MN^2)$.

3.4.2 Bitmap

This technique encodes in bitmaps all the information required to decide the degree of domination of all the objects. An object x whose local scores are $s_1(x), s_2(x), ..., s_M(x)$ is mapped to an n-bit vector, where n is the total number of distinct values over all lists.

Let n_i be the total number of distinct values in the ith list (i.e. $n = \sum_{i=1}^{M} n_i$). For the dataset in Example 1, for example, there are $n_1 =6$ and $n_2 =5$ distinct values in the first and second lists and n $=11$. Assume that $s_i(x)$ is the jth largest score in the ith list; then, it is represented by n_i bits, where the $(j-1)$ leftmost bits are 0, and the remaining ones 1. Table 9 shows the bitmaps for objects in Example 1. Since $s_1(x_2)$ is the largest value in the first list, all bits of it are 1. Similarly, since $s_2(x_2)$ is the 4th largest in the second list, the leftmost 4-1=3 bits of its representation are 0, while the remaining ones are 1.

Table 9. The bitmap of the dataset in Example 1

Object	Local scores	Bitmap representation
X_1	(0.92, 0.87)	(011111, 00011)
X_2	(0.95, 0.87)	(111111, 00011)
X_3	(0.88, 0.95)	(000111, 11111)
X_4	(0.87, 0.90)	(000011, 01111)
X_5	(0.89, 0.85)	(001111, 00001)
X_6	(0.86, 0.88)	(000001, 00111)

Consider now that we want to know the degree of domination of an object, e.g. x_5 with bitmap representation (001111, 00001). The leftmost bits whose value is 1 are the 3th and the 5th, in the first and second lists, respectively. The algorithm creates two bit-strings, $c_1(x_5) = 110010$ and $c_2(x_5) = 111111$, by juxtaposing the corresponding bits (i.e. 3th and the 5th) of every object. Let $A(x_5) = c_1(x_5) \& c_2(x_5) = 110010$. The rightmost bits whose value is 0 of x_5 are the 2th and the 4th, in the first and second lists, respectively. Then, the algorithm creates another two bit-strings, $d_1(x_5) = 110000$ and $d_2(x_5) = 111101$, by juxtaposing the corresponding bits (i.e. 2th and the 4th) of every object. Let $B(x_5) = c_1(x_5) \mid c_2(x_5) = 111101$. The 1's in the result of $C(x_5) = A(x_5) \&$ $B(x_5) = 110000$, indicate the objects that dominate x_5, i.e. x_1 and x_2. Obviously, the degree of domination of any object x equates the number of 1's in the result of $C(x)$. Both the time cost and extra spaces needed of bitmap are $O(MN^2)$.

In our experiments, we use brute-force algorithm to fulfill pre-computations because it's easy to implement.

4 Experiments

Our algorithms are implemented in C++. We perform our experiments on a Duo T2130 1.86GHz PC with 1GB of memory. We use both synthetic and real dataset to evaluate NRA, DNRA and ADNRA algorithms. The metrics we measure is the number of sorted accesses performed since the middleware cost is the number of sorted accesses performed times the cost per sorted access.

4.1 Description of Datasets

We do experiments on five synthetic datasets and one real dataset. All generated local scores belong to the interval [0, 1]. The five synthetic datasets are produced to model different input scenarios; they are UI, NI, EI, CO and AC, respectively. UI, CO and AC are generated using the same methodology as [5]. UI contains datasets where object's local scores are uniformly and independently generated for the different lists. NI contains datasets where object's local scores are normally and independently generated for the different lists. EI contains datasets where object's local scores are exponentially and independently generated for the different lists. CO contains datasets where object's local scores are correlated. In other words, the local score $s_i(x)$ of an object x is very close to $s_j(x)$ with high probability, where $i \neq j$. To generate an object x, first, a number u_x from 0 to 1 is selected using a Gaussian distribution centered at 0.5. x's local scores are then generated by a Gaussian distribution centered at u_x with variance 0.01. Finally, AC contains datasets where object's local scores are anti-correlated. In this case, objects that are good in one list are bad in one or all other lists. To generate an object x, first, we pick a number u_x from 0 to 1, like we did for CO datasets. This time, however, we use a very small variance, so that u_x for different x are very close to 0.5 and to each other. The local scores of x are then generated uniformly and normalized to sum up to u_x. In this way, the overall scores of all objects are quite similar, but their individual scores vary significantly.

Table 10. Default settings of experimental parameters

Parameter	Default values
Number of objects , i.e. N	100,000
Number of lists, i.e. M	5
k	20
K	20
Aggregate function	summation

For synthetic datasets, our default settings for different parameters are shown in Table 10. In our tests, the default number of data items in each list is 100,000, i.e. N=100,000. Typically, users are interested in a small number of top answers, thus we set $k = 20$ as k's default value. DNRA needs to pre-compute the K-skyband and unless otherwise specified we set K =20 since we set $k = 20$. Like many previous works on top-k query processing, such as [12], we choose the aggregate function as the sum of the local scores. In half of our tests, the number of lists, i.e. M, is a varying parameter. When M is a constant, we set it to 5 since most top-k algorithms are evaluated on the dataset with no more than 5 lists.

For real dataset, as did in [12], we choose El Nino dataset (http://kdd.ics.uci.edu), which contains oceanographic and surface meteorological readings taken from a series of buoys positioned throughout the equatorial Pacific. The data is expected to aid in the understanding and prediction of El Nino/Southern Oscillation (ENSO) cycles. We neglect the objects missing some fields. The remaining dataset contains 93935 objects. We chose 7 lists to test our algorithms. And we normalize the dataset with the formula: $\dfrac{s_i(x) - Min}{Max - Min}$, where $s_i(x)$ is x 's ith local score.

4.2 Experimental Results

4.2.1 Effect of the Number of Lists

In this section, we compare the performance of our algorithms with NRA over the datasets described in section 4.1 while varying the number of lists.

Over the datasets we considered, with the number of lists increasing up to 12 and the other parameters set as in Table 10, Fig.5-10 show the results measuring the number of sorted accesses performed. The results show us that both our algorithms perform several orders of magnitude fewer sorted accesses than NRA. The reason is that our algorithms already get some information about the objects through pre-computation and they only access the potential objects that can be top-k answers. As M becomes small, the advantage of our algorithms over NRA increases. The reason for this increase is that the K-skyband contains fewer objects as M becomes smaller. Over UI and CO, the ratio of the number of sorted accesses performed by ADNRA to that performed by DNRA is nearly 2/3. And the ratio nearly decreases to 1/2 over NI, EI and AC. Over El Nino Data, although the ratio is a little larger, ADNRA still performs significantly fewer accesses than DNRA. The reason why ADNRA outperforms DNRA is that ADNRA classifies the objects into N categories while DNRA only classifies objects into two categories. After ADNRA accesses $D_0, D_1, \cdots, D_i$, the value of t is already relatively big, which makes it perform fewer accesses on D_{i+1} .

4.2.2 Effect of k

In this section, we study the effect of k, i.e. the number of top objects requested, on performance. Since the number of top objects requested varies with different users, we need to set the parameter K in pre-computation of DNRA as a sufficiently large const, i.e. the upper bound of the number of top objects requested. In our experiments below, we set $K=100$, and the other parameters as in Table 9 except that k varies from 10 to 100.

Fig.11-16 show the results of our experiments over the considered datasets. The results show that both our algorithms perform orders of magnitude fewer accesses than NRA. For DNRA and ADNRA, the number of their accesses both increase slightly with k over all the considered datasets. But the situation is different for NRA.

The number of accesses performed by NRA increases with k over UI and CO, almost does not increase over NI and EI Nino data and even fluctuates over EI and AC. The predominance of ADNRA over DNRA becomes more apparent as k becomes smaller. The reason is that when k is small, i.e. $k<K$, DNRA may perform some useless accesses. Specifically, DNRA may still access those objects whose degree of domination is no less than k, but those objects can not be top-k answers for any increasingly monotone aggregate function. However, ADNRA will never access those objects.

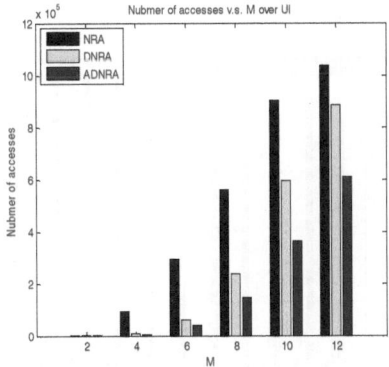

Fig. 5. The number of accesses v.s. the number of lists over UI, k=20

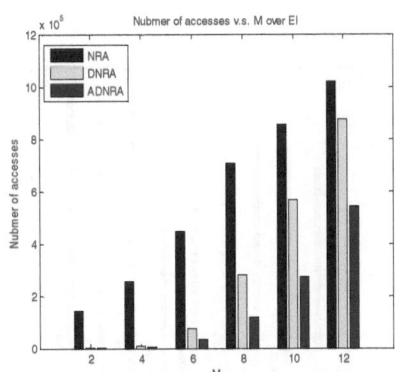

Fig. 6. The number of accesses v.s. the number of lists over NI, k=20

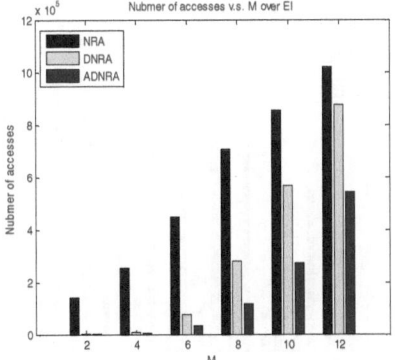

Fig. 7. The number of accesses v.s. the number of lists over EI, k=20

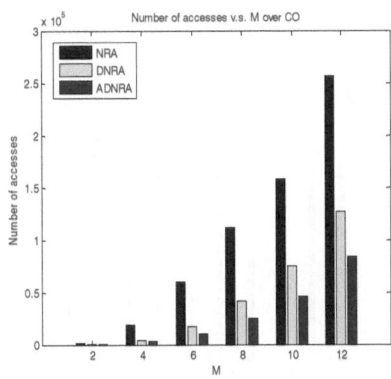

Fig. 8. The number of accesses v.s. the number of lists over CO, k=20

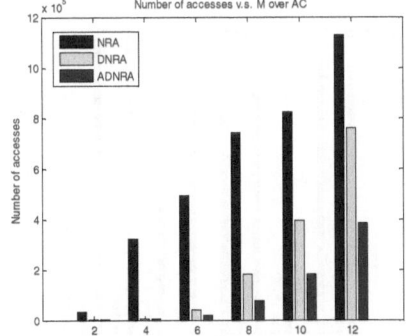

Fig. 9. The number of accesses v.s. the number of lists over AC, k=20

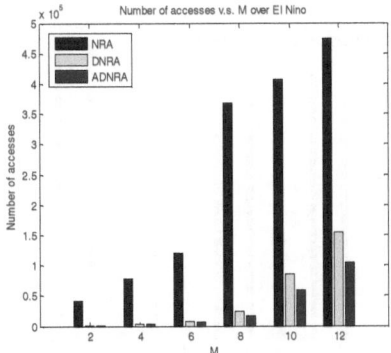

Fig. 10. The number of accesses v.s. the number of lists over El Nino Data, k=20

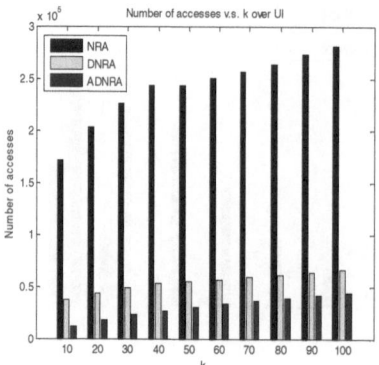

Fig. 11. The number of accesses v.s. k over UI, $M=5$

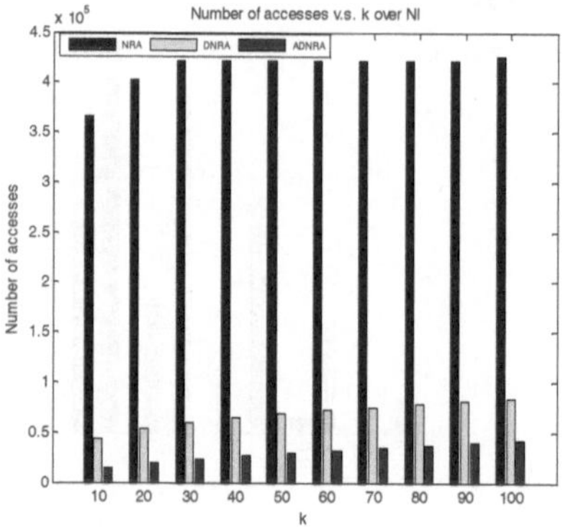

Fig. 12. The number of accesses v.s. k over NI, $M=5$

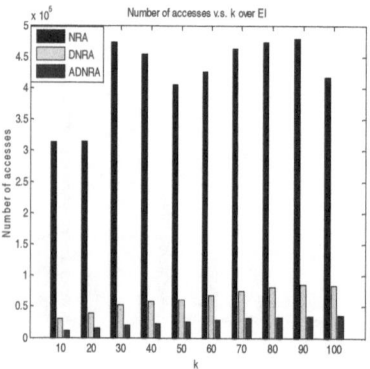
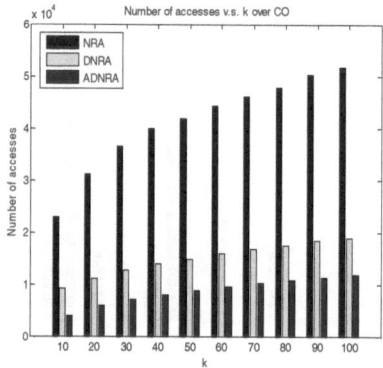

Fig. 13. The number of accesses v.s. k over EI, $M=5$

Fig. 14 The number of accesses v.s. k over CO, $M=5$

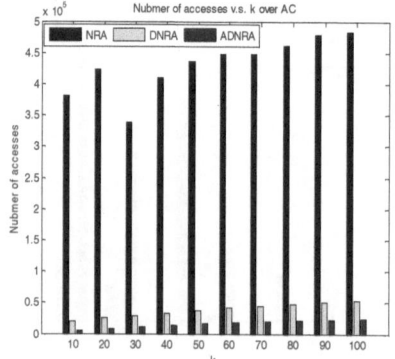
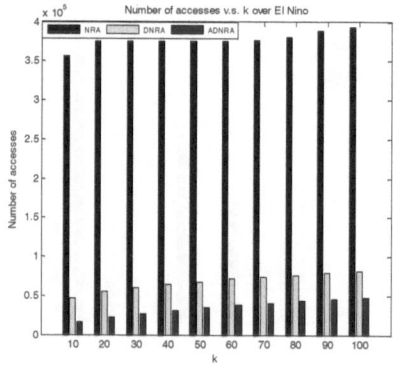

Fig. 15. The number of accesses v.s. k over AC, $M=5$

Fig. 16. The number of accesses v.s. k over El Nino Data, $M=5$

4.3 Summary

Our experiments illustrate that DNRA and ADNRA do several orders of magnitude fewer sorted accesses than NRA, both on synthetic datasets and real dataset. The reason is that our algorithms classify objects and reduce the accessing scope. As M becomes smaller, the decrease of sorted accesses becomes more significant. The reason is that the K-skyband contains fewer objects as M becomes smaller. Algorithm ADNRA does much fewer sorted accesses than algorithm DNRA. For some instances, ADNRA performs 50% fewer accesses than DNRA. This could be explained by the fact that DNRA only classifies objects into two categories depending on whether they belong to the K-skyband or not while ADNRA takes a further step to classify the objects into N categories according to their degree of dominations.

5 Related Works

Efficient processing of top-k queries is both an important and hard problem that is still receiving much attention. *Skyline* (skyline is a special instance of K-skyband, where K=1) computation is another kind of queries that is also attracting much attention.

There are intrinsic relations between the two kinds of queries. Some papers have tried to use these kinds of relations to address top-k queries, such as [15] and [16]. In [15], A.Vlachou et al. proposed a framework called SPEERTO to support top-k query processing over horizontally partitioned data stored on peers organized in a super-peer network. The key idea of SPEERTO is that each peer computes its K-skyband as a pre-processing step and each super-peer maintains and aggregates the K-skyband sets of its peers to answer any incoming top-k query. Essentially, SPEERTO classifies objects into two categories depending on whether they belong to the K-skyband or not. Our work makes a further step to classify objects into N categories according to their degree of dominations.

In [16], L.Zou and L.Chen proposed an indexing structure, called DG (Dominant Graph). Based on that, they proposed *Traveler* algorithms to answer top-k queries. Our work is different from [16] mainly in two aspects. Firstly, the models of dataset we use are different. The dataset in [16] consists of one list with N data items which are like ($x, s_1(x), s_2(x), ..., s_M(x)$), where x is an object, $s_i(x)$ is x's ith local score. And each data item can be random accessed. However, the dataset in our paper consists of M lists with N data items, which is more general. And each data item can be only sorted accessed. Secondly, both our works are based on the classifications of the objects, but our methods to classify objects are different. DG uses *Maximal layer* [17] to classify objects while we use degree of domination to classify objects (*Note:* the first Maximal layer contains the same objects as sub-dataset D_0, which are the skyline objects of the dataset).

We did not compare our algorithms with *Traveler* algorithms directly because they have different methods to access data item, i.e. *Traveler* algorithms use random access to access data item while we only use sorted access. Actually, authors in [16] compared *Traveler* algorithms with TA and CA [1], but they did not compare them with NRA. Certainly, *Traveler* algorithms can also be used in cases where data item can only be sorted accessed and our approaches can also be generalized to cases where random access is possible.

6 Conclusions and Future Works

In this paper, we propose DNRA and ADNRA algorithms to address top-k queries, both of which are based on the partition of the dataset. DNRA classifies the objects into two categories depending on whether they belong to the K-skyband or not. And it only accesses the K-skyband objects when answering top-k queries. Furthermore, ADNRA classifies the objects into N categories according to their *degree of domination*. And it only accesses k categories in order to find the top-k objects. Experimental comparisons show that our algorithms perform several orders of magnitude fewer sorted accesses than NRA and that ADNRA performs significantly fewer sorted accesses than DNRA on some datasets. The reason why our algorithms outperform NRA is that they already know some information about the objects through pre-computation and they only access those potential objects that can be the real top-k. DNRA is powerful in top-k system where k is a constant. ADNRA can be used in any top-k system where the aggregate function is increasingly monotone and k is a constant or not.

As M becomes larger, D_0 and D_1 contain more and more objects, which results in our algorithm ADNRA performs more and more accesses. In the future, we plan to propose some kind of method to continue classifying objects in D_0 and D_1 in order to make ADNRA stop earlier. Furthermore, the variation of ADNRA using dataset-level-parallel policy is fit for parallel environments, so we will optimize it by parallel computing in our future work. Specifically, we first distribute the sub-datasets $D_0, D_1, \cdots, D_{k-1}$ onto k processors; secondly, let the ith processor computes in parallel the top-$(k-i)$ objects in D_i, and store them in Y_i; thirdly, we combine $Y_0, Y_1, ..., Y_{k-1}$ to get the final top-k answerers.

Acknowledgement

This work is supported by the National Science Foundation of China under the grant No.60533020 and No.60873210. This work is also supported by the Science Research Fund of MOE-Microsoft Key Laboratory of Multimedia Computing and Communication (Grant No. 06120801).

References

1. Fagin, R., Lotem, A., Naor, M.: Optimal aggregation algorithms for middleware. In: PODS Conf. (2001)
2. Guntzer, U., Balke, W.-T., KieSling, W.: Towards efficient multi-feature queries in heterogeneous environments. In: IEEE Int'l Conf. on Information Technology, ITCC (2001)
3. Ilyas, I.F., Aref, W.G., Elmagarmid, A.K.: Joining ranked inputs in practice. In: VLDB Conf. (2002)

4. Ilyas, I.F., Aref, W.G., Elmagarmid, A.K.: Supporting top-k join queries in relational databases. In: VLDB Conf. (2003)
5. Börzsönyi, S., Kossmann, D., Stocker, K.: The skyline operator. In: ICDE Conf. (2001)
6. Balke, W.-T., Nejdl, W., Siberski, W., Thaden, U.: Progressive distributed top-k retrie-val in peer-to-peer networks. In: ICDE Conf. (2005)
7. Kimelfeld, B., Sagiv, Y.: Finding and approximating top-k answers in keyword proximity search. In: PODS Conf. (2006)
8. Babcock, B., Olston, C.: Distributed top-k monitoring. In: SIGMOD Conf. (2003)
9. Cao, P., Wang, Z.: Efficient top-k query calculation in distributed networks. In: PODC Conf. (2004)
10. Akbarinia, R., Pacitti, E., Valduriez, P.: Reducing network traffic in unstructured P2P systems using Top-k queries. Distributed and Parallel Databases 19(2) (2006)
11. Akbarinia, R., Pacitti, E., Valduriez, P.: Processing top-k queries in distributed hash tables. In: Kermarrec, A.-M., Bougé, L., Priol, T. (eds.) Euro-Par 2007. LNCS, vol. 4641, pp. 489–502. Springer, Heidelberg (2007)
12. Yuan, J., Sun, G.Z., Tian, Y., Chen, G.L., Liu, Z.: Selective-NRA Algorithms for Top-k Queries. In: APWeb/ WAIM Conf. (2009)
13. Tan, K., Eng, P., Ooi, B.: Efficient Progressive Skyline Computation. In: VLDB Conf. (2001)
14. Papadias, D., Tao, Y., Fu, G., Seeger, B.: Progressive skyline computation in database systems. ACM Transactions on Database Systems 30(1), 41–82 (2005)
15. Vlachou, A., Doulkeridis, C., Norvag, K., Vazirgiannis, M.: On Efficient Top-k Query Pro-cessing in Highly Distributed Environments. In: SIGMOD Conf. (2008)
16. Zou, L., Chen, L.: Dominant Graph: An Efficient Indexing Structure to Answer Top-K Queries. In: ICDE Conf. (2008)
17. Cormen, T.H., Leiserson, C.E., Rivest, R.L., Stein, C.: Introduction to algorithms. MIT Press, Cambridge (2001)

Using Multi-threading and Server Update Pushing to Improve the Performance of VNC for a Wall-Sized Tiled Display Wall

Yong Liu, John Markus Bjørndalen, and Otto J. Anshus

Department of Computer Science, University of Tromsø
{yongliu,jmb,otto}@cs.uit.no

Abstract. Display walls are wall-sized, high-resolution displays, typically built using several computers, each driving a projector or an LCD. The VNC (Virtual Network Computer) model is a simple way of creating desktops large enough for display walls by using a centralized virtual frame buffer. However, performance suffers significantly when the resolution increases due to the centralized server locating and compressing updates for the display computers. Another problem is that the display computers request and receive updates independently, resulting in an inconsistent view. TiledVNC is developed to better adapt VNC to a display wall and improve performance over an existing implementation, TightVNC. The changes include multi-threading, a server push update protocol, and pushing updates for the same frame to all viewers. To evaluate our system, we play two videos on our 22 megapixel display wall. Compared to TightVNC, TiledVNC increases the frame rate with up to 46% for a 6.75 megapixel video.

Keywords: TiledVNC, TightVNC, display wall, VNC, performance, high resolution.

1 Introduction

Display walls [14] are large, wall-sized, high-resolution displays constructed by tiling a number of smaller LCD displays or projectors driven by several computers. While a single display typically support a few megapixels, all the displays taken together add up to typically from twenty to several hundreds of megapixels. This allows for having a lot of data and information available simultaneously. Many windows from several applications can be displayed, or the whole display wall can be dedicated to high-resolution visualizations. When viewed at a distance, overview and coarser structures become visible; while viewed up close, users can read the text and see finer details. The size of the display wall lets a single user walk along the wall to view different parts of the data being displayed, and it lets multiple users have space enough either to work using different regions of the display wall or together in a collaborative manner. The size in combination with a high pixel count gives a display wall many more usage areas than a standard projector projected at a distance onto a large screen to create a large image.

P. Mueller, J.-N. Cao, and C.-L. Wang (Eds.): Infoscale 2009, LNICST 18, pp. 306–321, 2009.
© Institute for Computer Science, Social-Informatics and Telecommunications Engineering 2009

By having a standard desktop expanded to fill a display wall, the users will be able to use unmodified legacy applications while taking advantage of the large size and pixel count. However, standard operating systems don't support having several PCs and displays and coordinating them into a display wall with a correspondingly large desktop. A simple approach to create a large enough desktop is to use the VNC (Virtual Network Computer) model [11]. A VNC server maintains a virtual desktop with dimensions matching a display wall. The applications run on the same computer as the VNC server, but they only see what they believe to be the normal X server. Each display wall computer runs a VNC viewer requesting updates from the server corresponding to its tile of the virtual desktop, and physically displays it. We have used this approach for several years, and it is also used in the NCSA Display Wall In a Box (http://www.ncsa.uiuc.edu/Projects/DWiB/).

VNC transfers updates as compressed pixel data. The advantage is that this is portable across platforms and simplifies implementation of the viewers compared to solutions that forward graphics API calls to the clients. The main drawback is overhead. Applications render into the server's virtual frame buffer, and the VNC server needs to keep track of dirty regions[1] in the virtual frame buffer. Large dirty regions result in large updates. These must be compressed and then transmitted to the viewers. However, the VNC server uses no graphics hardware support to do this. Consequently, encoding is done by the CPU with the frame buffer for the virtual desktop in the computer's random access memory. If no compression is used, the pixel copying and processing is reduced, but now the network can become a bottleneck.

Another problem with using VNC for a display wall is that the tiles update independently of each other, whenever the individual VNC viewers request an update. Because of this, the tiles can sometimes display content from different frames making text and images display inconsistently across the tiles.

Other approaches to using a display wall may give better performance, but have drawbacks. Linking an application running on some computer with a modified graphical library that transparently will redirect output to the display wall can improve the performance in comparison with VNC [6]. This is because the library transmits graphics commands instead of the much larger amount of pixel data to the display computers. The drawback is that the dependence on specific libraries limits the number of applications which can be used without changes.

Modifying applications to run fully or partially on the computers that drive the individual displays may provide the best performance, but requires access to the source code of the application. This may be too complex and time-consuming depending on the application. The individual copies of the application need to be synchronized, data may need to be exchanged, and user input and other I/O have to be solved on an application-by-application basis.

We believe that using VNC is a simple and flexible approach to providing users with a familiar desktop environment where standard applications can run

---

[1] Regions that have been modified since the last update sent to one or more viewers covering that region.

unmodified. For static documents, like windows which rarely are updated and moved around, a low frame rate is not a significant problem. For dynamic documents like videos, animations and complex web sites, the frame rate becomes low enough to frustrate the user. The performance and the consistency of each frame across the tiles should be improved to better support a wider range of display wall usage scenarios.

2   Related Work

Distributed Multihead X, XDMX [4], makes it possible to create a high-resolution display wall desktop. Client applications connect to a front-end X server, which transparently transmits X commands from its clients to a set of back-end X servers running on the computers of the display wall. No data compression is used. In XDMX the back-end servers are meant to receive only their part of the data. This is very important for dynamic documents like videos, web sites with animation and similar to reduce network traffic and achieve good frame rates. We have observed a high startup time to have a static document like a high-resolution 25-megapixel image displayed. However, after the initial startup time, panning the image around is very smooth.

MultiStream[9] is a system using freely available video encoders to create lossy videos on-the-fly of a desktop, and then stream the videos to a display wall or PCs for play-back using common media players. The system is transparent to the applications. However, when used to create a video of the large desktop of a display wall, capturing and encoding the pixels are CPU intensive, and the performance suffers.

In the Chromium approach [6] a set of individual tiles of a display wall are made to appear as a single display to the applications. Display output from applications using OpenGL is transparently redirected to the display wall. The advantages include that applications don't have to be changed, and the model is flexible in that it can be used both for single process and multiple process parallel applications. A limiting factor is that the applications must use OpenGL. We have also experienced performance limitations when using Chromium on a game with more than four tiles [12].

SAGE [7] is a flexible and scalable software approach to sending display output from applications to a display wall. However, applications are required to be rewritten with the SAGE application interface library. Xinerama [15] is an extension to the X window system using multiple graphical devices to create one large virtual display. However, it requires the graphical devices to coexist on a single computer. These approaches are designed to let an application display to a display wall. They are not suitable as a way to do a high resolution display wall desktop.

3   Applying VNC to a Display Wall

A display wall is comprised of several computers and projectors (see Figure 1). The projectors are physically aligned into a matrix, and (rear-) projected onto a

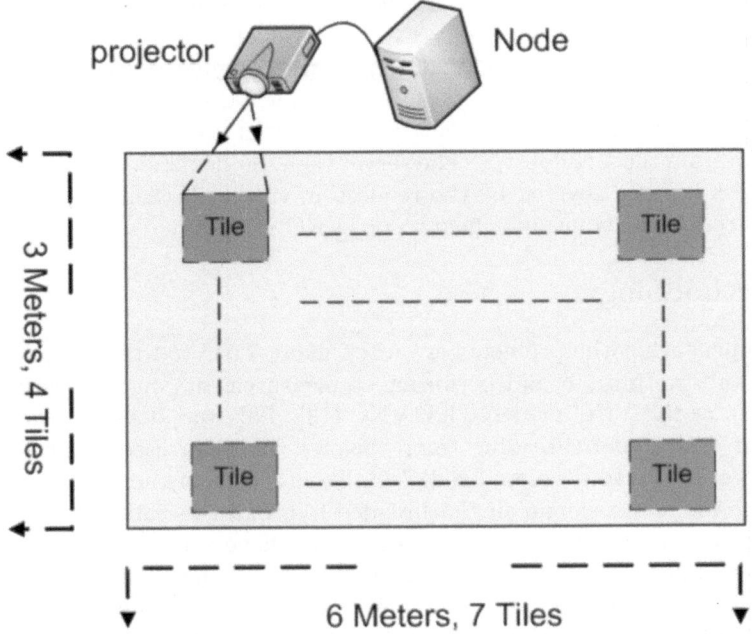

Fig. 1. The Architecture of Display Wall. Each projector is plugged into a computer that displays one tile of the desktop.

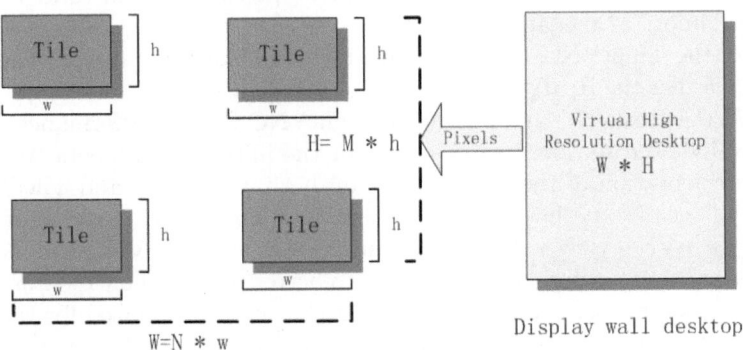

Fig. 2. The Architecture of Display Wall Desktop

screen. The VNC (Virtual Network Computer) system is a simple way of creating a desktop large enough to fill a display wall. See Figure 2. A VNC server runs on a computer together with the applications displaying to the desktop.

The VNC server handles a virtual desktop large enough to fill the display wall. Each display computer runs a VNC viewer requesting desktop updates from the server for the area of the desktop corresponding to its tile, and displays it.

When an application needs to produce output to the desktop, it uses normal X library calls to request the X server to output pixels. This call is, transparently to the application, sent to the VNC server which updates the virtual desktop correspondingly. To get updates, a VNC viewer polls the VNC server. Based on its position in the projector matrix, each viewer requests the corresponding pixel area from the VNC server. The server then, on demand, checks for updates in the desktop area covered by the requesting viewer. If there are updates, the server encodes and transmits them to the VNC viewer.

4   Methodology

To document what the problems are when using VNC to drive a desktop for a display wall, we initially did performance measurements on an existing implementation of the VNC model, TightVNC [13]. This was done on a single core computer with hyper-threading (more below). We then used the insight from these experiments to develop TiledVNC. Because one of the modifications was to change the server from a single-threaded to a multi-threaded model, we used a quad-core computer to let the multi-threading have better effect than it would have on a single-core computer. We therefore did a complete new set of experiments both on TightVNC and TiledVNC to allow us to compare them directly and see how the modifications impacted performance and why.

For the experiments we use a display wall with 28 computers, each with a projector. The network is a gigabit switched Ethernet. The screen is 6 meters wide and 3 meters high for a total area of $18m^2$. Onto this screen we rear-project in a 7x4 matrix. Each projector has 1024x768 pixels giving in total 7168x3072 pixels, or almost 22 megapixels.

We use the TightVNC 1.3.9 implementation of the VNC server. The display nodes run either the RealVNC [1] viewer or a VNC viewer we have implemented. We found the RealVNC viewer to give TightVNC better performance than the TightVNC viewer and decided to use it for the initial experiments. We use our own implementation of the VNC viewer on both TightVNC and TiledVNC for the second set of experiments. Our viewer gave TightVNC better performance than the RealVNC viewer. Using the same viewer for TightVNC and TiledVNC in the second set of experiments was done to better remove the viewer as a factor. Another reason for using our own viewer is that it is customized for the display wall domain, removing all keyboard and mouse handling. Our own viewer use the SDL [2] cross-platform multimedia library.

The display wall computers run 32-bit Rocks 4.1 Linux on a cluster of Dell Precision WS 370s, each with 2GB RAM and a 3.2 GHz Intel P4 Prescott CPU.

For the initial set of experiments on TightVNC the VNC server runs on a computer identical to the display node computers running the viewers, and also with Rocks 4.1 Linux. For the second set of experiments on TightVNC and TiledVNC we used a quad-core 3.8 GHz Intel Xeon CPU and 8 G RAM memory. The operating system is 64-bit Redhat Linux RHEL 5. While the TightVNC server could only use one thread, we configured the TiledVNC server to use four threads to handle updates.

To emulate updates to a high-resolution desktop we use two videos of 3 and 6.75 megapixel. We play the videos using a media player, one at a time, at the computer running the VNC server, and display them to the VNC virtual desktop. The VNC viewers request updates from the VNC server as often as they can manage, and display them physically to the display wall tiles.

We made the two videos using FFmpeg [5], and at the resolution 2048x1536 (R1) and 3072x2304 (R2). The videos are encoded as MPEG4 at 30 FPS, each video lasting 120 seconds for a total of 3600 frames. The VNC server compression ratio using hextile encoding on the videos is about 5.

The R1 video covers exactly four (two by two) tiles and its area is $2.6m^2$. This area is representative for the area used by several typical streaming applications on the display wall. At nine tiles (three by three) the R2 video covers an even larger area of the display wall.

We use ffplay [5] as the video media player. The media player runs at the same computer as the VNC server, displaying into the virtual desktop. It plays images one by one, and does not drop images because of timeouts. This is important, as the computer and VNC server cannot keep up with the 30FPS framerate, slowing down ffplay and extending the time spent on playing back the video.

For each experiment we define a virtual frame buffer (a desktop) at the VNC server matching the configuration of the video we play back, and at a color depth of 32 bits. By doing this we get each video to exactly cover the whole VNC virtual desktop, avoiding complicating issues arising from having the video play back partially on more than four (or nine) tiles of the display wall.

In [10] a method is described using slow-motion benchmarking to measure thin-client performance. Following the same ideas to benchmarking, we use two videos. While these videos played back well on all the computers we had available, a 22 megapixel video did not, making it impractical to use it in the experiments. However, the lower resolution videos do reflect interesting collaboration settings where full desktop updates are rare. One such setting is collaboration using many static documents and a few videos and web sites with animations.

We have three performance metrics:

FPS: "Frames per second" as seen at the display wall or at the VNC server. This is the number of updates received by the VNC viewers or by the VNC server per second. While we measure and calculate the FPS per tile, we only report on the average FPS over all four or nine tiles. Higher is better. The FPS for the server is computed as the number of video frames (3600) divided by the time it takes ffplay to actually play the video (which will be longer than 120 seconds).

UFP: "Updated frames percent": The percentage of all video frames played back by the media player which is received by the VNC viewers. First, we count the accumulated average number of updates sent to the VNC viewers until a video finishes. We then, because each video is 3600 frames long, divide the accumulated average of frame updates by 3600 to compute the UPS. This is possible since ffplay does not drop frames, and will draw every frame on the desktop. UFP is 100% when each update is seen by all viewers, and is less than 100% when the application updates the VNC virtual frame buffer faster than the viewers get updates. The higher the UFP, the less updates are missed by the VNC viewers. Higher is better.

"Time": This is the time we measured it took for ffplay to play back into the virtual frame buffer the 120 seconds long video. Closer to 120 is better.

5   Problems When Using VNC for a Display Wall

To document the performance behavior encountered when applying VNC to a high-resolution desktop for a display wall, we did a set of experiments measuring the performance of TightVNC.

5.1   Performance Results for TightVNC

The results are shown in Table 1. The media player, ffplay, at the VNC server computer attempts to play back the videos at 30 FPS. The measurements show that even for the lowest resolution 3 megapixel video (R1) only 8.1 FPS is received by the display wall viewers.

Table 1. Performance of Display Wall Desktop. The numbers show the Frames Per Second (FPS) and Updated Frames Percent (UFP) for two resolutions: 2048x1536 (R1) and 3072x2304 (R2).

Video Resolution	2048x1536 (R1)	3072x2304 (R2)
FPS	8.1	4.3
UFP	67%	99.5%
Time	297	836

We observe that the media player has enough resources to play back into the virtual frame buffer, 33% more frames are displayed at the VNC server than what the VNC server sends to the VNC viewers.

We believe that this slowdown is in part due to the application updates being delayed in the VNC server while the VNC server is busy handling the VNC clients. TightVNC is single-threaded, and is not able to handle XLib requests while compressing and sending data to VNC viewers. Another factor is that the media player and the VNC server run on the same host, competing for resources.

In the case of the higher resolution 6.75 megapixels video (R2), the FPS decreases to 4.3 while at the same time almost all of the frames written to the virtual frame buffer get sent to the VNC viewers.

In practical terms, a user viewing the videos on a display wall will experience that the 120 seconds long videos need 297 and 836 seconds, respectively, to play back.

5.2   Discussion and Conclusion

The network bandwidth could have been a bottleneck in these experiments because the 6.75 megapixel video has frames with 27MB per frame. However, pixel compression reduces the network traffic, and with a compression ratio of about five we can achieve about 20 FPS on a network with 1000Mb/sec bandwidth (which is about what a gigabit Ethernet can support). However, to find out if pixels can be compressed, each pixel must be compared at least once. Using the CPU and memory (instead of a graphics card) adds to the latency of X operations. We observe that VNC is slow when large areas of the desktop needs to be updated. Modified pixels must be encoded to reduce the network bandwidth consumed when transferring updates to the viewers, but this encoding turns into a bottleneck for large display walls. The single-threaded implementation of the server contributes to the scalability issues as it cannot benefit from newer multi-core CPUs. We conclude that a multi-threaded model is needed to benefit from multi and many-core architectures.

The media player attempts to play back at 30 FPS, but, for the R2 video, only 4.3 FPS is actually written to the virtual frame buffer. The VNC viewers have enough resources to queue up new update requests before the media player is finished updating a frame. The VNC server has enough resources to send all of these updates to the viewers.

If a viewer requests an update when a dirty region is registered for that viewer, the server will immediately compute and return an update. If there is no update available, the server will place the viewer on a waiting queue. The first XLib update that modifies a region corresponding to the viewer will start a timeout timer for the viewer. At timeout, a set number of milliseconds, the server will compute an update packet and send it to the client. This allows the VNC server to aggregate multiple small updates before sending updates to the viewer. However, this does not work well for the large frame updates generated by the R2 video. For large updates the time of compressing and initiating transferring it to a viewer is more than the default update timeout delay of 40ms. After an update is sent, the timers for the other waiting viewers have expired, and the server has to send the next of these updates immediately.

A high UFP is good if the server and viewers manage to provide this without slowing down the application too much, but our measurements show that the media player is slowed down severely. As a result, the 2-minute (3600 frames) R2 video plays in 14 minutes, when displayed on the R2 desktop.

We have observed that the desktop does not keep the display wall consistent. The tiles in the display wall are updated independently of each other because the VNC server handles update requests from a viewer without considering recent or pending updates for the other viewers. This can result in some tiles having older output than other tiles, and happens more frequently when the load of the server increases. We conclude that VNC model is not well suited when used to support a desktop for a display wall, which have a number of tiles that we want to keep consistent, and that a solution for this problem is needed.

Please see [8] for more details about the performance problems encountered when using VNC for a display wall desktop and on how we improved the performance of TightVNC without changing the VNC model and update protocol.

6   Improving TightVNC

To adapt VNC to a display wall and improve performance, we did several changes, and used the TightVNC implementation of VNC as a starting point for the resulting TiledVNC system.

To utilize multi-core architectures, we change the VNC server from being single-threaded to multi-threaded.

To control the load on both the server and client side we change the update protocol of the VNC server from a viewer pull to a server push model. The server initially waits until all viewers connect to it, and then the server periodically pushes updates to the viewers.

To reduce the period when tiles show content from different frames, we only push updates for the same frame to all viewers. This was simplified by the server push model.

We also remove the mouse and keyboard input handler from all viewers because in the case of a display wall using VNC all input devices can be connected directly to the VNC server computer instead of to the viewers. We do not report further here on the detailed effect of this change.

6.1   From Single-Threading to Multi-threading

Figure 3 illustrates the architecture of the TiledVNC multi-threaded VNC server. The idea is to have a set of threads waiting on a timer. When a timeout happens, the threads get a task from a pool of tasks. Each task indicates an area of the virtual frame buffer corresponding to a tile of the display wall. A thread scans the frame buffer for dirty regions that needs to be updated, and if there are any, it will compress the data and send it to the corresponding viewer. Then the thread goes to the pool of tasks and gets a new area to check. A counter is used to keep track of the number of remaining tasks. When all tasks are done, the threads block for the next timeout.

We implemented the server in C, using the Pthread [3] thread package. We use a Pthread monitor condition variable to have threads wait.

The period between timeouts, the delay, lets the server control its load, and impact the performance.

Different numbers of threads can be used. However, in this paper we only report on using four threads, that is, one thread per core of the computer running the VNC server.

6.2   From Viewer Pull to Server Push

A VNC server usually uses a viewer pull model. The server waits for requests for updates from the VNC viewers, and services them as soon as they arrive.

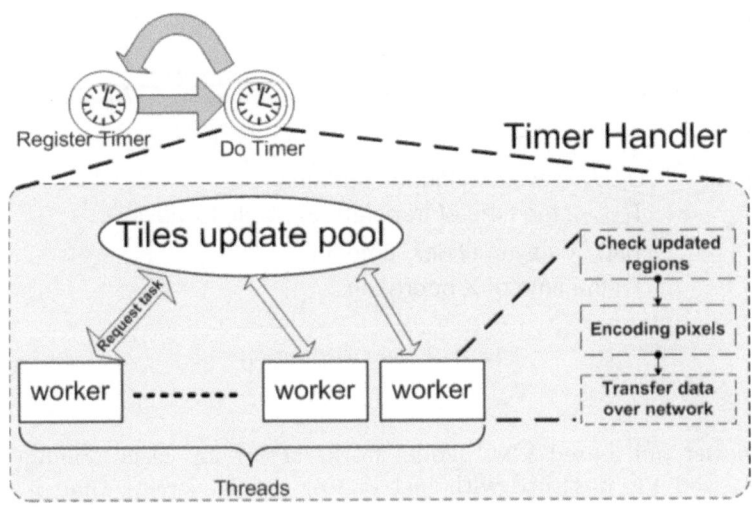

Fig. 3. Multi-thread Display Wall Desktop

If the server finds an update it is sent as soon as possible. This approach lets the viewers request an update only when they are ready, and the server only has to send updates, and thereby creating network traffic and using bandwidth, when there are viewers ready to receive. However, by just requesting an update, a viewer enforces the server to look for updates and encode them as soon as possible.

If we analyze some interesting permutations of resolution, network bandwidth, and number of viewers we find:

Low desktop resolution, low network bandwidth, few viewers: Even when a high level of compression is used, the low resolution and small number of viewers do not give the server a too high load, and the media player (in our case) gets more CPU resources. The server can keep up with the requests from the viewers. The result is a relatively good frame rate.

High desktop resolution, low network bandwidth, many viewers: A high level of compression is needed, and this together with the high number of viewers give the server a high load, and the media player gets less CPU resources. The server cannot keep up with the requests from the viewers. The low bandwidth will further delay the receiving of updates. The result is a very low frame rate.

High desktop resolution, high network bandwidth, many viewers: A high level of compression is needed, and this together with the high number of viewers give the server a high load, and the media player gets less CPU resources. The server cannot keep up with the requests from the viewers. However, the high bandwidth will mean that the network is not the bottleneck, and will not reduce the frame rate further. The result is still a low frame rate.

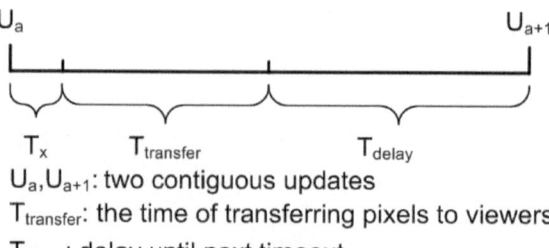

U_a, U_{a+1}: two contiguous updates
$T_{transfer}$: the time of transferring pixels to viewers
T_{delay}: delay until next timeout
T_x: the time of X operation

Fig. 4. Time Distribution

The viewer pull based VNC model works better for usage domains with a standard sized PC desktops with just one or a few viewers, than it does for a high-resolution display wall desktop with potentially many more viewers. A high-resolution VNC server with multiple clients spends more time on encoding pixels than transferring the pixels over the network. The many viewers also force the server to service them as soon as possible. Consequently, the server has little influence over its own work load. The performance of the VNC server is impacted by the frequency of updates.

The time ΔT between two contiguous updates is the sum of T_x, $T_{transfer}$ and T_{delay}, as shown in Figure 4.

T_x and $T_{transfer}$ are insignificant for the standard PC desktop resolution case. When the size of the desktop increases, T_x and $T_{transfer}$ grow larger. T_x in particular can become large in the high resolution. T_{delay} is the duration between updates. During this time the media player application may also get more CPU resources because the server may wait idle for new viewer requests or for the timeout. Reducing the update frequency will reduce the server load. This can be achieved by increasing T_{delay}.

We have changed the viewer pull model to a server push model to let the server have better control over its work load and the update rate. The assumption is that the viewers always will have more resources available than they need to display the updates sent from the server.

6.3 Consistency between Tiles

The viewer pulls update protocol used by VNC, when used in a tiled display wall, results in a possibility for viewers displaying content from different frames. This is because each viewer requests and gets updates independently of each other. The server push update protocol makes it simple to reduce the period when tiles show content from different frames by simply pushing updates from the same frame to all viewers before the next frame is pushed out. Even if viewers receive the updates at slightly different times, the updates are from the same frame. This works well as long as the viewers have resources enough to receive and display all updates. This is a realistic assumption for a display wall with many viewers, and a heavily loaded server.

7   Comparing TightVNC vs. TiledVNC

To document the impact of changing VNC in the way described above, and to be able to do comparisons, we did a set of experiments measuring the performance of TightVNC and TiledVNC on the same platform and using our VNC viewer.

7.1   Performance Results

The result from the experiments is shown in Figures 5, 6 and 7.

The X-axis is the delay between timeouts, T_{delay} in millisecond. The Y-axis is the frame rate (FPS) or the updated frames percent (UFP).

The results show that the best frame rate as seen by the **viewers** for the 3 megapixels video was achieved when updates were done every 30ms. In this case TiledVNC increased the frame rate to 14 FPS, or about 34% more than TightVNC. About 80% of the updates done at the server side were displayed at the display wall.

The best frame rate as seen by the viewers for the 6.75 megapixels video was achieved when updates were done more rarely, at 70ms. In this case TiledVNC increased the frame rate to 6 FPS, or about 46% more than TightVNC. About 100% of the updates done at the server side were displayed at the display wall.

TiledVNC is performing better than TightVNC in all cases, but when the delay between updates increases, the frame rate decreases for both systems to between 3-6 FPS.

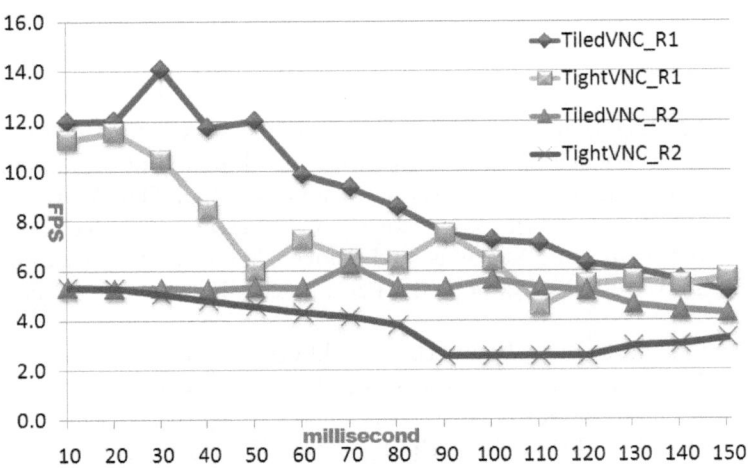

Fig. 5. FPS at the Display Wall

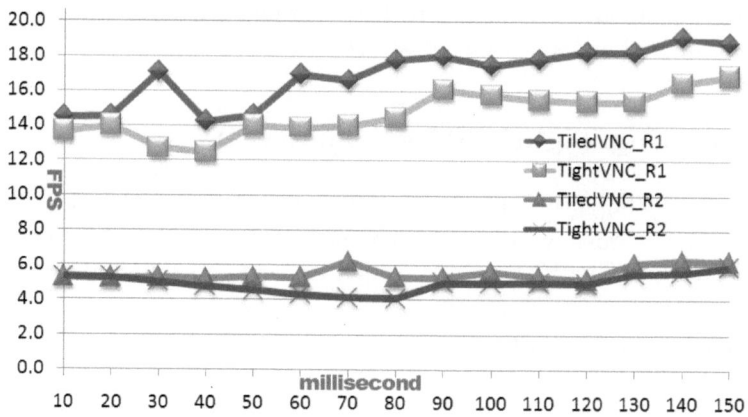

Fig. 6. FPS at the VNC Server

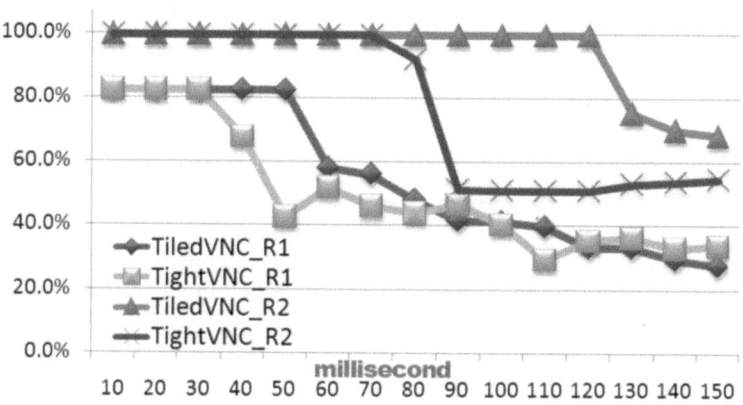

Fig. 7. UFP

The results show that the best frame rate at the **server** for the 3 megapixels video was achieved when updates were done every 140ms. In this case TiledVNC achieved a frame rate of 19 FPS, about 15% better than TightVNC.

The best frame rate at the server for the 6.75 megapixels video was achieved when updates were done at 70ms and above 130ms. In this case TiledVNC increased the frame rate to about 6 FPS, but this is only slightly better than TightVNC.

TiledVNC is performing better than TightVNC in all cases, but less so than as seen by the viewers. At the server, when the delay between updates increases, the frame rate increases for both systems when playing the R1 video from about 14-15 to 17-19 FPS. However, for the R2 video, the frame rate stays at around 5-6 FPS almost independently of delay time. Playing back R2 and running the server seems to saturate the computer used. In this case a faster computer should give better performance.

Table 2. Time to Play Back a 120 Seconds Long Video

T_{delay}	30 ms	70 ms
TiledVNC_R1	211	216
TiledVNC_R2	679	579
TightVNC_R1	283	257
TightVNC_R2	712	869

From Figure 7, it can be seen that TightVNC begins earlier to skip frames than TiledVNC. This is because TightVNC uses a single core, while TiledVNC benefits from using all four cores. However, both systems have the same UFP at delays below 30 and 70 ms respectively for R1 and R2.

In practical terms, a user viewing the videos on a display wall will experience that the 120 seconds long videos takes longer to play back. TightVNC need for the best cases 257 and 712 seconds, respectively, to play back R1 and R2. For TiledVNC the videos take for the best cases 211 and 579 seconds to play back.

Comparing the results for TightVNC in Table 2 with Table 1, the performance is improved because of the more powerful computer used in the last set of experiments, and because using 30ms or 70ms give better performance than the default 40ms used in the first set of experiments.

7.2 Discussion

Although the performance of TiledVNC is better than TightVNC, it still suffers from low FPS. One main reason is that updating the virtual frame buffer has no hardware (GPU) support. However, we still benefit from multiple cores. The compression rate of the Hextile encoding used by TightVNC and Tiled-VNC is about 5. When $T_{delay} = 30ms$, TiledVNC sends about 34 MB/sec and 29 MB/sec into the network when playing back respectively the 3 and 6.75 megapixels videos. The gigabit Ethernet can support about 100MB/sec. With more cores the multi-threaded TiledVNC should be able to push more updates into the network. For the 3 megapixel video, we estimate that using eight cores may give us about 19 FPS. This is about 45MB/sec, and still less than what a gigabit Ethernet will support. This is interesting because it indicates that there are performance benefits for TiledVNC to be expected from more cores, and it is simpler to update to a computer with more cores than to update the whole network.

The TiledVNC server used only four threads to scan for and compress updates. For future experiments we will document the effect of using more threads.

8   Conclusion

VNC is a simple way of supporting a high-resolution desktop for a tiled display wall. It will allow legacy applications to run as before, but displaying to a much larger desktop than a standard sized PC desktop.

We have done a set of experiments on TightVNC to identify the performance behavior and bottlenecks when using VNC to support a high-resolution desktop for a tiled display wall. Based on the results we changed VNC from single to multi-threaded model, and changed the update protocol from a viewer pull model to a server push model. We also achieved to keep the viewer content more consistent across frames. We then did a set of new experiments on the new TiledVNC system to document the impact on performance coming from these modifications. We used a 3 megapixel and a 6.75 megapixel video to emulate frequent updates to a display wall.

The new TiledVNC has better performance than TightVNC in all cases. Best case frame rates are improved about 34% and 46% when playing demanding videos at 3 and 6.75 megapixels. Even though the best frame rate at 14 FPS is about half of the 30 FPS the videos were made to play at, this will be enough in many situations where the updates to the display wall desktop are much less frequent than the frequent updates generated by a video covering the whole desktop.

The main bottleneck is the load on the computer running the VNC server and media player. Looking for updates in the virtual frame buffer and compressing them before sending the data to the viewers saturate the resources. However, we expect the multi-threaded TiledVNC to track well the progress of multi-core architectures, and also be able to benefit from further performance boost from a graphical processing unit (GPU). We are working on GPU support for VNC.

Acknowledgements. This work has been supported by the NFR funded project IKT 2010 159936: SHARE - A Distributed Virtual Desktop for Simple, Scalable, and Robust Resource Sharing across Computer, Storage, and Display Devices.

References

1. RealVNC, http://www.realvnc.com/
2. Simple DirectMedia Layer, http://www.libsdl.org/
3. Butenhof, D.R.: Programming with POSIX threads. Addison-Wesley Longman Publishing Co., Inc., Boston (1997)
4. Faith, R.E., Martin, K.E.: Xdmx: distributed multi-head x, http://dmx.sourceforge.net/
5. FFmpeg, http://ffmpeg.mplayerhq.hu/
6. Humphreys, G., Houston, M., Ng, R., Frank, R., Ahern, S., Kirchner, P.D., Klosowski, J.T.: Chromium: a stream-processing framework for interactive rendering on clusters. ACM Trans. Graph. 21(3), 693–702 (2002); 566639
7. Jeong, B., Renambot, L., Jagodic, R., Singh, R., Aguilera, J., Johnson, A., Leigh, J.: High-performance dynamic graphics streaming for scalable adaptive graphics environment (2006); 1188568 108
8. Liu, Y., Anshus, O.J.: Improving the performance of vnc for high-resolution display walls. In: CTS 2009: The 2009 International Symposium on Collaborative Technologies and Systems (2009)

9. Liu, Y., Anshus, O.J., Ha, P.H., Larsen, T., Bjørndalen, J.M.: Multistream a cross-platform display sharing system using multiple video streams. In: 28th International Conference on Distributed Computing Systems Workshops, ICDCS 2008., pp. 90–95 (2008)
10. Nieh, J., Yang, S.J., Novik, N.: Measuring thin-client performance using slow-motion benchmarking. ACM Trans. Comput. Syst. 21(1), 87–115 (2003)
11. Richardson, T., Stafford-Fraser, Q., Wood, K.R., Hopper, A.: Virtual network computing. IEEE Internet Computing 2(1), 33–38 (1998); 613221
12. Stødle, D., Hagen, T.-M.S., Bjørndalen, J.M., Anshus, O.J.: Touch-free multi-user gaming on wall-sized, high-resolution tiled displays. In: PerGames 2007: Proceedings of the 4th International Symposium on Pervasive Gaming Applications, pp. 75–83 (2007)
13. TightVNC, http://www.tightvnc.com/
14. Wallace, G., Anshus, O.J., Bi, P., Chen, H., Chen, Y., Clark, D., Cook, P., Finkelstein, A., Funkhouser, T., Gupta, A., Hibbs, M., Li, K., Liu, Z., Samanta, R., Sukthankar, R., Troyanskaya, O.: Tools and applications for large-scale display walls. IEEE Computer Graphics and Applications 25(4), 24–33 (2005)
15. Xinerama, http://sourceforge.net/projects/xinerama/

Author Index